THE AMERICAN
EXPERIMENT

THE AMERICAN EXPERIMENT

Essays on the Theory and Practice of Liberty

Edited by

Peter Augustine Lawler
and
Robert Martin Schaefer

Rowman & Littlefield Publishers, Inc.

ROWMAN & LITTLEFIELD PUBLISHERS, INC.

Published in the United States of America
by Rowman & Littlefield Publishers, Inc.
4720 Boston Way, Lanham, Maryland 20706
3 Henrietta Street
London WC2E 8LU, England

British Cataloging in Publication Information Available

Library of Congress Cataloging-in-Publication Data

The American experiment : essays on the theory and practice of liberty
/ edited by Peter Lawler and Robert M. Schaefer.
p. cm.
Includes bibliographical references and index.
1. United States--Politics and government. 2. United States-
-Constitutional history. 3. Political science--United States-
-History. I. Lawler, Peter Augustine. II. Schaefer, Robert
Martin.
JK21.A434   1994   320.973—dc20   93-49433   CIP

ISBN 0-8476-7903-9 (cloth : alk. paper)
ISBN 0-8476-7904-7 (paper.: alk. paper)

Printed in the United States of America

The paper used in this publication meets the minimum requirements of
American National Standard for Information Sciences—Permanence of
Paper for Printed Library Materials, ANSI Z39.48–1984.

Contents

Acknowledgments

First of all, we would like to thank our authors for their first-rate contributions. We would also like to thank them for their patience and cooperation. The discipline required for professors to write on an introductory level is not to be minimized.

Much of the work in getting the chapters in shape for publication was done by Bob's colleagues and staff at the University of Mobile. We are especially indebted to the technical expertise of Krista Risner and careful proofreading of Cathy Collier. At Berry College, Kathy Gann, as usual, contributed in many ways. Jen Siebels and Katie Cauthen also edited and proofread. Terri Schaefer was enormously helpful in proofreading.

Jonathan Sisk at Rowman and Littlefield showed great confidence in and gave maximum support to this project from the very beginning. Lynn Gemmell, our copy editor, worked quickly but with extraordinary concern for quality and detail. We are grateful to them both.

Last, but most, we relied on the love, charm, and good humor of four women, Rita, Catherine, Terri, and Maggie.

Introduction

Peter Augustine Lawler and
Robert Martin Schaefer

In a very obvious sense, this might be the most diverse introduction to American government ever. The twenty-nine chapters, the product of twenty-nine authors, provide a great variety in style, perspective, and opinion. This book will hold your interest and provoke you to think for yourself.

Most of our authors are active and experienced teachers of political science. Each of them was asked to "write up" his or her most effective class or series of classes. So the chapters reflect the author's particular passion for the subject. They are often contentious, even polemical, and we sometimes disagree with their conclusions. But they are always well informed and instructive.

Our aim was to have you experience each teacher on his or her best day. Of course, we did not realize this aim perfectly, but we are sure that it has given this book more character and animation than is usually true of other introductions to American government. This book does have some unity of purpose and approach. It comes from the strong interest almost all our authors have in political philosophy. This book is both more philosophical *and* more constitutional than other introductions.

Philosophy and constitutionalism inform the common sense that Americans bring to political life. Our authors use the language American citizens and statesmen have actually used in arguing with one another about principles and policy. They avoid, as much as possible, the impersonal and somewhat lifeless language of ideological systems and social science.

American political life has been organized under the same Con-

1

stitution for more than two hundred years. During that time, the Constitution has only rarely been amended. Its fundamental principles, arguably, have not changed. The most important of the amendments are the Thirteenth, Fourteenth, Fifteenth, and Nineteenth, which extended the implementation of those principles to blacks and women. These amendments may be understood to have perfected the Constitution of 1787, which had already avoided racism and sexism by making neither racial nor gender-based distinctions.

The greatest constitutional change was the Fourteenth Amendment. But, properly interpreted, its purpose was simply to apply the Constitution's original principles about equal citizenship to state law. It nationalized American political life in the service of those principles. Similarly, the Fifteenth and Nineteenth Amendments were also nationalizing commands to the states about blacks and women voting.

Americans quickly became accustomed by their Constitution to make almost all political disputes legal and finally constitutional ones. They almost never question the Constitution itself. They argue over how it is to be applied to a particular issue or practice. Americans most commonly ask: Is it constitutional? And they quite commonly disagree on answers to that question.

The broadest and deepest versions of this question have concerned the general direction of national policy. Was slavery or its expansion constitutional? Is the welfare-regulatory state constitutional? Such questions are constitutional and political, and so not merely legal. They are never answered authoritatively by the Court, although it always tries.

These most comprehensive or *regime* questions have characteristically been answered by presidential elections. Some of these elections, extraordinary events that political scientists call *critical elections* (1800, 1860, 1936, and perhaps 1828 and 1896), are marked by great political intensity or animosity, including rhetorical extremism. The rhetorical battle is, at heart, a contest over principle, with one party accusing the other of subverting the Constitution's true intention.

Such battles indicate the inherent difficulties of a written constitution. Citizens and statesmen must not only interpret the powers and limits set down by the Constitution, but must also apply these guidelines to future exigencies. War, foreign policy, economic depression, and other issues must be resolved in light of a constitution that is general in nature. Americans are confronted with the twofold task of preserving the Constitution, and thereby order, while simultaneously attempting to promote justice—which many times requires great change.

Naturally, there has been, and always will be, disagreement over the meaning of specific clauses in the Constitution and the principles that underlie the Constitution. These heated arguments—culminating, in one case, in civil war—over the meaning and application of constitutional principle are characteristically based on interpretations of the Constitution in light of principles, for the most part, only implicitly found there. These great principles are liberty and equality. For their understanding of these principles, Americans have used as their authority the Declaration of Independence. The Declaration, as Abraham Lincoln said, is *the* American statement of abstract principle, and the Constitution is its application. The ideas expressed in the Declaration form the lens through which we read the Constitution.

This American perception of the need to interpret the Constitution in light of abstract principle is one reason why this book is both philosophical and constitutional. The Declaration's principles, as they flowed from the pen of Thomas Jefferson, were derived from the writing of the political philosophers. Jefferson's thought had many influences, including classical authors such as Cicero, Aristotle, and Epicurus. But his primary debt as a political thinker was to the modern English political philosopher John Locke.

All the leading statesmen of the founding generation were unusually open and indebted to Locke and the other modern philosophers. Generally, the Founders viewed their political activity as part of the Enlightenment, the modern effort to bring the principles of philosophy directly to bear on political life. So they viewed the Constitution as largely a practical application of their understanding of the philosophers' political wisdom, much of which is summarized in the Declaration's "self-evident" truths.

The first of these truths is "all men are created equal." They are all equally free beings. The Declaration suggests that because a human being is free by nature, he originally exists in a state of nature without subordination to government. In this state, according to Locke, his primary concern is the preservation and comfort of his precariously situated body. Hence, man consents to government because he has the right to preserve himself, but he is not able to do so effectively without government's help.

Jefferson's second self-evident truth, the inalienability of rights, clarifies this definition of equality by reminding us that man's body is not the only element of man's nature worthy of preservation. The second self-evident truth amounts to a definition of what it means to be a human being. Man is the being with rights. Whenever we think clearly about him, we think about rights. In this respect, the Declaration distinguishes man from the other animals and from God.

Animals, strictly speaking, do not have rights, because they are not aware that they have or need them. They are not aware of their essential vulnerability or their mortality. God, strictly speaking, does not have rights, because, for him, self-preservation is not a problem. He has no need of rights. The human being, like the other animals, has a body. But he is also like God insofar as he is self-conscious and rational and so is aware of his true situation. This mixture of qualities produces the being with rights, the one who reasons in light of his natural situation as a being with a body.

So the Declaration is based on a theology, even if an incomplete one. This theology is not specifically Christian. It is based on what human beings can know about their natures independently of divine revelation. The idea that the truth required to determine the purpose and limits of government is self-evident suggests that there is no political need to rely on revelation. Self-evident means, plainly, evident to the self, or what one can know without outside assistance.

The Declaration does not say that all truth, or even all truth that human beings might know, is self-evident. Certain truths must be held as self-evident for a people to establish itself as a political community that secures rights effectively. Jefferson and the other Founders tended to believe that a government based on revelation would not produce such a community. It would inevitably be undermined by unnecessary and often extreme political controversy. Human beings, as Locke observed, will always disagree on the meaning of revelation. The best chance for peaceful agreement is to limit the political relevance of theology to what we know by nature.

But notice that the Declaration's theology, by defining God, limits man. If man imagines himself to be a god, he will stop being concerned with his own rights or the rights of others. He will stop thinking clearly about his own situation, and so about what he can and ought to do to improve that situation. He will also tend to oppress others, because he will stop seeing them as beings with rights. Much of the tyranny that has plagued the world in our century—certainly that of the communists and the fascists—came from abandonment of the theology that comes from defining man as the being with rights. Those who imagined they were gods—or like a god in their power and wisdom—attempted to reduce others to nothing but animals.

The Declaration goes on to list some of the rights human beings possess by nature: life, liberty, and the pursuit of happiness. Life comes first. In the state of nature the free individual is concerned primarily with his own self-preservation. Even liberty is, first of all, the freedom to choose the means to preserve oneself. After consent to government, liberty becomes primarily the freedom to choose how to earn one's living. The only limit to liberty is the rights, the life and liberty, of others.

The separation of religion and politics, a fundamental American principle, begins as a requirement of peace and freedom. But it can turn out to be good for the soul too. Human beings are left free to believe as they are directed by their consciences. This principle of separation fits well with the biblical view that human beings are free from government by virtue of their duties to a personal Creator.

The third right the Declaration mentions, the pursuit of happiness, is hard to distinguish from liberty. If an individual is free, we can assume that he will use his freedom to pursue happiness as he understands it. Liberty must mean, in part, the freedom to define happiness for oneself, or not to have it defined by government. The right to the pursuit of happiness is far from a guarantee of happiness. It suggests, of course, that human beings will never be perfectly happy in this life. The attempt of government to remedy that imperfection would be a violation of the right to pursue happiness for oneself.

It is also self-evidently true, according to the Declaration, that human beings have a right to "alter or to abolish" existing government and "institute" a new form of government that, in their view, better secures their rights. Jefferson means to call to mind Locke's teaching regarding rebellion as a justification for the American revolution. He adds that human beings are so constituted that they will exercise this right rarely and reluctantly. This resistance to resistance, as Locke observes, comes from a prudent realization that revolution is a dangerous return to the state of nature.

The violation of rights that leads to revolution ought to be so great that individuals perceive little or no difference between life under existing government and their fearful existence in the state of nature. Fear of government can actually be worse. There is nothing on earth more terrifying than a completely arbitrary, tyrannical government. But government ceases to protect rights when it becomes *either* too strong or too weak. When government is too weak to secure law and order, people become too afraid of each other, or at least become fearful of the lawless among them. A government deserving of our consent is strong but limited.

The Declaration says that people have the right to revolution because the foundation of government is consent. There are occasions when consent might reasonably be withdrawn. The foundation of consent does not necessitate democratic government, or the people's participation in the making of laws. It is the effective protection of rights.

So the Declaration suggests that democratic government, because of its propensity to violate minority rights, is not always worthy of our consent. The Declaration does not say how a democratic government might be constituted to protect the equal rights of all. Its purpose was not to establish a new form of government. For the way the Founders finally answered this question, we must turn to the Constitution.

The procedure usually followed by our authors is to understand the Constitution with the assistance of the authoritative exposition of its achievements, *The Federalist*.

The Federalist's defense of the Constitution presupposes the Declaration's principle that the purpose of government is the protection of liberty or the natural diversity of human individuality. Government that protects the rights of all equally and effectively is good or just. The twin threats to good government in America are weakness or incompetence and the oppressive rule of a majority faction. The Constitution, in *The Federalist*'s eyes, is the foundation for strong, stable, properly limited, but still democratic government.

Our authors also usually recognize that it is insufficient to understand America's constitutional achievement simply through the Declaration's principles and *The Federalist*'s analyses. They turn often to the most profound book written on America as a regime, Alexis de Tocqueville's *Democracy in America*. Tocqueville shows that the American defense of rights against the excesses of democracy cannot be explained without a more comprehensive account of what the Americans received as an inheritance from the English. He discusses the contributions of three of these inheritances at length: religion, the family, and local government. Without participation in these institutions, Americans would be too individualistic to think or act effectively on behalf of human liberty.

Volume 1 of Tocqueville's *Democracy* is concerned primarily with how American democracy controls "the tyranny of the majority," or the assertiveness of the democratic ruling group. Volume 2 is concerned far more with the possibility that the Americans might completely surrender their human assertiveness or individuality. Tocqueville's fear is the emergence of a despotism of "schoolmasters," who will rule human beings so apathetic and passive that they have fallen below the level of humanity. Volume 2, in effect, criticizes the American Founders for not seeing clearly enough that the weakness of the free individual might cause him to be unable to defend individuality or human liberty.

Tocqueville, *The Federalist*, and the Declaration are guideposts for the authors' interpretation of American political principles, the Constitution, and contemporary issues. Our book is divided into three sections. The chapters in the first section consider America's fundamental principles. They show, in various ways, how liberty is reconciled with equality or democracy in theory and practice. They include extensive discussions of *The Federalist*, but also the Anti-Federalist and Tocquevillian criticisms of certain dangers to liberty latent in the constitutional system.

The chapters in the second section examine American political institutions. As *The Federalist* explains, the American Constitution depends for its effectiveness on well-designed institutions more than on human virtue or character. Virtue and character are unreliable without institutional support and encouragement. Some of the chapters concern the three institutions—president, Congress, and Court—that make up the separation of powers system. Others concern institutions that the Founders did not intend but have become part of our political system, the bureaucracy and political parties.

Each of our authors is impressed by two facts. First, the constitutionally designed institutions now function somewhat differently than the Founders intended. Second, the institutions they did not design are to some great extent shaped by the institutions they did. The key question for Americans, finally, is not whether institutions function today as the Founders intended. It is whether the way they do function serves or undermines constitutional purposes.

The third section considers some of the policies that continue to divide Americans. Here the authors examine policy alternatives with constitutional principles in mind. But they are not afraid to ascend, when necessary, to discussions of human nature.

These policy analyses make clear that contemporary dilemmas are often manifestations of perennial problems associated with the fundamental political choices our Founders made. Our successes and failures with respect to race, gender, the family, and so forth reveal both the greatness and the imperfections of the American experiment. Even a constitutional and philosophically informed regime falls short of wisdom and complete justice. Part of the greatness of America is its capacity for self-criticism.

One purpose of this book is to replace the textbook in introductory American government courses. We assume that most professors who use it will supplement it with the reading of primary sources, such as *The Federalist* and Court opinions. We also assume that in most courses not all of the chapters will be covered.

But this book is meant to be much more than a textbook. It can be read profitably by anyone seeking a sound, interesting introduction to American politics.

Part One

Founding Principles

1

What Is Politics?

William B. Cody

The serious study of American government and politics presupposes that we know what politics is. But many, if not most, of the common usages of the term *politics* completely ignore the essential nature of politics. So we cannot give a definition of politics until we identify its essential character.

Our word politics is derived from the Greek word *polis*. *Polis* is most frequently translated into English as "city-state." But the best English equivalent is actually "native country" or "fatherland," so long as we bear in mind that it refers to a community of limited area and population. Today political scientists frequently refer to any independent state, regardless of size or population, as a polity.

Politics is also derived from the Greek word *politeia*, which is usually translated as "constitution," but it means much more. *Politeia* refers to the way of life of the *polis* (or polity) and those who take part in governing and communal life and why they are permitted to do so. It refers to the basis of the actual ordering of the political community.

More comprehensively still, *politeia* refers to "a community of what people honor."[1] The *politeia* of a particular polity defines that which the community collectively holds or believes to be worthy of respect, preference, praise, or rewards. *Politeia* also defines what that community holds to be worthy of condemnation, blame, penalties, or punishments. The *politeia* is a statement, frequently implicit, of what the community finds worthy of honor or of contempt. So *politeia* is concerned with those shared notions of what is deserved, what is just, and what is good. Within a given polity, political rule is entrusted to those whom the *politeia* indicates "justly deserve" the honor of ruling. The community grants the honor of ruling to that element of the population which is deemed to be most important to the life of the polity.

For example, if a political community were formed around the notion that the wealthiest individuals of the society should be made rulers because their contributions are the most important to the life of the polity, then the form of government for that polity would be a *plutocracy* (rule of the wealthy). If, on the other hand, the political community determined that the military leaders of the society are entitled to rule, and made them rulers because they make the greatest contribution to the polity, then the form of government for that polity would be a *timocracy* (rule of the military).

Other forms of government are created by other *politeias*. In some polities the religious leaders of the community are held to be the most important members of the society and are granted political leadership of the polity. A polity ruled by its religious leaders is called a *theocracy*. In other polities the community seeks to honor the most virtuous or best of its citizens by granting to them the right to rule. This rule of the best, or most virtuous, citizens is called *aristocracy*.

Sometimes political scientists use the term *oligarchy* to refer to any polity in which the rule is placed in the hands of the few, regardless of the means used for selecting the few. By contrast, if the *politeia* accepts of the rule of the majority because the contribution of each individual citizen is equally honored for its own sake, the polity is called a *democracy*. One final form of rule is *tyranny*, the uncontrolled and self-interested rule of one person over the polity. The *politeia* which supports a tyrannical government is typically one of fear or acceptance of the force which accompanies such rule. That which is honored (or at least accepted) in a tyranny is violence and force.

Frequently, the *politeia* of a given polity directs that the honors of the society be distributed among different, and even competing, groups. Control over one aspect of government may be given to the majority, control of another to the wealthy, and control of yet another to the best or the religious. When this occurs to such a degree that it is impossible to determine which group ultimately controls the government, the government is called a *mixed regime*. In practice, the *politeias* of most regimes distribute honors to more than one group, although often one of those groups has ultimate control and defines the government. For example, a regime in which the majority controlled some aspects of governing, and the wealthy and the military controlled others, but all important and ultimate control was in the hands of the majority would still be called a democracy.

When we cannot isolate clearly where the ultimate control of the government in a polity lies, we truly are looking at a mixed regime. Today there are probably more mixed regimes in the world than any other type, and many would argue that the government of the United States is a mixed regime.

The concern with shared values involving justice and issues of right and wrong remains at the center of all politics. Political decisions are based on the decision-makers' notions of what is just or what is right in a given situation. That does not mean that all political decisions are based on high moral grounds. While the question of what is good, or right, or just may be addressed from the standpoint of principle, it may also be asked from the standpoint of power or self-interest. A ruling group may consistently use its self-interest as the sole basis for choosing between competing political alternatives. When it does so, the ruling group is saying that it is good, right, or just for its individual interests to dominate society. In a tyranny, the ruler typically is said to govern in that way.

Politics in this broad sense permeates all of society. It is at the heart of all human existence. Politics decides what will be taught in schools and who will teach it. Politics decides who, if anyone, will be allowed to own private property in the community. It decides who will be allowed to vote—one, or a few, or all. Politics even decides who will be allowed to marry and procreate and who will be allowed to worship as they see fit.

Everyone is aware of the existence of polities in which private property is outlawed, or ones in which marriage and procreation are strictly limited, or in which freedom of religion is nonexistent. American students frequently have a hard time seeing these decisions as political because they assume that they are a part of our individual freedom. We Americans often assume that it is an individual's personal right to marry whomever one pleases, or not to marry at all. Americans also tend to believe that people have the right to worship as they see fit, or not to worship at all. We tend to see such choices as our rights and to deny the authority of government to interfere with them! But the decision that these areas are matters of personal choice and beyond the reach of government are, in themselves, political decisions based upon the shared values, or *politeia*, of Americans.

In fact, decisions in all of these areas have been limited by various governments in America over the years. It is only in the past few decades that the last state laws against interracial marriages disappeared. Generations of American students, regardless of their wealth, were precluded from attending educational institutions, both public and private, in much of the country unless they were of the "appropriate" race and sex. Likewise, in colonial times and even in the early years of the republic, several states had established religions. Even today there are severe restrictions on what one may do on the basis of religion, as opposed to what one may believe. For example, one may believe that human sacrifice is an essential religious ritual, but one would be guilty of a crime if he engaged in such a ritualistic murder in the United States. Politics is deeply involved in even the most personal aspects of human life.

In order to fully grasp this concept of politics we must understand that, to the ancient Greeks, a human being's "natural place" was living in a *polis*. They thought that a truly human existence consisted of living in community with other human beings, sharing ideas and conversations concerning right and wrong, and good and evil. The Greek philosopher Aristotle explicitly stated that "man is by nature a political animal."[2] He explained that creatures of human form are not living a human existence if they are living without such a community. Aristotle added that one living outside of the *polis* by choice or nature was "either a beast or a god."[3] Human life and politics fall somewhere between beasts and gods.

To begin again from a slightly different perspective, all political action aims at either preservation or change. When dealing with political action, we are dealing with actions in relation to the members of our community, or, at the very least, sharing our space. In the political context, the question of what is best, or what is the good, is inevitably asked with regard to the relationships between the members of the community.[4] Regardless of whether one is pursuing preservation or change, one seeks the better alternative. Such pursuits lead to the question, implicitly or explicitly, of which alternative is better. Constantly seeking the better alternative inevitably leads one to the question of what is best or what is the good. When one encounters such questions, one is drawn to consider how the best or the good can be attained once it is identified.

The way in which a polity (or a people) answers these questions (What is the good? What is best?) and their political auxiliary (What is justice?) determines the type of polity it is or will be. The polity's answers to these questions *is* the *politeia* of that polity, society, or community. Accordingly, how a society answers those questions molds the sort of society it will be. In order to understand the government and politics of any people, we must begin with at least a tentative answer to how that people would answer the fundamental political questions: What is just? What is the good? What is right? Politics is again revealed to be centered on shared notions of what is worthy of honor (as being best, or just, or the good).

We can now give a working definition of politics. *Politics is the realm of human activity concerned with the communally shared notions of what is deserving of honor and blame and society's authoritative means of determining and implementing such shared notions.*

What About Power and Politics?

Some scholars and political analysts view *power* as the central concept of politics. They argue that power, and not the shared values of the community, defines all politics just as wealth defines all economics. These advocates of power politics claim the title of "political realists" to distinguish themselves from the "political idealists," who do not acknowledge power as the central concept of politics.

To understand the position of the political realists, we must first grasp the essentials of power and politics.

The leading academic proponent of power politics in the twentieth century is Hans J. Morgenthau.[5] According to Morgenthau, political realists believe that politics is an autonomous field of human endeavor, governed by its own rules, and not dominated by any other field. From this point of view, politics may be influenced by such things as economics, religion, ethics, or law, but politics is not dominated or controlled by any of these other fields. Politics is an independent realm of human activity.

For political realists the central concept and organizing principle of politics is power. Morgenthau defines *power* as "man's control over the minds and actions of other men."[6] Power is one's ability to replace another's will with one's own so that he does what you want him to do rather than what he would otherwise do. Accordingly, power is a psychological relationship between those who exercise it and those over whom it is exercised.

To understand this concept of power, one must bear in mind that power is not the same as force. Power is a psychological relationship between two minds, whereas force is a physical relationship between two bodies. Although power relationships may involve explicit or implicit threats of physical violence, if physical violence is actually used in the relationship, it is a relationship of force and not of power.

In addition, power must not be confused with mere influence. Influence refers to one's ability to affect another's decision, which stops short of actually *controlling* the other's will or decisions. Power involves a psychological control over the actions of others which stops short of physical violence, but extends beyond the ability to influence another's decision.

Morgenthau acknowledges that power exists in many relationships in nonpolitical settings. There are power relationships within the family, between parents and children, and between spouses. Power relationships also exist in the workplace and various other social institutions. While recognizing the presence of power in other human institutions, Morgenthau notes a profound difference between power in those places and power in the political realm. Power is simply one aspect of those other relationships, but not the most important part.

In politics power is the central concept around which all else revolves. Morgenthau distinguishes those other forms of power from political power by saying that politics deals with the power of holders of public authority, rulers, and other political leaders. Even with this limitation, politics has quite broad implications since "holders of public authority" is not necessarily limited to those holding official public offices. A robber may exercise power over you on a deserted street without holding public office.

Despite his primary focus on power, Morgenthau admits that power is the means to political ends and not an absolute end in itself.[7] While power considerations and calculations are crucial for political realists, power is almost always guided by other ultimate aims. Although power is the immediate aim in most political settings, it is sought as the means to some other end. For Morgenthau, power is always the immediate aim of international politics, but it is sought for the sake of pursuing other goals such as wealth, national self-determination, or glory.

Ultimately, even for the political realists, the essence of politics is focused on the shared values of the community. The goals for which power is sought and for which it is used are derived from the values shared by the political community involved. Most political realists ignore this fact, and even Morgenthau refuses to focus much attention on it. But Morgenthau does acknowledge that a purely political man, as he defines him, would be a beast.[8] In the twentieth century the fascists and the Nazis were the most explicit and willing proponents of power politics in practice. But their ends were among the most ideological or value-laden ends ever pursued by any nations—the vindication of Italian culture and the triumph of the Aryan race, respectively.

Political realists will not emphasize this point, and for good reason. Political realism was reborn in the wake of the destruction of World War II. It was an effort to remind politicians of the dangers involved in ignoring power in their pursuit of ideological ends— world brotherhood and democracy. The political realists focus on power because they have witnessed the destruction that resulted when many of the nations of the world sought to denigrate the role of power in politics. Morgenthau understood what he was doing. But some of the present-day advocates of power politics seem to have lost sight of it.

What Is the Political System?

In recent decades, many contemporary political scientists have written about politics from the standpoint of the *political system*. These writers view the political system as a mechanical device, like a machine or a computer, or a biological organism, such as a plant or animal, which carries out certain functions in response to various stimuli. The efficiency and the effectiveness of various political systems in performing their functions are the principal interests of these advocates of the systems approach to politics. Basically, the systems approach is an attempt to apply the general systems theory, which was developed to deal with mechanical devices and biological organisms, to the study of political life. The leading proponent of the systems approach to politics is David Easton.[9]

The primary focus of the systems analysis of politics is to study the political system's stimuli and responses in an empirical way. In the terminology of the systems approach, the stimuli of the political system are called *inputs*, and the responses are referred to as *outputs*. One goal of this approach to the study of politics is to reduce politics to the study of things, inputs and outputs, which can be measured and counted. By doing this one can avoid the problems of dealing with such difficult concepts as shared values or even power.

A second goal of this approach is the creation of a value-free political science, so that the science of politics can become more like the physical and biological sciences. While power is not quite so abstract a term as values or "what ought to be honored," it does present serious problems of recognition and measurement.[10] Accordingly, both the power approach and the communal values approach tend to be denigrated by the political behavioralists who seek to quantify the study of politics and reduce it to a study of precisely measured inputs and outputs in an effort to become more scientific.

Despite the reluctance of the systems theorists to deal with the values that are inherent in the political realm, Easton still finds it necessary to define the political system in terms of "the authoritative allocation of values for a society."[11] The effort of the systems approach to isolate politics from shared values of the community fails. Just as Morgenthau found it necessary to accept a fundamental role of values in politics, so, too, does Easton. Ultimately, the political system emerges as an abstraction rather than a reality. The political system allows us to glimpse only a part of the realm of politics, and not even its essence—shared or communal values.

Democracy and Totalitarianism

For most of the twentieth century the world has witnessed a contest between two competing political camps—liberal democracy and totalitarianism. These camps, unlike their predecessors in earlier centuries, were based on political ideologies, or universalized political ideas concerning how all society ought to be arranged and ruled. These political ideologies differed from earlier ideas on politics (or *politeias*) because they professed to be founded upon universal truths, discoverable by human beings and applicable to all human situations. The earlier ideas on politics had been specific to certain locations and human communities. These earlier ideas were viewed as being subject to change as conditions varied and were not thought to be applicable all peoples or nations.

The first modern ideology to emerge was *democracy*. The spread of democratic ideas in the eighteenth and nineteenth centuries ushered in the era of political ideology which would come to full bloom in the twentieth century. During the twentieth century, evolving democratic regimes faced a series of challenges from various competing ideologies which dominated political life in other polities. Among these challengers to liberal democracy were *fascism* in Italy, its more virulent cousin *Nazism* in Germany, and *communism* in the Soviet Union.

There are many differences between fascism (including Nazism) and communism but they shared some important characteristics. They each were endorsed by at least one powerful state which was willing to export their newfound political "truths" by force, if necessary. They were all convinced that their "universal truth" was *the* universal truth to replace the now outdated democracy. Because they were convinced of the ultimate truth of their doctrines, they established totalitarian states to suppress all other competing ideas by force. Because of these similarities, these new regimes are frequently lumped together under the heading of *totalitarianism*.

What Is Democracy?

Democracy can be broadly defined as a form of government in which the ultimate decision-making authority rests with the majority of the people living under it. Since the early nineteenth century democracy has been widely embraced as the model of good political rule and a goal to be strived for by all nations. Democracy emerged as the apparent victor in a long struggle against *authoritarianism*, the form of government in which rulers tolerate little or no public opposition and in which the rulers cannot legally be removed from office by the public. The form of democracy which emerged victorious was *liberal democracy*, a version of democracy, or majority rule, which is based upon the "natural rights," or liberties, possessed by all human beings. The majority rules, but it cannot violate individual rights.

The emergence of democracy as the model for all political rule made it necessary for virtually all rulers to put forth at least some claim of democratic justification for their rule. As a result, the term democracy has been used to describe several different forms of political regimes in recent times.

Direct democracy is used to describe political rule in which all, or most, of the citizens directly participate in the making of the important decisions of the community and the running of public affairs. Direct democracy is the classical democracy described by Aristotle. It is the democracy practiced in the ancient Greek *polis* and in the small New England townships. Direct democracy is also the democracy of small clubs and private associations. Because direct democracy requires the regular and frequent direct participation of most members or citizens, this form of democracy is limited to very small political entities.

Representative democracy refers to those governments in which the political leaders are selected on the basis of an open competition for the votes of the citizens. The people are the foundation of all political power. But their direct participation is limited primarily to the election of representatives to carry out their governing functions, including the making of law. Representative democracy is the form of government practiced in the United States and Western Europe, as well as in other parts of the world today. Representative democracy has also been evolving in central and Eastern Europe during the past few years. The use of popularly elected representatives to carry out the functions of government makes this form of government practicable in countries with large territories and populations, where direct democracy could not be used.

Democratic centralism describes those governments which claim to rule on behalf of the people or in the people's true interests, even though the leaders are not competitively elected or directly accountable to the citizenry. Under democratic centralism the democratic legitimacy of the established regime is not based on the democratic method of making all important decisions, as in direct democracies. Nor is its democratic legitimacy based on the democratic mode of selecting the important decision-makers, as in representative democracies. Rather the democratic legitimacy in democratic centralism is founded on the presence of effective leaders who claim to base their decision on the true interests of the people. Under democratic centralism, it is the *ends* of government rather than the *means* which legitimate the claim of democracy.

Democratic centralism has been used to justify the rule of the Communist party in the Soviet Union and in other communist states. Likewise, democratic centralism was a cornerstone of both Italian fascism and German Nazism. All actions of those states were justified in the name of the people and as being for the sake of the people. It is, in short, often justification for totalitarianism. Democratic centralism has also been used to justify traditional authoritarian regimes, particularly in developing countries or countries newly emerging from a colonial experience.

Democracy has taken on many meanings in the twentieth century. Some of these meanings are more or less compatible with traditional understandings of democracy, while others were not. The essential point is that the acceptance of democratic principles was so widespread in the twentieth century that even the most dictatorial of regimes were forced to find some method of claiming to be democratic. No government could claim legitimacy without showing its connection to the people.

What Is Totalitarianism?

Totalitarianism refers to governments in which authoritarian rulers recognize no limits to their powers and attempt to regulate every aspect of human life. Totalitarian governments are highly centralized and refuse to recognize or tolerate political parties holding different opinions. Totalitarianism refers to the totality of the aspects of society which the government seeks to control, as well as to the degree of control sought by the central authority. Totalitarianism emerged in the twentieth century as an outgrowth of the old forms of authoritarianism. Technological breakthroughs in the fields of communications, transportation, and military weaponry and tactics radically increased the abilities of governments to exercise control over their subjects. While totalitarianism was strengthened by technological developments, it was justified by the emergence of democratic centralism.

By the end of the nineteenth century, democracy could not be ignored or openly opposed, even by its severest critics, the old authoritarians. Many of the older regimes made concessions to the democratic elements of society in order to maintain some aspects of their former powers. These concessions were frequently made involuntarily, under a threat of force by advocates of democracy or in the wake of violence. The governments of the world were becoming more democratic, at least in appearance.

At the same time, severe critics of the liberal democratic movement also emerged. These critics asserted that liberal democracy and the accompanying economic order of private capitalism were actually enslaving people in a new way by giving them a false liberty or freedom. New forms of government were proposed which would operate in a totalitarian way in order to rid the people of false liberal democratic ideas and to rule in the best interests of the people. These totalitarian movements claimed that only they could rule in the true interests of the people. They argued that liberal democracy and capitalism had conspired to give people a false view of the world so that the people would forge their own chains and believe that they were free and happy in them. These totalitarian movements took two basic forms: fascism and communism.

Although fascism and communism would come to share many of the same totalitarian principles, the two forms of movement were very different from one another in other important aspects. During the height of the fascist movements, greater antagonism was exhibited toward their communist counterparts than toward their liberal democratic opponents. Likewise, the communists tended to be no more tolerant of fascists than of liberal democrats. In many ways fascism and communism represent two opposite poles of totalitarianism.

Under fascism the state becomes the center of all human life. The state gives all meaning to human existence. Fascists claim that liberal democracy corrupts human beings by focusing on the individual. This focus on the individual leads to a preoccupation with personal freedom and achievement which ultimately denies people the opportunity to become a part of the greatest human endeavor—the state. Fascism calls upon human beings to give up their ephemeral, false individual freedom and enables them to become a part of the state, the ultimate human enterprise.

Only through the state, the fascists claim, may human beings know true power and gain the ultimate human recognition by dominating other humans. Only through the state can a human being aspire to immortality by becoming a fully integrated part of the state, an immortal entity of human creation. The true fascist human being would be totally immersed in the state. One would gain all identity through the state and would see the highest human end as dying in the service of the state.

One particularly virulent form of fascism which emerged in the twentieth century was Nazism. *Nazism* is the form of fascism that was promoted by the National Socialist German Workers Party under the leadership of Adolf Hitler. Nazism took the basic tenets of fascism one step farther by introducing the notion of racism. Under the Nazis, it was not simply the state which was preeminent, but a particular race of people who were naturally superior and entitled to rule over the world. The claimed natural superiority of the German people, or the Aryan race, was used to justify their absolute control over all political, economic, and cultural activities. This claim was used by the Nazis to justify the domination, and even the extermination, of non-Aryan peoples.

At the other pole of totalitarianism is *communism*. Totalitarianism is not an essential part of the theory of communism developed by Karl Marx and Friedrich Engels. But as communism developed as a political regime in the Soviet Union under Vladimir Lenin and Joseph Stalin, totalitarianism emerged as an essential feature of the communist movement. Under communism, the state is not the ultimate goal, as it is for the fascists. The state possesses its enormous powers under communism to rid the people of the selfish and destructive attitudes which had developed under the extended rule of capitalists and liberal democrats. In the long run, the state will disappear when the last vestiges of capitalist thought or ideologies have been cleansed from the earth.

The ultimate goal for communists is the equality of human beings with regard to material possessions. Since communists view the world as being controlled by the material realm, material equality will result in total equality. For the communists, all value is derived from labor, which is the sole property of the human who performs it. Accordingly, no one should be allowed to profit from another's labor. So the idea of profiting from the labor of others is one of the principal capitalistic ideas that needs to be eradicated.

The communists envision a day when all will be allowed to enjoy the product of their own labor and exploit the value of no one else's labor. When that day finally arrives, there will emerge a society composed of equal, unselfish, sharing individuals. At that time, the communists argue, there will be no need for the state to regulate human affairs. However, until that time arrives, there is a great need for a totalitarian state to protect the people from selfish ideas and the enemies of the people. This communist conception of the state is quite different from that of the fascists.

In 1994, totalitarianism appears to be in retreat in much of the world, as the old communist states continue to crumble, and a zeal for democracy and capitalism spreads into the vacuums they left. But totalitarian regimes continue to exist in Cuba and in parts of Asia and elsewhere. Monumental changes have taken place in the world as a result of the revolution of 1989 in Eastern Europe. Despite the apparent demise of Soviet communism, one cannot now know whether totalitarianism will die out altogether or find some future revival. While there is some basis for great optimism for the future prospects for world peace and an end to ideological conflict, the future remains less than certain as political conflicts and economic uncertainties continue to dominate current events throughout the world.

Conclusion

The essence of politics is shared notions of justice and shared answers to questions concerning what is good and right. Efforts to avoid this conclusion lead one to abstractions which fail to address the essence of politics. Such efforts also present the danger of misunderstanding the vital political questions which we face in our everyday existence and which frequently have life and death consequences. If we hope to understand anything of significance about politics, we cannot ignore these questions of values, regardless of the difficulties they present. Proponents of "political realism" (power politics) and the systems approach to politics fail to the extent that they attempt to divorce the study of politics from the study of political values.

The ideological conflicts which forged the history of the twentieth century have been a stark reassertion of the centrality of values for politics. The promise of the revolution of 1989 to end the cold war and ideological conflict in the twenty-first century must not blind us to the centrality of values in politics. Rather, the end of ideological conflict, if it is here, offers a new challenge for us to understand the role of values in politics in new nondogmatic ways. The absence of a cold war in which each side must unthinkingly adhere to its own ideology for mere survival presents an opportunity for true reflection with regard to political values in a more open and searching way. Today's challenge is to exercise that new freedom responsibly and with the seriousness it deserves.

What is politics? As stated previously, politics may be defined as the realm of human activity concerning the shared notions of what is worthy of honor and blame and society's authoritative means of determining and implementing such shared notions. This definition has its roots in antiquity, but nothing in the past two thousand years has done anything to reduce its essential truth. On the contrary, a great deal of what has transpired in the intervening score of centuries has reconfirmed that this understanding of politics is one which grasps its essential character and nature. It is also one which is needed for the future of humankind.

Notes

1. I am deeply indebted to the late Howard B. White of the New School for Social Research for this formulation of the esssential nature of politics. See also Leo Strauss, "On Aristotle's Politics," *The City and Man* (Chicago: Rand McNally, 1964), pp. 13–49; and Leo Strauss, "On Classical Political Philosophy," *What Is Political Philosophy?* (originally published 1959; Westport, Conn.: Greenwood Press, 1973), pp. 78–94.

2. Aristotle, *Politics*, trans. Carnes Lord (Chicago: University of Chicago Press, 1984) (1253a3), p. 37.

3. Ibid. (1253a25–28), p. 37.

4. See generally Aristotle, *Nicomachean Ethics*, trans. Martin Ostwald (Indianapolis: Library of Liberal Arts, 1962) (1094a1–1096a10), pp. 3–9.

5. See generally Hans J. Morgenthau, *Politics Among Nations*, 6th ed., rev. by Kenneth W. Thompson (New York: McGraw-Hill, 1985).

6. Ibid., p. 32.

7. Ibid., pp. 31–32.

8. Ibid., p. 16.

9. See generally David Easton, *A Framework for Political Analysis* (Englewood Cliffs, N.J.: Prentice-Hall, 1965); David Easton, *A Systems Analysis of Political Life* (New York: Wiley, 1965).

10. See Morgenthau, Chapters 8–10.

11. Easton, *Framework*, p. 50.

Suggested Reading

Aristotle. *Nicomachean Ethics*. Translated by Martin Ostwald. Indianapolis: Library of Liberal Arts, 1962. Book I.

Aristotle. *Politics*. Translated by Carnes Lord. Chicago: University of Chicago Press, 1984. Books I and III.

Cohen, Carl, ed. *Communism, Fascism, and Democracy: The Theoretical Foundations*, 2nd ed. New York: Random House, 1972. See pp. 80–98 (on Marxism), 128–54 (on Leninism), 328–44 (on Italian fascism), 374–90 (on Nazism), 396–424 (on liberal democracy).

Easton, David. *A Framework for Political Analysis.* Englewood Cliffs, N.J.: Prentice-Hall, 1965.

Morgenthau, Hans J. *Politics Among Nations*, 6th ed. Revised by Kenneth W. Thompson. New York: McGraw-Hill, 1985. Chapters 1–10.

Strauss, Leo. "On Aristotle's *Politics.*" *The City and Man.* Chicago: Rand McNally, 1964.

2

The American Revolution

Paul A. Rahe

I

Was America's war for independence and the establishment of the American republic a revolution? Some, on both the left and the right, doubt it. Though mistaken, they have a case to make. There was, after all, considerable continuity in America between the old order and the new—and not just in population, language, manners, mores, and the like.

The American colonists were, in local affairs, self-governing prior to 1776, much as they would be thereafter. The principles on which they governed themselves bore a striking resemblance to those held by their British cousins across the seas, as they always had. For the king in Parliament, who had borne responsibility for intercolonial relations, overseas commerce, and imperial defense, the colonists simply substituted a national government of their own devising. Some property did change hands in the course of their struggle for independence, and the laws of inheritance underwent an alteration in a number of places. But neither event was a great social transformation. If the Americans consistently termed their war of national liberation a revolution, it was arguably a sign of an inflated sense of self-importance on their part.

One fact is certain. When Parliament passed the Stamp Act in February 1765 and Britain's colonists in North America mounted a campaign of massive resistance against the imposition of modest duties on legal documents, newspapers, pamphlets, playing cards, and the like, they were persuaded that they were acting to defend their traditional rights and privileges as Englishmen against what we would now call a revolution from above. Few, if any, then imagined that to preserve those inherited rights and privileges they would have to give up being Englishmen altogether. No one then spoke, at least not in public, of setting a radically new course.

Had Parliament's repeal of the Stamp Act in February 1766 brought the matter to a close, as many Americans at the time presumed it had, they could in the aftermath have adapted to their own situation the remarks that Edmund Burke later made concerning the behavior of the English in the course of the Glorious Revolution of 1688 and 1689:

> What we did was in truth and substance, and in a constitutional light, a revolution, not made, but prevented. We took solid securities; we settled doubtful questions; we corrected anomalies in our law. In the stable, fundamental parts of our constitution we made no revolution,—no, nor any alteration at all.[1]

Of course, the colonists did eventually declare their independence. But even this radical step can be interpreted in a conservative light. When Parliament repealed the Stamp Act, it stopped well short of endorsing the principle summed up in the colonists' slogan: "no taxation without representation." It, in effect, repudiated that principle in passing the Declaratory Act, which specified that the king in Parliament "had, hath, and of right ought to have, full power and authority to make laws and statutes of sufficient force and validity to bind the colonies and people of *America*, subjects of the crown of *Great Britain*, in all cases whatsoever."[2] Nothing could persuade the colonists to be satisfied with the claim advanced in Parliament that the latter's members represented not those who actually elected them but the nation as a whole. The colonists did not believe that they were *virtually* represented in and by a legislative body containing no members directly accountable to them at election time.

As a consequence, Parliament's subsequent imposition of the Townshend duties on tea and other items of trade stirred renewed resistance. And when, in reaction to the Boston Tea Party and other acts of resistance, Parliament passed and implemented the Coercive Acts—closing Boston harbor, suspending the constitution, altering the method of selection for the governor's council, and otherwise restricting local self-government in Massachusetts—the Americans were forced to choose between their allegiance to Great Britain and a reassertion and defense of their inherited rights and privileges as Englishmen. Here again, their revolution can be interpreted as an attempt, made under impossible circumstances, to restore what was essential in the prior status quo.

In any case, it may have been inevitable that Britain's colonies on the Atlantic seaboard of North America would eventually strike out on their own. If the revolutionary firebrand Thomas Paine is to be believed, this was the view of nearly everyone in England and America in the late eighteenth century. More than a century before the Stamp Act crisis, one Englishman had suggested that when Europe's "Colonies in the *Indies*" came "of age," they would "wean themselves" from their respective mother countries.[3] In 1722, in *Cato's Letters*, the radical journalists John Trenchard and Thomas Gordon took up this observation and recast it as a warning to Britain's rulers that as the colonies grew more prosperous and populous, they should take care to retain their loyalty. Citing "the corrupt State of human Nature," they denied that there was any prospect that the colonies would remain subject to the mother country any longer than it suited their purposes.

In the end, Trenchard and Gordon contended, when a colony has become "too powerful to be treated only as a Colony," one must, if one wishes to maintain close ties, "imitate the Example of Merchants and Shopkeepers; that is, when their Apprentices are acquainted with their Trade and their Customers, and are out of their Time, to take them into Partnership, rather than let them set up for themselves in their Neighbourhood."[4] Francis Hutcheson reiterated this observation in 1755, dismissing as "unnatural" the notion that "a large society, sufficient for all the good purposes of an independent political union," should remain "subject to the direction and government of a distant body of men who know not sufficiently the circumstances and exigencies of this society."[5]

By the time Hutcheson penned these words, the thirteen colonies had already come to form a large society, sufficient for all the good purposes of an independent political union and capable of establishing a partnership on more or less equal terms with Great Britain. It was with this fact in mind that Benjamin Franklin, in 1754, proposed his Albany Plan of Union with its provisions that America be represented in Parliament and that the colonies be united for the common defense under a council presided over by a nominee of the British crown, made up of representatives elected by the colonial assemblies, and authorized to impose taxes. In principle, at least, it should have been perfectly possible for the American colonies to have achieved effective autonomy or even to have found their way to independence without carrying out a revolution. The key to understanding why this proved impossible and what made the American Revolution genuinely revolutionary is found in the Declaratory Act's assertion of the absolute supremacy of the king in Parliament. In later years, John Adams would deny that the war for independence was even a "part of the Revolution." It was, he insisted,

> only an Effect and Consequence of it. The Revolution was in the Minds of the People, and this was effected, from 1760 to 1775, in the course of fifteen Years before a drop of blood was drawn at Lexington. The Records of thirteen Legislatures, the Pamp[h]lets, Newspapers in all the Colonies, ought [to] be consulted, during that Period, to ascertain the Steps by which the public Opinion was enlightened and informed concerning the Authority of Parliament over the Colonies.[6]

To grasp what was at stake in the struggle over the authority of Parliament, one must pause to consider more fully the mixed character of the British regime and the manner in which trimming statesmen in Great Britain had managed to strike a balance between the contradictory principles informing that country's politics. One must also consider the reasons why this balancing act could not be sustained in America, and the choice of principles ultimately made by the colonists.

The polity that emerged in England in the wake of the Glorious Revolution was a mixed regime. It was remarkably successful in practice, but it remained vulnerable throughout because it was grounded in and sanctioned first principles which were diametrically opposed and utterly incompatible. To all appearances, this polity was medieval. There was an hereditary monarch who reigned by the grace of God. In some measure, he even ruled, and he styled himself the Defender of the Faith as his more recent predecessors had. There was an hereditary, landed aristocracy. In passing property from one generation to another, the aristocracy practiced primogeniture, denying daughters and younger sons an equal share in the inheritance—all for the purpose of empowering the firstborn son. Large parts of its estates were entailed and so could not be sold or given away. And the members of this aristocracy were accorded by right of birth, if not by recent royal nomination, the privilege of sitting in Parliament's House of Lords.

There was also an established church with bishops appointed by the king and graced with political privileges comparable to those of the aristocracy. There was a House of Commons as well. This more democratic branch of the government exercised considerable influence and power. Its members were, however, elected not by the general public to represent constituencies of similar population but by corporations which had been accorded this privilege by royal charter in ages past. A number of populous cities were unrepresented while some of these ancient corporations were so lacking in population that they were called "rotten boroughs." Many members of Parliament owed their seats to noble patrons. It was not uncommon for the king's ministers to influence votes in the House of Commons by a shrewd distribution of lucrative offices and honors.

Religious toleration had been instituted. But the measure passed into law as an act of royal and parliamentary indulgence, not as a legal confirmation of the rights of conscience, and it afforded no protection at all to Catholics, to Socinians (biblical unitarians), to Deists (philosophical unitarians), and to nonbelievers. The attempt to unite all Protestants within a single, latitudinarian church had been rejected by the Anglican clergy, and the Test and Corporation acts barred Protestant Dissenters from public office.

Edmund Burke was not being entirely disingenuous when he denied that the Glorious Revolution was what we would now call a revolution. As he put it,

> The nation kept the same ranks, the same orders, the same privileges, the same franchises, the same rules for property, the same subordinations, the same order in the law, in the revenue, and in the magistracy,—the same lords, the same commons, the same corporations, the same electors. The Church was not impaired. Her estates, her majesty, her splendor, her orders and gradations, continued the same.[7]

And yet there were those who insisted that the Glorious Revolution had been what the name suggests it was. After all, there had been a change of personnel at the top, and that change had been effected in an highly irregular fashion. Not even the eloquence of an Edmund Burke could disguise the fact that King James II had been deposed by his subjects. One could call the event an "abdication" and leave it ambiguous whether James's departure from the throne was constituted by his abuses as king or by his flight to

France. But nothing could hide the fact that William of Orange had arrived in England with a sizable army unbidden by the king, that leading aristocrats and serving officers had broken their oath of allegiance to James and had rallied to the Dutch invader's cause, and that William's claim to succession on the throne was, on hereditary principles, indefensible.

Well might adherents of the Tory party, steeped as they were in devotion to altar and throne, recoil in the face of the betrayal of God's anointed king which they had sanctioned and even connived at. They appealed to the necessity of the case, to the rights of conquest, and to Providence in a vain attempt to settle their own consciences. As loyal Anglicans, they could perhaps console themselves with the fact that, with the succession of an aggressively Catholic king, they had been forced to choose between altar and throne. But there was nothing in the principles of the old Tory party to sanction such a choice on the part of men who considered themselves heirs to the royalist Cavaliers of the English Civil War.

The Tories' Whig opponents were committed to religious liberty and the parliamentary cause. So they were on firmer ground when they dismissed all claims of divine right and defended the revolution as an act of legitimate, popular resistance to tyranny. Some eighty years after the Glorious Revolution the Swiss observer Jean Louis de Lolme contrasted the United Kingdom with "almost all the States of Europe." Elsewhere "the will of the Prince holds the place of law," but in Great Britain the "English, placed in more favourable circumstances, have judged differently." In his view, their verdict had been reached once and for all at the time of their revolution when "the true principles of civil society were fully established." By expelling James II for violating his coronation oath, they confirmed "the doctrine of Resistance, that ultimate resource of an oppressed People." By excluding the Stuart family with its penchant for despotism, they "determined that Nations are not the property of Kings." In 1688 and 1689, "the principles of Passive Obedience, the Divine and indefeasible Right of Kings, in a word, the whole scaffolding of false and superstitious notions, by which the Royal authority had till then been supported, fell to the ground."[8]

But even the Whigs found it expedient in the end to play down the revolutionary character of what they had done and to look the other way when many of their Tory compatriots refused to take an oath asserting the legitimacy of William's rule. As Burke's shrewdly calculated misrepresentation of the revolution suggests, Whigs and

Tories alike eventually took to heart the advice profferred to conspirators by Niccolò Machiavelli:

> He who desires or wishes to reform the condition of a city and wishes that it be accepted and that it be able to maintain itself to everyone's satisfaction is forced to retain at least the shadow of the ancient modes so that it might seem to the people that the order has not changed—though, in fact, the new orders are completely alien to those of the past . . . And if the magistrates change from those of old in number, authority, and term of office, they ought at least to retain the name.[9]

The French philosopher Montesquieu, after visiting England early in the eighteenth century, described the British regime as "a republic" that "conceals itself under the form of a monarchy."[10] A restoration of the legitimate Stuart line remained a serious possibility half a century after James II's deposition, but only because the English were never fully reconciled to what they had done and could never face up to the consequences.

As the testimony of Montesquieu and Lolme suggests, visitors from the continent of Europe were inclined to dismiss as mere subterfuge the surviving trappings of the old regime. They supposed that, in Britain, they had come face to face with a radically new political order portending the future of the human race. In contrast, Americans who crossed the Atlantic were prone to suppose that they had sailed into the distant past. Although they tended to take pride in their heritage and to stand in awe at the splendor of the English court, they were also inclined to be decidedly uncomfortable with the medieval institutions and practices that remained intact.

II

There were, in fact, two Englands—the world of hierarchy and ordered ranks described with such enthusiasm by Burke, and another polity, which he found it expedient to pass by largely unnoticed. In the shadow of the establishment, there survived a class of Protestant Dissenters, lukewarm Anglicans, believing unitarians, religious agnostics, and barely concealed atheists. These were more at home in the cities and towns than in the country shires, and they were closely connected with the rapidly expanding commercial sphere

dominated by artisans, merchants, agricultural improvers, and those
in the learned professions. This class exercised an influence all out
of proportion to the meager numbers of those within it. Its adherents championed and propagated a radical doctrine which derived
political legitimacy neither from divine right nor from tradition but
from the consent of the governed.

John Locke was this doctrine's most respectable and consistent
exponent. The appeal to prescription or tradition he ignored as needing
no refutation. He focused his attack on the doctrine of divine right.
In the first of his *Two Treatises of Government*, he debunked the
case made on behalf of absolute monarchy by the old Tory defenders of patriarchal government. They contended that ordinary human beings are like children and that both nature and the Bible
dictate their subjection to the tutelage of those who happen to be
in authority over them. In his *Second Treatise*, Locke argued that
all human beings are by nature free and equal, that no one has been
given by nature or nature's God the right to rule others against their
wishes. So all legitimate human authority derives from the consent
of the governed, and governments have been established by human
beings for their own convenience—to safeguard their lives, their
liberty, and the property that they hold in the fruits of their labor.

From these premises, Locke concluded that public office is a trust.
It is perfectly appropriate that the governed hold accountable those
on whom they have conferred this trust. Citizens have the right to
resist oppression and to overthrow and replace governments hostile to or neglectful of the limited ends for which those governments were established. In defense of this revolutionary doctrine,
Algernon Sidney and Colonel Richard Rumbold were martyred.
Rumbold summed up its proponents' creed more succinctly than
anyone else either before or thereafter when, on the scaffold, he
denied that the mass of mankind are born with saddles on their
backs and a favored few booted and spurred, ready to ride them
legitimately by the grace of God.

At the end of the seventeenth century and in succeeding decades,
the radical banner was held high and the doctrine of consent was
taught by a host of talented polemicists. They championed what
they called "the Country" against those closely associated with "the
Court" in the reigns of King William, Queen Anne, and their Ha-
noverian successors George I, George II, and George III. A number of considerations explain the remarkable influence exercised
by these radical Whigs and their disaffected, country-Tory admir-

ers. They were better educated than their clerical opponents and more skilled in the new art of polemical journalism. Their arguments were more consistent with the findings of modern science than those of the high Anglicans. And—most important—it was difficult if not impossible to justify the established order on the basis of indefeasible hereditary right doctrine and unlimited passive obedience.[11]

By the time of the Stamp Act crisis in the mid-1760s, the radical Whig doctrine espoused by John Locke had found a place within the authoritative exposition of the British constitution propounded in William Blackstone's *Commentaries on the Laws of England.* Already, in 1741, the Scottish philosopher David Hume had hazarded two closely related observations. In one place he noted, "There are few men of knowledge or learning, at least, few philosophers, since Mr. LOCKE has wrote, who would not be ashamed to be thought" to belong to the Tory party.[12] Elsewhere, he remarked that "there has been a sudden and sensible change in the opinions of men within these last fifty years, [brought about] by the progress of learning and of liberty."

Most people, in this island, have divested themselves of all superstitious reverence to names and authority: The clergy have much lost their credit: Their pretensions and doctrines have been ridiculed; and even religion can scarcely support itself in the world. The mere name of *king* commands little respect; and to talk of a king as GOD's vice-regent on earth, or to give him any of those magnificent titles, which formerly dazzled mankind, would but excite laughter in every one. Though the crown, by means of its large revenue, may maintain its authority in times of tranquillity, upon private interest and influence; yet, as the least shock or convulsion must break all these interests to pieces, the royal power, being no longer supported by the settled principles and opinions of men, will immediately dissolve. Had men been in the same disposition at the *revolution*, as they are at present, monarchy would have run a great risque of being entirely lost in this island.[13]

Hume's obituary for the doctrine of the divine right of kings erred only in being premature. Prior to Hume's death, a serious convulsion did take place within the realm ruled under the British crown. As he had foreseen, the monarchy collapsed. With it, in time, all religious establishments likewise gave way. But these events transpired, not in Great Britain but in its colonies on the other side of the Atlantic Ocean—for there, "the progress" of what Hume meant by "learning" and "liberty" greatly exceeded anything known in the mother country. There the new way of thinking espoused by John Locke and the radical Whigs found particularly fertile ground.

III

Just as there were two Englands, so also were there two Americas. In the colonies, the trappings of the old regime were much less visible than in the mother country, but they were still present. There was no royal court, and there were no lords. And yet all but two of the colonies sported proprietary or royal governors who were armed with a viceregal prerogative more impressive on paper than the powers wielded in Britain by the king. These governors conducted affairs in a manner suggestive of the pomp and circumstance familiar in the mother country. In the process, they set the tone for those socially prominent in the colonies.

Some colonists found it hard to bear the behavior of those within the entourage of the governors with their "Airs of Wisdom and superiority" and their "fribbling Affectation of Politeness."[14] But many were caught up in the rivalry for stations of honor. If anything, as the decision for independence approached, the concern with hierarchy and the competition for rank was growing more rather than less intense. In May 1774, Joseph Edmundson, the Mowbray herald extraordinary of the English College of Arms, was asked to prepare rules of precedency spelling out for those within a colonial governor's entourage precisely where they stood.

As there were no lords in America, so also were there no bishops. But the Anglican clergy of the colonies were, in principle, no less beholden to the bishop of London than those residing near to hand. As the Revolution approached, there was a campaign under way to tighten up church discipline, to strengthen the hand of the clergy against their lay patrons, and to that end to secure the appointment of a bishop to serve in America. Many of the colonists were Dissenters, especially in New England. But where they were in the majority, their sect was the established church. This state of affairs gave them a stake in the inherited order not shared by Dissenters in England. The colonies had all been founded with a religious end in mind. The voyage of the *Mayflower* was undertaken first and foremost "for the Glory of God, and Advancement of the Christian Faith" and only secondarily for "the Honour of our King and Country."[15] All of the early colonial charters resolutely sound this theme.

The religious establishments that did exist in the colonies had over time become far more tolerant of religious outsiders than were the national churches in England, Scotland, and Ireland. But this tolerance served only to mitigate, not to alter the fact that most of the colonists were living within an ecclesiastical polity. To a great extent, the clergy retained respect, and their pretensions and doctrines seemed impervious to ridicule. In the colonies, there was no lack of what Hume termed a "superstitious reverence to names and authority."

One did not find in America the vast disparities of wealth so visible in Britain, but there were rich and poor nonetheless. In most of the colonies, there was an abundance of virgin land, although this did not altogether eliminate dependency among whites. Tenant farmers could be found in New York's Hudson Valley and in New Jersey. A great many immigrants first came to America as indentured servants—bound by contract to labor for those who had paid for their passage across the Atlantic. Others became such under the pressure of poverty soon after their arrival. The fact that tenant farmers were the exception and that indentured servitude was a temporary state did not prevent the growth of an ethos of political and social deference. In the South, the prevalence of Negro slavery gave an aristocratic cast to the whole society.

Patriarchy's hold on the American political imagination may have been, by European standards, quite tenuous, but it did exist. Husbands and fathers dominated colonial families to a considerable degree, and in one fashion or another their authority was reinforced by the law. This circumstance, together with the Americans' inherited and unquestioned allegiance to England's king, nourished in some quarters the confusion between paternal and political authority that the experience of childhood nearly always instills. The fact that the king was far away and never to be seen may have loosened, but did not eliminate, his hold on public sentiment. Well into 1775, though armed conflict with the forces of the crown was already under way, George Washington and the officers of the Continental Army were still drinking toasts to the monarch's health.

There was, of course, another side to the story, and it deserves particular emphasis here. For if the Americans operated, as their British cousins did, under a hybrid settlement that combined distinct and incompatible principles and practices, it is only fair to remark that, in the New World, the mix of medieval and modern was much less favorable to what remained of the ancien régime. It may have taken what John Adams termed a "Revolution . . . in the Minds of the People" to persuade the colonists to renounce "the Authority of Parliament over the Colonies." But America was, from the outset, far closer to being a radical Whig paradise than the mother country was.

In a great many respects, the colonies were already independent states by the time of the Stamp Act crisis. They had their own representative assemblies. In most ways they actually managed their own affairs. Ultimately, all were subject to the purview of the authorities in London. But apart from enacting navigation acts to regulate commerce between America, Britain, and Europe, Parliament rarely had any compelling reason to insist on meddling in local affairs. When the authorities in the mother country did intervene, they could often be convinced to side with the assembly against the governor. The governor usually occupied his office for a short period of time before returning to Britain, while the former represented interests not likely to disappear.

Whatever their expectations may at first have been, the appointed governors soon discovered that in America the legislature really was supreme. In part as a consequence of a program of reform pressed on the authorities in London in the late 1690s by John Locke, in part as a result of local initiative and legislation, the appointed governors had very little in the way of patronage with which to manipulate the colonial assemblies. In addition, there were no rotten boroughs in the New World and no prospect that they would ever emerge. Those who represented a given locality in the colonial assembly paid close attention, even when not under instruction, to the sentiments of their constituents.

The strength of the religious establishments was undercut by a religious revival. The Great Awakening, occasioned by George Whitfield's triumphant evangelical tour of America, had intensified religious sensibles in every colony. In its aftermath, there occurred a splintering of the traditional sects. By the time of the Revolution, the colonies which had religious establishments found their establishments under sustained assault.

The religious revival had had another surprising consequence. Religious enthusiasm is not ordinarily conducive to the spread of a reasonable Christianity like that espoused by John Locke, and the first Great Awakening can hardly be said to have been friendly to coldly rational religion. But, as David Hume had pointed out, enthusiasm inspires self-confidence, and it renders its supporters "free from the yoke of ecclesiastics" and inclined to "great independence in their devotion" and even to "a contempt of forms, ceremonies, and traditions."[16] When the novelty wears off and religious enthusiasm wanes, the independence of mind initially fostered by enthusiasm can open the way for enlightenment, as had happened in England.

In America, something of this sort also took place. Initially, disgust at the excesses of Whitfield's admirers drove more conventional Anglicans and Dissenters in the direction of rational religion. Later, as the ardor of the enthusiasts cooled, many of them stumbled onto the same path. A remarkably high proportion of those prominent in the Revolution were unorthodox Christians, if not Deists outright. In political affairs, despite the persistence in many quarters of a "superstitious reverence to names and authority," many American ministers and laymen evidenced the self-confidence, the independence of mind, the contempt for forms, ceremonies, and traditions, and something of the sense of mission and destiny that had distinguished the enthusiasts in days gone by.

Although religion had played a preeminent role in the founding of the colonies, most had been from the start entrepreneurial enterprises as well. The establishment and development of the colonies had been very much a part of a scheme for the promotion of commerce and progress in the arts, which had been devised early in the seventeenth century by Sir Francis Bacon, the first great advocate of the scientific revolution. Through much of the seventeenth and eighteenth centuries, the colonial system was managed by men such as John Locke who shared Bacon's hopes for economic and technological development. In part as a consequence of their efforts to encourage immigration, the American population grew at far too fast a rate to be compatible with the maintenance of traditional, comparatively uniform religious communities.

Subsistence farming was quite common and perhaps even predominant in the Northeast. But the same cannot be said for the South. Well before the Revolution, the colonies had become in both spirit and fact pretty much what they were meant to be from the start: dynamic, commercial societies intimately tied by trade to the mother country. In the colonies, self-made men, such as Benjamin Franklin, were more plentiful than they had been anywhere in the world at any previous time in human history. As was only natural, these entrepreneurs found thoroughly congenial the new economic thinking of Bacon and Locke and the political outlook that went with it.

Like their cousins on the other side of the Atlantic, educated Americans tended to be familiar with the writings of John Locke. These works confirmed their inclination toward an independence of mind in matters religious, moral, and political. No political work was to be found in more colonial libraries than Locke's *Two Treatises of Government*. In the sermons, pamphlets, and newspapers published in America during the decisive period stretching from 1760 to 1776, none was as often cited, quoted, paraphrased, plagiarized, and applied to the crisis that arose. Locke's sly exploitation of religious rhetoric enabled unsuspecting clergymen throughout the colonies to present his novel political doctrine to their parishioners as the teaching of St. Paul.

Of course, there was a host of literate individuals in America who never bothered to read Locke's dense political tract. But a great many of these imbibed his teaching concerning the natural rights of man and his doctrine of jealous anticipation, resistance, and revolution from other, more entertaining sources produced in England by Locke's radical Whig admirers. Self-respect and a sense of their own dignity as Englishmen gave the colonists a powerful motive for resenting Parliament's attempt to tax them without expressly securing their consent. And the Lockean first principles so visible in the political books they read provided them with a theoretical justification appealing to nature and nature's God to support their right to self-government.

In reading these works, the Americans also came across the schemes of political architecture pioneered during England's Great Rebellion, adapted under the Restoration by Locke and his fellow Whigs, and further elaborated after the Glorious Revolution as a critique of the machinations of England's Court party by the radical Whigs and their successors. This aspect of the colonists' Whig heritage had a profound impact on the conduct of public affairs within the colonial assemblies. It shaped the rhetoric of corruption and conspiracy that had already come to characterize American public debate decades before the Stamp Act was passed.

Lockean first principles added force to the Americans' instinctive annoyance at Parliament's clumsy attempts at an encroachment on their traditional rights. And the teaching concerning political architecture that they had also imbibed encouraged them to renounce the authority of the succeeding British administrations on the grounds that Parliament was a corrupt and unrepresentative body lacking political legitimacy even at home.

IV

As a result of careful statesmanship on the part of trimming politicians through a series of generations, the British managed to obscure and conceal, if not ultimately resolve, the contradictions inherent in their hybrid political regime. As Edmund Burke and his Court Whig predecessors intended, the sanction of tradition made it difficult and even perhaps impossible to separate institutions and practices that argument could not logically bring together and justify by appeal to a common principle. As William Blackstone's *Commentaries on the Laws of England* suggests, the British managed to satisfy Tories and Whigs alike by avoiding an appeal to first principles, by attributing to the king in Parliament an "absolute despotic power,"[17] and by defending that attribution and the overall shape of British politics and society by an appeal owing more to tradition than to reason.

With regard to America, Burke advocated a trimming strategy designed to achieve a similar end. "Leave America to tax herself," Burke pleaded in Parliament.

> I am not here going into the distinctions of rights, nor attempting to mark their boundaries. I do not enter into these metaphysical distinctions; I hate the very sound of them . . . Leave the rest to the schools; for there only may they be discussed with safety. But if, intemperately, unwisely, fatally, you sophisticate and poison the very source of government, by urging subtle deductions, and consequences odious to those you govern, from the unlimited and illimitable nature of supreme sovereignty, you will teach them by these means to call that sovereignty itself in question. When you drive him hard, the boar will surely turn upon the hunters. If that sovereignty and their freedom cannot be reconciled, which will they take? They will cast your sovereignty in your face. Nobody will be argued into slavery.[18]

Burke warned his colleagues that the Americans exhibited the same "fierce love of liberty" that typified the English. With an eye

to the issue that had occasioned the struggle under way, he reminded
them that "the great contests for freedom" in their own country
"were from the earliest times chiefly upon the question of taxing."
He impressed on his fellow members of Parliament the fact that
the religion of those in New England was "a refinement on the
principle of resistance," dubbing it "the dissidence of dissent, and
the protestantism of the Protestant religion." He pointed out to them
the manner in which the prevalence of slavery in the South rendered that region's whites stubborn adherents of the cause of their
own liberty. And he emphasized that, in the colonies, there were a
great many lawyers, versed in a study which "renders men acute,
inquisitive, dexterous, prompt in attack, ready in defence, full of
resources. In other countries, the people, more simple, and of a
less mercurial cast, judge of an ill principle in government only by
an actual grievance; here they anticipate the evil and judge of the
pressure of the grievance by the badness of the principle. They augur
misgovernment at a distance, and snuff the approach of tyranny in
every tainted breeze."[19] Burke spared no pains in his quest to bring
home to his colleagues the folly of making policy for the colonies
on the basis of an abstract principle of parliamentary sovereignty
that, in other circumstances, he thought it prudent and proper to
assert. But, in the situation, his fellow members of Parliament did
not see fit to adopt his shrewd advice.

This left the Americans in a quandary. John Adams discerned
what was at stake from the outset. In 1765, this young lawyer sought
to set the struggle with Parliament in the context of world history
in his *Dissertation on the Canon and Feudal Law*. Behind Parliament's imposition of the stamp tax, he discerned "a direct and formal design . . . to enslave all America." He readily conceded that
the Reformation, the Great Rebellion, and the Glorious Revolution
had left the alliance between designing clerics and ambitious kings
in Great Britain "greatly mutilated." But he nonetheless contended
that, in that island kingdom, this "wicked confederacy" was "not
yet destroyed."

To the forebears of his fellow colonists, Adams attributed "an
utter contempt of all that dark ribaldry of hereditary, indefeasible
right—the Lord's anointed—and the divine, miraculous original of
government with which priesthood had enveloped the feudal monarch in clouds and mysteries, and from whence they had deduced
the most mischievous of all doctrines, that of passive obedience
and non-resistance."

To his contemporaries Adams addressed an appeal, calling on them to abandon that "timidity" which made them "afraid to think."

> Let it be known that British liberties are not the grants of princes or parliaments, but original rights, conditions of original contracts, coequal with prerogative and with government; that many of our rights are inherent and essential, agreed on as maxims and established as pre-liminaries even before a parliament existed.

And Adams called on his fellow colonists to "search for the foundations of British laws and government in the frame of human nature, in the constitution of the intellectual and moral world."[20] He demanded that the colonists abandon respect for prescription and put asunder what the Court Whigs and Edmund Burke had worked so hard to bring together. He asked them to embrace one England and repudiate the other—which, whether he then confessed it or not, was to call for revolution.

Few, if any, among Adams's contemporaries relished the prospect of the colonies severing their ties with the mother country, and they recognized the need for what they termed a common "superintending power." They reasserted radical Whig principles that established popular self-government as a matter of right rather than revocable privilege and that grounded this right in nature as well as in the particular history of the English constitution. But they also sought some way to reconcile their assertion of this right with an allegiance to Great Britain.

In the very first pamphlet provoked by the Stamp Act crisis, James Otis took up the suggestion advanced by Benjamin Franklin that the Americans be given representation in Parliament, arguing that this body could then legitimately tax the colonists. Otis's proposal turned out to be unacceptable to both parties to the dispute. Many of the colonists entertained grave misgivings. It was common practice in America for a representative's constituents to give detailed instructions to the man whom they elected to the assembly. In an age in which it took three months to sail from the New World to the Old, it would be extremely difficult to hold accountable representatives who resided at so great a distance.

Otis's proposal was unacceptable to Parliament because it would have opened up a can of worms. It would have undone the compromise worked out within Britain's political class in the first quarter-century following the Glorious Revolution. It would also have dis-

pelled the illusion of historical continuity and the sense of tradition that even those within Parliament most sympathetic to the Americans thought it essential to sustain.

It would have been politically impossible for Parliament to extend representation to the colonies overseas while at the same time
maintaining the rotten boroughs at home and denying representation to Manchester, Birmingham, Sheffield, and other populous
English localities which elected no members to Parliament. As Lord
Mansfield put it in the House of Lords in 1766, "Every objection
. . . to the dependency of the colonies upon Parliament, which arises to it upon the ground of representation, goes to the whole present
constitution."[21]

In his testimony before the House of Commons in 1766, Benjamin Franklin sought another expedient. He suggested a distinction between internal taxation designed to produce a revenue, which
no one could lawfully impose on the colonists but the colonists
themselves, and duties aimed solely at the regulation of trade, which
Parliament could impose in its capacity as the empire's superintending power. He contended that the Americans would recognize
the dictates of necessity and, in effect, give tacit consent to Parliament's exercise of a power to enact such duties as required for the
survival of the empire, for this is what they had always done in the
past.

It was on this presumption that Parliament repealed the Stamp
Act and then imposed on the colonists the Townshend duties. Had
this system of tariffs not been designed to raise a revenue, the
colonists might have left well enough alone. But it was perfectly
clear that, under the guise of regulating trade, Parliament had gone
in search of revenue, and so the colonists ultimately judged the
compromise suggested by Franklin unworkable. As John Dickinson
would ultimately point out, the colonists could trust no one but their
own duly elected representatives: "the money *said* to be taken from
us for our defence, *may be employed* for our injury."[22]

Finally, in desperation, as resistance to the collection of the
Townshend duties provoked Parliament to pass the Coercive Acts,
figures such as Thomas Jefferson, John Adams, James Iredell, and
James Wilson sought another way out. They refused to acknowledge that Parliament had any right to legislate for the colonies at
all. They asserted that the colonial assemblies were Parliament's
equals. And they contended that the empire was held together by a
common executive. As Wilson put it, "the different members of the

British Empire are distinct states, independent of each other, but connected together under the same sovereign."[23]

Though ingenious, this expedient was even less workable than the suggestion that the colonists be given representation in Parliament. In addressing their appeals directly to George III, the colonists called into question the fundamental principle underlying the Revolution Settlement, as expressed in the coronation oath of William of Orange and his wife, Mary, who promised "to govern the people of this kingdom of England, and the dominions thereunto belonging, according to the statutes in parliament agreed on, and the laws and customs of the same."[24] No one in Parliament, Whig or Tory, would have been willing to concede to the monarch the capacity to act contrary to the wishes of Parliament in any sphere at all, and George III knew better than to think that he could get away with the attempt.

The only expedient that might have worked was the one suggested by Edmund Burke. Parliament might have continued to take for granted its own supremacy. The colonists, in their turn, might have continued in their presumption that an assembly in no way accountable to them could in no way pretend to speak for them and represent their interests. And the peace between them could nonetheless have been maintained as it had been before 1763. But this would have been possible only if Parliament had practiced restraint and refrained for prudential reasons from exercising the power and authority that it arrogated on principle to itself. Such a policy, requiring as it did the subordination of heartfelt principle to the demands of prudence, required statesmanship of an unusual kind. In the late 1760s and early 1770s such trimming statesmanship was lacking.

V

In declaring independence, the Americans grasped the nettle which the English had refused in 1688 and 1689, and they embarked on a journey that would eventually require them to jettison all that smacked of the old regime. As they approached the fateful decision, Thomas Paine published his famous pamphlet *Common Sense*, encouraging them with the thought that their cause was "in great measure the cause of all mankind," that their struggle for independence marked "the birthday of a new world," and that they actually had it in their

"power to begin the world over again."[25] When the Americans selected a design for the Great Seal of the United States of America
they made its principal theme the assertion that 1776 marked the
beginning of a *novus ordo seclorum*—"a new order of the ages."

No one ever spoke more eloquently of the revolutionary implications of America's Declaration of Independence than Thomas
Jefferson, its primary author. Not long before the fiftieth anniver-
sary of its adoption and signing, Jefferson received an invitation,
asking that he journey from Monticello to Washington, to join in
the festivities held to commemorate the event. Because he was ill,
he was unable to attend. In fact, like John Adams, he died on the
day of the great celebration. Although weakened by disease, the
aged statesman marshalled his meager physical resources, and in
his last surviving letter, he described the choice made on the Fourth
of July 1776 in language echoing the words uttered by the Whig
martyr Colonel Richard Rumbold as he was about to be executed
in 1685 for the role he had played in the Rye House Plot:

> May it be to the world, what I believe it will be, (to some parts
> sooner, to others later, but finally to all,) the signal of arousing men
> to burst the chains under which monkish ignorance and superstition
> had persuaded them to bind themselves, and to assume the bless-
> ings and security of self-government. That form which we have
> substituted, restores the free right to the unbounded exercise of rea-
> son and freedom of opinion. All eyes are opened, or opening, to the
> rights of man. The general spread of the light of science has already
> laid open to every view the palpable truth, that the mass of mankind
> has not been born with saddles on their backs, nor a favored few
> booted and spurred, ready to ride them legitimately, by the grace of
> God.[26]

Thomas Paine had been correct when he asserted that America's
cause was "in great measure the cause of all mankind." By step-
ping in where their English forebears had feared to tread, the
Americans set an example that would, they fully hoped and expected, set the world on fire.

In their Declaration of Independence, the former colonists sought
to achieve three ends: to present themselves to the world as a single "People" united under a government worthy of recognition and
support, to elaborate the fundamental principles justifying their
assumption "among the Powers of the Earth, [of] the separate and
equal Station to which the Laws of Nature and of Nature's God

entitle them," and to demonstrate "to a candid World" that, in assuming that station, they had not sinned against "Prudence," which dictates "that Governments long established should not be changed for light and transient Causes."

In making their case, the Americans acknowledged the existence of "Political Bands" which had "connected" them with their British brethren, but they denied that Parliament had ever exercised any lawful authority over them. Parliament's passage of legislation concerning the colonies they termed an attempt "to extend an unwarrantable Jurisdiction over us." The "Political Bands" which they found it "necessary" to "dissolve" were constituted solely by their common allegiance to the crown. The bill of particulars that they drew up, asserting the existence of "a long Train of Abuses and Usurpations," evincing "a Design to reduce them under absolute Despotism," was therefore lodged against "the present King of Great Britain." It was not just "their Right," they asserted, "to throw off such Government, and to provide new Guards for their future Security." It was "their Duty" as well.

The former colonists could claim such a right and acknowledge such a duty because they were a "People" and recognized certain "Truths to be self-evident":

> that all Men are created equal, that they are endowed by their Creator with certain unalienable Rights, that among these are Life, Liberty, and the Pursuit of Happiness—That to secure these Rights, Governments are instituted among Men, deriving their just Powers from the Consent of the Governed, That whenever any Form of Government becomes destructive of these Ends, it is the Right of the People to alter or to abolish it, and to institute new Government, laying its Foundation on such Principles, and organizing its Powers in such Form, as to them shall seem most likely to effect their Safety and Happiness.[27]

Here, compressed within a single paragraph replete with phrases lifted almost verbatim from the pages of the second of John Locke's *Two Treatises of Government*, lay the assertion that made the Americans' war of national liberation a revolution with radical implications, requiring that they "begin the world all over again" and institute "a new order of the ages."

Some of the radical implications of the principles embraced in the Declaration of Independence, notably those concerning the enslavement of men and women of African descent, the Founders

left for the most part to future generations to effect. Others, notably those concerning the institution of a new government and the
organization of its powers in a form conducive to their own safety
and happiness, they faced squarely. On the eve of independence, at
the behest of the Continental Congress, the former colonies set out
to revise their laws or to draft new constitutions reflecting the abolition
of the monarchy and the establishment of a confederation of republics on American soil in such a manner that "the exercise of
every kind of authority . . . under the said crown [of Great Britain]
shall be totally suppressed, and all the powers of government exerted, under the authority of the people of the colonies."[28]

VI

In taking up the burden of self-government, the former colonists
had to keep in mind the fact that, in justifying their right to independence on the basis of Locke's argument, they had made a profound and lasting decision concerning the legitimate purpose and
limits of government in the fledgling United States. Thomas Paine
summed up what was to be the almost-official American view in
the first two paragraphs of *Common Sense* when he told his readers, "Society is produced by our wants and government by our
wickedness; the former promotes our happiness *positively* by uniting our affections, the latter *negatively* by restraining our vices ...
Society in every state is a blessing, but government, even in its
best state, is but a necessary evil."[29]

James Wilson echoed Paine's sentiments when he dubbed government "highly necessary" and then qualified his statement by
adding, "to a fallen state."[30] Few, if any, Americans thought that it
was the task of the government to define and provide for human
happiness. But it was universally agreed that it is the government's
duty to protect and promote its pursuit, and the acquisition and use
of property were deemed central to that pursuit.

As early as 1764, James Otis cited "the great law of *self-preservation*" and contended that the "*end* of government" is "the *good*
of mankind" and that "above all things" it exists "to provide for
the security, the quiet, and happy enjoyment of life, liberty, and
property." He insisted that "there is no one act which a government can have a *right* to make that does not tend to the advancement of the security, tranquillity, and prosperity of the people," and
he added that "if life, liberty, and property could be enjoyed in as

great perfection in *solitude* as in *society* there would be no need of government."[31] Four years later, in a letter to Britain's secretary of state penned by Samuel Adams, the Massachusetts House of Representatives traced the principle of representation to the fact that it "is acknowledged to be an unalterable law in nature that a man should have the free use and sole disposal of the fruit of his honest industry, subject to no controul."[32]

In 1775, when Alexander Hamilton condemned "the pretensions of parliament," he emphasized the fact that those pretensions "divest us of that moral security, for our lives and properties, which we are entitled to, and which it is the primary end of society to bestow."[33] George Mason sounded the same theme in the Virginia Declaration of Rights, and John Adams did so in the Massachusetts Constitution of 1780. Their language can be found echoed in the bills of rights adopted in Pennsylvania, Vermont, and New Hampshire, and there are provisions in the constitutions of Maryland and of North and South Carolina presupposing the same concern for the protection of property rights. From the outset of the Revolution, constitutionalism was conceived primarily as a formal, legal instrument to limit legislative discretion, contain democratic passion, and thereby safeguard the natural rights of man—especially the right to acquire and retain property.

In dropping the customary reference to property from the Declaration of Independence, Thomas Jefferson did not mean to deny that its acquisition and possession are among man's inalienable rights. In 1779, in his revisal of Virginia's laws, he noted the inclination of "wicked and dissolute men" to commit "violations on the lives, liberties and property of others" and then observed that what "principally induced men to enter into society" and what accounts therefore for government's "principal purpose" is the desire for "the secure enjoyment of these."[34] If he chose in the new nation's founding document to emphasize "the Pursuit of Happiness," it was because he took industry and labor deployed in happiness's pursuit to be more fundamental than the property they produced.

So, when James Madison later derived "the rights of property" from "the diversity in the faculties of men" and grounded his defense of the constitution proposed by the Philadelphia convention on the premise that "the first object of Government" is "the protection" of the "different and unequal faculties of acquiring property," he was simply drawing out the implications of the fundamental doctrine so elegantly spelled out by Jefferson.[35]

Although there was a consensus as to the ends of government, there was much dispute with regard to the means best suited to achieving those ends. When Alexander Hamilton presented to Congress his famous *Report on the Subject of Manufactures*, he envisaged an exceedingly active role for government in the economic sphere, contending that its promotion of manufacturing would furnish "greater scope for the diversity of talents and dispositions, which discriminate men from each other."

Hamilton thought it a proper task for government to "cherish and stimulate the activity of the human mind, by multiplying the objects of enterprise"[36] Jefferson disagreed, finding in government supervision of the economy a tyrannical potential. If government was a necessary evil, it should be kept to a minimum. In his first inaugural, he identified as "the sum of good government . . . a wise and frugal Government, which shall restrain men from injuring one another, shall leave them otherwise free to regulate their own pursuits of industry and improvement, and shall not take from the mouth of labor the bread it has earned."[37] On the question dividing Jefferson from Hamilton, Americans have been at odds ever since.

VII

The Americans' ultimate success in establishing constitutions capable of meeting the criteria spelled out by Thomas Paine, James Wilson, George Mason, Thomas Jefferson, James Madison, Alexander Hamilton, and the like obscures the boldness required of them at the time. There had been republics before, and the Americans took heart from their example and sought, as best they could, to learn the lessons evident from their various histories. They could not, however, ignore the fact that all previous republics had failed.

The republican experiment undertaken in mid-seventeenth-century England after the execution of Charles I had proved to be an embarrassment. And however impressive and splendid the republics of ancient Greece and Rome may have been, the example they set did not merit emulation. Alexander Hamilton spoke for his compatriots when, in *The Federalist*, he observed, "It is impossible to read the history of the petty Republics of Greece and Italy, without feeling sensations of horror and disgust at the distractions with which they were continually agitated, and at the rapid succession of revolutions, by which they were kept in a state of perpetual vibration, between the extremes of tyranny and anarchy."[38]

When David Hume cited "reason, history, and experience" against John Locke's claim that human beings are capable of fashioning governments for themselves, he had a case to make.[39] But the prospect which Hume took to be sobering, the former colonists found exhilarating and even intoxicating, for they welcomed the challenge. Well before the American experiment could have been considered a success, John Adams openly rejoiced in the fact that the nascent American states had "exhibited, perhaps, the first examples of governments erected on the simple principles of nature." He believed that, "if men are now sufficeintly enlightened to disabuse themselves of artifice, imposture, hypocrisy, and superstition, they will consider this event as an era in their history," for it "will never be pretended that any persons employed" in establishing the new American governments "had interviews with the gods, or were in any degree under the inspiration of Heaven, more than those at work upon ships or houses, or laboring in merchandise or agriculture." Instead, "it will forever be acknowledged that these governments were contrived merely by the use of reason and the senses." In Adams's estimation, "Thirteen governments thus founded on the natural authority of the people alone, without a pretence of miracle or mystery, and . . . destined to spread over the northern part of that whole quarter of the globe, are a great point gained in favor of the rights of mankind."[40]

Of course, to gain this point the Americans would have to make a success of self-government. Though they managed to extract from the British by force of arms a recognition of their independence, it was in the 1780s by no means clear that their republican experiment would succeed. As early as 1783, George Washington had expressed grave misgivings. In early June, on the eve of his retirement as general of the armies, he addressed a circular to the governors of the states. It was intended to be his last official communication, his farewell address.

In this open letter, Washington congratulated his fellow Americans on their great victory and reminded them that there was much left to do. They had won the war, and they could lose the peace. "It is yet to be decided," he noted, "whether the Revolution must ultimately be considered as a blessing or a curse: a blessing or a curse, not to the present age alone, for with our fate will the destiny of unborn Millions be involved." This great question remained to be decided in part because there was a serious prospect that the end of the war would bring a relaxation of the Union, "annihilating the cement of the Confederation" and allowing the United States "to become the sport of European politics."[41]

Four years would pass before Washington's call received an answer, and that answer was made manifest only when civil strife between rich and poor, between creditors and debtors, and between frontier separatists and defenders of the former colonies' territorial integrity threatened chaos in each and every one of the states. Had it not been for Shays' Rebellion in western Massachusetts (1787), the state legislatures and the Continental Congress might have ignored the request of Alexander Hamilton, James Madison, and the other delegates to the abortive Annapolis Commercial Convention that a federal convention be called to amend the Articles of Confederation. It is not an accident that the constitution which that federal convention eventually produced explicitly guarantees to each of the states a republican government and includes provisions denying to these subordinate polities the right to issue money and to impair the obligation of contracts. Experience had demonstrated that the legislatures sitting in the various state capitols were not to be trusted, and patriots like John Jay and John Marshall were beginning to wonder whether human beings really are "incapable of governing" themselves.[42]

In a sense, as John Adams suggested, the revolution was over by the time that independence was declared. It had taken place, as he said, "in the Minds of the People" in the period stretching "from 1760 to 1775, . . . before a drop of blood was drawn at Lexington," and it concerned "the Authority of Parliament over the Colonies" and the legitimate scope of government. It was, however, one thing to define government's authority and to specify its scope, and it was another to construct a workable regime compatible with the pertinent definitions and specifications. To justify republican government, one has to demonstrate that it is possible to reconcile wisdom with popular consent. And so to begin to understand American politics, one must not only ponder the decision concerning first principles made in 1776: one must consider as well the great debate that took place in 1787 and 1788 concerning the political architecture proper to a modern republic.

Notes

1. Edmund Burke, "Speech on the Army Estimates," 9 February 1790, in *The Writings and Speeches of the Right Honourable Edmund Burke* (Boston: 1901) III 225–27.

2. "The Declaratory Act," 18 March 1766, in *Prologue to Revolution: Sources and Documents on the Stamp Act Crisis, 1764–1766*, ed. Edmund S. Morgan (New York: 1973) 155–56.

3. James Harrington's *Oceana*, ed. S. B. Liljegren (Heidelberg: 1924) 19–20.

4. John Trenchard and Thomas Gordon, *Cato's Letters, or Essays on Liberty, Civil and Religious, and Other Important Subjects*, 6th ed. (London: 1755) IV 3–12: no. 106, 8 December 1722.

5. Francis Hutcheson, *A System of Moral Philosophy in Three Books* (London: 1755) III.viii.12.

6. Letter from John Adams to Thomas Jefferson on 24 August 1815, in *The Adams-Jefferson Letters: The Complete Correspondence Between Thomas Jefferson and Abigail and John Adams*, ed. Lester J. Cappon (Chapel Hill: 1959) II 454–56.

7. Edmund Burke, "Speech on the Army Estimates," 9 February 1790, in *The Writings and Speeches of the Right Honourable Edmund Burke* III 226–27.

8. Jean Louis de Lolme, *The Constitution of England, or an Account of the English Government*, 3rd ed. (London: 1781) 55–61.

9. Niccolò Machiavelli, Discoursi sopra la prima deca di Tito Livio 1.25, in *Tutte le opere*, ed. Mario Martelli (Florence: 1971) 108.

10. Charles-Louis de Secondat, Baron de La Brède et de Montesquieu, De l'esprit des lois 1.5.19, in *Oeuvres complètes de Montesquieu*, ed. Roger Caillois (Paris: 1949–51) II 304.

11. See the Letter from the Earl of Chesterfield to Philip Stanhope on 7 February 1749, in *The Letters of Philip Dormer Stanhope, Earl of Chesterfield, with the Characters*, ed. John Bradshaw (London: 1926) I 195.

12. David Hume, "Of the Parties of Great Britain," in *Essays Moral, Political, and Literary*, ed. Eugene F. Miller (Indianapolis: 1985) 614.

13. David Hume, "Whether the British Government Inclines More to Absolute Monarchy, or to a Republic," in *Essays Moral, Political, and Literary* 51.

14. See, for example, *The Diary and Autobiography of John Adams*, ed. L. H. Butterfield (Cambridge, Mass.: 1961) I 250, 358.

15. "The Mayflower Compact," 11 November 1620, in Documents of American History, 8th ed., ed. Henry Steele Commager (New York: 1968) 15–16.

16. David Hume, "Of Superstition and Enthusiasm," in *Essays Moral, Political, and Literary* 73–79 (esp. 75).

17. William Blackstone, "Commentaries on the Laws of England (Oxford: 1765–69) I 156–57.

18. Edmund Burke, "Speech on American Taxation," 19 April 1774, in *The Writings and Speeches of the Right Honourable Edmund Burke* II 72–73.

19. Edmund Burke, "Speech on Moving Resolutions for Conciliation with the Colonies," 22 March 1775, in *The Writings and Speeches of the Right Honourable Edmund Burke* II 120–27.

20. John Adams, *A Dissertation on the Canon and Feudal Law* (1765), in *The Works of John Adams*, ed. Charles Frances Adams (Boston: 1850–56) III 447–64 (esp. 450, 454, 458–59, 463–64).

21. See George Bancroft, *History of the United States of America, from the Discovery of the Continent* (New York: 1882–86) III 191.

22. John Dickinson, *Letters from a Farmer in Pennsylvania* (1767–78), in *The Political Writings of John Dickinson*, ed. Paul Leicester Ford (Philadelphia: 1895) I 366.

23. James Wilson, *Considerations on the Nature and Extent of the Legislative Authority of the British Parliament* (1774), in *The Works of James Wilson*, ed. Robert Green McCloskey (Cambridge: 1967) II 721–46 (at 745n).

24. See "Coronation Oaths (old and new), 1685 and 1689," in E. Neville Williams, *The Eighteenth Century Constitution, 1688–1815: Documents and Commentary* (Cambridge: 1960) 36–39.

25. Thomas Paine, *Common Sense* (14 February 1776), in *The Complete Writings of Thomas Paine*, ed. Philip S. Foner (New York: 1945) I 3, 45.

26. Letter from Thomas Jefferson to Roger C. Weightman on 24 June 1826, in *The Writings of Thomas Jefferson*, ed. Paul Leicester Ford (New York: 1892–99) X 390–92.

27. The Declaration of Independence, 4 July 1776, in *The Papers of Thomas Jefferson*, ed. Julian P. Boyd (Princeton: 1950–) I 429–32.

28. *Journals of the Continental Congress, 1774–1789*, ed. Worthington Chauncey Ford et al. (Washington, D.C.: 1904–37) IV 342, 357–58: 10 and 15 May 1776.

29. Thomas Paine, *Common Sense* (14 February 1776), in *The Complete Writings of Thomas Paine* I 4.

30. James Wilson, "Of the Study of the Law in the United States," 1790, in *The Works of James Wilson* I 87.

31. James Otis, T*he Rights of the British Colonies Asserted and Proved* (1764), in *Pamphlets of the American Revolution, 1750–1776*, ed. Bernard Bailyn (Cambridge: 1965–) I 425–26.

32. Letter from the House of Representatives of Massachusetts to Henry Seymour Conway on 13 February 1768, in *The Writings of Samuel Adams*, ed. Harry Alonzo Cushing (New York: 1904–8) I 190–91.

33. Alexander Hamilton, *The Farmer Refuted, &c.*, 23 February 1775, in *The Papers of Alexander Hamilton*, ed. Harold C. Syrett (New York: 1961–79) I 88.

34. The Revisal of the Laws, 18 June 1779: 64. A Bill for Proportioning Crimes and Punishments in Cases Heretofore Capital, in *The Papers of Thomas Jefferson* II 492.

35. Alexander Hamilton, James Madison, and John Jay, *The Federalist*, ed. Jacob E. Cooke (Middletown, Conn.: 1961) 58: no. 10.

36. Alexander Hamilton, "Report on the Subject of Manufactures," 5 December 1791, in *The Papers of Alexander Hamilton* X 254–56.

37. Thomas Jefferson, "First Inaugural Address," 4 March 1801, in *A Compilation of the Messages and Papers of the Presidents, 1789–1897*, ed. James D. Richardson (Washington, D.C.: 1896) I 321–24 (at 323).

38. *The Federalist* 50: no. 9.

39. See David Hume, "Of the Original Contract," in *Essays Moral, Political, and Literary* 465–87 (esp. 474).

40. John Adams, A Defence of the Constitutions of Government of the United States of America (1787–88), in *The Works of John Adams* IV 292–93.

41. George Washington, "Circular to the States," 8 June 1783, in *The Writings of George Washington*, ed. John C. Fitzpatrick (Washington, D.C.: 1931–44) XXVI 483–96 (at 485–86).

42. Letter from John Jay to Jacob Reed on 12 December 1786, in *The Correspondence and Public Papers of John Jay*, ed. Henry P. Johnston (New York: 1890–93) III 221–22; and Letter from John Marshall to James Wilkinson on 5 January 1787, in *The Papers of John Marshall*, ed. Herbert A. Johnson et al. (Chapel Hill: 1974) I 199–201.

Suggested Reading

Bailyn, Bernard. *The Ideological Origins of the American Revolution.* Cambridge: Harvard University Press, 1967.

Becker, Carl. *The Declaration of Independence: A Study in the History of Political Ideas.* New York: Vintage Books, 1942.

Greene, Jack P. *Peripheries and Center: Constitutional Development in the Extended Polities of the British Empire and the United States, 1607–1788.* Athens: University of Georgia Press, 1986.

Morgan, Edmund S., and Helen M. Morgan. *The Stamp Act Crisis: Prologue to Revolution.* New York: Macmillan, 1962.

Rahe, Paul A. *Republics Ancient and Modern: Classical Republicanism and the American Revolution.* Chapel Hill: University of North Carolina Press, 1992.

Wood, Gordon S. *The Creation of the American Republic, 1776–1787.* Chapel Hill: University of North Carolina Press, 1969.

Wood, Gordon S. *The Radicalism of the American Revolution.* New York: Alfred A. Knopf, 1992.

3

Federalism

Kenneth M. Holland

The United States is the first and oldest federal democracy in the world. The constitutions of federal democracies differ from those of countries with a centralized, or unitary, political system. The former grant only certain powers to the national government, with the constituent units—called by various names, including states, provinces, republics, cantons—retaining many of the powers they had exercised as independent nations prior to their decision to federate, or form a league or association with other independent countries. The principal motives for sovereign states to come together in this way are to increase trade among themselves and to boost their military power.

Countries with unitary constitutions, such as Great Britain, France, and Japan, are not the products of federation and do not divide power between levels of government. Many countries have since imitated the American experiment with a two-tiered political system, including Switzerland, Canada, Australia, Mexico, Russia, Germany, and India. The nations of Western Europe currently are attempting to strengthen their economic and political union, with many on the continent hoping a United States of Europe eventually will emerge.

But modern federations are notoriously unstable. Federalism by its nature is a dynamic process, neither easily defined nor maintained.[1] Federations always seem to be struggling against either dissolution or consolidation. Examples of both tendencies are easy to find. In 1991 the Union of Soviet Socialist Republics, despite the vigorous efforts of then President Mikhail Gorbachev, was dis-

mantled by its member states. The year 1992 witnessed the breakup of Yugoslavia, and on January 1, 1993, Czechoslovakia split into
the Czech Republic and Slovakia. A powerful separatist movement
in Quebec is casting doubt on the future of the Canadian confederation.

The U.S. federal system is in no danger of disintegration. The
more likely result is that the United States will follow the lead of
the Australian, German, Mexican, and Indian federations, where
the states have lost most of their former autonomy to an increasingly powerful central government. Is this a trend worth caring about?
In order to answer this question, we must first understand how the
Framers of the Constitution intended federalism to contribute to the
welfare of the American people and to the other ends which the
Constitution seeks to achieve. Then we must inquire whether, regardless of its original virtues, federalism is an outdated concept,
ill suited for the demands of the twenty-first century.

The Birth of Federalism

The delegates at the Constitutional Convention in 1787 were divided
into two camps, each led by a Virginian. The advocates of a consolidation of the states under a unitary national government were
led by James Madison. The proponents of the continued sovereignty of the states, united in a confederation for the limited purposes
of trade and defense, were inspired by George Mason.

The basis for this division was a disagreement over what form
of government would protect rights and secure liberty. Those opposed to a consolidation of the states, who later called themselves
Anti-Federalists, were persuaded by the French philosopher Montesquieu's teaching that liberty was safe only in a small republic,
that large countries inevitably degenerated into dictatorships, or
despotisms. Those who favored a unitary political system like that
of Great Britain or France pointed to the class warfare to which
petty republics were inevitably subject, resulting in unjust laws,
persecution of minorities, and political instability. This disagreement was fundamental enough that by July the convention was near
a breakup.

The Connecticut delegation came forward with what came to be
known as the Great Compromise, a compromise which made agreement on a constitution possible.[2] Under this agreement the consti-

tution would blend unitary, or national, features with arrangements usually associated with a loose confederacy of sovereign states. The heart of the compromise was the manner in which seats in the two houses of Congress were distributed. The sixty-five seats in the House of Representatives would be allocated to the states according to their populations. The twenty-six seats in the Senate would be allocated equally among the thirteen states, as if the Senate were an international assembly of sovereign nation-states.

These institutional features mean that the Constitution set up a hybrid, a mixture of what had always been regarded as two irreconcilable systems: a unitary national government and a league of independent states. The concept was so novel that there was not even a term to describe it. Even as late as the 1830s, the French writer Alexis de Tocqueville could say that the American Constitution is "neither exactly national nor exactly federal; but the new word which ought to express this novel thing does not yet exist."[3]

In 1787 the words "federal" and "confederal" were interchangeable. Madison stressed the new system's novelty when he argued that the "compound government" formed by the Constitution must "be explained by itself, [and] not by similitudes or analogies."[4] The Constitution simply refers to it as "a more perfect Union." Madison described the product of the Philadelphia compromise as a regime that was "in strictness, neither a national nor a federal Constitution, but a composition of both."[5] It was a scheme "partly national, partly federal."[6]

The Constitution's national features include (1) the ability of the Congress to make laws affecting individuals, such as tax and conscription laws, in contrast to confederal bodies which typically are confined to decrees and requisitions directed at the member states; (2) representation in the House of Representatives by population, whereas in federations the member states typically have an equal voice, regardless of wealth or population; and (3) the ability of Congress to make policy, such as establishment of a system of federal trial courts to determine civil and criminal cases, in areas other than commerce and defense, the traditional concerns of confederal bodies.

But, as Madison emphasized, the limited scope of the general government's legislative powers was a critical element of the compromise that generated a sharp contrast between the U.S. Congress and the British Parliament. While Parliament enjoyed plenary and unlimited power, the Congress of the United States was confined to those powers specifically enumerated in the Constitution and such powers as reasonably could be implied from it. The states would retain all their legislative prerogatives not so delegated by the Constitution to the United States.

The principal issue during the ensuing campaign of 1787–88 in the states to ratify the plan was the Anti-Federalist charge that because of the scope of the powers granted and the lack of adequate safeguards, the federal government would not remain within the bounds of its enumerated powers. It would swallow up the reserved powers of the states and degenerate into an elected despotism. In order to quiet these apprehensions, the proponents of the Constitution, who called themselves the Federalists, promised to amend the Constitution immediately after ratification. In the First Congress, which began sitting in 1789, Madison introduced twelve amendments, ten of which were successful and were appended to the Constitution in 1791. The amendments, as a whole, emphasized the enumerated character of the powers of Congress. The Ninth and Tenth Amendments reiterated the point that the states retained all rights and powers not delegated by the Constitution to the federal government.

Each of these ten provisions, which by the 1880s came to be known as the Bill of Rights, stressed the limits the convention had placed on the executive, legislative, and judicial officers of the national government and, by implication, the expanse of the powers retained by the states. What the Congress was prohibited from doing, the state legislatures were free to do. For example, while the Congress could not incorporate a Church of the United States, the states were free to make religious establishments, as in fact several did. In *Barron v. Baltimore* (1833), the Supreme Court reminded the public that none of the prohibitions in the first ten amendments applied to the states.

By the 1840s "federalism" was commonly used to describe the American political system, and the general, or national, government was typically referred to as the federal government. But we do not often follow Canadian and Australian practice by describing our country as a federation.

The Sovereignty of the States

Under a federal constitution, the states possess what are called reserved powers. The source of these powers is the people of the state, who delegate them to the state government by means of a state constitution. The states of the United States of America are self-governing political communities, possessing all the features of an independent state except a foreign service, including a legislature, an executive, a judiciary, the power to tax and punish, and a militia. As William Johnson of Connecticut said at the Constitutional Convention, the states are distinct "political societies."[7] The original thirteen states existed before federation and could exist again as independent states if the federation were to dissolve, as in Yugoslavia.

The Constitution recognizes the sovereignty of the states in these ways:

(1) acknowledgment in Article VII that the act of joining the union was voluntary on the part of each state;

(2) the confinement of the federal authority to those powers enumerated in Article I, powers whose exercise is in the mutual interest of all the states;

(3) the retention by the states, acknowledged in the Ninth and Tenth Amendments, of their authority to deal with the vast bulk of their internal affairs;

(4) the equality of the states in the Senate, regardless of their relative wealth, strength, or size.

Federalism Distinguished from Decentralization

Many countries which are not federations resemble the United States in the way they administer government. The similarity arises because the central government in countries with unitary constitutions often does not make all political decisions but delegates authority down to various kinds of local governing bodies, such as regional, county, or municipal councils. Although such decentralized administration may resemble federal arrangements, the distinction between federalism and decentralization is fundamental.

No matter how much the counties of England, the departments of France, or the prefectures of Japan may resemble the states of Germany, America, or Australia or the provinces of Canada, they are mere subdivisions of the national government which exist primarily for administrative purposes. Because they are creatures of the national authority, the national government can modify their powers, redraw their boundaries, or abolish them at any time. Prime Minister Margaret Thatcher's abolition of the Greater London Council, the governing body for metropolitan London, is a case in point.

Local officials exercise the authority of the national government, not that of their region or city. At any time, the central government could bypass them and require all contact between individual citizens and government agencies and officials be with the national authority. If the local units disappeared, the national government would continue to operate, since it is in no respect dependent on them for its existence. Local government exists for reasons of efficiency and responsiveness. General national policies often need to be adapted to take into account local variations and needs. Officers of the central government posted outside the national capital are the eyes, ears, mouths, and hands of the central authority, enforcing laws, collecting taxes, and observing and reporting the level of public satisfaction with the regime.

In the United States, by contrast, the original states existed before federation, were not creatures of the central authority, and would continue to exist if the central authority were to be dissolved. And at least for the first one hundred fifty years of the nation's history, the states existed essentially for the purpose of self-government, not administration of central government programs. In fact, if the states ceased to exist, the United States of America would also cease to exist, because it is a federation of states.

Not all the Framers of the Constitution believed that federalism is superior to decentralization. Although known as the Father of the Constitution, Madison, as we saw, actually attempted to persuade the Constitutional Convention to replace the confederacy with a unitary national government employing decentralized administration. In *Federalist* 10 and 51, which address the problem of the tyranny of the majority, he was careful not to praise the virtues of divided sovereignty. He praised instead the economic and religious diversity which would characterize a country, like the United States under the proposed constitution with an extensive territory, republican constitution, and commercial orientation.

The concept of the large, commercial republic, as Madison describes it, is perfectly compatible with a unitary national government. The pluralism advocated is a medley of social classes, religious sects, occupations, professions, industries, technologies and types of property, no one of which is large enough or sufficiently geographically concentrated to control the government. All legislation, therefore, will be the product of temporary coalitions of these various interests. As compromises within the coalition, laws, Madison believed, would approximate "justice and the general good."[8]

The Supreme Court's Role as Guardian of the Constitution

The Founders of the American federation designed the Supreme Court to guard the Constitution. Because one of the principal elements of the country's basic law is the division of powers between two levels of government, the Court's responsibility is to preserve the federal structure. Because of the constant, and inevitable, struggle for power between the states and the national government, and because of the general language used in the Constitution to divide powers, the Court's responsibility to preserve the mixed nature of the Constitution is one of its most difficult challenges. To be effective, the justices must first determine which force is currently dominant— dissolution or consolidation—and then develop a judicial strategy to prevent the breakdown of the compound into one of its elemental modes—a unitary political system or confederation of sovereign states.

The principal weapon with which the Framers armed the justices for this battle is judicial review. In numerous instances since the founding, the Supreme Court of the federation has declared acts of the national legislature invalid on the grounds that it had exercised a power not authorized by the Constitution and reserved to the states.[9] But judicial review has in fact more often been used by the Court against acts of the states found to be inconsistent with the federal Constitution, laws, or treaties than against intrusive federal action. This fact only underscores the role of the Court as the balance wheel of the federal system, tasked with the responsibility of maintaining as far as possible a healthful balance between state autonomy and national control.

There are at least six distinct understandings of the federal principle held at one time or another by a majority on the Court, each dominant during a particular historical period.

The Constitution as a Nation-Building Instrument (1801–1835)

The chief justiceship of John Marshall was marked by the assertion of federal power over the states. The key principle was that the federal Congress's powers as granted by Article I, Section 8 were supreme over those of the states. The powers reserved to the states by the Tenth Amendment (1791) did not restrict the national government. It was but a tautology, neither granting nor restraining powers. The only restrictions came from explicit prohibitions on the national government, such as the First Amendment's prohibition on laws abridging freedom of speech, and from the fact that the legislative powers of the national government were enumerated.

But Marshall limited the scope of the doctrine of enumerated powers in *McCulloch v. Maryland* (1819),[10] dealing with the power of Congress to charter a bank. He said that Congress enjoys not only the powers explicitly granted but those that could reasonably be implied from the Constitution. Animating the Marshall Court's generous view of the scope of federal power was the assumption that the single greatest threat to the public interest and the rights of minorities, especially the rights of property holders, was the state legislatures.

Federalism as a Weapon in Class Conflict (1836–1864)

Chief Justice Roger Taney, heading the Court from 1836 until 1864, took a very different view of the constitutional division of authority. Beginning with the assumption that the federal government was overly sensitive to the demands of the wealthy, the Taney Court resolved many conflicts between state and federal power in favor of the states. The contrast with Marshall's approach is clearest in decisions concerning the scope of the states' power to make regulations affecting commerce among the states, a power which the Marshall Court denied to the states on the ground that interstate commercial regulation was a monopoly of the U.S. Congress under Article I. By contrast, the Taney Court held that the states could, in the absence of federal law, regulate interstate and foreign commerce, either as a state regulation of commerce or as an exercise of police power—the power to protect the health, safety, welfare, and morals of the people.

Taney, in sharp contrast with Marshall, took a narrow view of Article I, Section 10's prohibition against state laws impairing the obligation of contracts.[11] Decisions of the Taney Court had the effect of allowing state government intervention in the market in the name of equal opportunity for all classes.

Dual Federalism (1865–1937)

In *Hammer v. Dagenhart* (1918),[12] the Supreme Court invalidated a congressional statute that restricted the transportation in interstate commerce of goods produced by child labor, even though Congress was explicitly granted the power in Article I, Section 8 to regulate commerce among the states. The Court held that "the local power always existing and carefully reserved to the States in the Tenth Amendment" was a positive restriction on the otherwise valid powers of Congress.

So the Tenth Amendment was read by the Court as saying that "Congress shall make no law destroying powers the states exercised before ratification of the Constitution." This reading made the Tenth Amendment analogous to the language of the First Amendment, which prohibits Congress from infringing on freedom of the press under any circumstances. This principle of interpretation became known as *dual federalism*. The federal government could not intrude on powers reserved to the states, and the state governments could not encroach on powers delegated by the Constitution to the federal government.

The States' Failure to Protect the Disadvantaged (1938–1975)

As a result of President Franklin Roosevelt's attempt to pack the Supreme Court with justices supporting the New Deal, the Court, admitting defeat, abandoned its defense of state sovereignty and returned to the Marshall approach. In the words of Justice Harlan Stone in *United States v. Darby Lumber* (1941),[13] in which the Court upheld the federal minimum-wage and maximum-hours law, the Tenth Amendment "states but a truism that all is retained which has not been surrendered." The Court announced that the states were no longer part of its special constituency. Through their participation in the affairs of the federal government, such as the election of U.S. senators, the Court said, they were perfectly capable of protecting their own interests. Groups excluded from the political process, on the other hand, such as racial minorities, the poor, and political dissidents, were in need of judicial protection.

The decisions of the Warren Court (1954–1969) assumed that the states were far greater threats to justice and the interests of the "underdogs" of American society than was the federal government. State legislatures came under comprehensive federal judicial control.

The "New Federalism" of the Nixon Court (1976–1984)

Republican Richard Nixon, elected president in 1968 partly because of popular reaction against the hostile attitude of the Warren Court to states' rights, appointed a number of politically conservative justices. The Court reversed direction on the state/federal issue in *National League of Cities v. Usery* (1976).[14] It invalidated a congressional attempt to apply the minimum-wage and maximum-hours provisions of the Fair Labor Standards Act to state governments and their political subdivisions because of the threat it posed to federalism. The law, said Justice William Rehnquist, threatened the states' "separate and independent existence," which he treated as a check on the power of Congress analogous to the First Amendment's ban on acts abridging freedom of speech or press. Significantly, Rehnquist did not rely on the Tenth Amendment but on "the total structure created by the Constitution" as the basis of this restriction.

The Return to Judicial Restraint in State–Federal Conflicts (1985–Present)

The Rehnquist doctrine did not long endure. In *Garcia v. San Antonio Metropolitan Transit Authority* (1985),[15] the Court overruled *National League of Cities*. A 5–4 majority held that the "traditional governmental functions" test for the scope of federal power over the states was unworkable and inconsistent with the true meaning of Article I and the Tenth Amendment. The Fair Labor Standards Act, said Justice Harry Blackmun for the Court, did not violate any specific constitutional provision. The states must rely on the political process, not the Constitution or the Supreme Court, to preserve their historic role in the federal system.

This posture of the Supreme Court is not likely to change despite the fact that the Court between 1968 and 1992 acquired a solid conservative majority. Developments in the 1980s and 1990s have worked to reduce the interest of conservatives in preserving the rights of the states. Although the Republican party maintained its control over the executive branch of the federal government, many municipalities and states came under the control of liberal Democrats and even, in a few jurisdictions, socialists.[16] Charles Fried, President Reagan's Solicitor General during his second term, is an example of these conservative nationalists. He advocated "severe

federal restrictions" on such "Luddite and leveling impositions" as
rent-control schemes, affirmative-action policies and racial set-aside
ordinances.[17]

The Fourteenth Amendment and
the Conquest of the States

Since 1925 the Supreme Court has often acted as though the three
Civil War amendments—Thirteenth, Fourteenth, and Fifteenth—
fundamentally altered the original relationship between the states
and federal government. Through the doctrine of incorporation, the
Supreme Court by the 1960s had produced a decisive shift in the
federal balance. This doctrine teaches that the Fourteenth Amendment's due process clause included, or incorporated, the fundamental individual rights and liberties enumerated in the Bill of Rights.
Because the language of the Fourteenth Amendment explicitly restricts the states, the Supreme Court in effect was overturning its
earlier decision in *Barron v. Baltimore* saying the Bill of Rights
does apply equally to the state and federal governments.

One of the ironies of this issue was that there was a space of
nearly sixty years between ratification of the amendment in 1868
and the first use of the incorporation doctrine in 1925, when the
Court applied the First Amendment's guarantee of freedom of speech
to the states.[18] Another thirty-six years elapsed before the Court
ventured beyond the First Amendment's protection of the democratic
freedoms of speech, press, and assembly to nationalize the Fourth,
Fifth, and Sixth Amendment rights of the criminally accused.

The scale of the reforms imposed upon the states by the Warren
and Burger Courts between 1954 and 1985 was enormous. The chart
on the following page shows some of the state policies struck down
by the Court under the Fourteenth Amendment during this period.
The only significant reprieve received by the states was in 1976
when the Supreme Court, in *Gregg v. Georgia* (1976), lifted the
moratorium on execution of the death penalty for murder.

Can the States Take Care of Themselves?

The Supreme Court has pointed to the privileged position held
by the states as an interest group within the national Congress and

State Policy	Case in Which Invalidated	Year
Racial segregation	*Brown v. Bd. of Education*	1954
Bans on sexually explicit publications	*Roth v. U.S.*	1957
Warrantless police searches	*Mapp v. Ohio*	1961
Prayer in public schools	*Engel v. Vitale*	1962
Legislative districts of unequal population	*Reynolds v. Sims*	1964
The death penalty	*Furman v. Georgia*	1972
Criminalization of abortion	*Roe v. Wade*	1973
Patronage dismissals of government employees	*Elrod v. Wade*	1973
Racial quotas in university admissions	*Regents v. Bakke*	1978

their capacity in the political arena to prevent or correct abuses of power by the federal government.[19] But this premise of state privilege, standing for the proposition that the states are quite capable of tending to their interests through the ordinary political process and in no need of special attention from the courts, is questioned by many state governors and legislators. They claim that the provisions cited by the Supreme Court are, in fact, ineffective as ways of protecting state autonomy.

The Erosion of the States' Influence in Washington

From the beginning the capacity of the Senate to act as a states' house, where proposed legislation would be evaluated from the point of view of how it affected each state in its corporate capacity, was eroded by the phrase in Article I, Section 3 stating that "each senator shall have one vote." This was a notable departure from the practice in the Continental Congress which met during the Revolution, in the Congress which sat under the Articles of Confederation (1781–1788), and in the Constitutional Convention, where the delegations from each state cast a single vote. By giving each senator a separate and independent vote, the Constitution makes it unlikely that the senators from each state will ordinarily cooperate in order to identify and effect the interests of their state.

The development of political parties, unanticipated by the constitutional Framers, has further eroded the value of the Senate as a states' house. Often a single state will have one Republican senator and one Democratic senator. When this happens, the state's senators will cast opposing votes on many bills of importance to the state. Most devastating of all to the premise of state privilege is the Seventeenth Amendment (1913), which altered the manner in which senators are chosen, substituting popular election for selection by state legislature. As a result, Republican and Democratic senators tend to represent different constituencies within the same state, each typically part of a larger nationwide interest group.

Exacerbating these tendencies is the full-time career nature of service in the Senate, the concentration of well-financed and organized lobbying organizations in Washington, and the dependence of senators on campaign contributions from these organizations. Nearly all senators maintain their primary residence near the nation's capital because they regard their job as a federal lawmaker as their career and because the Congress is in session year-round. The location of their roots is evidenced by the fact that when they leave the Congress, many senators choose to continue to live in the Washington area rather than return to their home state.

Washington is also home to hundreds of lobbying groups, employing some of the most talented lawyers and technical staff in the country. Although many are federated organizations, consisting of state chapters, they tend to present a unified front to the various components of the federal government. Senators are dependent on these organizations not only for information and voting cues but also for money to finance their sexennial reelection campaigns. Legislation authorizing the formation of political action committees (PACs) by labor, industry, and ideological associations has accelerated congressional dependence on interest group contributions.

The constitutional weakness of the states is not the only source of their growing lack of clout in Washington. The sheer growth in the size and functions of the federal government since the 1930s has further muted the voice of the states. The pressures for centralization of both policy-making and the raising and distribution of public revenue have grown exponentially since the Great Depression and World War II. From the point of view of equality—which in recent decades has won numerous victories over liberty in its struggle to be the paramount moral principle of the Constitution—it is unacceptable that a citizen's access to public goods should depend upon the accident of where he or she resides within a country. The increasing competitiveness of world trade has brought new pressures to bear upon federal systems to harmonize and unify state and federal policies, such as taxation, consumer protection, occupational safety and health, education, and transportation. The centripetal pressures exerted on the states and Canadian provinces by the 1988 Free Trade Agreement between the United States and Canada are likely to increase with the addition in 1994 of Mexico to form a North American Free Trade Agreement.

Federalism's Virtues as Revealed by Experience and Scholarship

Although the writings and speeches of the federal Fathers shed insufficient light on the virtues of a regime which is "partly federal, partly national," a number of prominent scholars have concluded that federalism enjoys distinct advantages over both centralized and decentralized unitary systems.

First, it can now be seen that federalism contributes significantly to the achievements of the ends of Madison's large commercial republic. It increases the variety of competing entities, for each of the states constitutes a distinct interest. Any person or group which attempts to articulate the national interest will generate opposition from those entrusted with the interest of their state.

Citizens will develop loyalties and attachments to their states which will work against organization of interests or classes on a national scale, those which Madison treats as the most dangerous to justice and liberty. In countries with federal systems, labor unions and industries will tend to organize along federal lines, with largely self-governing chapters in each state. Studies have shown that such fragmentation weakens the influence of the national organizations on government and weakens class conflict at the national level.[20]

Second, federalism generates greater and more meaningful opportunities for democratic participation than even the decentralized mode of political organization. The relatively high degree of participation produces heightened feelings of political involvement and effectiveness. So federalist regimes suffer less than unitary systems from public apathy.

Third, federalism can work as an important structural barrier to excessive social and economic control by government. Unitary political systems like that in Great Britain have exposed their population to relatively unchecked government.

Fourth, experience indicates that federations encourage innovation. The states, in their competition with each other for people and enterprises, are willing to try new approaches and solutions. But the cost of a policy failure is limited to the one or two states which are first to try the experiment. The multiplication of levels of government also makes public policies more contestable, ensuring shorter lives for bad programs.

Fifth, free-market economists have found that competition among the constituent jurisdictions of a federation makes it easier for citizens to satisfy their preferences. The states compete to attract businesses and skilled workers by offering what they are looking for—including high-quality medical care, good schools, safe streets, clean air and water—at a price lower than that of their competitor states.[21] Citizens able to relocate have more choices available and at a more reasonable cost.

Sixth, competition among the states holds down the degree of government intrusion into the economy, thus contributing both to economic growth and to individual freedom.[22] Individuals and businesses will tend to avoid or flee jurisdictions with onerous regulations.

Seventh, federalism encourages competent government. People are more willing to delegate power when that power will be divided between two levels of government than if all of it were to go to the states or to the national government alone. Under the Articles of Confederation, for instance, both the states and the confederal Congress were too weak to govern effectively.

Eighth, centralized democracies run the risk of the national legislature being dominated by regionally concentrated factious majorities. The existence of a states' house can operate as an effective barrier to control of the legislative process by one region of the country. Historically, one of the key purposes of federation has been to prevent the largest, wealthiest, and most powerful state or states from dominating their smaller neighbors. In the absence of the Senate, California, for instance, with its fifty-two seats in the House of Representatives, would exert enormous influence over the Congress.

Ninth, federalism generates greater variety and diversity than unitary systems. The existence of state governments tends to preserve regional and policy differences. Although contiguous, New Hampshire and Vermont offer visitors contrasting ambiences, the former promoting laissez-faire policies and the latter a social welfare approach.

Tenth, commentators stress the capacity of federalism to preserve communities, which act as a healthful respite from the alienation and anomie endemic to large, impersonal modern nations.[23] It is easy to feel anonymous and excluded in the midst of a crowd of strangers. Many states and counties work hard to preserve their small towns and villages and to make them attractive places in which to live, work, and raise families.

So there may be a fortunate coincidence between what is desirable in itself—the federal structure—and the Constitution of the United States. It is not surprising, then, that Presidents Carlos Salinas de Gortari of Mexico and Boris Yeltsin of Russia, when in the early 1990s they set about to introduce democratic and free-market reforms in their countries, said that a revitalization of federalism was vital to their project.

Federalism in Action: Environmental Policy

Does American federalism actually exhibit these virtues? Or would a unitary system be fairer and more efficient? Evidence from a variety of policy areas, including environmental protection, suggests that although the costs of divided sovereignty are high, the benefits gained, both tangible and intangible, are substantial.

Critics contend that federal systems impede the achievement of common-good objectives, such as clean air and water, for three reasons. First, the constitutional dispersion of powers fragments interest groups, making it difficult for organizations representing the environment such as the Sierra Club and Greenpeace to mobilize their members. The existence of two layers of government, moreover, multiplies the number of points where environmental initiatives, such as banning chlorofluorocarbons, can be vetoed. In a country like Great Britain where all political power originates from the central government, public interest groups like those active in the environmental movement need to have but one office in the nation's capital and need the support of only one level of government.

Second, competition among the states for economic growth also drives regulation to its lowest common denominator. Firms, unhappy with the strict environmental standards in California, can move to a state such as Arizona or Nevada with more permissive pollution regulations. The mere threat of such moves is enough to force California to lower its standards. In Britain the central government sets economic development policy for the entire country, and local governments cannot offer financial incentives to potential investors more attractive than other jurisdictions. Environmental regulations are uniform for the entire country.

Finally, both the state and federal governments avoid taking necessary action, such as requiring municipalities to construct adequate waste-water treatment facilities, by disclaiming or shifting responsibility to another level of government or claiming lack of constitutional authority. If a river is polluted, the state can blame Washington and Washington can say it's the state or local government's responsibility to clean it up. The British Parliament enjoys complete, or plenary, legislative authority and holds the chief administrators, or ministers, accountable for completion of the mission assigned to their department. There is little opportunity for buck passing.

From the point of view of protecting the environment, then, unitary systems, such as that of Great Britain or Japan, are superior, say the critics.

Federalism: The Environment's Friend

But these criticisms are not particularly applicable to environmental policy-making in the United States. They overlook the fact that federalism, by encouraging participation in politics, has helped generate effective environmental interest group politics. Countries with unitary constitutions do not support nearly as many pressure groups. In Britain and Japan, achievement of such goals as preserving wilderness depends on initiatives within rather than outside government. But politicians and bureaucrats suffer from inertia and tend to move slowly.

Federalism has also encouraged innovation and policy experimentation in the environmental area. Republican Presidents Ronald Reagan and George Bush believed that strict pollution regulations were hurting many companies, many of whom were choosing to relocate to Mexico and other Third World countries to avoid the high costs of compliance. So the period 1980–1992 was one of reduced federal environmental policy aggressiveness.

But the slowdown occurred primarily in the Republican-controlled executive branch of the federal government. Many of the Reagan–Bush policy retreats were blocked by the Democratic-controlled Congress, by the federal courts, and by state and local governments. At the same time, other policy advances were initiated by the Congress and certain states, which the White House could not stop. Environmental advocates, like other interests that felt unwelcome in Washington, sought relief from state and local governments, which, under our federal system, have broad powers to enact environmental regulations on their own and to exceed many federal environmental standards.

The experience of the past two decades suggests that it is possible to achieve clean air and water and strive toward ecologically sustainable development within a political system of divided powers and responsibilities. Federalism does seem compatible with the realization of important public goods, such as a healthful environment, sound education, and a growing economy.

Notes

1. Kenneth Wiltshire, *Planning and Federalism: Australian and Canadian Experience* (St. Lucia: University of Queensland Press, 1986), p. 87.

2. Thus, Connecticut proudly and rightly calls itself "the Constitution State."

3. Alexis de Tocqueville, *Democracy in America*, ed. Phillip Bradley, 2 vols. (New York: Random House, 1945), 1:165.

4. James Madison, "Outline," in *The Writings of James Madison*, ed. Gaillard Hunt, 9 vols. (New York: Putnam's, 1910), 9:351.

5. *Federalist* 39.

6. *Federalist* 39.

7. Max Farrand, ed., *The Records of the Federal Convention of 1787*, 4 vols. (New Haven: Yale University Press, 1937), 1:461.

8. *Federalist* 51.

9. Examples include *Hammer v. Dagenhart (The Child Labor Case)*, 247 U.S. 251 (1918); *National League of Cities v. Usery (State Employees Wage Case)*, 426 U.S. 833 (1976): *New South Wales v. Brewery Employees' Union of New South Wales (The Union Label Case)*, 6 CLR 469 (1908); *New South Wales v. The Commonwealth (The Incorporation Case)*, 169 CLR 482 (1990).

10. 17 U.S. (4 Wheat.) 315 (1819).

11. See Taney's opinion for the Court in *Charles River Bridge v. Warren Bridge*, 36 U.S. (11 Pet.) 419 (1837).

12. 247 U.S. 251 (1918).

13. 312 U.S. 100 (1941).

14. 426 U.S. 833 (1976).

15. 469 U.S. 528 (1985).

16. Burlington, Vermont, for example, under the mayorship of socialist Bernard Sanders.

17. Charles Fried, *Order and Law: Arguing the Reagan Revolution—A Firsthand Account* (New York: Simon and Schuster, 1991), pp. 186–87.

18. *Gitlow v. New York*, 268 U.S. 652 (1925).

19. See *Amalgamated Society of Engineers v. The Adelaide Steamship Co. Ltd. (The Engineers' Case)*, 28 CLR 129 (1920), at 151 and *The First Uniform Tax Case*, 65 CLR 373 (1942), at 429.

20. Trevor Matthews, "Federalism and Interest Group Cohesion: A Comparison of Two Peak Business Groups in Australia," 20 *Publius* (Fall 1990): 105–28; Alan C. Cairns, "The Governments and Structures of Canadian Federalism," 10 *Canadian Journal of Political Science* (December 1977): 719–20.

21. Philip J. Grossman, "Fiscal Competition Among States in Australia: The Demise of Death Duties," 20 *Publius* (Fall 1990): 145–59.

22. Geoffrey Brennan and James M. Buchanan, *The Power to Tax: Analytical Foundations of a Fiscal Constitution* (Cambridge: Cambridge University Press, 1980).

23. See Daniel J. Elazar, "Mason Versus Madison: Developing an American Theory of Federal Democracy," in *Federalism: The Legacy of George Mason*, Martin B. Cohen, ed. (Fairfax, Va.: George Mason University Press, 1988).

Suggested Reading

Diamond, Martin. "The Ends of Federalism." *Publius* 3, no. 2 (Fall 1973).

———. "*The Federalist* on Federalism." *Yale Law Journal* 86 (May 1977).

Kincaid, John. "From Cooperation to Coercion in American Federalism: Housing, Fragmentation and Preemption, 1789–1992." *Journal of Law and Politics* 9 (Winter 1993): 333–430.

Madison, James, Alexander Hamilton, and John Jay. *The Federalist Papers,* 10, 39, 51. New York: New American Library, 1961 (1788).

Zuckert, Michael P. "Federalism and the Founding: Toward a Reinterpretation of the Constitutional Convention." *Review of Politics* 41 (Spring 1986): 166–210.

4

The Federalist

Thomas S. Engeman

The Congress that adopted the Declaration of Independence on July 4, 1776 also submitted the Articles of Confederation to the states for their approval. For the next eleven years (1777 to 1788), until the ratification of the new Constitution, the Articles of Confederation provided the legal basis for American government, although the Articles were not formally ratified until 1781.

In principle, the authority created by the Articles was strong. Certainly, the formal powers of Congress were extensive, but the "confederal principle," making Congress merely an agent of the sovereign state governments, led to anything but competent national power. The inability of Congress to legislate over individual citizens resulted in its subservience to the state governments. Because Congress could only request the reluctant states to arm and to fund the national government, the states had the authority to determine the actual power of Congress.

Most, but not all, Americans of the time thought the government under the Articles of Confederation too weak. After a preliminary meeting in Annapolis in 1786, another convention was summoned by Congress to consider reform. Meeting in Philadelphia during the summer of 1787, a relatively small convention of only fifty-five delegates drafted our present Constitution.

The representatives at the Philadelphia convention decided to replace the confederal government of articles with a largely national government. This national government, not the states, would be sovereign, having the ability to define the constitutionality or legality of its own powers and actions. Through the Supreme Court, the national government would be able to override state statutes infringing on its legitimate activities. The Framers wished to ensure that it was the people and not the state governments who consented to the new Constitution. So they insisted that the voters select representatives to special state ratifying conventions.

The Federalist Papers is the product of the often intense political debates over ratification in the state conventions. With New York State's powerful Governor George Clinton vehemently opposed to the new Constitution, Alexander Hamilton, a New Yorker, requested the aid of John Jay (the great diplomat) and James Madison (the Father of the Constitution) to help him write a series of newspaper articles. These articles would bring to the Federalist cause the most thoughtful and persuasive arguments in support of the Constitution.

The eighty-five articles composing *The Federalist* were published by most of the newspapers in the New York City area. The first thirty-six papers were quickly bound into Volume I of *The Federalist* and circulated throughout the thirteen states. Almost immediately it acquired the reputation it has enjoyed ever since: the best single commentary ever written on the meaning of the Constitution and the political science (and thought) of its Framers.

Like many of the political essays of this period, *The Federalist* was published under a pseudonym. The three authors chose Publius, a Roman hero and savior of the Roman Republic. When discussing *The Federalist*, I will frequently refer to it as written by Publius. I will do so for the sake of convenience and to convey the unity of the original project. The original readers did not know who wrote the essays, nor did the three authors wish their collaborative authorship known. Considerable planning also went into ensuring the continuity of Publius's argument throughout the work.

The Intellectual Background

Alexander Hamilton, James Madison, and John Jay were men of political action. They were trained in the period of political ferment that began almost immediately after the French and Indian War in 1763, and they had each occupied positions of power and trust since the early days of the Revolution. In light of their long and distinguished public service, it is natural that Hamilton, Madison, and Jay would make political prudence and experience their watchwords in framing a new constitution.

Nevertheless, Publius recognized that the political situation in what Alexis de Tocqueville called the "first new nation" had certain unusual and novel features. In particular, the Framers of the new Constitution thought a stable popular government was now a practical possibility, although it had not been in the past. Publius assumed that the new science of nature—the new physical science of Isaac Newton and the new political science of the most "enlightened" authors of Europe such as John Locke and David Hume— had improved human understanding of both nature and politics. According to *Federalist* 9, Publius confirms, "the science of politics, like most other sciences, has received great improvement."

The major features recently discovered or improved in "the science of politics" are these: (1) separation of powers; (2) "representation of the people in the legislature by deputies of their own election," or the "republican principle"; (3) bicameralism of the legislative branch; (4) life appointments of judges, facilitating the separation of judicial power from executive and legislative power; and (5) the most important—"the ENLARGEMENT of the ORBIT within which such systems are to revolve."

The enlargement of the orbit is the most novel of these features. It abandons the central idea of the republican thought of the time that the only reliable bases for democratic politics are personal knowledge of the character of one's fellow citizens and active political participation. Altogether, the principles of the new political science "are means, and powerful means, by which the excellencies of republican government may be retained and its imperfections lessened or avoided" (*Federalist* 9).

Publius's thought must be located in the new political science of the enlightened authors of Europe. The Enlightenment's great promise was that scientific progress—especially when publicly taught or popularized—would result in a parallel progress in society and politics. At its most extreme, it hoped that scientific progress would issue in a utopia where the necessity of government in any form would be vastly reduced or eliminated altogether. Often identified with the French Enlightenment, enlightened utopianism was certainly represented in the founding generation (if imperfectly so) by Thomas Paine and Thomas Jefferson.

But Publius repeatedly ridicules this enlightened utopianism. Neither human nature nor society is capable of fundamental transformation in the manner embraced by this form of enlightenment

(*Federalist* 6). Men are too passionate and nations depend too much on established opinions and prejudices to become a "philosophical race of kings." As Publius says, "The most rational government will not find it a superfluous advantage to have the prejudices of the community on its side" (*Federalist* 49).

In opposition to the utopianism of the French Enlightenment, the English Enlightenment, found in writers such as John Locke, argued that man's passionate nature could not be changed. To a degree, passion can be rationally guided so that men can govern themselves with some degree of rationality. Enlightened political science strengthens man's understanding of society's permanent and aggregate interests—as opposed to the individual's immediate self-interest, not to mention his personal preferences and aversions.

In addition to the prudent rationalism of the English Enlightenment, Publius also seems to have been influenced by the even more traditional liberalism of David Hume and other thinkers of the Scottish Enlightenment, and by Baron de Montesquieu. Unlike John Locke, who argued that men could make governments anew based on consent and natural rights—life, liberty, and the pursuit of property (or happiness in the Declaration of Independence), David Hume argued that rights and liberties could safely (or really) develop only in practice, through political experience. In Hume's view the historical practice of political societies determines their politics, not a theoretical formulation of the political good.

Publius stands closer to the English Enlightenment when he argues that the Enlightenment gives statesmen useful tools to understand human nature and to create political institutions, now permitting the realization of republican self-government. But he is faithful to both Locke and Hume when he adds that the Enlightenment does not change man's natural passions. For this reason, a knowledge of history or practical experience is necessary to learn how human nature actually manifests itself. Knowledge acquired merely from theoretical writers may describe human nature accurately, but unless one has actual experience of man's passionate nature, such bookish wisdom cannot reasonably guide political life. Publius repeatedly avers, "Experience is the oracle of truth; and where its responses are unequivocal, they ought to be conclusive and sacred" (*Federalist* 20). Experience, however, is not always unequivocal; reason must then be our true guide (*Federalist* 14).

The People and Their
Ambitious Representatives

Like the other members of his generation—including the great democrat Thomas Jefferson—Publius accepted a distinction between levels of human ability. Relatively few men have a taste or stomach for political life. Only the "ambitious" seek political office despite its clear difficulties. According to Publius, the summit of ambition is the love of fame: "the ruling passion of the noblest minds" (*Federalist* 72). The arrangement of the constitutional offices aims to ensure that the ambitious who are elected through the political process will be the wise and virtuous. But even wisdom and virtue are not always reliable. Passionate human nature being what it is, the separation of powers will help guarantee that the representatives, once in office, remain responsible.

Publius believes the success of the new Constitution depends on the success of the representative or "the republican principle." Republicanism means for Publius not only government by representatives, but government by a few or the best of the people, elected by the people to represent the people as a whole.

Publius relies on the abilities of the best to govern as the people's representatives. The Constitution gives representatives sufficient political power and independence from public pressure to ensure that they can govern effectively. The four-year presidential and the six-year senatorial terms, and the indefinite term of "good behavior" for federal judges and justices of the Supreme Court, demonstrate that Publius sought a political fabric capable of withstanding the utmost uncertainty and depredation of human affairs: wars, depressions, mass immigrations, and instability of public opinion.

But "the new science of politics" is a democratic form of republican government. Although opposed to direct democracy—where all the people participate in the assembly—the Framers recognized that popular consent is the only legitimate and effectual basis of republican political power. All public power derives either directly through election from the people or indirectly through appointment by popularly elected officials. For example the president names (and the Senate confirms) members of the Supreme Court.

By creating a Constitution based on popular government while encouraging the most talented to rule in the public interest, Publius believes he has successfully combined the antagonistic ancient

principles of equality or democracy and human excellence or aristocracy. The improved science of politics solves the problem of
class conflict. In the small, ancient republics, class conflict resulted either in civil war between the people and the aristocrats or in
the imposition of a political tyranny by one class over the other.

Nevertheless, the opponents of the new Constitution, the Anti-
Federalists, were the first—but hardly the last—to pronounce the
new Constitution dangerous to both political liberty and popular
self-government. The independent power of the new representatives
was thought to defend the interests of the wealthy. In the view of
the Anti-Federalists and their more recent followers—the "Progressive" intellectuals of this century—the new Constitution represented not the completion of the Revolution but the subversion of the
Revolution by those very economic elites most distrustful of genuine democracy.

The Shape of a Successful
Democratic Republic

What are the specific social and political institutions Publius
believes will allow the new Constitution to be both a popular and
a good or stable government? What are the improvements in the
science of politics, and the new models "of a more perfect structure," permitting "enlightened friends of liberty" not to have to
abandon republican governments as indefensible?

In Publius's analysis the single greatest improvement in the science of popular government is the enlightenment of society itself
in "the enlargement of the orbit," or the extended commercial republic. As Publius says, "in the extent and proper structure of the
Union, therefore, we behold a Republican remedy for the diseases
most incident to Republican government" (*Federalist* 10).

"The extended commercial republic" is the solution to the problem of factional majorities or majority tyranny. Previous popular
governments failed because of the antagonisms within the populace. This tendency to civil war or the oppression of the minority
of the people by the majority of them—what Publius calls majority
tyranny—must be curbed if popular government is to succeed.

Publius's solution to majority faction or tyranny is more moderate majorities. In *Federalist* 10, Publius makes the case for a great
variety of economic interests and religious and political "sects."

When no interest or sect can hope to form a majority on its own terms, then moderate majorities become possible. Each interest and sect lowers its expectation about its likely success in the political process and begins to contemplate a moderate compromise with potential allies in a majority coalition.

The danger of majority tyranny exists as long as immediate economic, political, or religious advantage can be obtained by simple electoral majorities. If two or three economic interests or sects can monopolize public policies—for example, farmers, industrialists, and bankers, or labor unions, minority groups, and intellectuals—they will harm the interests and rights of the minority, who are not part of the coalition. But if business and labor interests are sufficiently diverse, they will inevitably associate with different political groupings. The political groupings must include differing religious, charitable, ethnic, and economic interests; then the possibility of a majority faction or tyranny is vastly reduced.

The broad-based, moderate coalitions Publius envisions assume two new political developments within "an extended area." First, numerous religious sects will result from the separation of Church and State and the expected fragmentation of the religious faiths. Second, the multiple economic interests Publius desires will arise as a consequence of modern economic development with its principle of ever increasing division of labors. The limited economic classes and interests of the feudal system were insufficiently diverse to produce the large number of interests Publius seeks.

In other words, only a modern, liberal society produces the numbers and kinds of sects and interests necessary to "make it less probable that a majority of the whole will have a common motive to invade the rights of other citizens" (*Federalist* 10).

But the mere satisfaction of competing interests is *not* the end of democratic government. On the contrary, these "interested" moderate majorities are the means enabling representatives to pursue the "permanent and aggregate interests" or the common good of the community. On many various and differing issues, sects and interests can be divided and reunited to win support for policies impossible to obtain from unenlightened or "nonextended" majorities united primarily by political ideology, class hatred, or serious religious sectarianism. These rational and long-term policies are often indirectly related to the immediate self-interest of the interests.

After Publius's radically new solution for fractious and tyranni-

cal majorities, he proposes other solutions to the structural difficulties encountered in the creation of a successful Constitution. Let
us look at the most important of these:

(1) The new Constitution will rule over citizens, not states. The
ineffectiveness of the Articles of Confederation resulted from its
defect in this respect, so that national decisions were nullified by
state inaction and resistance. An effective union of the states requires a government capable of breaching the barrier of the state
governments, making state citizens national citizens responsible to
national laws.

(2) The new Constitution will have all necessary powers to achieve
the ends given to the national government. According to *Federalist*
23, Publius argues:

> The *means* ought to be proportioned to the *end*; the persons, from
> whose agency the attainment of any *end* is expected, ought to pos-
> sess the *means* by which it is to be attained.

How much constitutional power is necessary to ensure sufficient
energy, especially for security matters?

> These powers ought to exist without limitation: Because it is im-
> possible to foresee or define the extent and variety of national exi-
> gencies, or the correspondent extent and variety of the means which
> may be necessary to satisfy them.

With such flexibility the government will have the necessary energy to govern competently.

(3) Although the new Constitution will be national and will be
energetic or strong, it will also be a limited government. It will be
limited in various ways.

(a) The purposes assigned to the national government are limited in their number and ends. Purposes not assigned to the federal
government are reserved to the states and individuals respectively.
Neither the national nor the state governments should intrude any
further than necessary in the areas reserved for individuals or private associations. This principle is the separation of "state and
society." While the separation of "state and society" neither can
nor should be absolute, it is a statement of a fundamental belief
that individuals and society (free associations: religious, economic, educational, and charitable) should be independent of governmental control to the extent possible and reasonable.

The separation of state and society is founded on two different sorts of arguments. A state unwilling to permit freedom of religion, political association, speech and other natural rights violates man's natural freedom and ultimately becomes tyrannical over him. A government usurping natural rights and freedoms will also prove less competent in ordering society than will rational individuals and free associations. This is true in many areas of human activity, especially so in economic affairs.

(b) Another limit to *The Federalist*'s strong national government is federalism. State and local governments are independent of the national government. Publius argues that the separation of national and state governments will encourage efficiency and oversight in public policy, while protecting the liberties of the governed. Federalism accomplishes this end by encouraging the voters to transfer their political allegiance from national to state and local representatives, or vice versa, depending on their confidence in the justice and desirable influence of the different levels of government (*Federalist* 39). For example, as long as some state governments were perceived as corrupt and racist, reformers in the early and middle decades of the twentieth century demanded greater national control of economic regulation and policies affecting race. In the 1970s and 1980s an electorate grown cautious of national expansion elected national leaders promising to return power and influence to the states. Most state governments were no longer perceived as corrupt and undemocratic.

American federalism is energized through the voters' ability to elect officials who may strengthen or weaken national power versus state and local power. Federalism encourages a useful "competition" between levels of government, giving voters somewhat greater control over government than a purely centralized system would allow.

(c) Another device designed to ensure both rational and nonoppressive government is the separation of powers. Significantly, Publius introduces the separation of powers not as a check on governmental abuse, but as a protection of the energy and power of government. (Only then is separation of powers considered as a security against the oppression of the people by their representatives.) Without separation of powers the legislative branch—the "legislative vortex" he calls it—would destroy the independence of the executive and the judiciary (*Federalist* 48).

The weakening or reabsorption of the executive into the more powerful legislative branch would cripple the energy and effectiveness of the government while increasing the likelihood that the legislative branch would become ever more arbitrary in executing "the popular will." The balance of power secured through the effective separation (and cooperation) of the three governmental powers avoids the weakness and irrationality associated with essentially legislative governments.

Publius's most novel device ensuring the separation of powers is wholly political. In *Federalist* 51 he argues that neither constitutional barriers nor virtue and morality are sufficient to guarantee the long-term separation of powers. So in addition to the restraints of morality or character, and the formal or parchment barriers in the Constitution, Publius looks to the conjunction of constitutional means (or powers) and personal motives to effect the separation. Publius wishes to counteract ambition with ambition. If a congressman wishes to be reelected or to become a senator, it becomes his interest to do his job well. He cannot win popular trust and esteem (or protect the interests and liberties of his constituents) by ceding power to the executive or judicial branch. Similarly, no president will win distinction by ceding his constitutional powers to Congress. Hence all three branches have the power and the interest to guard jealously their political and constitutional turf from the intrusion of other ambitious politicians.

(4) Publius believes his greatest constitutional construction is the presidency. "There is hardly any part of the system which could have been attended with greater difficulty in the arrangement of it than this" (*Federalist* 67). The intrinsic difficulty in the arrangement of presidential power was compounded by the Anti-Federalist opposition to the very existence of the presidency. The Anti-Federalists identified the presidency with a return of the English monarch, and inevitably, the end of democratic politics as the president-as-monarch in their nightmares practices the arts of corruption and manipulation to concentrate power.

But Publius is wholly committed to an energetic executive.

> Energy in the executive is a leading character in the definition of good government. It is essential to the protection of the community against foreign attacks: it is not less essential to the steady administration of the laws . . . A feeble executive implies a feeble execution of the government. A feeble execution is but another phrase for a bad execution: And a government ill executed, whatever it may be in theory, must be in practice a bad government. (*Federalist* 70)

One cannot find in Publius's constitution the executive of virtually unlimited implied powers which Alexander Hamilton, operating in support of George Washington's administration, later claimed to find there. Publius's executive is one of great energy and initiative. But he remains tethered by the constitutional language of Article II and the enabling legislation and oversight of the Congress.

Publius undertakes the difficult task of arranging the executive because it is that constitutional office which will enable the new government to function as the source of a national and effective public policy. The Framers had learned from the Articles of Confederation the imbecility of merely legislative government.

(5) In the American constitutional system the legislature becomes the most powerful bulwark against governmental tyranny. The essential power is executive; executive power alone gives governments energy and coherence. But the strong executive Publius envisions requires a sufficiently strong legislature to protect the liberties of the people and maintain effective political oversight and dialogue with the executive. This is the reason Publius makes Congress the court of impeachment of the federal judiciary and the president. A small, unelected Supreme Court would not have the political weight to guarantee that a popularly elected president would obey the impeachment verdict and leave office voluntarily (*Federalist* 65).

In some sense Publius expects the House of Representatives to serve as the "tribunes" of the people. Popular liberty is the chief purpose of the House of Representatives:

> First. As it is essential to liberty that the government in general, should have a common interest with the people; so it is particularly essential that the branch of it under consideration, should have an immediate dependence on, & an intimate sympathy with the people. Frequent elections are unquestionably the only policy by which the dependence and sympathy can be effectually secured. (*Federalist* 52)

In contrast to the House of Representatives, the Senate is not concerned with the immediate happiness of the people. It is concerned with the "knowledge of the means by which that object can be attained" (*Federalist* 56). The Senate is expected to provide no less than wisdom in deliberation, stability, and a locus of national interest and national character in foreign relations.

The Senate—along with the Supreme Court and the president—

is one of the "permanent" constitutional offices. Publius expects the permanent institutions to attract persons of the highest character and capacity, those who have proven worthy of the popular trust. Within these permanent offices, representatives have sufficient power and independence to permit them to seek the "permanent and aggregate interests of the community," not merely the electorate's immediate interests.

Congress is given the most formal power under the first Article of the Constitution. Congress has the power of the purse, to raise taxes, regulate commerce, and coin money or control the currency. Through its treaty ratifying power it shares in foreign policy. Through the power of impeachment it has the ability to even the score, especially with the executive. Finally, Congress is granted the sweeping power "to make all laws necessary and proper for carrying into Execution the foregoing powers."

(6) The Supreme Court is the final branch of the new Constitution in Publius's presentation. His description of the Court is novel in at least one respect. John Marshall argued in *Marbury v. Madison* (1803) that the Court had the power to rule on the constitutionality of the actions of the other branches (Congress and the president). One of the most important bases of the Court's argument in *Marbury* was *Federalist* 78, for here is one of relatively few places where the Framers made it clear (publicly, or outside the closed Constitutional Convention) that judicial review was part of their intention. Not only has judicial review strengthened the position of the Court in our constitutional system, it has greatly enhanced the importance of the Constitution itself.

(7) Immediately after discussing the Supreme Court's position in the Constitution (*Federalist* 78 to 83), Publius turns to the politically vexed question of a written bill of rights. The opposition of Publius, as well as of the convention, to a bill of rights has generally been accorded little notice, probably because of the immediate passage of such a bill in the First Congress in the form of the first ten Amendments to the Constitution.

Several aspects of Publius's argument against a bill of rights are noteworthy. However, his most fundamental argument is that the entire Constitution is a bill of rights and that only moderate majorities and moderate governments can protect citizens' rights in the long run. Mere "parchment barriers" will not protect individuals and minorities against determinedly oppressive majorities.

Conclusion: The English
and Scottish Enlightenment

The political institutions Publius proposes are prudential adaptations and, in some cases, genuine developments and novelties from the major liberal authors—especially John Locke, David Hume and Baron de Montesquieu—who inspired the Framers. Publius argues correctly, I think, that his reliance on these authors is one of a statesman long familiar with constitutional design as well as affairs of state. Unlike the intellectuals and reformers who design constitutions in the isolation and abstraction of their secluded "cabinets" or studies, Publius has been guided by experience, his own and what can be learned from the study of human nature in the course of political history, especially in the American experience with self-government.

Another approach to his perspective is to consider Publius's suggestion that he is preserving and completing the devotion to virtue of the ancient political thought of Plato and Aristotle (although he clearly rejects the ancient attempt to found politics on virtue instead of reason or interest). As he says:

> There are men who could neither be distressed nor won into a sacrifice of their duty; but this stern virtue is the growth of few soils: And in the main it will be found, that a power over a man's support is a power over his will. (*Federalist* 73)

Publius takes a more prudential position than the ancients. Better and more enlightened men will be virtuous, but they will not be irrationally so. They will rarely act from duty or disinterested motives. Publius assumes that the new science of nature and politics has strengthened the prudential character of citizens and states, and so even virtue is enlightened. When discussing the presidency, Publius warns that one of the major disadvantages to limiting the number of presidential terms would be to lessen "the inducements to good behavior" of the lame duck incumbent.

For Publius, interest—hopefully rational, comprehensive, and long-term interest—is a more reliable basis for the opinions and behavior of majorities and their representatives than is morality, piety, or virtue. By "lowering the standards" of human endeavor, Publius is attempting to realize the goals of self-government or republicanism sought by the ancients.

Publius's moderate, modern realism (and his optimism) are also based on his recognition that the people as well as their representatives possess sufficient virtue to justify the desire for popular, representative government.

Virtuous and enlightened individuals will always arise. Virtue and honor have "been found to exist in the most corrupt periods of the most corrupt governments" (*Federalist* 76). While in other forums the Framers advocated an education to morality and religion, Publius confines his discussion (in *The Federalist*) to the perfection of political institutions.

Arguably, the success of the institutional devices Publius recommended—such as an "extended commercial republic," the refinement of the republican or representative principle, and separation of powers—resulted from Publius's serious regard for experience. It might also be argued that this regard for the Constitution's political success, and the prudential maxims of the writers of the Scottish Enlightenment, may have attenuated the Framers' concern for the formal attention to natural rights characteristic of American liberals of this period.

Detecting this change of emphasis, the Anti-Federalists responded to it by demanding (and obtaining) a Bill of Rights, as three-quarters of a century later, Abraham Lincoln demanded that the Constitution be read in light of the natural rights doctrine of the Declaration of Independence. In Abraham Lincoln's judgment, the Framers' prudential accommodation with slavery—required to achieve political unity and the acceptance of the new Constitution—had outlived its usefulness. Slavery needed, finally and definitely, to be put on the road to ultimate extinction. The intention of the Framers regarding the eventual abolition of slavery now needed to be fulfilled.

But this supposed tension between a more radically enlightened and egalitarian Declaration of Independence and a restrained, prudential, and inegalitarian Constitution is much more apparent than real. It is more proper and certainly more correct to say that Publius sought political institutions capable of combining the Enlightenment's demand for liberty, equality, and self-rule *with* an energetic and stable government. As a statesman, Publius recognized that good political theory (the natural rights doctrine of the Declaration of Independence) could be realized only through the extraordinary political prudence demanded by the drafting, ratification, and establishment of the Constitution.

The realism or pragmatism of the Framers' Constitution was, as Abraham Lincoln later said, the "Frame of Silver" necessary to support the "picture" or the purpose of the American founding. In the picture, Lincoln said, were the "Apples of Gold"—the original natural rights and liberties promised by the Declaration of Independence and the American Revolution.

Suggested Reading

Adair, Douglass. *Fame and the Founding Fathers: Essays by Douglass Adair*. New York: Norton, 1974.

Carey, George. *The Federalist: Design for a Constitutional Republic*. Urbana: University of Illinois Press, 1989.

Epstein, David F. *The Political Theory of The Federalist*. Chicago: University of Chicago Press, 1984.

Kesler, Charles R., ed. *Saving the Revolution: The Federalist Papers and the American Founding*. New York: Free Press, 1987.

Pangle, Thomas L. *The Spirit of Modern Republicanism: The Moral Vision of the American Founders and the Philosophy of Locke*. Chicago: University of Chicago Press, 1988.

5

The Federalist versus the Procedural Republic

Kenneth L. Grasso

In the eyes of its Founders, the American republic was a nation with a mission. This mission was to prove to the world that self-government with justice was possible, that democratic government could be good government. Free institutions, they wished to show, need not bring forth tyranny or anarchy, but it can effectively secure justice, order, freedom, and the common good. If the democratic revolutions sweeping today's world are any indication, then the American experiment in self-government has been a success. We have proved to the world that free institutions can work, that democratic government *can* be good government.

Recent decades, however, have witnessed a far-reaching change in the nature of the American body politic. America has been largely transformed from what might be termed a "republic of common aims" into what might be called a "procedural republic."[1] By a republic of common aims, I mean a democratic society united by a common view of what a human being is and of the political and moral principles and goals to which the body politic is dedicated. By a procedural republic, in contrast, I mean a society grounded in a consensus of a purely procedural nature, a consensus limited to the procedures to be used in making political decisions. While contemporary Americans may agree about the structure of our political and legal institutions, we no longer agree about the way of life we aspire to create and sustain, about the political and moral ends these institutions should serve. "What is in short supply today," as one recent study has pointed out, "is . . . not consensus on the rules of the game but a sense of purpose as to what one should achieve by playing the game."[2]

Is this development a welcome one? After all, as Robert Bellah, one of America's most eminent sociologists, has written:

> It is one of the oldest sociological generalizations that any coherent and viable society rests on a common set of moral understandings about good and bad, right and wrong, in the realm of individual and social action. It is almost as widely held that these common moral understandings must also in turn rest upon a common set of religious understandings that provide a picture of the universe in terms of which the moral understandings make sense.[3]

Sociologists have long concluded that a stable and vigorous society requires more than a procedural consensus. It requires substantive agreement about the nature of man and the moral and political ends and principles to which the society is dedicated.

Surprisingly, however, the rise of the procedural republic has prompted relatively little concern. In part, this fact can be explained by the impact on the contemporary American public mind of several influential theories of democratic government. The rise of the procedural republic, these theories suggest, should not generate concern for two reasons.

The first reason has to do with the very nature of the American experiment in democracy. America, it is contended, was intended by its Founders to be a procedural republic. This view received one of its classic expressions in a famous dissenting opinion written by one of the most influential figures in the history of the Supreme Court, Oliver Wendell Holmes. The Constitution, he said, "was made for people of fundamentally differing views."[4] The Constitution, in this view, was designed for a people who disagree fundamentally about the moral and political goals to which the American polity should be committed. It was intended to supply a set of rules regulating conflicts over this very question. It was intended to be a peace accord, establishing a framework within which such conflicts could be conducted without recourse to violence.

The second reason has to do with the nature of democratic government itself. A commitment to proceduralism, it is argued, is precisely what separates free from unfree societies. The hallmark of a truly democratic society is that it has neither an official truth, an orthodoxy, on which it insists nor a conception of the good life which it seeks to "impose" on its citizens. Agreeing to disagree on such matters, the citizens of a free society are united only by their acceptance of a set of rules governing the making of decisions and resolution of conflicts. A commitment to proceduralism, in this view, is a defining attribute of a free society.

I want to take issue with both of these contentions. The rise of the procedural republic marks a break with the American political tradition, a dramatic departure from the theory of democratic government on which the American experiment in self-government rests. It also constitutes a threat to the very future of American democracy. My argument will begin with an examination of *The Federalist*.

The Problem of Self-Government

The fundamental theoretical problem *The Federalist* faced is reconciling self-government with justice. "Justice," according to Publius in *Federalist* 51, "is the end of government. It is the end of civil society. It even has been, and even will be pursued, until it be obtained, or until liberty be lost in the pursuit."

Yet historically popular governments have not proved themselves capable of effectively securing justice and the common good. As a matter of fact, it is "impossible" to read their histories without "feeling sensations of horror and disgust" at their perpetual vacillation "between the extremes of anarchy and tyranny" (*Federalist* 9). If free government is to have a future—if it is to "be rescued from the opprobrium under which it has so long labored" (*Federalist* 10), if its cause is not to be abandoned as "indefensible"—a way must be found of creating a type of democratic government that can effectively secure justice and the common good.

If democracy is to be made safe for the world, a means must be devised to overcome the vices which have almost always issued in the collapsed democratic governments. In his discussion of the deficiencies of the American governments of his era, Publius identifies three such vices. The first is the tyranny of the majority, the fact that in popular government "measures are too often decided, not according to the rules of justice . . . but by the superior force of an interested and overbearing majority." The second is the proclivity of free governments to paralysis as a result of the fragmentation of the body politic into a multiplicity of conflicting groups, the tendency in such societies for "the public good" to be "disregarded in the conflicts of rival parties." The third vice results from the first two: the chronic "instability" of democratic governments (*Federalist* 10).

These vices of democracy are but symptoms of a deeper and hitherto "mortal" disease: faction. Because the "latent causes of faction are . . . sown in the nature of man," no society will be immune to this disease. But if the causes of factionalism cannot be eliminated, the effects of factionalism can be controlled. Publius's solution to this problem hinges on the introduction of a scheme of representation and the diversity resulting from the larger society (i.e., the "extended sphere") that representation makes possible.

How do representation and extended sphere assist us? The effect of representation, he argues, can be

> to refine and enlarge the public views, by passing them through the medium of a chosen body of citizens, whose wisdom may best discern the true interest of their country, and whose patriotism and love of justice, will be least likely to sacrifice it to temporary and partial considerations. (*Federalist* 10)

A representative assembly consisting of representatives of exceptional wisdom and moral character would be better equipped to enact laws advancing justice and the common good than would their constituents if the latter were to make the laws themselves.

Extending the sphere acts to divide the society into "so many parts, interests, and classes of citizens." As a result, no one group will be large enough to dominate the political process because no group will be large enough to constitute by itself a majority. By preventing the existence of a majority interest, the republic's diversity, in short, acts to prevent the emergence of a majority faction. The fact that a majority must encompass a number of different groups, a multiplicity of different interests, will "render an unjust combination of a majority of the whole, very improbable, if not impractical." "In the extended republic of the United States, and among the great variety of interests, parties and sects which it embraces," concludes Publius, "a coalition of a majority of the whole society could seldom take place on any other principles than those of justice and the general good" (*Federalist* 51).

Today, some writers interpret this line of analysis as an early version of the procedural republic. For *The Federalist*, they conclude, politics is reduced to a struggle among competing interests over the allocation of scarce values—over the divvying-up of the spoils, as it were—conducted according to the rules of the game given by the Constitution. The republic's diversity will assure that no single group is capable of imposing its views on others, of translating all its demands into law. So majorities will necessarily consist of loose and ever shifting coalitions of groups.

To form such coalitions, compromise will be essential. To achieve some of their goals, groups are going to have to both forgo some of their own goals and support other groups in the achievement of theirs. Laws and public policies will be the outcome of amoral compromises between essentially self-seeking groups united only by an acceptance of the procedural guidelines—the rules of the game established by the Constitution.

Yet a moment's reflection will reveal that even the limited portion of Publius's argument just examined is difficult to square with this reading. Consider, for example, Publius's discussion of representation and the role of representatives. In seeking representatives of extraordinary wisdom and virtue to "refine and enlarge public views," he suggests a nobler conception of business of politics than the divvying-up of the spoils. And if this account seems to explain how Publius hopes to avoid majority tyranny, it doesn't explain how Publius's solution will enable us to establish a strong government capable of securing justice and the common good. Publius's whole solution can be seen only through further exploration of how Publius expects the republic's diversity to influence the decision-making process.

The difficulty in forming a majority that results from the republic's extensiveness (and consequent diversity), reinforced by certain institutional expedients (the famed "auxiliary precautions" of bicameralism, staggered elections, separation of powers, checks and balances, etc.), slows the decision-making process in ways that have important and salutary implications for the quality of the decisions made. "In the legislature," according to *Federalist* 70, "promptitude of decision is oftener an evil than a benefit. The differences of opinion, and the jarring of parties in that department of government . . . promote deliberation and circumspection, and secure to check excesses in the majority." Similarly "the oftener . . . [that a] measure is brought under examination, the greater the diversity in the situations of those who are to examine it, the less must be the danger of the errors which flow from want of due deliberation, or of those missteps which proceed from the contagion of some common passion or interest" (*Federalist* 73).

Thus, diversity works to prevent the formation of a majority around a single particular interest (and thereby to reduce the likelihood of the emergence of a majority faction) and so to make the consideration of the good of the whole community possible. Simultaneously, drastically slowing the decision-making process helps assure that decisions are not made in the heat of passion. The public is given a chance to calm down. More than this, slowing the decision-making process creates a window of opportunity for the thorough airing of all points of view, for the give-and-take of public debate, criticism, fact-finding, and the assessment of long-range effects. It acts, in short, to make deliberation possible.

Publius's solution to the problem of self-government requires the construction of a democratic system in which the laws do something more than merely reflect the will of the people. He seeks to create a system in which they embody "the cool and deliberate sense of the community," in which they embody the reason of the people (*Federalist* 63).

Implicit in Publius's line of argument is a distinction between political proposals resulting from sheer acts of will, from interest and passion, and those resulting from reasoned judgment, from deliberation. "It is," he writes, "the reason of the people that ought to control and regulate the government. The passions ought to be controlled and regulated by the government" (*Federalist* 49). The reason why Publius seeks majorities which emerge as an outgrowth of a process of deliberation is not mysterious. Factions, it will be recalled, have their origins in interest and passion. The deliberative process Publius seeks acts to bring factious demands before the bar of reason. Factious proposals—proposals having their origin in interest and passion—will find it difficult to survive the test of this deliberative process. Proposals for which no justification may be advanced other than the passion or self-interest will be exposed. Deliberation thus functions as a filter, acting to filter out demands emanating from interest and passion.

But slowing the decision-making process does not itself guarantee that the type of serious deliberation Publius seeks about how the good of the whole community might best be advanced will actually take place. It merely creates the potential for such deliberation. Whether or not this potential for "refining and enlarging the public views" through a deliberative process is realized will depend on the character of members of the representative assembly. Here again, Publius believes that our extended republic's size and diversity will be of assistance to us because it will help secure the selection of "proper guardians of the public weal" (*Federalist* 10).

A large republic, to begin with, will be more likely than a small republic to select a representative assembly consisting of legislators of the character Publius seeks, for the same reason that a high school of 10,000 students is likely to assemble a better football team than a school of 1,000. In both cases, the larger pool works, all other things being equal, to assure a greater number of candidates with the required characteristics. The republic's size creates "a greater probability of fit choice."

At the same time, the size of the legislative districts will make it "more difficult for unworthy candidates to practice with success the vicious arts by which elections are too often carried" (*Federalist* 10). The size of the republic's legislative districts will itself function as a barrier to both bribery and other forms of outright corruption, while simultaneously acting as an impediment to the success of mere demagoguery. (Whereas a single speech to a single audience may enable a demagogue to be victorious in a small district, a larger district will necessitate many speeches to many audiences. A larger district makes it more likely that demagogues will be exposed and that the voters will less likely to be passionately aroused by speeches.)

Publius's refusal to rely upon either "enlightened" statesmanship or moral and religious motives alone does not mean that they are irrelevant to the republican remedy he proposes. As his conception of the representative's role makes clear, he does indeed presuppose that enlightened statesmen will usually be at the helm. He is aware that his solution to the problem of self-government with justice presupposes a particular type of citizenry. It presupposes a citizenry capable of recognizing, and choosing to be governed by, representatives of the character Publius seeks. It presupposes, in the final analysis, a citizenry aware of the distinction between justice and injustice, and committed to doing justice. In short, it presupposes what Willmoore Kendall and George W. Carey have termed "a virtuous people."[5] As *Federalist* 55 suggests:

> As there exists a certain degree of depravity in mankind which requires a certain degree of circumspect and mistrust: so there are other qualities in human nature, which justify a certain portion of esteem and confidence. Republican government presupposes the existence of these qualities in a higher degree than any other form.

A debased populace, in other words, cannot govern itself with justice. Thus, diversity is only half the solution of the problem of self-government with justice. The other half had to do with enlightened statesmanship and moral character. Ironically, by dividing and thereby weakening factionalism, the republic's diversity is what enables enlightened statesmanship and the virtue of the American people to come to the fore.

Likewise, Publius neither embraces the view that politics is merely a struggle among competing factions regarding the divvying-up of the spoils nor seeks to reduce political decisions to amoral compromises between self-seeking interests. On the contrary, he insists that the superiority of the Constitution to the Articles of Confederation is found in the fact that it will establish a strong and energetic government capable of securing justice and the common good. To secure laws and public policies which effectively advance these goals, he seeks to create a decision-making process that can transcend factionalism. To create such a process he avails himself of the country's diversity (along with certain auxiliary precautions) to secure majorities which are the outcome not of bargaining among factions but of a deliberative process whose participants will be the citizens "who possess [the] most wisdom to discern and most virtue to pursue, the common good of society" (*Federalist* 57). The decisions of such majorities, he argues, will be consonant with the demands of justice and the common good.[6]

Publius's Republic of Common Aims

Given Publius's emphasis upon the far-ranging diversity of our extended republic, a few questions arise. In what sense, for example, can such a body politic be said to possess a "common good"? Is not such a polity little more than a collection of diverse groups pursuing their interests and united only by the agreed-upon mechanisms for resolving conflicts—the rules of the game—established by our constitutional system? Likewise, given our diversity, how can Publius so confidently generalize about the American people's moral character? Indeed, in what sense can the inhabitants of such a polity be said to be a "people" at all, much less a virtuous one?

If Publius's discussion emphasizes America's pluralism, it at the same time calls our attention to the horizon within which this pluralism exists. This pluralism occurs in the broader context of a "people" constituting a "community" possessing "permanent and aggregate interests." The political order established by the Constitution will not be inhabited by a mere collection of groups and individuals united only by geographical proximity and the acceptance of a common set of legal and political procedures. Rather, it will be inhabited by "one united people," by "a band of brethren united to each other by the strongest ties" (*Federalist* 2). Indeed, this community—whose common good the government is charged with advancing, and to whose well-being factions are a threat—is the ultimate source of political authority.

Despite the diversity found within their extended republic, the American people can be said to be a people because they are united by a common culture, a common way of life. "Providence," Publius writes, "has been pleased to give this one connected country, to one united people, a people descended from the same ancestors, speaking the same language, professing the same religion, attached to the same principles of government, [and] very similar in their manners and customs" (*Federalist* 2). At the heart of this common way of life will be found a body of common values and shared principles, a substantive consensus. The consensus embodies a shared understanding of what a human being is, of what is good and bad for human beings, of what structure of social relations ought to inform human life.

It is the deep formative influence exercised by this shared understanding on their collective and individual characters that enables Publius to speak of the American people as a virtuous people. The common conscience created by this shared understanding enables the American people to recognize, and motivates them to reject, the "wicked and improper" projects of factions.

The Constitution was not intended for "people of fundamentally differing views," nor was the unity it established to be purely procedural in nature. The political unity established by the Constitution was intended to build upon a preexisting cultural unity and the substantive moral consensus found at its center. This consensus provided the moral framework within which our institutions were meant to operate. It provided, in other words, the moral and political ends—the common aims—which these institutions were meant to serve, and the principles by which operations were to be guided and directed.

It was the formative influence of this common culture—combined with the republic's diversity and certain inventions of prudence—that Publius believes will enable America to reconcile democratic government with the demands of justice, freedom, order, and the common good. It is the centrality of this cultural consensus to the theoretical underpinnings of the American democratic experiment that makes it impossible to classify that experiment as merely a procedural enterprise.[7]

The Conditions of Freedom

To show that Publius was not a proponent of a procedural understanding of democracy does not resolve the question of the com-
patibility of the procedural republic with democratic government.
For our purposes, this whole problem may best be approached by
means of a question that *The Federalist* leaves unanswered: Why
is a virtuous people a precondition of a successful democracy?
Admittedly, the relationship between the effectiveness of democratic
institutions and the character of the people is a subject we seldom
reflect upon today. We tend to assume that laws and public policies
effectively securing justice, ordered liberty, and the common good
emerge automatically—as if by an invisible hand—from the processes of democratic government. We tend to imagine that—to borrow
a phrase from the great poet T. S. Eliot—that in democracy we have
discovered a system so perfect that nobody has to be good.

But a little reflection will reveal that nothing could be further
from the truth. If democracy historically has been so rare and fragile a form a government, it is because it demands so much of the
citizenry. In authoritarian regimes, order is imposed from the top
down, though force and fear. Eschewing such methods, a free society relies for its vitality on the willingness of the individuals and
groups that compose it to cooperate freely to secure the common
good, and to use the freedom given them in a responsible fashion.
"Just as the democratic society freely chooses its government," John
Middleton Murry writes, "so the democratic citizen must freely choose
to do his duty to the commonweal."[8]

A vigorous democracy thus requires the presence of what Daniel
Bell terms *civitas*—the "spontaneous willingness to obey the law,
to respect the rights of others, to forgo temptations of private en-
richment at the expense of the public weal—in short, to honor the
'city' of which one is a member."[9] Many examples could be offered to illustrate the importance of *civitas* to the vitality of a democratic polity. To offer but one, imagine for a moment the effect its
absence would have on the ability of a democratic polity to act
effectively to achieve its goals and address its problems. There can
be no denying that compromise is essential to democratic decision-
making. Yet whether or not compromise takes place will depend
heavily on the mind-set of the citizens and the attitude with which
they approach public affairs.

Will individuals and groups be responsible, exercising self-control in making demands on the government? Will they be willing to

sacrifice their own interests for the good of the community? Will they be willing to bear their fair share of the burdens, to pay their dues, as it were? If the answer to these questions is yes, then achieving the compromises that the polity needs in order to secure the common good should not, all other things being equal, be especially difficult. If, on the other hand, the answer is no, then securing the compromises the public good depends on is going to be difficult indeed, perhaps even impossible.

The absence of *civitas* will inevitably issue in a phenomenon that has been called "anomic democracy."[10] Without public-spiritedness and a sense of community, it is inevitable that the body politic will splinter into a multiplicity of narrowly self-seeking groups who view each other with fear and suspicion. The ever escalating and conflicting demands of these groups, in turn, will overload the political system. The result will be gridlock. Such a dysfunctional democratic government will be capable of giving, but it will not be capable of leading. It will be anxious to respond to the demands of these groups, but will be incapable of exercising the strong leadership necessary to secure the goods which constitute the substance of good government.

But there is an even deeper and more fundamental sense in which democracy requires a virtuous people. The moral foundation of democracy is found in the affirmation of an order of rights and justice which transcends the positive laws of the state and to which governments, majorities, and individuals alike are held accountable. This idea received classic expression in our Declaration of Independence:

> We hold these Truths to be self-evident, that all Men are created equal, that they are endowed by their Creator with certain unalienable Rights, that among these are Life, Liberty, and the Pursuit of Happiness—That to secure these Rights, Governments are instituted among Men, deriving their just Powers from the Consent of the Governed.

This affirmation, in turn, is rooted in a particular understanding of what a human being is. A human person, as John Courtney Murray has written, is a sacred being

> because he comes from God and goes to God; a creature whose basic dignity lies in his dutifulness towards God and who is endowed with the rights in order that he may lead this life of dignity. [11]

The rights of human beings are rooted in their nature and destiny: their dignity as bearers of the image and likeness of God; their possession of a destiny transcending the world; and the grave responsibilities with which they are charged by their creator.

In a democratic society, laws and public policies will, in the final analysis, reflect the convictions, the moral values, and the character of the citizens. Whether the decisions made by democratic processes are consistent with the moral and spiritual affirmations which lie at the heart of democracy will thus depend on the character of the citizens, on their internalization of these affirmations. Only to the extent that these affirmations are living reality in the minds and hearts of the citizens will it be a living reality in their public life. Do they know and strive to live in accordance with the orders of rights and justice? Do they understand the sacredness of man, and the imperatives this sacredness imposes on them as a people? If the answer to these questions is no, then democratic institutions and procedures will only be the instruments with which new forms of servitude and injustice will be forged.

Some would try to avoid this truth by relying on written constitutional guarantees of rights and on the power of unelected judges to enforce such guarantees against popular majorities. Yet the effectiveness of what Publius terms "parchment barriers" is questionable. After all, constitutional guarantees can be ignored or altered. And the judiciary will not, over the long run, be an obstacle to a highly determined and organized popular majority. Judges, as Publius points out, possess "neither force nor will" (*Federalist* 78), they must rely on the popularly elected branches to enforce their decisions. Moreover, insofar as judges are themselves chosen indirectly by the people, in the long run their views will reflect the views and values of the majority. There is no avoiding the truth of Lincoln's remark that in a system such as ours, public opinion is everything.

Indeed, the absence of a virtuous people not only renders democratic institutions and procedures incapable of securing justice, but renders the very existence of these institutions and procedrues precarious. To understand why this is the case, it is necessary merely to inquire why a society should go to the trouble creating and sustaining the characteristic institutions and procedures of democracy? The answer to this question lies not in the institutions and procedures themselves but in something beyond them. Elections, for example, are valuable as a means of securing the goal of self-government, as a means of institutionalizing the right of the people to govern themselves.

If our democratic institutions are to endure, we thus need, as John Hallowell has observed, "a philosophy in terms of which we can justify our democracy and our preference for it."[12] A people who lack a firm allegiance to the philosophy that supplies democracy's very moral foundation will be unable to justify these institutions intellectually, and unwilling to bear the burdens and make the sacrifices which are the price of freedom. Among such a people, free institutions have no more chance of enduring the changing tides and storms of political life than a sand castle has of enduring the changing tides and storms of the sea.

Conclusion

Faced with the disturbing implications of the rise of the procedural republic for the future of our democratic institutions, we can respond in one of two ways. On the one hand, we can do nothing to halt our slide into the abyss of the procedural republic. To respond in this way means to acquiesce in the continued devitalization of our democratic institutions.

On the other hand, we can attempt to escape the morass of the procedural republic by trying to recreate the type of substantive concensus on which the health of our democratic institutions depends. Admittedly, an undertaking of this magnitude will not be easy and its success is by no means assured. It presupposes nothing less than what Murray terms "a new moral act of purpose and a new act of intellectual affirmation comparable to that which launched the American constitutional commonwealth."[13] Yet it alone offers our democratic experiment the hope of a future worthy of its historic mission.

Notes

1. To the best of my knowledge, the term "procedural republic" was coined by Michael Sandel. See his essay "The Political Theory of the Procedural Republic" in *Constitutionalism and Rights*, edited by Gary C. Bryner and Noel B. Reynolds (Provo, Utah: Brigham Young University, 1987), 141–56. I borrow the term "republic of common aims" from Robert P. Hunt's "Moral Orthodoxy and the Procedural Republic" in *John Courtney Murray and the American Civil Conversation*, edited by Robert P. Hunt and Kenneth L. Grasso (Grand Rapids: William B. Eerdmans, 1992), 253.

2. Michael J. Crozier, Samuel P. Huntington, and Joji Watanuki, *The Crisis of Democracy* (New York: New York University Press, 1975), 159.

3. Robert N. Bellah, *The Broken Covenant* (Chicago: University of Chicago Press, 1992), xvi.

4. *Lochner v. New York*, 198 U.S. 45 (1905).

5. Kendall and Carey, *The Basic Symbols of the American Political Tradition* (Baton Rouge: Louisiana State University Press, 1970), 112.

6. For a much more detailed presentation of Publius's solution to the problem of self-government, see Kenneth L. Grasso, "Pluralism, the Public Good, and the Problem of Self-Government in *The Federalist*," *Interpretation* 15 (May/June 1987): 324–45. The best guide to *The Federalist*'s theory of politics is George Carey's *The Federalist: Design for a Constitutional Republic* (Urbana: University of Illinois Press, 1989).

7. For the importance of this cultural consensus to Publius's argument, see, in addition to the previously cited studies, Edward Milligan's *One United People: The Federalist Papers and the National Idea* (Lexington: University of Kentucky Press, 1990).

8. John Middleton Murry, "The Moral Foundations of Democracy," *Fortnightly* (September 1947), 168.

9. Daniel Bell, *The Cultural Contradictions of Capitalism* (New York: Basic Books, 1978), 245.

10. See Crozier et al., 158–68.

11. John Courtney Murray, S.J., "The School and Christian Freedom," *Proceedings of the National Catholic Educational Association* XLVIII (August 1951), 64.

12. John H. Hallowell, The Moral Foundation of Democracy (Chicago: University of Chicago Press, 1954), 67.

13. John Courtney Murray, S.J., *We Hold These Truths* (New York: Image Books, 1964), 22.

Suggested Reading

Carey, George W. *The Federalist: Design for a Constitutional Republic*. Urbana: University of Illinois Press, 1989.

Hallowell, John H. *The Moral Foundation of Democracy*. Chicago: University of Chicago Press, 1954.

Kendall, Willmoore, and George W. Carey. *The Basic Symbols of the American Political Tradition*. Baton Rouge: Louisiana State University Press, 1970.

Murray, John Courtney, S.J. *We Hold These Truths*. New York: Image Books, 1964.

6

The Constitutional Thought
of the Anti-Federalists

Murray Dry

Although they claimed to be the true federalists and the true republicans, the men who opposed the Constitution's unconditional ratification in 1787–1788 were called Anti-Federalists.

The leading opponents from the major states included Patrick Henry, George Mason, and Richard Henry Lee from Virginia; George Clinton, Robert Yates, and Melancton Smith from New York; John Winthrop and Elbridge Gerry from Massachusetts; and Robert Whitehill, William Findley, and John Smilie from Pennsylvania. They all agreed that the document produced by the convention in Philadelphia was unacceptable without some amendments. Since most state constitutions contained bills of rights, the need for a similar feature for the national constitution formed the Anti-Federalists' most effective argument against unconditional ratification. The national Bill of Rights is the result of that dialogue.

Nevertheless, the Anti-Federalists' major contribution to the American founding lay more in their critical examination of the new form of federalism and the new form of republican government than in their successful campaign for a bill of rights. The Anti-Federalists sought substantial restrictions on federal power, which the amendments subsequently adopted did not provide. Suspicious of a strong national government, these opponents nevertheless failed to agree on an alternative constitutional arrangement. Still, the legacy of the Anti-Federalists persists in our constitutional debates over federalism and republican government.

Anti-Federal constitutionalism finds its most thoughtful and comprehensive expression in the *Letters of the Federal Farmer* and the

Essays of Brutus, attributed to Richard Henry Lee and Robert Yates, respectively. Although authorship remains uncertain, these writers covered all major constitutional questions in a manner that required, and received, the attention of "Publius," the pen name adopted by Alexander Hamilton, James Madison, and John Jay, authors of the famous *Federalist Papers*.

This essay discusses Anti-Federal constitutionalism in three parts: federalism, the separation of powers, and the Bill of Rights.

Republican Government and Federalism

The Anti-Federalists claimed to be the true federalists because they were the true republicans. Consequently, we begin with their account of republican government and its relation to federalism.

The Anti-Federalists believed that to maintain the spirit of republican government, which was the best defense against tyranny, individuals needed to know one another, be familiar with their governments, and have some direct experience in government. Only then would the citizenry possess a genuine love of country, which is the essence of republican, or civic, virtue.

The Anti-Federalists espoused the then traditional view of republican government, reflected in the first state constitutions, which emphasized the legislative branch of government. With the first federal constitution, the Articles of Confederation, the states, through their legislatures, retained effective control of federal men and federal measures. The delegates to Congress were chosen by the state legislatures and were subject to being recalled. The federal power to raise taxes and armies not only required a vote of nine states but, even after such a vote, depended on state requisitions, which meant that the federal government depended on the good will of the states to execute the law.

In stark contrast, the constitution proposed by the Federal Convention in 1787 provided the basis for a strong national government. Elections to the House of Representatives would be by the people directly, not the states, and the federal powers over taxes and the raising of armies would be completely independent of the state governments. This new form of federalism necessarily produced a new form of republicanism, the "large republic." Furthermore, Publius did not shrink from providing a positive argument in support of it. *Federalist* 10 justified the new form of republicanism, not only as the price of union but as the republican remedy to the disease of majority faction, or majority tyranny.

Because the Federalists saw a major danger not from the aggrandizing of the ruling few but from the tyranny of the majority, they sought to restrain the influence of that majority in order to secure individual rights and the permanent and aggregate interests of the community. Such restraint was to be achieved through a large extended sphere, i.e., the constituencies of the federal government. These would be larger and more diverse than the constituencies of the states, and so would make majority tyranny more difficult, since more negotiation and compromise would be needed for any single faction to become part of a majority. In addition, the increased competition for office would produce better representatives and a more effective administration throughout the government.

Perhaps because he took republican government for granted, as a given in America, Publius understood it to require only that offices of government be filled directly or indirectly by popular vote. Furthermore, the representation of the people was satisfied by the fact of election, regardless of the contrast between the wealth and influence of the elected and the electorate.

To the Anti-Federalists, the people would not be free for long if all they could do was vote for a representative whom they would not know and who would be very different from them. Because the Anti-Federalists emphasized participation in government, they argued that a small territory and a basically homogeneous population were necessary for a notion of the "public good" to be agreed upon. The Anti-Federalists did not insist that every citizen exercise legislative power. But they did emphasize representation of the people in the legislatures and on juries. By "representation" they meant that the number of people in a legislative district must be small enough and the number of districts large enough so that the citizens will know the people they are voting for and be able to elect one of their own—one of the "middling class." This latter phrase referred to the large number of farmers of modest means. A substantial representation of this agricultural middle class was possible even in the large states and necessary for the character of the governors to reflect the governed. Under the proposed constitution, argued the Anti-Federalists, this kind of representation would be impossible at the federal level, where the districts would contain at least 30,000 people.

Likewise, by participating in local jury trials, in civil as well as criminal cases, the people in their states acquired a knowledge of the laws and the operation of government, and thereby, argued the Anti-Federalists, became more responsible citizens. It was feared that this responsibility would be lost when cases were appealed to the proposed national supreme court, which had jurisdiction on appeal over all questions of law and fact.

Because the Anti-Federalists believed that republican government was possible in the states but not in one single government for the entire country, only a confederacy, that is, a federal republic, could safeguard the nation's freedom. They understood such a form of government to have a limited purpose, primarily common defense. Hence, those who became Anti-Federalists originally favored limited amendments to the Articles of Confederation, rather than an entirely new constitution. When a new constitution became inevitable, they hoped to limit the transfer of political power from the states to the national government. They claimed to be the true republicans and the true federalists because they understood republican government to require a closely knit people attached to their government. They sought to grant only so much power to the federal government as was absolutely necessary to provide for defense. In this way, the distribution of governmental power, as between the nation and the states, would correspond to the distribution of representation.

And while the Anti-Federalists did argue for an increase in the federal representation, that by itself would not have satisfied the requirement of republican government, as they saw it, since the people would always be more substantially represented in their state governments. According to the Anti-Federalists, the Federalists were not federalists but consolidationists. The ultimate effect of the Constitution would be to reduce the states to mere administrative units, thereby eliminating republican liberty.

Federalism and the Constitution:
The Legislative Powers

Already fearful of the Constitution's threat to republican liberty, the Anti-Federalists vehemently objected to the large number of specific powers granted to Congress, especially the taxing power and the power to raise armies. They found the undefined grants of power in the "necessary and proper" and the "supremacy" clauses

(I:8,18 and VI:2) alarming as well. The government, Brutus claimed, "so far as it extends, is a complete one, and not a confederation," and "all that is reserved to the states must very soon be annihilated, except so far as they are barely neccessary to the organization of the general government." With the power to tax virtually unchecked, Brutus lamented that "the idea of confederation is totally lost, and that of one entire republic is embraced."

The Anti-Federalists attempted to draw a line between federal and state powers, conceding to the federal government only those powers which were necessary for security and defense. Their most common tax proposal would have limited the federal government to a tax on foreign imports, leaving internal taxes, both on individuals and on commodities, to the states. This limitation would guarantee the states a source of revenue out of reach of the national government. If this federal tax source proved insufficient, the Anti-Federalists proposed turning to the states for requisitions, as was the case under the Articles of Confederation.

Brutus warned, as well, that the power "to raise and support armies at pleasure . . . tend[s] not only to a consolidation of the government, but the destruction of liberty." The Anti-Federalists generally took the position that there should be no standing armies in time of peace. Brutus proposed a limited power to raise armies to defend frontier posts and guard arsenals to respond to threats of attack or invasion. Otherwise, he maintained, standing armies should only be raised on the vote of two-thirds of both houses.

Publius's rejection of this position was complete and uncompromising. The "radical vice" of the Confederation had been precisely the dependence of the federal power on the states. The universal axiom that the means must be proportional to the end required that the national government's powers be adequate to the preservation of the union (*Federalist* 15 and 23).

The Separation of Powers and Republican Government

The separation of powers refers primarily to the division of power among the legislative, executive, and judicial branches of government, but also includes bicameralism, or the division of the legislature into a house of representatives and a senate. In this part, we begin with the Anti-Federalists' general approach to the separation of powers, which will be followed by accounts of their views on the Senate, the executive, and the judiciary.

The Anti-Federalists attacked the Constitution's separation of powers from two different perspectives. Some, such as Centinel (a Pennsylvania Anti-Federalist), alleged that there was too much mixing and not enough separation; others, like Patrick Henry and the Maryland Farmer, asserted that there were no genuine "checks" at all. The first position opposed the special powers given to the Senate and the executive. The second argued that a true separation of powers depended on social divisions not available in the United States, such as an hereditary nobility as distinct from the common people. The English Constitution drew on such divisions; social class checked social class in a bicameral legislature, and each was checked, in turn, by an hereditary monarch. While the Federalists celebrated the filling of all offices by election directly or indirectly, some Anti-Federalists, including Patrick Henry, argued that such elections would result in the domination of the natural, or elected, aristocracy in all branches of government, not a true "checks and balances" system.

The Senate

The Anti-Federalists feared that an aristocracy would emerge from the Senate, taking more than its share of power. A small number of individuals, elected by the state legislatures for six years, and eligible for reelection, shared in the appointment and treaty-making powers with the executive, as well as in the lawmaking process with the House of Representatives. In order to prevent senators from becoming an entrenched aristocracy, the Anti-Federalists favored an amendment requiring rotation in office and permitting recall votes by the state legislatures. They also favored a separately elected executive council, which would have relieved the Senate of its share in the appointment power. None of these proposals was adopted.

The Executive

Anti-Federalist opposition to the office of president was surprisingly limited. While Patrick Henry asserted that the Constitution "squints toward monarchy," most of the Anti-Federalists accepted the unitary office and the "electoral college" mode of election.

The eligibility of the president to run repeatedly for office, however, did provoke substantial opposition, as did the absence of a special executive council, which would have shared the appointment power. Whereas Publius had argued that reeligibility provides a constructive use for ambition, Federal Farmer replied that once elected, a man will spend all his time and exercise all his influence to stay in office. The executive council would have weakened the power of the Senate, which concerned the Anti-Federalists even more than the president's power.

No Anti-Federalist expressed concern about the general phrase "the executive power," perhaps because it was unclear whether this was a grant of power or merely the name of the office. Some questioned the "commander-in-chief" clause, the pardoning power, and the authority to call either of both houses into the special session. But in light of the difficulties of governing without an independent executive, which the country experienced under the Articles of Confederation, and the common expectation that George Washington would become the first president, the Anti-Federalists let their objections go.

The Judiciary

While many Anti-Federalists failed to discuss it, Brutus's account of the judicial power anticipated the full development of judicial review as well as the importance of the judicial branch as a vehicle for the development of the federal government's powers, both of which he opposed. By extending the judicial power "to all cases, in law and equity, arising under this constitution," Article III permitted the courts "to give the constitution a legal construction." Moreover, extending the judicial power to equity as well as law (a division made originally in English law) gave the courts power "to explain the constitution according to the reasoning spirit of it, without being confined to the words or letter." Hence, Brutus concluded that "the real effect of this system will therefore be brought home to the feelings of the people through the medium of the judicial power."

Under the judicial power, the courts would be able to expand powers of the legislature and interpret laws in a way Congress did not intend. Brutus interpreted the grant of judicial power to all cases arising under the Constitution as a grant of judicial review. He opposed this grant, because he thought the judges, who were appointed for life, should leave it to Congress to interpret the constitutional reach of its powers. That way, if Congress misinterpreted the Constitution by overextending its powers, the people could repair the damages at the next election. Brutus approved of the Framers' decision, following the English Constitution, to make the judges independent by providing them with a lifetime appointment, subject to impeachment, and fixed salaries. But he pointed out that the English judges were nonetheless subject to revision by the House of Lords, on appeal, and to revision, in their interpretation of the constitution, by Parliament. Extending the judicial power to the American Constitution meant that there would by no appeal beyond the independent nonelected judiciary. Brutus did not think that impeachment for high crimes and misdemeanors would become an effective check, and while he did not mention it, he doubtless would have regarded the amendment process also as unsatisfactory.

Anti-Federalists including Brutus objected as well to the extensive appellate jurisdiction of the Supreme Court. Article III, Section 2 may have guaranteed a jury trial in criminal cases, but on appeal, the fate of the defendant would be up to the judges. The Anti-Federalists wanted to have the right of jury trials extended to civil cases and to have the results protected against appellate reconsideration.

Finally, Brutus objected to the "Madisonian compromise," which authorized, but did not require, Congress to "ordain and establish" lower courts. Except for the limited grant of original jurisdiction in the Supreme Court, judicial power, the Anti-Federalists argued, should have been left to originate in the state courts.

The Bill of Rights

The Anti-Federalists are best known for the Bill of Rights, since the Constitution would not have been ratified without the promise to add it. But the Bill of Rights was as much a Federalist as an Anti-Federalist achievement. The Anti-Federalists wanted a bill of rights to curb the power of the national government to intrude upon state power; the Bill of Rights, as adopted, did not address this question. Instead, it limited the right of government to interfere with individuals, and, as such, included provisions similar to those in the bills of rights in many of the state constitutions.

When the Federalists denied the necessity of a federal bill of rights, on the grounds that whatever power was not enumerated could not be claimed, the Anti-Federalists pointed to the Constitution's supremacy and the extensiveness of the enumerated powers to argue that there were no effective limitations on federal authority with respect to the states. None of the actual amendments, which were written up and guided through the House by Madison, followed the Anti-Federal proposals to restrict federal powers, especially the tax and war powers. As for what became the Tenth Amendment, Madison himself said that it simply clarified the existing enumeration of powers but changed nothing. Furthermore, when an Anti-Federalist tried to get the adverb "expressly" inserted before "delegated" in the amendment—"The powers not delegated to the United States by the Constitution, not prohibited by it to the States, are reserved to the States respectively, or to the people"—his motion failed by a substantial margin.

The Anti-Federalists' demand for a bill of rights derived from their understanding of republican government. Such a form of government was mild in its operation and a public proclamation of their rights kept the people aware of them. Consequently, the Bill of Rights, even in its Federalist form, reflects Anti-Federal constitutionalism. But the amendments did not restrict the major federal powers, over taxes, commerce, and war, or in any way limit implied powers. Furthermore, as Jefferson noted, in a letter he wrote to Madison in 1789, by emphasizing individual rights, the Bill of Rights put a legal check in the hands of the judiciary. In other words, before he opposed the power of judicial review, Jefferson seemed to take its existence for granted. He argued that writing a bill of rights into the Constitution would provide judicial protection of those rights. Neither Jefferson nor the Anti-Federalists seemed to realize how a federal bill of rights, by strengthening the federal courts, would thus serve to strengthen Federalist constitutionalism.

Conclusion

The Anti-Federalists lost the ratification debate because they failed to present a clear and convincing account of a constitutional plan that stood between the Articles of Confederation, which they acknowledged was unable to provide for the requirements of union, and the Constitution proposed by the convention, which they feared would produce a consolidation of power. And yet the periodic and contemporary constitutional debates over federalism, over the extent of legislative and executive power, and over individual rights and judicial review reflect the different conceptions of republican government that were developed in the founding dialogue over the Constitution.

Any strict construction of federal power has much in common with Anti-Federalist constitutionalism. During the founding debate, opponents of a strong national government wanted to amend the Constitution; after ratification, Anti-Federalists had no choice but to interpret the Constitution to require limited federal government. The contemporary controversies over abortion, pornography, and sexual practices among consenting adults, and the issues surrounding the religion clauses of the First Amendment, reveal disagreements over the scope of individual rights, on the one hand, and the legitimacy of government maintenance of community manners and morals on the other. These controversies resemble the founding debate over republicanism, where the Federalists focused on the security of individual rights and the Anti-Federalists expressed a greater concern for the character of republican citizenship, maintained in part through religion.

The recent debate over flag burning, which took place in 1989–90 in the federal courts and in Congress, illustrates the tension between the individual right to free, robust, uninhibited expression, and a patriotic requirement that the symbol of our country be treated with special respect. The Supreme Court's decisions, invalidating two different forms of flag protection laws, one state and one federal, followed the existing freedom of speech doctrine regarding the importance of "content neutrality": the government may not restrict expression in order to show preference for a given message, even one which symbolizes our country's dedication to freedom. After the Flag Protection Act was found unconstitutional, Congress voted for a constitutional amendment, but failed to pass it with the required two-thirds vote in the Senate.

Turning from a specific right to a structure of government issue, we find a substantial popular interest in term limitations for members of Congress. In the national elections in 1992, fourteen states passed referendums placing term limits on their members of Congress. This action is Anti-Federal in character in two ways: in its reliance on the direct governmental power of the people, in the form of a referendum; and in its enforced rotation in office. Because the Constitution provides for neither referendum nor enforced rotation, this form of term limitations is likely to be held unconstitutional in the federal courts, as it should be. Then we will get a chance to see whether the sentiment for Anti-Federal constitutionalism is strong enough in this context, as it was not in the flag-burning context, to support a constitutional amendment.

From both of these recent examples it is clear that notwithstanding the substantial changes during the past two hundred years in our country and our government, constitutional issues often have a relationship to our constitutional founding. Moreover, the Anti-Federal concerns about a popular structure of government and the moral qualities necessary for free government remain an important part of our constitutional polity. And while we cannot simply recite arguments from the past to settle current controversies, a familiarity with the constitutional debate at the founding may instruct us in our own deliberations concerning what is best for our constitutional polity.

Acknowledgment

This essay is reprinted, with revisions, from *this Constitution: A Bicentennial Chronicle*, Fall 1987, published by Project '87 of the America Historical Association and the American Political Science Association.

Suggested Reading

Dry, Murray. "The Case Against Ratification," in *The Framing and Ratification of the Constitution*, Leonard W. Levy and Dennis J. Mahoney, eds. New York: Macmillan, 1986.

————. "The Anti-Federalists and the Constitution," in *Principles of the Constitutional Order*, Robert L. Utley Jr., ed. Lanham, Md.: University Press of America, 1989.

Madison, James. *Notes of Debates in the Federal Convention of 1787* (discussion of the Virginia Plan, May 31–June 13).

Storing, Herbert J., ed. *The Anti-Federalist* (abridged by Murray Dry). Especially Brutus (essays I–VIII, XI) and Federal Farmer letters (I–VII).

Wood, Gordon S. *The Creation of the American Republic, 1776–1787*. Chapel Hill: University of North Carolina, 1969.

7

Religion and the Founders' Intentions

Thomas Lindsay

[The Establishment Clause] requires the state to be neutral in its relations with groups of religious believers and nonbelievers. . . .
—Justice Hugo L. Black, *Everson v. Board of Education* (1947)

. . . [N]othing in the Establishment Clause requires government to be strictly neutral between religion and irreligion. . . .
—Justice William H. Rehnquist's dissent in *Wallace v. Jaffree* (1985)

In this country, dispute over the proper relation between religion and politics, like the poor, seems always to be with us. Opposing views on the question today can be divided roughly into two camps. "Nonpreferentialists" argue that it is both constitutional and prudent for government to support religion generally. In this view (expressed in William H. Rehnquist's *Jaffree* dissent, above) the Constitution prohibits only government's preferential treatment of one or a few religions over others. In opposition stand "strict separationists," who (as suggested by Justice Hugo L. Black's opinion for the majority in *Everson*) find the establishment clause of the First Amendment to prohibit government support of any and all religion. This interpretation has been implemented by the Court, in large part, over the past half-century.

As one would expect in a constitutional order, our debate over religion and politics usually is over the Founders' intentions. That this turn to the founding produces opposing conclusions is perhaps also to be expected. While knowledge of and fidelity to the Founders' purposes is the surest single method of constitutional interpretation, such efforts on the subject of religion and politics face unique

119

difficulties. On this issue, ours might be said to be a heterogeneous founding. That is to say, the seeds of our current dispute were planted at the founding itself.

For this reason, both nonpreferentialists and strict separationists find among our Founders solid support for their competing positions. Separationists look primarily to the thoughts and actions of James Madison and Thomas Jefferson. Without denying the majesty of these two men, nonpreferentialists rely not simply on what they thought and did, but also on the compromises they were forced to make on the issue with other Founders opposed to the strict separation of Church and State. For nonpreferentialists, these compromises, especially those concerning the final language of the First Amendment's religion clauses, are the proper focus of constitutional interpretation. The substance of these compromises, they argue, governed constitutional interpretation of the religion clauses for our first one hundred fifty years as a nation.

The Case for Strict Separation: *Federalist* 10 on the Problem of Faction

Federalist 10 addresses the "mortal disease" of republican government, "faction."[1] A faction is any group, be it a majority or minority, which is animated by purposes contrary to the public good or private rights. It can be neutralized, Madison writes, by two methods: by "removing its causes" or by "controlling its effects." There are also two methods of removing faction's causes. The first method of removal, destruction of liberty, promises also to destroy political life. The "second expedient" consists in "giving to every citizen the same opinions," passions, and interests. But this possibility is "as impracticable as the first would be unwise," for it ignores the diversity fixed in human nature.

Natural diversity results from the coupling of liberty with fallible human reason. The marriage of error and freedom does not, of itself, produce faction. Citizens may approach their differences with indifference, or at least toleration, in light of the recognition of their shared fallibility. But, in human beings, reason is also mixed with self-love. Hence "opinions and passions will have a reciprocal influence on each other." Self-love and error prevent the separation of passion from opinion in political activity and so stand in the way of human unity or homogeneity.

Federalist 10 finds in human nature a further barrier to uniformity: "The diversity in the faculties of men" is no "less an insuperable obstacle." The right to acquire property originates in the natural diversity and inequality of human talents. Therefore government's "first object" is the "protection of these faculties," and with them, their fruits. But the protection of unequal and diverse talents gives rise to unequal and diverse fruits ("different degrees and kinds of property"). From the "influence" of this diversity and inequality in property on "sentiments and views" arises a corresponding division of society "into different interests and parties."

While "sown" in our "nature," the power of the two sources of faction—opinion and economics—varies with the "circumstances of society." So Madison proceeds to list the different expressions resulting from these two sources, beginning with the "reciprocal influence" of "opinions and passions."

> A zeal for different opinions concerning religion, concerning government, and many other points, . . . an attachment to different leaders ambitiously contending for preeminence and power; or to persons of other descriptions whose fortunes have been interesting to the human passions, have, in turn, divided mankind, . . . inflamed them with mutual animosity, and rendered them much more disposed to vex and oppress each other. . . . (*Federalist* 10)

The careful reader's attention cannot help but to be drawn to the obscurity of the last example of the list—the "persons of other descriptions." They are not political actors in the precise sense. They are "other" than the leaders "ambitiously contending for preeminence and power." Madison appears to be referring here to the world's great religious figures.

This interpretation of "persons of other descriptions" is supported by Madison's letter to Jefferson of October 24, 1787. This letter, written one month before *Federalist* 10 was published, is the virtual first draft of that paper. Madison, writing privately to his trusted friend, was more free than he would be in a public statement to speak his mind.

In this letter Madison rejects the usefulness of religion as a rights-protecting "restraint" on the "bulk of mankind who are neither Statesmen nor Philosophers." Not only does he reject religion that has "kindled into enthusiasm," but he also argues that "even in its coolest state," religion "has been much oftener a motive to oppression than a restraint from it." Is this a merely historical observation—to the truth of which a believer could agree—or does Madison regard the truth of his observation to follow from the very nature of revealed religion?

The letter's explicit criticism of religion is omitted from the published *Federalist* 10. This omission may be explained by the fact that Madison knew such criticism would inflame the sentiments of his overwhelmingly religious audience. Nevertheless, the basis for that criticism begins to emerge from *Federalist* 10's teaching on politics and human nature. Our examination of that essay left off questioning the identity of and reason for Madison's obscure reference to "persons of other descriptions."

If even the "coolest" religion is "much oftener" a source of, rather than a remedy for, faction, might Madison's persons of other descriptions refer to the great religious leaders who "kindled" the people's "interest" into "enthusiasm" and subsequently destroyed their followers' ability to "cooperate for their common good"? From a historical standpoint, it appears unlikely that Madison's description could apply to *other* than the world's great religious figures, for what persons, other than the political leaders already listed, have excited and continue to excite their followers to the point that they become "divided" and "inflamed"?

In the immediate sequel Madison finds the power of "animosities" such that, even absent a "substantial occasion," the "most frivolous and fanciful distinctions have been sufficient to kindle" "unfriendly passions" and the "most violent conflicts." Remember that the prior passage linked the power of persons of other descriptions to their appeal to the passions. Passion (used in *Federalist* 10 interchangeably with self-love), in its "connection" to reason, was listed earlier as one cause, if not *the* cause, of homogeneity's "impracticability." If the power of religious leaders lies in their appeal to the "passions," and passion in assemblies "wrest[s] the scepter from reason" (*Federalist* 55), might Madison view as primary among the "most fanciful" "distinctions" something like a Thirty Years' War over the issue of Protestantism versus Catholicism? That this is the case seems supported by Madison's argument in *Federalist* 37, in which he addresses the status of revelation.

The God of Revelation and the God of Nature

In *Federalist* 37, in an apparent digression, Madison reflects on the obscurity that must accompany all human communication:

And this unavoidable inaccuracy . . . [is proportional] to the complexity and novelty of the objects defined. When the Almighty himself condescends to address mankind in their own language, his meaning, luminous as it must be, is rendered dim and doubtful by the cloudy medium through which it is communicated.

While the divine is omniscient, its messages to humanity require the "cloudy medium" of speech. This alone does not deny the pious possibility that prophets can receive God's message through inspiration. But their attempt to communicate the divine way to uninspired humanity requires the cloudy medium of words, which "render dim and doubtful" the Almighty's meaning. The most striking inference to be drawn from this passage is this: If "inaccuracy" grows with the complexity and novelty of the object, the Bible, Torah, Koran, etc., in addressing subjects no less complex than the nature of and duties owed God, must exceed in doubtfulness.

My examination of Madison's private letters on this theme—which an essay of this size cannot reproduce—persuades me that *Federalist* 37 is an attack, if a somewhat veiled one, on the status of revelation as human knowledge and not simply the recognition, shared by many a believer, of the mysterious character of the divine.[2] If Madison denies human capacity to know the nature and existence of the commands of, and thus the duties toward, revelation's God, for him faction and bloodshed stemming from differences over the content of a dim and doubtful "oral tradition" are the height of irrationality (and must therefore be centered in the passions for Madison). We saw that *Federalist* 10 argued that it was the "fortunes" of persons of other descriptions that "have been interesting to the human passions." We see now why Madison locates this appeal in the "passions." After his analysis of revelation, what must Madison say of the reliability of the sources that report the "fortunes" of the religious founders?

If my identification of *Federalist* 10's "persons" is accepted, then its list of the opining causes of faction begins and ends with religion ("[a] zeal for different opinions, concerning religion" begins the list and "persons of other descriptions" ends it). *Federalist* 10 appears to disclose revealed religion—among the manifestations of the opining faculty—to be the literally first and last cause of oppression.

So, Madison appears to buy whole the Enlightenment critique of religion. But his doubt of revelation does not lead him to assert that man lacks transcendent moral and political guidance. Rather, he finds such in "the transcendent law of nature and of nature's God." This law is the "absolute necessity of the case"—"the great principle of self-preservation" (*Federalist* 43).

Nor does Madison's doubt of revelation prevent him from recognizing religion's usefulness. In a letter Madison explicitly grants the utility of religion.[3] How can this be reconciled with the October letter's censure of "even" the "coolest" religion? Madison apparently views as useful only revealed religion that squares with the "law of nature and of nature's God." The latter is deduced, he informs Beasley, by "reasoning from the effect to the cause." This is consistent with Madison's public rhetoric, which argues that the political conclusions from the laws of nature's God (religious toleration) harmonize simply with duty to revelation's God (Christian charity). This rhetorical tack taken to harmonize reason's political direction with certain of revelation's teachings appears necessary to "persuade" those referred to in the October letter as the "great bulk of mankind who are neither Statesmen nor Philosophers."

Understanding his belief in religion's utility, including the alleged harmony between nature's laws and revelation's duties, requires grasping his view of what we today call the "religious impulse." In an 1833 letter to the Reverend Mr. Adams, Madison writes: "There appears to be in the nature of man what ensures his belief in an invisible cause of his present existence, and anticipation of his future existence" (*Writings* 9: 484–87). He then rejects Adams's call for a stronger Church–State alliance with an argument that appeared ten years earlier in a letter to Professor Everett: "there are causes in the human breast, which ensure the perpetuity of religion without the aid of the law."[4]

Madison never says that the ineradicable belief in God is divinely implanted. He says only that it is found in human "nature." So strong are these notions that their support by law is unnecessary. He is able qualifiedly to grant religion's utility while denying the need for government to nurture it. The valid (equals moral) elements in religion are planted by nature, and hence require no support from government. At the same time, the destructive (equals irrational) elements in religion will be diluted considerably owing to this very lack of support.

Madison held that religion, while ineradicable, can be enlightened. It can be moved from reliance on an "oral tradition" toward "nature's God." So he attempted publicly to harmonize the biblical

God with nature's God. With the merging of revelation and the natural-rights doctrine, the latter's "more universal and persuasive application" promises to undermine the appeal of the former. But the great force behind Madison's project for liberty lies not in religious education per se, but in the effects on the souls of the citizens of life in an extended commercial republic. To this theme Madison devotes the remainder of *Federalist* 10.

Federalist 10's Solution to Faction

Federalist 10 finds the second major cause of faction to be "the various and unequal distribution of property." Madison's remedy to this cause relies on multiplying, in order to highlight, conflict over *kinds* of ("various") property, in contrast to *amounts* of property. Madison learned from Adam Smith that regulating "various interests" is the "principal task" of "modern legislation," and emerges only in modern, or democratized, commerce. The latter, unlike ancient commerce, affects the behavior, nature, opinions, and habits of the majority to an extent heretofore unachieved. Further, while democratized commerce inculcates commercial habits in the people generally, it serves also to focus their commercial allegiances on the various interests into which they have been fragmented, thereby downplaying sensitivity to and hence conflict over amounts of property. The democratization of commerce exercises both a uniting and a dispersing function, and the interaction of the two is instrumental in remedying the effects of faction.

In explaining his remedy to property-based faction, Madison further examines the relation of politics and religion. Crucial to this relation is that individuals focus on local pursuits and away from potentially fatal struggles over basic principles. The fragmentation required for liberty and served by multiplicity cannot exercise its intended effect in the absence of "opposite and rival interests," specifically, widespread acquisitiveness. This root of the "most common and durable" source of faction is also prerequisite to effective fragmentation of multiple interests. This channeling of rival interests remedies humanity's general lack of "better motives" (*Federalist* 55).

If natural selfishness cannot be simply negated, government, "the greatest of all reflections on human nature," must seek instead to moderate selfishness through multiplying its foci. The coalition process is driven by the citizens' recognition that, to satisfy their selfish aims, they must come down to the "brokerage level"—at which a majority composed of diverse interests, religions, and geographies can agree. Creating unity out of extraordinary multiplicity compels, for what need be only selfish reasons, the moderation of the most extreme claims of all. While *Federalist* 52 to 83 contain arguments for the need for "other-regarding" virtue in the people and in their representatives, the durability of selfishness appears to be the foundation on which *Federalist* 10 rests.

Religion enters this political analysis in this way. The fragmenting effects of multiple interests depend on acquisitiveness. But this poses a certain tension with an ethos that regards "lucre" as "filthy" and teaches that the love of money is the "root of all evil" (1st Peter 5:2). The character-forming effects of democratized commerce promise to weaken the soul's "crusading" tendency. It counters the call to subordinate this world and the body to higher pursuits. Selfishness made rational by institutional restraints is the ethos encouraged by the multiplicity of interests scheme—in obvious tension with the pronouncement: "How hardly shall they that have riches enter into the kingdom of God" (Luke 19:24).

Religion is affected politically not only by fostering acquisitiveness but also by multiplicity of sects. According to *Federalist* 10, a "sect may degenerate into a political faction" locally, but sect multiplicity will prevent its ranging across the nation. The political concern (liberty) requires that no majority religious faction be formed. The more religions the better, because each sect is smaller and more dispersed, and thus "unable to spread a general conflagration."

But this political concern is in tension with religion: Believers as believers desire their sect's enlargement at the expense of other sects. In this sense, Madison's requirement of sect multiplicity signals and implements the primacy of the political over the religious. True, religious multiplicity was a given in his day, but it was also much more than a constraint to which he had to accommodate himself. It was for him a blessing for liberty.

Multiplicity of interests and multiplicity of sects thus look to and require each other. The former dampens the other-worldly emphasis by which religion "kindle[s] into enthusiasm," supplying in its place capitalism's lower but more sober virtues, e.g., industry, mildness, and thrift. Sect multiplicity renders even this milder ("coolest") state of piety less capable of concerted action. This double blow was for Madison the foundation of his project to blunt religion's tendency to "oppress." In Madison's republic, the need to compromise whittles away at religion's extremes; majority formation amid economic and sect multiplicity requires appeals to the "more persuasive and universal" laws of nature. Clearly, he recognized that sources other than religion can equally destroy liberty "under different circumstances." But *Federalist* 10's list of the causes of faction begins and ends with religion owing to the particular circumstances he envisions: Given his aim to subordinate dispute over amounts to kinds of property, faction stemming from "opinion," religion in particular, most threatens republicanism, for revealed religion generally imperils the careful egoism on which the multiplicity of interests scheme depends.

The Case for Nonpreferential Support of Religion

In the latter half of the twentieth century, Madison's separationist project has come more and more to dominate Supreme Court interpretation of the religion clauses of the First Amendment. To give just a few examples, in *Everson*, as we have seen, the Court read the establishment clause to require government "neutrality" between religious belief and nonbelief. In *Engel v. Vitale* (1962), the Court decided that the establishment clause forbids public schools from so much as encouraging their students to participate in even nondenominational prayer. In *Abington Township v. Schempp* (1963), the Court also used the establishment clause to strike down state and municipal laws requiring Bible reading as well as daily recitation of the Lord's Prayer in public schools. Beginning with *Everson*, up to the present day, the tendency is to equate the "Founders on religion" with the views of those leading Framers—primarily Madison and Jefferson—who were both deists and supporters of radical Church–State separation.

But Madison's and Jefferson's views were not simply triumphant at the founding. Nonpreferentialists argue that focusing solely on Madison and Jefferson blinds us to the full picture of public opinion at that time. For nonpreferentialists, the very fact that Madison's religion-friendly rhetoric belied his private hostility to revealed religion demonstrates that Madison, ever the political man, knew well that the full public expression of his personal opinions or political goals would inflame the animosity of the majority of his fellow citizens.

For nonpreferentialists, the founding view begins to come better into focus when we examine the debates about and the ratification of the First Amendment, the opening words of which are "Congress shall make no law respecting an establishment of religion, or prohibiting the free exercise thereof. . . ." What was this intended to mean, and what was it supposed to do? In finding out, nonpreferentialists argue, the issues become more complex than is suggested by the modern Court.

On the one hand, Americans then were, as Alexis de Tocqueville noted, and are now, as poll after poll shows, a highly religious people. Clearly, freedom of religion, in pursuit of which many of the earliest colonists left the Old World for the New, was paramount among the ends sought by the First Amendment. On the other hand, a number of our leading Founders were not especially pious men. Madison, as we have seen, along with Jefferson, Washington, and some others, were, at most, deists. (Briefly put, deism, a "rational religion," denies knowledge based on revelation in favor of that gleaned through rational observation of nature.)

For these deists it was quite likely, nonpreferentialists grant, that the natural-rights teaching of the Declaration of Independence required no biblical foundation. The theory of political justice found in the Declaration was regarded as self-evident not on the basis of revealed truth but rather from the standpoint of the rational understanding of nature and human nature. Jefferson's Declaration of Independence, after all, speaks not of the laws of the Jewish or Christian God, but rather of the "Laws of Nature and of Nature's God."

But does granting these points paint us into the corner of the separationists' understanding of the American Founding? Nonpreferentialists stress the fact that the deist-separationists, while influential, did not get everything they wanted in the final language of the Constitution. In drafting the First Amendment, the secularists had to make important compromises with the Anti-Federalists, who were, by and large, very pious men. So it is in the substance of these compromises—not simply in the intentions of one camp or the other—that nonpreferentialists look to find the fuller picture of the public mind at the time of the founding. Sound constitutional interpretation, according to nonpreferentialists, must be guided by our knowledge of, not a few, but rather, the majority of those who participated in the founding. Ours, after all, was a democratic, not an aristocratic, founding.

On this reasoning, and without denying Madison's hostility to revealed religion, nonpreferentialists stress the fact that Madison failed in his attempt to get language protecting the equal rights of conscience in the First Amendment. That he failed was most likely due to the fact that the more pious members of Congress rejected this language because they suspected that it would come to compel government to be neutral between religion and atheism.

But while Madison was thwarted through the democratic amendment process, his project came to triumph 156 years later through judicial fiat. The modern Court, beginning with premises articulated by Justice Black in the landmark 1947 *Everson* case, now interprets the religion clauses as requiring government neutrality between religion and atheism.

From its beginnings in *Everson*, the movement toward radical separation of Church and State has proceeded rapidly. This radicalization has both fed on and fostered a principle of constitutional interpretation that is now accepted without question by many in today's intellectual culture. Stated generally, this train of thought argues that all views on morality owe to religion; therefore the separation of Church and State prohibits government legislation on moral matters.

Nonpreferentialists argue that the dominance of this view of the Constitution demonstrates how far we have come from the Founders' intentions. In addition to what we have already seen, they cite two historical facts as evidence against the new view. First, they consider the following statement, "Religion, morality, and knowledge being necessary to good government and the happiness of mankind, schools and the means of education shall forever be encouraged." The author of this statement (Article III of the Northwest Ordinance) was the American Congress in 1787. And the First Congress repassed this ordinance in 1789—the same Congress that gave us the religion clauses of the First Amendment. Second, the Constitution left to the states the "police power," which included the power of the states to legislate for themselves on moral matters—and legislate on moral matters the states did, and continue to do to this day.

Politics, Piety, and the Soul's Sustenance

For nonpreferentialists, the preceding account provides a fuller picture of public opinion at the founding. If this is the case, what was the origin of this opinion? Was it simply the product of the fact that we were then an overwhelmingly Protestant country? And if so, does our growth in religious as well as irreligious diversity mandate our departure from the traditional understanding of religion and politics? To answer these questions, nonpreferentialists turn to what they regard as perhaps the best single statement of the founding generation's view of the proper relation between religion and politics. It comes from President George Washington's Farewell Address, written with the substantial aid of Alexander Hamilton. It comes from the man who so embodied the American mind and spirit that he was drafted, over his own protestations, to become our first president. Precisely because we can grant Washington's deism, nonpreferentialists argue, his argument takes on a timeless—and therefore timely—character. He states,

> Religion and morality are essential props. In vain does that man claim the praise of patriotism who labors to subvert or undermine these great pillars of human happiness[,] these firmest foundations of the duties of men and citizens . . . Nor ought we to flatter ourselves that morality can be separated from religion . . . [C]an we in prudence suppose that national morality can be maintained in exclusion of religious principles? Does it not require the aid of a generally received and divinely authoritative Religion?

For our deist first president, religion offers indispensable benefits to politics. But in what precisely were those benefits thought to consist? According to nonpreferentialists, the view of Church–State separation that triumphed at the founding—the view on which both deists such as Washington and conventionally religious men could agree, the view that dominated judicial scholarship for our first one hundred fifty years as a republic—stressed what has been called "the religious foundation of legal freedom." In contrast, the modern Court tends to emphasize law as the protector of freedom *from* religion.

These two differing emphases and the reasons behind their differences explain the fundamental cleavage between the nonpreferentialist and strict-separationist positions. These differences rest, at bottom, on contrasting conceptions of human nature. Washington's Farewell Address asserts the laws' need for divine support. The traditional understanding of Church–State separation sought to allow for what has been designated the "maximum feasible" religious pluralism through support of not any one particular religion but rather of religion generally, for the principles and institutions upon which the Judeo-Christian ethic rests.

The phrase "Judeo-Christian ethic" is troubling to more than secularists today. Some very pious Jews and Christians stress the profound differences between Judaism and Christianity. Moreover, there is a multiplicity of conflicting sects all labeled "Christian." But, according to nonpreferentialists, one need not deny these substantial differences to affirm a moral-religious core on which all or nearly all Jews and Christians agree. This core consists largely in the moral precepts found in the Ten Commandments.

The Founders' support for such "general religion" sought to supply an element of political health that may be lacking in a people dedicated primarily to comfortable self-preservation. This religion consists of the one God beneath the variety of gods represented by America's multiplicity of religions. By upholding for public consumption and edification the moral teaching of one God, the traditional understanding of Church–State relations sought to inspire in citizens those virtues that flow from piety, such as self-restraint, courage, reverence for the old, and an ennobling sense of self-transcending awe. While desirable in any polity, nonpreferentialists argue that the public practice of such virtues is particularly required in democracies, which depend for their preservation on the ordered liberty of the politically authoritative multitude. Why?

In America the majority rules within the limits of a written constitution. But how far do these limitations reach? The Constitution can only restrain the majority temporarily. If it could simply and finally obstruct majority rule, we would cease to be a democracy. So not only can the majority do much of what it wills in accordance with the Constitution, it can also, when the Constitution presents itself as an obstacle, override any and all restraints through the amendment process. Stated simply, in this country there is nothing that a dedicated majority cannot do. How, then, to prevent majority tyranny? How to get the majority to stop thinking only of what it *can* do and to think more seriously about what it *ought* to do?

The only answer consistent with democratic principles appears to be that the majority must come to restrain itself. But self-restraint, like any virtue, requires moral education. From where is this education to come? For the majority of our Founders, argue nonpreferentialists, public morality requires religion. So, if political liberty demands a certain suppression of piety, it also requires its public inculcation. The Founders' support for general religion sought to reconcile the sometimes-contrary elements of liberty and order. On the one hand, our multiplicity of religions compels politically active sects to build interreligious coalitions, thereby diluting religious extremism and consolidating liberty. On the other hand, government support of the principles shared by the majority of religions supplies the moral order by which we distinguish liberty from license.

This "maximum-feasible-religious-pluralism" standard of the First Amendment's religion clauses results in the requirement that government be neutral or "nonpreferential" only *among* the various religions and not *between* religion and atheism. The traditional view aimed at the "maximum" in the name of liberty but limited that maximum in the name of "feasibility"; that is, diversity is circumscribed in pursuit of that unity upon which public morality relies. The strength of the traditional understanding lies finally in its reasoned recognition of both the tension and the support offered democratic liberty by religious piety. But the modern Court, according to nonpreferentialists, appears to have abandoned this view. All that is appreciated today are the reasons for separating, as opposed to marrying, religion and politics.

Notes

1. This section of my essay draws from my 1991 attempt at a more detailed examination of Madison in "James Madison on Religion and Politics: Rhetoric and Reality," *American Political Science Review* 85:4, 1321–37. My interpretation of *The Federalist* owes an immeasurable debt to the teaching and scholarship of the late Martin Diamond. Diamond was the first to uncover the true intentions behind Madison's rhetoric on the issue of the proper relation of Church and State.

2. See Madison's 1825 letter to Dr. Caldwell in *Letters and Other Writings of James Madison* (New York: Worthington, 1884), Vol. 3, pp. 504–5, and his letter to the Reverend Mr. Beasley, in *The Writings of James Madison*, G. Hunt, ed. (New York: Putnam, 1900–10), Vol. 9, pp. 230–31.

3. See the letter to Beasley cited above.

4. Cited in Robert S. Alley, ed., *James Madison on Religious Liberty* (Buffalo: Prometheus Books, 1985), p. 84.

Suggested Reading

Alley, Robert S., ed. *James Madison on Religious Liberty*. Buffalo: Prometheus Books, 1985.

Diamond, Martin. "The Federalist," in *American Political Thought: The Philosophic Dimensions of American Statesmanship*, Morton J. Frisch and Richard Stevens, eds. New York: Scribner's, 1971.

Diamond, Martin. *The Founding of the Democratic Republic*. Itasca: Peacock, 1981.

8

The Framers on the Limits of Limits: The Bill of Rights and the Constitution

Joseph M. Knippenberg

In the debates over jurisprudence and judicial philosophy that now take place whenever someone is nominated to the Supreme Court, one of the crucial bones of contention is almost always the status of the Bill of Rights as a limitation on the federal and state governments. Commentators also debate the role of the federal courts as expositors and guardians of the rights the Bill supposedly contains. So when Judge Robert H. Bork was nominated by President Ronald Reagan to the Supreme Court, the opposition focused on what they regarded as his constricted reading of the rights protected under the Constitution. Judge Bork, they argued, would roll back many of the rights won in the courts by blacks and women, among others.

Bork responded that judges were bound to enforce a reasonable reading of the Constitution. Where it was silent, as it arguably was in many of the cases where new legal rights—such as that to privacy—had been asserted by plaintiffs and recognized by the Court, judges were obliged to defer to the responsible majorities in the state and federal legislatures. In making this argument, Judge Bork hearkened back to what he said was the original understanding of the role of the judiciary in our constitutional system. We can learn a great deal about the merits of these opposing claims by returning to the founding.

Let me begin by reminding you of the classic American statement of our rights:

> We hold these Truths to be self-evident, That all Men are created equal, that they are endowed by their Creator with certain unalienable

135

Rights, that among these are Life, Liberty, and the Pursuit of Happiness—That, to secure these Rights, Governments are instituted among Men, deriving their just Powers from the Consent of the Governed, that whenever any Form of Government becomes destructive of these Ends, it is the Right of the People to alter or to abolish it, and to institute new Government, laying its Foundation on such Principles, and organizing its Powers in such Form, as to them shall seem most likely to effect their Safety and Happiness.

These words from the Declaration of Independence are so familiar that we no longer even think about their meaning. Please indulge me as I try to lay out their import for the question I have proposed. In the first place, we have our fundamental rights, not because the Bill of Rights says so, but by virtue of the fact that we are human beings. Those "human" or natural rights antedate the Bill of Rights, the Constitution, and, indeed, the Declaration of Independence. In terms found most recently in the confirmation hearings for Clarence Thomas, the Declaration of Independence is a "natural law"—not a positive law—document.

As the Declaration indicates, natural rights are to be enforced, not in courts, but by a people roused to their defense. In the first instance, each person has a right to decide for himself or herself how best to define and defend "Life, Liberty, and the Pursuit of Happiness." In practice, we find that we are most secure in association with others where each agrees to make some concessions for the sake of the community.

To leave the definition of our rights and responsibilities in the hands of judges is to deny the Declaration's claim that these rights are *unalienable*. We cannot legitimately give them up. We have them still, even if a government or some band of thieves tries to take them away.

This leads me to my third point: There's a difference between having a right and being able effectively to exercise it. Someone can deprive you of your life or liberty, but not of your right to life or liberty. If he takes away your life or liberty, he is injuring you, that is, acting unjustly. If nothing else, you can legitimately be indignant.

All of these considerations suggest that we need to find some way of protecting or preserving rights. That, indeed, is the purpose of government. According to the Declaration of Independence, in other words, government is a positive good, absolutely essential for the protection and preservation of our natural or human rights.

Of course, the Declaration also identifies government as a principal threat to our rights, but that does not alter the fact that we need governmental protection if we are effectively to enjoy them. The implication is that a good government must be powerful enough to protect us while being limited in such a way as to make it as unlikely as possible to threaten us.

This sounds like a paradox: a powerful, but limited government. Well, let me heighten the paradox: the government must not only have power, but virtually unlimited power. If we cannot define (that is, limit) the threat in advance, it would be a bad idea to limit the capacity of the government to respond. We would not have the protection when we were most in need of it.

Lest you think that I am pulling this doctrine out of a hat, consider the words of Alexander Hamilton, taken from *Federalist* 23:

> These powers [essential to the common defense] ought to exist without limitation, *because it is impossible to foresee or to define the extent and variety of national exigencies, and the correspondent extent and variety of the means which may be necessary to satisfy them.* The circumstances that endanger the safety of nations are infinite, and for this reason no constitutional shackles can wisely be imposed on the power to which the care of it is committed.

How, then, are we to understand the Bill of Rights, which, after all, is supposed to limit government in certain ways? Let me begin my explanation by remarking something obvious, but often unnoticed: The Bill of Rights consists of the first ten *Amendments* to the Constitution. When the Framers met to draft the Constitution in Philadelphia, they did not agree on the necessity of a Bill of Rights. Many of them thought, in other words, that the Constitution itself was sufficient to preserve the rights enunciated in the Declaration. (In addition, we cannot forget that what they thought they were remedying by proposing a new Constitution to replace the old Articles of Confederation was a government *too weak* to do its job.)

Rather than spend a great deal of time explaining how they thought that this new government—without being limited by a Bill of Rights— would protect rights, I shall restrict myself to a couple of observations. In the first place, and most importantly, it would be a *representative* government, answerable to the citizens every time they vote. This, needless to say, is one of the greatest controls on any government. If, like the erstwhile communist constitutions, you have an extensive bill of rights but no mechanism for making the government responsible to the people, you are likely still to have a tyranny. If rights are respected under these circumstances, it is only through the grace of the government.

A second safeguard is the separation of powers, maintained by a system of checks and balances. If one branch, or one part of one branch, were to attempt to gain too much power for itself, it would be in the interest of the other branches, not to mention in the interest of the people, to resist it and to make the effort to rein it in. By tying the dignity of the officeholder to the dignity of the office, the Framers sought to make "the private interest of every individual" the "sentinel over the public rights." The competing ambitions of the various officeholders would effectively limit the capacity of any part of the government to do harm.

Of course, much could be said about the circumstances under which both these devices are most likely to succeed, but I shall again limit myself to one observation. A government that represents, as simply and directly as possible, a tyrannically minded constituency is likely to be tyrannical. Representation and separation of powers work best with a fully enfranchised and very diverse citizenry, whose members are jealous of their rights and are unlikely to combine to form a monolithic majority. In other words, the institutional devices work best in a particular social setting, which is provided by a large commercial republic.

As a result of such considerations, among others, there was a fairly widespread opinion in Philadelphia that a Bill of Rights was not really necessary. Other devices, they thought, would be sufficient to protect our rights.

Indeed, some went further. James Madison, who eventually took responsibility for the adoption of the Bill of Rights as a leading member of the First Congress, thought the Bill would be least useful when it would be most needed. Let me try to reproduce his reasoning. Historically, he argued, bills of rights have been either weapons in a tug of war between a king and his people or, in effect, peace treaties ending that contest. When a government is not representative or responsible, the people have had to draw a line in the sand whose overstepping they would not tolerate. The king would either respect those limits or face popular opposition as the people rallied around the standard they had enunciated.

Now, in the United States we do not have a king. Of course, you could argue—and more than a few did—that a Bill could serve the people against an oppressive central government just as it had served against a king. If the government overstepped these bounds, the people could rebel. Under the circumstances, the government would likely back off.

Madison was dubious of this argument. He thought that a tyrannical central government was only one of the threats Americans faced and that it was far from the most important one. The great difficulty he saw was tyranny of the majority, that is, tyranny of the government acting on behalf of a tyrannically minded majority, doing the bidding of "the people" against a beleaguered minority. It would certainly be difficult to use the Bill of Rights to rally the people against themselves.

He and his colleagues had other reservations about the Bill as well. I shall mention just two. In the first place, an explicit list of limitations on governmental power would be misleading and perhaps even mischievous, for it would distract attention from the fundamental character of the Constitution as a limited grant of power.[1] The Constitution says that "Congress shall have power" to do only those things mentioned in Article I, Section 8. Whatever falls outside a reasonable construction of those clauses is not within the purview of Congress.

But if you focus attention on the Bill of Rights as the crucial limit on the government's power, you may give credence to the mistaken conclusion that, in the absence of the explicit limitation, Congress *would have had* that power. People might think that if you did not say "Congress shall make no law respecting an establishment of religion," Congress would have had the power to do so, even in the absence of a positive grant of power in Article I, Section 8. And where the Bill of Rights is silent, they might conclude that the governmental action is permissible, whatever the limits in the original grant of power.

The Framers wrote the Ninth and Tenth Amendments to prevent such a mischievous reading of the Constitution. The Ninth asserts that the list of rights is not exhaustive and the Tenth insists that the grant of power to the federal government is limited.

Madison's other very different reservation has to do with the consequences of the legalism that such a Bill would likely inspire. Remember Hamilton's stricture about the unlimited nature of the threats with which the government might have to deal. Absolute prohibitions would be very difficult to respect, especially in a time of crisis. A Bill of Rights would, under those circumstances, either hamstring and defeat a basically decent government or be ignored.

It is disproportionate to respect a right in one instance if the likely consequence is the defeat of a government that usually or regularly respects rights. Abraham Lincoln states a version of this view very well:

> [C]ertain proceedings are constitutional when, in cases of rebellion or Invasion, the public safety requires them, which would not be constitutional when, in absence of rebellion or invasion, the public Safety does not require them—in other words, . . . the constitution is not in [its] application in all respects the same, in cases of Rebellion or invasion, involving the public Safety, as it is in times of profound peace and public security . . . I can no more be persuaded that the government can constitutionally take no strong measure in time of rebellion, because it can be shown that the same could not lawfully be taken in time of peace, than I can be persuaded that a particular drug is not good medicine for a sick man, because it can be shown to not be good food for a well one.[2]

Furthermore, if you find that you regularly have to abridge or ignore supposedly absolute prohibitions, you might end up being altogether cynical about them. They would thus lose their force and fail to accomplish what they are supposed to.

About this time I expect that you are wondering how we ever came to have a Bill of Rights, if this is what some of the most influential Framers thought. The simple answer is "ratification politics." Although you rarely hear about them, there was a substantial group of people opposed to the new Constitution. We call them "Anti-Federalists," a label that is both helpful and misleading. It is misleading to the extent that it implies that the opposition was coherent, unified, and cohesive. It is accurate insofar as it implies that they knew better what they were against than what they were for. They did not have a well worked-out alternative to the new Constitution, but they could still make mischief.

And the Federalists thought that in the ratification of the Constitution, time was of the essence. Hence they co-opted the Anti-Federalists' most respectable complaint—the absence of a Bill of Rights in the new Constitution—and promised to remedy this supposed defect as soon as the new Congress convened. Needless to say, this clever political stroke deprived the Anti-Federalists of their best issue and paved the way for the ratification of the new Constitution.

In other words, Madison was sufficiently politic to put up with something of which he was not extraordinarily fond—the Bill of

Rights—in order to get something he really wanted—the Constitution. Indeed, he was even willing to find a silver lining in this very small cloud. As an educational tool, he thought, the Bill of Rights could do some good. It would help remind the people that the ultimate purpose of government is the protection of rights.

Of course, we typically regard the Bill of Rights as a great deal more than that today. It is, we often think, the principal pillar supporting all our rights. Therein hangs another tale, which I have time only to summarize. There is one matter about which some Anti-Federalists were perhaps prescient: they were very suspicious of judicial review, worrying that the federal judiciary would not be answerable to anyone in its interpretation of the Constitution. While I would argue that there are ways of controlling the judiciary, beginning from the recognition that nothing in the Constitution makes federal judges the exclusive or final arbiters of its meaning, they have won for themselves a major, even dominant, role as the authoritative expositors of the Constitution. When we think of limits on government, we tend to think of those placed on the so-called political branches by the courts in their role as guardians of our constitutional rights.

In addition, there is the Fourteenth Amendment, whose due process clause has been interpreted substantively as applying the Bill of Rights to the states, thereby opening up a whole new arena for judicial review and judicial activism. Until this happened—that is, for roughly one hundred years of American judicial history under the Constitution—the Court only rarely found any laws unconstitutional. The Bill of Rights was understood to apply only to federal actions (e.g., "*Congress* shall make no law . . .") and the well-constructed federal government did not often overstep its bounds.[3] That is not to say that the states could violate individual rights with impunity; they were usually confined at their own level within the same sorts of limitations as the federal government was in its.

So, our belief that the Supreme Court's enforcement of the Bill of Rights is the most important bulwark of our liberties has more to do with certain accidents of American constitutional history— with the rarely checked arrogation of power by the Supreme Court, to put it simply—than with the so-called original intentions of the Framers. As we can see, Judge Bork is indeed simply following the Framers when he insists that limited and good government depends more on the prudence and responsibility of officials elected by a well-informed citizenry than on the vigilance of judges.

In this connection, an example may be helpful. According to Bork, one of the principal reasons that recent nominations to the Supreme Court have occasioned such heated battles in the Senate is that pro-choice forces have sought to defend against the overturning or revision of the 1973 *Roe v. Wade* decision that established a constitutional right to an abortion. Proponents of that decision have repeatedly suggested that confirmation of additional "conservative" or "strict constructionist" judges will ultimately lead to a situation in which abortion is again illegal in America. They frequently leave the impression that the right to abortion depends entirely on the judiciary, failing to acknowledge that overturning that decision will not in and of itself make abortion illegal. Rather, the matter would be returned to the state and (perhaps) federal legislatures, which would be responsive to the wishes of their diverse constituencies. Given the way in which American public opinion is currently divided, and given the organizational capacities of both the pro-choice and pro-life camps, it is very unlikely that any sort of absolute ban on abortion would be passed under these circumstances. Majority coalitions built on compromises would set the policy, a situation perfectly consistent with Madison's (and Bork's) expectations.

Indeed, it might be possible through the amendment process to entrench the right to abortion in the federal or state constitutions, a procedure that at least would settle the question so unambiguously as to avoid reliance on the interpretive whims of judges and on the shifting character of judicial alignments. So, a return to original intent would restrict only the judiciary's ability to limit (or, for that matter, extend) governmental power, not the government's power to limit itself or the people's power to limit government.[4]

I would like to close with a plea for a sense of perspective. Judicial enforcement of the limits contained within the Bill of Rights is an important means of protecting us against certain kinds of governmental abuses. But it is crucial that we not forget three other considerations: that the defense of our rights often depends on the vigorous exercise of governmental power against predators abroad and at home; that the Supreme Court is neither the sole nor necessarily the most reliable barrier standing between us and tyranny; and that judges are as capable as politicians of usurping power and being unfaithful to the Constitution. (In this connection, it is sufficient to mention the infamous 1857 *Dred Scott* decision.)

More often than not, a well-constructed and responsible government will act on behalf of the public good, rather than against it. If we focus too much on the occasional threats that government poses, we may prevent it from doing a great deal of good. And finally, if we trust too much in the beneficence and self-restraint of judges, we may upset the system of checks and balances that is essential to good government and the protection of our rights.

Notes

1. The government may well be limited in its responsibilities, but still have plenary powers to carry out those responsibilities.

2. Abraham Lincoln, Letter to Erastus Corning, June 12, 1863.

3. To be sure, the federal courts did have to adjudicate jurisdictional disputes between the federal and state governments, as happened most famously in *McCulloch v. Maryland*, where the Supreme Court decided that no state could obstruct a federal attempt to carry out a responsibility legitimately within the federal sphere.

4. As Judge Bork observes, certain arguably unconstitutional extensions of the authority of the federal government—in which the judiciary has acquiesced—have become so woven into the fabric of our national life that it would be too disruptive to roll them back. To this extent, the jurisprudence of original intent must always be governed by the political prudence of judges. Its princial result would be to end the untrammeled expansion of judicial authority.

Suggested Reading

Bork, Robert H. *The Tempting of America: The Political Seduction of the Law.* New York: Simon and Schuster, 1990.

Goldwin, Robert A., and William Schambra, eds. *How Does the Constitution Secure Rights?* Washington, D.C.: American Enterprise Institute, 1985.

Licht, Robert A., ed. *The Framers and Fundamental Rights.* Washington, D.C.: AEI Press, 1991.

Lincoln, Abraham. Letter to Erastus Corning, June 12, 1863.

Madison, James. Letter to Thomas Jefferson, October 17, 1788, and Address on the Bill of Rights (April 8, 1789), *Annals of Congress*, 1st Session.

McDowell, Gary. "Were the Anti-Federalists Right? Judicial Activism and the Problem of Consolidated Government," *Publius* XII (1982), 99–108.

9

Two Challenges to
Democratic Responsibility

Sarah Baumgartner Thurow

The inherent imperfection of human beings is a perennial cause of conflict. We are close enough to perfection to know what it is. But we are far enough from perfection that our attempts to achieve it usually do more harm than good. Philosophers, poets, and theologians have called us to perfection and warned us against the danger of thinking that we can achieve it. Therefore the political question may be how to organize our common life to allow for the pursuit of perfection without succumbing to the demands of tyrants who assert that it must be achieved.

The same problem arises when we think about war and peace among men. Conflict comes from difference. People who are all the same have no reason to disagree and therefore no reason to fight. But who is to say what shape that sameness is to have? Most of the fiercest conflicts have been over the claims of different nations, religions, or ideologies to know the truth, a truth binding on everyone.

The imperfection of the human condition is also seen in suffering. No one wants to suffer from hunger, poverty, or indignity. Compassionate people want to relieve the suffering of others. The quest for the perfect abolition of suffering is the "soft" side of the perfection sought through the subjugation of everyone to a single view of the truth.

James Madison in his analysis of factions, in *Federalist* 10, comes to the conclusion that it is better to let differences persist and to work to contain, mediate, and moderate the conflict rather than to try to eliminate it altogether. Karl Marx, in *The Communist Man-*

145

ifesto, holds that suffering and conflict can and should be abolished through human effort. This chapter will compare Madison's and Marx's analyses to show how the American Constitution embodies a conscious choice to live with the imperfections and conflicts of human nature rather than to try to abolish them.

Alexis de Tocqueville in the last part of his *Democracy in America* warns democratic nations of the danger of a new kind of despotism which enslaves men's minds by providing easily and gently for their material needs. The second part of this chapter will examine the contemporary administrative welfare state in the light of Tocqueville's view of "soft despotism" to show how accurate he was in predicting this tendency in our regime. Finally, I will offer some reflections on how we might avoid the temptation of succumbing to "soft despotism" by recovering the understanding and embracing the principles of democratic responsibility expressed in *The Federalist*.

Liberty, Equality, and Responsibility

The two principles espoused by all democratic governments are liberty and equality. The claim of a government to be based on the twin principles of liberty and equality is most often made with an assumption that these principles are compatible, that there is no difficulty in having both. But liberty and equality, far from being mutually supportive principles, have been throughout history the source of the deepest and most divisive conflict within popular governments.

Liberty, as Tocqueville observes, must be won with effort and sacrifice and maintained with constant vigilance.[1] Left free, human beings are always ready to enslave one another. Another danger is that the excessive love of liberty leads readily to anarchy, or the breakdown of all social order.

But equality seems self-perpetuating and wholly safe. Human beings who are equal will always resist being made unequal. Democratic people find it almost impossible to believe that there could be too much equality, or that there are dangers in the progress toward ever more equality.

With respect to the goods of liberty and equality, liberty "occasionally gives sublime pleasure to a few," but everyone enjoys the daily pleasures of equality. Superior and ambitious men love liberty because it allows them to display and enjoy their abilities. Those with ordinary talents and drive are relatively indifferent to its benefits. They may actually dislike it because they fear losing out in competition. But everyone can enjoy not having any superiors. The easy-going life of equality is comfortable for everyone.

Neither liberty nor equality is unique to democracy. Equality may be found in the most despotic of regimes, where everyone is equally enslaved under one man. Liberty may be found in an aristocracy, where men are allowed to exercise natural or artificial inequalities freely. What gives the democratic republic its special appeal is its promise to make men "perfectly free because they are entirely equal, and . . . perfectly equal because they are entirely free" (DA 503).

Now, this ideal of perfection ought to make us suspicious from the start. But it is an enduring ideal which has motivated democratic revolutions from the American Revolution to both the most recent Marxist guerrilla movement and the anticommunist revolution of 1989. As an ideal it can't be beat. The trick is its implementation. The real achievement of the democratic republic lies in its balancing of liberty with equality so that each is enjoyed as much as the other, even if neither is enjoyed perfectly.

Two more distinctions must be made clear before we turn to Madison and Marx. Neither liberty nor equality is itself a simple thing. Liberty, properly understood, does not mean freedom to do anything one pleases, but rather freedom from submission to the arbitrary will of other men. It is best obtained by a rule of law in which all citizens participate in making the laws and the laws apply equally to all citizens. So there is a sense in which liberty is dependent upon equality. But equality is itself a complex phenomenon.

Equality can be understood as equality of conditions or equality of rights. Equality of conditions refers to a sameness in the way human beings live such that no one is noticeably richer, more powerful, more honored—or even, carried to its extreme, wiser, more talented, or more successful in anything. Equality of rights refers to a legal system in which there are no special privileges and no special obligations for certain individuals or groups over others. Equality of rights corresponds to equality of opportunity, while equality of conditions corresponds to equality of results.

From this pair of distinctions, we can begin to see how it is that the democratic republic balances liberty and equality. When liberty consists in equal participation in making the law and equal obligation to obey it, and equality is understood in terms of this equal opportunity to shape the common good, citizens can be both free and equal because they are not *perfectly* either. They have sacrificed the perfect freedom of being without any ruler and the perfect equality of conditions of sameness for the imperfect, but just, freedom and equality of self-government.

Self-government requires responsibility. In a despotism, monarchy, or aristocracy, the majority of the people do not concern themselves with government because they have no freedom to do so. Their conflicts with one another are decided by powers above them and outside of their control. Their well-being or suffering is largely beyond control. Such people can live in peace and comfort or in danger and poverty, depending on the benevolence of their rulers. But in a democratic republic people must settle their own conflicts and provide for their own well-being themselves because they are the government. Even when a constitution establishes a system of representation, the people must see to it that their representatives are responsible to them. They must take responsibility for their representatives.

Hard Despotism: A Comparison of the Principles of Madison and Marx

The problem of conflict between human beings is as old as mankind and has always been the basic political problem, whether in terms of defending the community from outside attack or in terms of keeping peace within. Practical politicians and diplomats have sought to manage the conflict, while men of political imagination have sought to discover the perfect regime in which the problem of conflict would be solved once and forever.

In *Federalist* 10 Madison takes up one of the alleged defects of popular self-government, its tendency to deteriorate into factional conflict. Without the overruling power of a king, the critics of popular government argue, the country will have no way to control the violence of competing groups. Monarchy, therefore, is a better regime because it is better at keeping peace. Madison agrees that factional strife is the greatest danger to the preservation of the United States, but he argues that the form of government constructed by the Constitution will provide "a republican remedy for the diseases most incident to republican government." He shows how the Constitution reduces the danger of factions.

Karl Marx sought to envision and to bring about the end of this pattern of conflict in the one regime that would make government no longer necessary.[2] Contrary to what is often alleged, the founders of communism were not out to establish a new form of despotism, but rather the most perfect democracy. Their motto might as well have been the passage quoted above from Tocqueville: to make men "perfectly free because they are entirely equal, and perfectly equal because they are entirely free." Marx was as dedicated to freedom and equality as the goals of government as were our own Founding Fathers. The real difference between *Federalist* 10 and *The Communist Manifesto* is Madison's conscious choice not to try to end conflict once and for all, and Marx's opposite choice.

Madison's Definition of Faction

Madison defines a faction as

a number of citizens, whether amounting to a majority or minority of the whole, who are united and actuated by some common impulse of passion, or of interest, adverse to the rights of other citizens, or to the permanent and aggregate interests of the community. (*Federalist* 10)

This definition has three crucial components.

(1) A faction may be either a majority or a minority of the whole citizenry. When we use the word faction today, we usually mean a group that is less than a majority, an "interest group" or a lobby. We think that what is wrong with factions is that they are in opposition to the majority will. Realizing that the majority of the citizens might act as a faction opens our eyes to the most subtle but also most potentially destructive force in a democratic republic, the majority faction.

(2) What unites a faction may be either an "interest" or a "passion." That is, a faction may be composed of people who all hope to profit or fear to suffer as a result of some government policy, or it may be composed of people who have a strong feeling about an issue or principle. An example of the former would be a corporate lobby; of the latter, the Ku Klux Klan or the neo-Nazi party.

(3) What makes such a united group into a faction, however, is the character of their shared interest or passion. To be properly a

faction, a group's shared interest or passion must be either *adverse to the rights of other citizens* or *adverse to the common good of the community.* It is easier to think of examples of the former, but more difficult to think of examples of the latter for the same reason that majority factions are hard to identify. In a democratic republic the majority determines what is considered to be the common good. Our Constitution sought to provide as much guidance as possible to the majority with respect to what the Framers thought was the common good, but without depriving the majority of their rule. The Framers also sought to temper majority rule because they knew that majorities sometimes do not perceive their own good.

Treating the Disease of Faction by Eliminating the Causes

Madison uses a medical analogy to talk about faction. He begins with the observation that there are two ways to deal with a disease: you can remove the causes or you can control the effects. Obviously anyone who knew how would prefer to remove the causes, and we would not regard anything less as a real cure. But some diseases cannot be cured, for example the "disease" of aging, which is part of our nature. Sometimes, even when a cure is possible, the cure may be worse than the disease.

The causes of faction are in the differences among human beings which bring them into conflict. There are two ways to remove these causes: either prevent people from acting on their differences, or remove the differences by making everyone the same.

To prevent people from acting on their differences is comparatively easy. Take away their liberty. Without the liberty to act, it does not matter how much hostility there is among the people. Madison compares this cure to putting out a fire by removing the air. Fire cannot burn without air, but neither can people breathe. Liberty is like air to the fire of faction, but it is also the life-breath of the democratic republic, without which it dies. This cure would be like cutting off your head to cure a headache.

But Marx is not so quick to reject this method. In the first place, he does not believe that the liberty that feeds the fire of faction is true liberty, but rather part of the belief system of the dominant class in his time, a "bourgeois liberty." Because people's ideas are determined by their economic class, bourgeois men cannot conceive of real liberty. Only those like Marx who have been enlightened by seeing the dialectic of history and can rise above their class interest by looking to history's end can know what true liberty looks like. When a communist state appears to be taking away liberty, it is only the delusion of the bourgeoisie who think their "bourgeois liberty" is real. In fact what is happening is the creation of true liberty (CM 26).

Marx argues that the result of the revolutionary overthrow of bourgeois rule and the establishment of the dictatorship of the proletariat will be perfect peace. This final revolution will create a new society in which there will be no more classes and therefore no more conflict. Perfect equality will ensure perfect freedom and together they will constitute perfect peace. With such an end in view, surely even apparently harsh means are justified (CM 31).

The second way to remove the causes of faction, according to Madison, is to make everyone the same, to give to every citizen the same opinions, passions, and interests. But Madison concludes that this is as impracticable as the removal of liberty is undesirable. Differences of opinion, passion, and interest stem from three sources: (1) the fallibility of human reason, (2) the connection between reason and self-love and between opinions and passions, and (3) the diversity of natural faculties. These passions are part of human nature. Short of changing that nature they cannot be wholly removed. Marx agrees, but he proposes to do precisely what Madison rejects as impossible, namely, change human nature.

(1) One source of differences of opinion, passions, and interests lies in the *fallibility of human reason.* Human beings, even if their intentions are good, make mistakes. Even if some have reasoned their way to the truth about some matter, the truth, by itself, does not produce agreement. In any human community, agreement must depend on both persuasion and compromise, and it will never be complete.

How does Marx deal with the fallibility of reason? He says his own reasoning is absolutely correct:

> The theoretical conclusions of the Communists are in no way based on ideas or principles that have been invented, or discovered, by this or that would-be universal reformer. They merely express, in general terms, actual relations springing from an existing class struggle, from a historical movement going on under our very eyes. (CM 23)

Anyone who disagrees with Marx, who does not see the rational truth of "historical movement," must be irrational. This premise is the rationale for confining political opponents in insane asylums in

Marxist regimes. It also explains the necessary hostility of Marxism toward religion, the attempts on the part of Marxists, especially in Latin America, to co-opt Christian principles as identical to their own, and the forceful opposition to Marxist regimes on the part of Islamic fundamentalists. There cannot be more than one absolute truth in men's hearts.

(2) The second source of differences of opinions, passions, and interests that Madison identifies is that there is a *connection between reason and self-love which creates a reciprocal relationship between opinions and passions*. What he means is this: Suppose you are a man taking a course on human excellence, and your professor proceeds to present very convincing evidence that women are superior to men. Even if the argument seems sound, you would have an incentive not to believe it because of what it would do to your self-esteem. It is simply human nature to want to think well of oneself and also to assume that what one loves is truly the best. Opinions are almost always shaped by self-love.

How does Marx handle this fact? He begins with the assertion of the materialist principle that ideas are derived from economic conditions and not vice versa. He says that what is called liberty, for example, in a feudal society is not the same thing as what a bourgeois democracy would call liberty. Neither one is true liberty, which is to be found only in the communist society he is working to bring about. Marx justifies a program of indoctrination, once called "enlightenment" and nowadays popularly called "consciousness raising," in which people who believe their liberty is being taken away are made to understand that what they called liberty was not liberty and the new regime which they perceive to be taking liberty away is actually giving it to them. This indoctrination aims to sever the natural connection between reasoning and self-love which prevents a person from accepting as true something that seems to him to be aimed at his subjugation.

(3) The third source of differences of opinions, passions, and interests is in the *diversity of natural faculties*. People differ in the things they do well, in their natural gifts and talents, as well as in the skills they are able to acquire. From this diversity of faculties comes a diversity of types of property. And, Madison says, "the most common and durable source of factions has been the various and unequal distribution of property."

Madison agrees with Marx on the immense importance of private property and class differences as the causes of conflict. The real difference is in what they chose to do about property as the principal cause of conflict.

For Madison, differences in property are the result of not interfering with the free use by human beings of their natural differences in abilities and tastes. These differences in property include not only the difference between rich and poor, but also the difference between agricultural and industrial ways of life, the tastes of professionals and artisans, even the difference between those ambitious for wealth and those content with what they have. It is not only how much property one has that matters. Even more important is what kind of property one has and how one regards property altogether.

True to his materialist and determinist premises, Marx proposed to eliminate differences of opinion by eliminating differences of property, both by the well-known expedient of abolishing all private ownership and by this less well-known and more complex system aimed at breaking the connection between work and material well-being. The communist regimes in Russia and Eastern Europe tried to run farms as if they were factories and to make doctors work under the same conditions as store clerks. They found that hostility smoldered just under the surface despite the nobility of the idea of each producing what he can and receiving what he needs.

Treating the Disease of Faction by Controlling the Effects

Madison concludes that the causes of faction are "sown in the nature of man." They are always ready to become active because of zealous leaders, competition among factions, and all the ordinary differences that arise in the conduct of life. The only way to prevent these latent differences from becoming active is to eliminate liberty. So the role of free and democratic government is not to eliminate conflict but to regulate it. It must be incorporated into the very processes of government itself.

Here we come to our last point of comparison with Marx. He included in his project a plan for operating within a bourgeois democratic republic until the revolution would establish communism and the Bolsheviks in the USSR perfected a form of communist rule that maintained the structures of republican government. Within the competition of factions, the Communist party would arise as the vanguard of the revolution and the voice of the proletariat, but more importantly, as the "universal" faction, the one party which is not a faction because it stands for the absolute truth and the inevitable movement of history. The members of a party "consider themselves far superior to all class antagonisms. They want to improve the condition of every member of society; . . . [and in their critical function they] attack every principle of existing society" (CM 40–41). In other words, the Communist party was to provide an agency exactly like enlightened statesmanship or the judgment of a divine king necessary to resolve all factional disputes correctly. That this party might remain a minority even after the revolution did not matter, for the rule of a minority who know the truth is better than the rule of a majority who are in error.

Madison suspects anyone claiming such perfection of judgment. He is even more convinced that people must exercise their own political judgment to keep their liberty. So he rejects any reliance on enlightened statesmen. He turns instead to a structure of government designed to control and diminish the worst effects of factional conflict: the large republic.

Madison identifies two ways of controlling the effects of a majority faction. Either you can prevent the existence of a factious passion or interest in a majority of the people at the same time, or you can prevent such a factious majority from acting. In a pure democracy or a small republic the people tend to be more homogeneous in their interests and passions, and the majority rules more directly than in a large republic, where those in government office must necessarily represent a larger constituency. First, a large republic allows for the selection of the best characters as representatives by the simple fact that there are more to choose from. Second, a successful candidate will have to convince a larger and more diverse group of people that he or she will really look after their interests well. Third, the federal system requires majority decisions on two different levels for major measures to become effective. The states were expected to provide a check on the federal government and vice versa so that a majority faction to control the whole country would have to be able to take control of government at both levels.

All three of these factors make it difficult for a majority to act as a faction: good representatives will be more likely to see and act for the common good despite what their electorate thinks they should do. The need to gain widespread support to get elected will force representatives to compromise among the factions supporting them, and the difference between state and federal interests and perspectives on the common good will make it unlikely that a single faction could succeed in becoming a majority in both governments (which requires also taking control of both houses of both legislatures).

Finally, the very size of the republic itself will mitigate against majority faction. The larger the population, the more diverse its opinions and interests are likely to be. Majorities will have to form around compromise positions, and these are not likely to be factious, that is, opposed to the rights of some part of the citizenry. Similarly, there is a kind of trust that where government must be by compromise, deviations from the common good will not be too great. Even if a majority of the people should come to share an opinion or interest adverse to the rights of other citizens or to the common good, it would be difficult for them to organize for action if they are dispersed around a large territory. If they are concentrated in one region, they might take control of the state governments there, but their power in the federal government would be concentrated in the representatives from those states, who would not comprise the majority of the Congress, especially in the Senate.

In summary, then, Madison finds in the large federal republic established by the Constitution the "republican remedy for the republican disease." Since eliminating the causes of this disease would entail either the sacrifice of liberty or the transformation of human nature, Madison chooses to control the effects. Marx, in contrast, chooses to seek the elimination of the cause of conflict through the transformation of human nature by means of a regime of total control in which everyone is ultimately to be conformed to the truth.

Soft Despotism: The Hidden Form of the Republican Disease

As we observed at the beginning of this chapter, the two principles underlying all forms of popular government are liberty and equality. One way of describing the difference between the Madisonian and the Marxian understandings of government would be to say that Madison prefers a liberty in which factional conflict requires constant vigilance to an equality in which there is no conflict because there are no differences that matter between people, while Marx prefers the opposite, to put an end to conflict by making human beings all the same.

The Framers of the Constitution saw themselves as engaged in an experiment to prove whether people really can govern themselves without recourse to a monarch or degeneration into anarchy. They built into the Constitution safeguards against both contingencies. They felt quite sure that the people's love of liberty would be the best defense against a tyrant, but they were more uncertain that they had provided adequate security against anarchy. Foreign observers were convinced that the United States could not hold together, nor even individual states remain stable for long. Our early history shows that unity and stability were not easily maintained even with the strong federal government introduced by the Constitution.

When he visited the United States in the early nineteenth century, Alexis de Tocqueville wanted to see how the experiment was working. Even more he wanted to study democracy in America because he believed that this was the wave of the future, the form of government destined to prevail throughout Europe, if not the whole world. With this observation, he agreed with Marx, his contemporary. Where Tocqueville differs from the communists is his deep concern for the preservation of liberty and the necessity of making the new equality compatible with it.

Tocqueville was capable of envisioning the new form of government called democracy as the same sort of perfection of liberty and equality that the communists sought. But the communists held onto the vision and used it to justify every sort of violence against their opponents. Tocqueville regarded the vision as just that, a vision. It is something to be looked up to and ardently desired perhaps, but approached with care for the present good and a realistic assessment of what is to be expected from human nature. This combination of vision and prudence is what makes Tocqueville's work so relevant to us today. He showed America of the nineteenth century both its faults and its possibilities, and possibilities both good and bad. It is remarkable how accurately he predicted the changes we have undergone in the past century.

We turn to Tocqueville to help see how we have changed our constitution—our way of life—even without changing our Constitution—our formal structure of government. As we see how closely the changes of the past half-century fit his model of "soft despotism," we will consider whether we have in fact been undergoing a "soft" revolution. We will consider how the form of government may have been changed from the original democratic republic into something like a "bureaucratic republic" or even a "despotism" of the kind Tocqueville describes. In addition, we will consider what might be done to recover the democratic republic intended by our Constitution.

The Growth of a New Form of Despotism

In Part Four of the second volume of *Democracy in America*, Tocqueville argues, contrary to ancient opinion, that the greatest threat to democratic government does not come from anarchy, or from too much liberty, the danger of which is easily seen and guarded against. He develops a description of a new kind of despotism, one growing out of the democratic love of independence itself. It insidiously transforms liberty into servitude without its victims even realizing what is happening to them. Precisely because it grows out of the love of equality and independence and because it takes control by "soft" means, this despotism is more dangerous than the ancient kind, harder to foresee and prevent, and almost impossible to cure once it has taken hold. To use Madison's medical analogy, this is the cancer of republican government, a disease so insidious and powerful that only the most radical treatment may be effective.

There are three factors which affect the rise of democratic despotism: attitudes of individualism and independence, administrative centralization, and the demise of secondary powers. We will look at each of these in turn.

(1) *Democratic peoples have a natural taste for individualism and independence.* Where citizens are equal in their political rights and responsibilities and also more or less equal in their economic and social conditions, they are inclined to obey their own will, considering themselves the best judge of their interests. In addition, democratic people tend to be mostly middle class. Most of them must spend most of their time making a living. They lack the leisure to attend to public business. Because their material well-being is dependent on business, and business requires a peaceful and orderly state, they are inclined to ignore politics as a waste of valuable time so long as everything is stable. Revolutionaries and political activists typically come from the upper class and find their

followers among the lower class. The alliance of wealthy aristocratic families such as the Kennedys with the interests of the working class within the Democratic party for the sake of promoting economic and social reform is one example of this general rule.

Democratic people, holding fast to their equality, recognize no personal obligations or rights between individuals such as existed in the feudal system. In the stratified society of the feudal age, inequalities among people carried with them very definite rights and duties, which were reciprocal and personal. The lord of the manor had the right to the labor of his serfs, and they to his protection against outlaws as well as against the neighboring nobility. An individual belonged not primarily to a class, but to the family he was born into and the family he was born to serve or to protect. Obedience was less to law than to a person, and patriotism was indistinguishable from personal loyalty.

The change wrought upon social relations by the demise of the feudal hierarchy and the rise of equality meant that each individual became a separate entity, free of personal obligations to any specific other person (even the bonds of the nuclear family became weaker), but also without the right to expect aid from any specific other person. People, Tocqueville says, became independent but weak.

In this condition, an individual in need would not go to his neighbor. His neighbor no longer had a socially enforced responsibility to help him, and his pride in being equal and independent would not let him stoop to becoming "beholden" to another. Instead he would look to the government to aid him. Because the government was not vested in any particular individual, being beholden to it would not be shameful and did not threaten his sense of independence. The government was also significantly more capable of helping him than any individual because it controlled the resources of the whole society. Finally, democratic government could be trusted to treat everyone equally, to enforce obligations or give aid without distinguishing among persons.

So out of the determination to remain independent of each other, human beings become dependent on the government, on a fictitious person thought to be incapable of oppressing them precisely because of its impersonal character. Tocqueville makes a telling observation when he says that "democratic peoples often hate those in whose hands the central power is vested, but they always love that power itself" (DA 673). We all complain of the stupidity or incompetence or just plain unfriendliness of the people who run the various governmental agencies we look to for our Social Security checks, our Medicare certification, or our licenses to practice our professions. Consider how we complain that social workers and regulatory agencies don't pay sufficient attention to the people they are supposed to be protecting. There seems to be tacit agreement that all this supervising and protecting and regulating is a good thing, we just don't like having to get it from identifiable people with all the usual faults of human nature. Whenever possible we are always ready to substitute some more restrictive rule or procedure or turn things over to a computer for the sake of uniformity and impartiality. It seems everyone hates "the bureaucracy" but no one is willing to give up the things it provides.

(2) *Tocqueville distinguishes between governmental centralization, which is compatible with liberty, and administrative centralization, which is not* (DA 87–98). Governmental centralization is another way to describe what we know as the federal structure of our government. Matters that concern the nation as a whole are decided in Washington by the legislative and executive representatives of the whole people, and judicial judgments relating to those laws and acts are made by federal courts. In theory at least, all other decisions are made on the state and local level. Administrative centralization, on the other hand, refers to the management of the details of local affairs by the central government.

Tocqueville praises governmental centralization as essential to the longevity and prosperity of a nation, a thought that was clearly in the minds of the Framers of our Constitution. Administrative centralization, on the other hand, is rarely a good thing. When the central government tries to administer the day-to-day details of local affairs, we find that the following things tend to happen: (1) A bureaucracy must be created both in the capital, where the rules and decisions are made, and in the localities, where they are enforced and implemented. (2) A superficial uniformity is created because all the localities are supposedly under the same rules and administration, but since local conditions vary widely, this uniformity is not real. (3) This system generates injustice as people come to perceive unequal treatment where there was supposed to be uniformity, and as people find that the same treatment is not equal in the contexts of different communities. (4) This system generates inefficiency and wastes resources as people far from a situation try to understand and make judgments about it.

Administrative centralization contributes to the development of soft despotism by teaching people to look to the central government to meet their needs. It also teaches them to value and expect equality more than liberty. Administrative centralization not only encourages the citizens to expect the government to run their lives, but it also places this administration in a government farther from them and therefore even less personal. Administrative centralization also emphasizes the equality of uniform regulation over the liberty of local responsibility.

When local governments are no longer responsible for the most important decisions affecting the lives of their citizens, interest in serving in local government or even in electing local officials declines. The Framers, and especially their Anti-Federalist critics, saw local government as the training ground for democratic citizenship. Remove the opportunity and the incentive for participating in self-government, and soon you will have very few citizens who understand liberty as anything other than being allowed to do as they please or equality as anything other than getting an equal share of the goods a benevolent but impersonal government gives out.

(3) *With the end of a stratified society came also the demise of the secondary powers which used to stand between individual citizens and the central government.* In aristocratic regimes the central power was the monarch, but this power was limited and checked by the power of the nobility and the clergy. The common people could appeal from one of these powers against another. In addition, responsibility for most of the things we think of as government was decentralized and divided among a variety of private or semiprivate institutions. Local needs were met by local powers.

Tocqueville gives a catalogue of the various rights and responsibilities which had already in his time been "wrested . . . from classes, corporations, and individuals . . . [and] have invariably been concentrated in the hands of the government" (DA 680). What is remarkable about this list is how many of these things we have so come to take for granted as governmental powers that we are startled to think that they once rested in private hands.

Charity

There are many people today who still think of charity as a private responsibility, and private charities still exist. But most of what used to be called charity and was practiced by private individuals for the sake of their moral well-being is now called public welfare and is the principal business of our government. Even the character of charitable giving and receiving has changed with, on the one hand, compulsory taxes used to aid the needy, and on the other, a doctrine of entitlement which looks less to neediness than to membership in a group defined as having a right to benefit in some particular way from the wealth collected in the taxes.

This system actually bears some resemblance to the feudal notion of rights and responsibilities belonging to persons by virtue of being born to a class or station in life—with the significant difference that today it is totally depersonalized. Once a man was identified by the manor to which he had been born and the lord to whom he owed fealty. Now he is identified by bureaucratic classification according to race, sex, physical handicap, language, etc.—characteristics which place him in a subgroup and tend to keep him there just as effectively as a serf or a nobleman was tied to the land he was born on.

Education

Tocqueville's description of the rise of public education presents an uncanny echo to much of what is being said today about its—deserved or deplored—demise. "The state . . . takes the responsibility for forming the feelings and shaping the ideas of each generation. Uniformity prevails in schoolwork as in everything else; diversity, as well as freedom, is daily vanishing" (DA 681). In the growing practice of homeschooling we see a revolt against the uniformity of centralized administration, but we also see something of the same concern in the fights to save the public schools as expressions of the standards of the local community.

Religion

Tocqueville describes the state taking control over religion, not by establishing a state religion to which everyone must conform but by taking away the power of religious leaders to speak and act as an independent force in society. His description applies to both the open hostility to religion in the (democratic) communist nations and the secularization in the name of toleration in the (non-communist) democratic nations. The constitution of the former Soviet

Union guaranteed freedom of religious worship equally with atheistic practice, but in the name of liberty prohibited religious instruction.

Public welfare

Tocqueville remarks that where aristocracies tended to leave individuals too much at the mercy of their own mistakes and the vicis-
situdes of fortune, democratic governments undertake even to "make
them happy against their will" (DA 681). The Social Security system can serve as an example. At one time it was generally agreed
that everyone should save up for hard times, that this was a virtue
and a responsibility and part of being a good citizen. But when too
many people found themselves without adequate savings or resources
in the Depression, it was decided that the government should in
effect force people to be virtuous and take care of themselves. But
now that we have lived with this "forced virtue" for a while, it has
lost all connection with virtue and taking care of oneself. It has
become both a tax and an entitlement. That is, those who pay into
their FICA accounts tend to look upon this not as prudently saving
up for their own future but as a tax imposed upon them to support
the present retired population. Similarly, those who receive Social
Security checks tend to regard them as something due to them because
they are in need, rather than as the income from their own prudently saved resources.

Regulatory agencies

Tocqueville reports at some length all the various economic activities coming under government control, from banks to labor relations, and the multiplying of specialized courts to deal with cases arising under the new complex of rules and regulations. Once
again what is especially noteworthy is not that these things were
not cared for under aristocratic rule, but that they have been depersonalized, made public, and administered by the central governmental bureaucracy.

Public works

Tocqueville's list of "roads, canals, ports, and other *semipublic*
works" (DA 686, emphasis added) speaks for itself. It is almost
inconceivable to the modern mind that these things might be left to

private initiative to provide, even though we have ventured to turn over such things as the postal service to private management in the hope of greater efficiency. Regardless of who actually does the work, we still expect the central government to see that it is done right, that is, uniformly and equally.

Soft Despotism: A Prediction of the Future or Description of the Present?

What are the features of this new despotism, which Tocqueville foresaw and which we are arguing is coming into being among us today? Tocqueville's own words describe it most effectively:

> The citizens are perpetually falling under the control of the public administration. They are led insensibly, and perhaps against their will, daily to give up fresh portions of their individual independence to the government, and those same men who from time to time have upset a throne and trampled kings beneath their feet bend without resistance to the slightest wishes of some clerk. (DA 688)

Tocqueville points to an irony in the rise of "soft" despotism:

> In the heat of the democratic revolution, men busy destroying the old aristocratic powers which opposed it displayed a strong spirit of independence. But as the triumph of equality became more complete, they gradually gave way to the instincts natural to that condition, strengthening and centralizing the power of society. They had sought to be free in order to make themselves equal. But in proportion as equality was established by the era of freedom, freedom itself was thereby rendered more difficult to attain. (DA 689)

This new despotism differs from past despotisms in three ways:

(1) Past despots always relied on secondary powers to administer their empires. The new despotism, because it is voluntarily accepted by its subjects, requires less power to administer, and the new techniques of bureaucratic management as well as technological advances Tocqueville did not imagine make it easier to administer a large territory. The totalitarian regimes of Nazi Germany and Stalinist Russia are good examples of the old despotism combined with the new, using the new techniques for mass control and the new ideologies of equality and public welfare to reinforce the old absolute rule of the tyrant.

(2) Despotism has always been understood to have a degrading

effect on the character of its subjects, from the Greek judgment of the barbarians who were less than human because they did not know how to rule themselves, to the philosopher Montesquieu's observation that people who have once lived under a bad regime may be incapable of living under a good one. But under the new despotism the people actually desire and promote the change in their character:

> Over this kind of men stands an immense, protective power which is alone responsible for securing their enjoyment and watching over their fate. That power is absolute, thoughtful of detail, orderly, provident, and gentle. It would resemble parental authority if, father-like, it tried to prepare its charges for a man's life, but on the contrary, it only tries to keep them in perpetual childhood . . . It provides for their security, foresees and supplies their necessities, facilitates their pleasures, manages their principal concerns, directs their industry, makes rules for their testaments, and divides their inheritances. Why should it not entirely relieve them from the trouble of thinking and all the cares of living? (DA 692)

For the sake of happiness, conceived as freedom from want, discomfort, and insecurity, people are willing to give up the exercise of free choice and turn over their choices to experts who will choose better than they could. What they don't realize is that such perfect security is impossible even under expert rule. But more importantly, they do not realize that by not exercising their free choice they will become less and less capable of making free choices and less and less capable of living with the uncertainty of being their own masters. So even when they come to dislike the life their masters have chosen for them, they may find it impossible to give up the security of having someone else be responsible.

> [L]iberty is less necessary in great matters than in tiny ones . . . Subjection in petty affairs, is manifest daily and touches all citizens indiscriminately. It never drives men to despair, but continually thwarts them and leads them to give up using their free will. It slowly stifles their spirits and enervates their souls . . . It really is difficult to imagine how people who have entirely given up managing their own affairs could make a wise choice of those who are to do that for them. (DA 694)

(3) The new despotism is "elective" in two senses of the word. As we have seen above, the regime itself is chosen. It is also ad-

ministered by elected "despots." It is not even correct to call the administrators of the new despotism despots. They are as much subject to the despotism they administer as are those who elect them, although they may believe themselves to be its masters. For the despotism is in the system, the complex of rules and procedures created for the sake of guaranteeing perfect security for everyone equally. Consider how difficult it has proved, even for the most adamant reformer, to reduce the federal bureaucracy or cut federal spending.

> Our contemporaries are ever a prey to two conflicting passions: they feel the need of guidance, and they long to stay free. Unable to wipe out these two contradictory instincts, they try to satisfy them both together. Their imagination conceives a government which is unitary, protective, and all-powerful, but elected by the people . . . Under this system the citizens quit their state of dependence just long enough to choose their masters and then fall back into it . . . They think they have done enough to guarantee personal freedom when it is to the government of the state that they have handed it over. (DA 693)

Antidotes to the New Despotism

Have we with the best of intentions so changed our character that we no longer have the qualities needed to undo the changes? Have we escaped the "hard" despotism of Marxian tyranny only to fall into the "soft" despotism of a mistaken quest for perfect security? Tocqueville makes a few observations about American democracy which suggest that he at least thought we would be more resistant to the new despotism than his European compatriots. We might still take heart from these qualities of our way of life, and where they are weak, strengthen them.

From Tocqueville's perspective the one most important force resistant to the new despotism and to any despotism is the presence of strong secondary powers in society. Strong secondary powers are organizations, groups, and even individuals whose power and authority come from a source other than the government. The best example of such a power is organized religion. The principle of separation of Church and State can be interpreted and enforced in such a way as to weaken religion by banning it from the public sphere. But it can have the opposite effect by allowing and even

encouraging religious spokesmen to address public issues in public, and religious communities to take responsibility for the material and moral welfare of their members.

Clearly this involves a sacrifice of the equality of uniformity,
for different religious communities will choose different ways of
life. But even the conflict between what the country as a whole
considers right and what different communities within it consider
right can become itself an exercise of liberty and self-government.
Remember Madison's conclusion that the best way to deal with the
existence of factions was to involve them in the governing process
itself, not to eliminate the conflict under a uniformity of passions,
interests, and opinions.

A second force of resistance to the new despotism is, ironically,
a free press. The irony of trusting to the press to oppose the new
despotism comes from our experience that the media—as we now
call the press—are often just as unified and just as enslaved by the
ideology of security as the rest of us. After all, their livelihood
depends upon pleasing us and it is easy to see what their role in a
"soft" despotism would be: entertain the people so they won't bother
to think. When they insist on thinking, do it for them and get it
over quickly and painlessly.

We could add in this category the institutions of higher education. They too have the potential to challenge our complacency in
ways that might free us. But they also seem to have bought into
the new despotism, for they have become one of the loudest voices
for conformity to the ideology of equal and perfect security and
governmental responsibility for people's choices, even to what
opinions they are allowed to have about each other.

A third force that could oppose the new despotism is the courts.
The courts have always occupied a position close to that of the
enlightened statesman or the power above society that Madison
mentioned in *Federalist* 10, and rightly so. For it is the responsibility of the courts to take time to consider carefully the will of
the majority with respect to the common good as expressed in the
laws and to protect individual rights from majority faction. If the
majority has implemented a plan that is in fact contrary to the common
good and to the rights of individuals because it has the effect of
depriving people of the capacity for self-government, free choice,
and personal responsibility, then it ought to be the duty of the courts
to declare such a plan unconstitutional.

So long as the courts in a democratic republic understand their
duty as preserving that form of government because it is the form

that best protects the people's well-being, they will be self-limiting. When they come to believe that the form of government is itself deficient and in need of correction, they change from being a part of the system of justice and a check on majority tyranny to being truly a power above and independent of the people. Unfortunately, today the Supreme Court seems more inclined not merely to reinforce the new despotism but to set itself up as the despot, the paternal power who knows better than anyone else what we need in order to be secure, equal, and happy despite our opinions and despite our political traditions.

Finally, the force which Tocqueville took for granted, but which may be the one best hope today, is local government. As we noted above, it was through participation in local government that the Framers expected the citizens to learn how to be citizens, to learn how to govern themselves by governing themselves. As Tocqueville noted, it is in the small matters of everyday life that liberty may be most important. When those small matters come under a myriad of rules and regulations enacted by representatives you may never meet, or even by unelected members of regulatory agencies, it is difficult for people to govern themselves. When the prevailing ideology tells you to trust the experts in Washington to look after your well-being and to accept sacrifices for a common good determined by a distant and impersonal bureaucracy and Supreme Court, people find it difficult to exercise their own judgment about what is just and good for themselves and the community they live in.

As Madison was well aware, people left free to choose in accordance with their passions and interests will come into conflict with one another and will make mistakes even when they find agreement. But Madison and the other Founders believed that it was a better and more truly human life to live in the midst of this imperfection. They believed we should use our liberty to work out compromises, to aid each other out of free compassion, to unite freely to work for a common good, and to suffer together from our mistakes, rather than to give up our natural freedom and our political liberty to any despot, even one who knows best.

Notes

1. Alexis de Tocqueville, *Democracy in America*, ed. J. P. Mayer (Garden City, N.Y.: Doubleday, 1969), pp. 504–5. All further references to Tocqueville will appear in the text in the following form: (DA pages).

2. Karl Marx and Friedrich Engels, *The Communist Manifesto* (New York:

International Publishers, 1987). All further references to this work will be given in the text in the following form: (CM pages).

Suggested Reading

Madison, James, Alexander Hamilton, and John Jay, *The Federalist* 1, 10, 51.
Marx, Karl, and Friedrich Engels. *The Communist Manifesto.*
Tocqueville, Alexis de. *Democracy in America*, Vol. 2, Part 4.

Part Two

Institutions

10

Congress: Representation and Deliberation

William F. Connelly Jr.

Americans love to hate Congress. Perhaps in the larger scheme of things, this is as it should be. Indeed, Congress may have been designed to be our national lightning rod and the butt of our jokes. Humorists Mark Twain and Will Rogers, among others, targeted the Congress of their times as "the best money can buy" and members of Congress as our "only indigenous criminal class." Even congressmen poke fun. Nineteenth-century Speaker Thomas B. Reed once observed that House members "never open their mouths without subtracting from the sum total of human knowledge." Today comedian Jay Leno and humor columnist Dave Barry just as easily find ready fodder for their amusing barbs in the performance of our national legislature.

For Congress, these may be the best of times and the worst of times. In recent years, it enthralled and educated the American public during three days of serious deliberation leading up to the Persian Gulf War. But the same Congress also gave us the embarrassing and infuriating spectacle of the Clarence Thomas–Anita Hill hearings, the House Bank and Post Office controversies, and the Senate's Keating Five scandal. Compounding such folly, Hill mandarins voted themselves midnight pay raises, authorized $22,000 for marble floors in congressional elevators, and reconsidered a "five-year budget summit accord" after only three months, all while the national debt soared. By its actions and inaction, Congress may be adding fuel to the fire of voter discontent.

So today Congress seems to be not so much the butt of our humor as the object of our scorn. George Bush, Bill Clinton, and Ross

171

Perot all lambasted Congress during the 1992 election season. Bush characterized Congress as dominated by "PACs, perks, privileges, partisanship, and paralysis." Clinton eagerly targeted a Congress dominated by his own party in criticizing "the brain dead politics in Washington" and "the stranglehold the special interests have on our elections and lobbyists have on our government." And, of course, blasting those fools on the Hill was central to the campaign of billionaire H. Ross Perot.

While Perot has most recently given voice to heightened voter discontent, the conventional critique of Congress has been fairly constant over time. Members of Congress are seen as beholden to special interests, addicted to PAC money, blinded by the perquisites of power, and interested only in reelection. Congress, in this view, is biased against change, oriented toward the status quo, and burdened by unnecessary partisanship. In a nutshell, Congress is out of touch and gridlocked.

While there certainly may be an element of truth to this conventional wisdom on Congress, the criticism needs to be placed in context. Congress may reflect the American people with all our strengths and weaknesses. In criticizing Congress, perhaps we are deflecting criticism from ourselves. The Founders designed Congress to represent our diversity as a nation and to deliberate, or think twice and three times, before acting. Contrary to the conventional wisdom, Congress may be gridlocked today precisely because it is *too much* in touch with the diverse interests making up our nation. Congress may be slow to promote change because there is no national consensus on what change is needed.

Congress is easily misunderstood. We need to go beyond the conventional wisdom to take a fresh look at Congress. We need to separate the wheat from the chaff, the fair from the unfair criticism, and we need to place that criticism and the calls for reform in context. For the critique to be accurate and any reforms to be appropriate and successful, we must understand the institutional and cultural contexts within which individual members of Congress operate.

Three Levels of Analysis

Congress is a complex institution. We need to analyze it at three levels: individual, institutional, and environmental. Individual analysis looks at members' individual incentives for acting as they do. For example, are congressmen self-interested or public-spirited? Institutional analysis recognizes that individuals operate within institutions that structure their behavior. Does the institution of Congress, for example, reward self-interested or public-spirited behavior among members? Finally, Congress itself functions within a larger political system or environment which, in turn, influences the institution's performance. Congress cannot be understood, for example, without taking into account the influence of the president, public opinion, and pressure groups.

Individual Analysis

Political scientist David Mayhew contends that one can best understand Congress by beginning with the assumption that all members at all times are "single-minded seekers of reelection." Mayhew's self-interest model of congressional behavior may be a useful starting point. But ultimately it remains incomplete and cannot adequately explain the enormous complexity of the policy process. First, a desire for reelection forces congressmen to be attentive to the needs of others, namely, voters. Second, a member's voting constituency may be sufficiently diverse to force him to choose between the demands of different groups. What course of action will best serve his reelection ambition may not always be clear.

Richard Fenno broadens Mayhew's analysis, arguing that members of Congress may, in fact, have three goals: reelection, power within the institution, and good public policy. Once elected, a member may not settle for the ceaseless pursuit of reelection for its own sake; he may want influence within the institution. His ambition may even include advancing a principled policy agenda. Fenno's analysis of individual motivation suggests that members may be moved by both personal ambition and institutional imperatives. At a minimum, members are constantly confronted with a conflict between their parochial reelection or constituency interests and the collective responsibility of Congress to the nation. Congressmen are torn between being the agents or advocates of narrow particular interests and being trustees seeking to advance the national interest. In other words, every member is both a representative for a part of the nation and a lawmaker for the whole nation. In Fenno's words, members must regularly choose between their "homestyle" and their "hillstyle."

Ultimately, individual analysis by itself is incomplete. We must look at the influence of the institution itself on the behavior of members, as well as the political environment within which Congress functions.

Institutional Analysis

Institutional analysis is based on the premise that Congress is more than the sum of its parts, and that Congress, as an institution, will have, as James Madison put it, "a will of its own." The Founders understood that institutions can influence the behavior of individuals and that institutions can be structured so as to curb the selfish tendencies of men and promote the public interest. Constitutional structures can pit ambition against ambition and, perhaps more importantly, promote institutional loyalty and a sense of institutional responsibility.

Most politicians elected to Congress, for example, naturally will be inclined to defend the institutional prerogatives of Congress against the president. Similarly, senators will be quick to defend the Senate against encroachments by the House, and vice versa. As political parties and committees came to play a role in Congress, members of parties fought for their party's interest, and members of congressional committees sought to protect the institutional prerogatives of their committee. In each instance, the "self-interests" of the members were redefined. They, in effect, adopted new constituencies apart from the original constituency that elected them to Congress. Members are constantly confronted with the dilemma of serving different, overlapping, and often conflicting constituencies, and so are forced to choose between conflicting loyalties. By virtue of their participation and involvement with these different institutions, members gain a stake in the success of each and they learn the art of compromise. Members learn to identify with the institution, and they develop a sense of "team spirit."

Much of the common criticism of Congress today misunderstands the design and function of the institution. For example, Congress is not the president. The Founders understood that different institutions do different things. They designed Congress to be a legislature and the presidency to be an executive. Stated simply, Congress is better at talking (i.e., deliberating) and the president is better at executing or acting. To criticize Congress for not acting with the energy or dispatch of the executive is to miss the point. We need to judge Congress by what a legislature is designed to do.

Herbert Storing understood that the separation of powers is "not aimed primarily at mutual checking but at the efficient performance of certain kinds of tasks," based on the assumption that "all governments perform certain kinds of functions, which are best performed in distinctive ways and by distinctive kinds of bodies."[1] For example, making general laws requires a detailed knowledge of the diverse interests, opinions, and passions of the people. Many representatives, frequently elected, can perform this function better than one individual, especially if they deliberate in open session. On the other hand, executive action is more naturally the preserve of one person, especially if it requires energy, secrecy, and dispatch. Similarly, the judiciary is more judicious for being independent and appointed, not elected, for what amounts to life tenure. The structure of institutions and their "different modes of election" determine what kind of power or function each can best exercise.

The functional separation of powers means that the two political branches can compete while they complement one another. The competition between the president and Congress introduces more energy into the policy process. The competition also invites a more open and public deliberation between the branches, which in turn invites greater policy responsiveness. But the separation of powers also creates a greater need for Congress to be both responsible and responsive. Congress is a more powerful legislature with national responsibility because of its independence from the executive.

Unlike parliamentary legislatures, Congress never surrenders its responsibility to the executive. Only in our separation of powers system could the legislature, for example, declare the executive's annual budget proposal "dead on arrival." Because the separation of powers has removed the executive from exercising decisive control over the legislative process, Congress has needed to develop its own internal structures for fulfilling its responsibility. In part, the committee system and party leadership fill the vacuum left by the legislature's independence from the executive in a separation of powers system.

The Separation of Powers

Critics often misunderstand the nature of the separation of powers. The checks and balances are not all there is to the separation of powers. The separation of powers does not merely limit the abuse of power, it also provides for the effective use of power. Congress is a powerful national legislature because of the institutional independence afforded by the separation of powers. The institutional independence or separation of Congress from the executive means that as a legislature it has more affirmative responsibility for policy-making than its counterpart in a parliamentary system. The U.S. Congress is the only major national legislature that clearly exercises an active, policy-making role. The institutional independence of Congress also makes its members more responsive to voters than to parties or presidents. After all, congressmen owe their election more to their constituents than to their party or president.

Ironically, it is precisely the institutional independence of the president and Congress that makes them need one another so much. In a sense, the president and Congress are two halves of a whole. They complement one another and need one another. By itself, Congress is not a complete policy-making process. So the president looms large in the congressional environment.

Functions of Congress

The two key functions of Congress are representation and deliberation. The proper exercise *and balance* of these two functions enables Congress to legislate effectively. Congress cannot act as efficiently as the executive because the president is one person, while Congress is 535 representatives of enormously diverse legislative districts and states. But for this same reason Congress is better than the president at representing the diversity of America, and Congress is better at deliberating among those diverse interests. Remember, Congress is meant to be deliberate in its deliberation. And unlike the British Parliament, Congress is not very good at forcing a national consensus where no consensus exists.

To criticize members of Congress for effectively representing local, parochial interests is to fail to appreciate the fact that in one sense the Constitution intends such a narrow focus, especially in the House. Congressmen are elected from legislative districts which are by definition more narrowly focused than the nation. Senators represent states which, again, are inevitably more parochial than the nation as a whole. The Founders meant to ground the deliberations of Congress in local interests.

Representing Diversity

The local or parochial orientation of Congress distinguishes our national legislature from the British Parliament. For Congress, local concerns typically supersede ideological concerns, and paro-chial interests commonly take precedence over party principle. Congress's strength as a legislature is rooted in its particularity, which may be appropriate given the conditions and circumstances of American political culture. Alexis de Tocqueville, the author of the classic *Democracy in America*, notes that different forms of government may be appropriate or inappropriate for a nation de-pending on its history, circumstances, and political context. Our separation of powers system may be a more fitting form of repre-sentative democracy for the United States than a pure parliamenta-ry form of government, especially given the enormous diversity of the country.

Fenno's research for his book *Homestyle* included extensive travel with members in their districts. He concluded "that any claim by anybody to have a feel for the whole country would be preposter-ous. For ill or good, no one can comprehend the United States. Only institutionally, not individually, can it be done."[2] The partic-ularity of Congress, and the tendency of its members to reflect parochial interests, may be a virtue rather than a weakness of our legislative process. Reformers, with their desire to create a legisla-tive process more inclined to reflect broad national concerns or broad ideological differences, may be ignoring the insights of Tocqueville and Fenno.

Still, the Founders hoped for more from their constitutional in-stitutions than a mere ambition checking ambition, or a channeling of the competition among the contending factions. They wanted their institutional structures to promote deliberation, to enable the peo-ple's representatives to "refine and enlarge the public view." In *Federalist* 71 Hamilton suggests that the "republican principle re-quires that deliberate sense of the community" should prevail. Hamilton argues that when "the *interests* of the people are at vari-ance with their *inclinations*," it is the duty of elected representa-tives to do what the people need rather than merely cater to what they want.

The Founders did not assume, as we so often do today, an easy identification between interests and inclinations, or needs and de-sires, whether of an individual, a group, or the nation. They recog-nized that reason must arbitrate between inclinations in order to arrive at interests. They did not expect that legislators exercising a merely instrumental judgment would be reduced to choosing the best means to the ends demanded by factions or simple majorities.

Rather, the Founders knew that legislating requires drawing conclusions and choosing ends. They understood that persuasion is the
crucial link between inclinations and decisions. They sought to
promote deliberation through the structure of their institutions, though
they recognized that it would be difficult to hear reasoned discourse
above the din and clamor of vying factions.

With Congress the Founders succeeded tolerably well in promoting
deliberation. Not that the Senate, the self-proclaimed "greatest
deliberative body in the world," is all deliberation and no din. As
with the House, the constant clamor of contentious groups and the
bargaining and compromising of differing interests are the stuff of
daily life in the Senate. To be certain, neither chamber offers what
public interest groups like Common Cause demand, namely pure
deliberation on the merits of public policy in some sort of ideal
Olympian aloofness. Nevertheless, reasoned discourse and persuasion do play a role whether in House committees or on the Senate
floor. Congress is not merely some kind of institutional barometer
registering the force of prevailing interest group pressures. The
structure of Congress promotes deliberation, although within the
context of a political environment consisting of thousands of contending organized interests.

In the final analysis, the challenge for Congress is to balance its
representative function with its deliberative function. Again, the
problem today may not be that Congress is out of touch, but rather
that Congress is too much in touch or too responsive to narrow
interests. Congress may be gridlocked precisely because as a legislature it is too responsive to narrow, parochial constituent concerns and therefore not readily able to legislate responsibly in the
national interest. The budget deficit comes to mind.

Bicameralism

A key constitutional principle governing the behavior of Congress is bicameralism, which divides the legislature into the House
and Senate. Like sibling rivals, the House and the Senate are so
close they are forever fighting. Consequently, some see bicameralism as a serious defect in the machinery of Congress. Since at least
the Progressive era of the early twentieth century reformers have
sought to overcome this supposed flaw in our national legislature.
But such reformers fail to appreciate the virtue of this "defect."
Indeed, the Framers of the Constitution intended this defect. Mad-

ison observed that in a republican government "the legislative authority necessarily predominates." In *Federalist* 51 he went on to suggest, however, that

> the remedy for this inconveniency is to divide the legislature into different branches; and to render them, by different modes of election and different principles of action, as little connected with each other as the nature of their common functions and their common dependence on the society will admit.

By dividing Congress into the House and Senate, the Founders sought not simply to "weaken," but also to strengthen Congress as an institution. Madison did see bicameralism as a means of limiting legislative power relative to the executive branch. But he also saw it as a way to strengthen the legislative functions. Again, in principle, a legislature should represent diversity and deliberate openly. Two chambers chosen by different modes of election can better represent, although somewhat redundantly, the needs of their constituents. Furthermore, two chambers motivated by different principles of action will inevitably clash. House and Senate conflict and competition augment the twin virtues or functions of a legislature.

Bicameralism succeeds in making Congress more effectively representative of our enormous diversity as a nation and more deliberative in adjudicating among our differing interests and opinions. Bicameralism also makes Congress more dynamic by providing alternative avenues for participation by members and groups in the policy process. Ultimately, broad-based consensus, not efficiency, may be a better measure of congressional effectiveness in policymaking.

House and Senate Rules and Procedures

The House and Senate are two very different legislative bodies representing two distinct national majorities, or at least two differently organized national majorities. The broad-based consensus needed to pass legislation requires cobbling together different coalitions in the House and Senate (both on the floor and in committee). In this sense, Congress operates by complex majority rule, usually called coalition building, rather than simple majority rule.

As noted above, the roots of House and Senate differences are found in their distinct constitutional structures. Senators represent states. Members of the House represent smaller districts made up of approximately 600,000 voters. The smaller, more intimate Senate has only 100 senators, while the larger, more boisterous House has 435 members. Senators have fewer colleagues and many more constituents than the typical House member. So congressmen may be closer to their constituents and senators may be closer to their colleagues. Finally, senators serve six-year terms; congressmen serve only two years. These simple constitutional differences make for two immensely dissimilar and mutually distrustful legislative bodies.

The Constitution also assigns different functions to these different structures. For example, the frequently elected House has responsibility for originating changes in tax policy. In practice, this means that the tax writing committee in the House, the Ways and Means Committee, is generally more influential in tax policy than its counterpart, the Senate Finance Committee. Conversely, the Constitution grants the Senate a greater role in the formation of foreign policy by dint of its role in voting on treaties and executive nominations. The more prestigious Senate Foreign Relations Committee is generally more influential than its counterpart, the House Foreign Affairs Committee.

The enormous differences between the House and Senate almost cannot be overstated. The two institutions are so different they are constantly suspicious of one another. The contrast between the two chambers can best be described as follows: The governing or operating principle of the House is conflict; that of the Senate is consensus. The House is much more partisan than the smaller Senate, where members constantly strive for comity and cooperation.

The rules of the House provide for majority rule. Senate rules reinforce the individual rights of members. The heavily rule-bound House is more efficient than the more deliberative Senate. House members tend to specialize in their committee work, while senators tend to be legislative generalists. Finally, the legislative process in the House is committee-centered; House committees are the workshops of Congress. The legislative process in the Senate is centered on the floor, making Senate committees less important in influencing legislation. The two chambers even have differing characteristic vices: the House tends to be more autocratic and the Senate more chaotic.

The House and Senate control the flow of legislation from committees to the floor in largely different manners. Generally speaking, the House Rules Committee strictly structures floor debate by attaching a "rule" to bills ready for floor consideration. The "rule" details the amount of time for debate, who will manage that time, and whether the bill will be "open" or "closed" to amendments on the floor. In recent years the Democratic majority in the House has increasingly resorted to "closed rules" to control floor debate. House Republicans see such efforts as denying them due process and a role in legislating.

The Senate is very unlike the House in allowing for freewheeling and wide-open floor debate. The Senate structures floor consideration of bills by negotiating "unanimous consent agreements" or UCAs. Unanimous consent agreements are just what they sound like—agreements to consider legislation agreed to unanimously. All senators, Democrats and Republicans, can play a role in this process normally worked out by the majority and minority leaders. It is remarkable that the Senate accomplishes anything at all.

Given the relaxed germaneness rules governing the relevancy of amendments to bills in the Senate, any senator can tack almost any amendment onto almost any bill. Similarly, individual senators can temporarily delay legislation from reaching the floor by means of silent "holds." A minority of senators also can indefinitely delay bills by use of the infamous filibuster, where members exercise their right to virtually unlimited debate on legislation. Differences in floor procedure go a long way in explaining how parties and committees differ in the House and Senate.

Parties and Committees

Congress organizes itself for action along two distinct, and perhaps contradictory, lines: party and committee. Party leaders and committee leaders often conflict. Dan Rostenkowski (D., Illinois), the powerful chairman of the House Ways and Means Committee, rarely kowtows to his party's leaders. Likewise, Jim Leach (R., Iowa), as Banking Committee ranking member (or vice chairman as Republicans like to say), is known for his independence from the dictates of his more conservative Republican colleagues. Party leaders have little control over the electoral fate of congressmen, hence committee leaders and, for that matter, rank-and-file committee members often exhibit little allegiance to the party line.

The constant competition among party and committee leaders makes Congress appear chaotic and congressional leadership seem nonexistent. Some critics go so far as to suggest that leadership in Congress is really "followership" and that legislative leaders are "slaves" to their membership. But Congress should not be judged by executive leadership standards. Leadership in Congress is not of an executive nature because Congress is not the president. Leadership does exist, although it tends to be free floating. Depending on the issue and timing, leadership can come from party leaders, committee leaders, or presidents.

Generally, House leaders tend to be more powerful than Senate leaders. The disparity between chamber leadership is in part a function of the Constitution. The Constitution mentions three legislative leaders—the speaker of the House, the president of the Senate (who is also vice president of the United States), and the president pro tempore of the Senate, who chairs the Senate floor proceedings in the absence of the Senate president when engaged in his executive branch duties. Because of the separation of powers, the constitutional leadership of the Senate tends to be weak, unlike the speaker of the House who actively manages floor debate.

Because the presiding officers of the Senate are weak, much responsibility for managing floor debate devolves to the majority and minority leaders who try to work in concert on the floor. A good illustration of the difference between House and Senate leadership can be seen in the "right of recognition" each possesses. The House speaker, currently Tom Foley (D., Washington), has an *active* right to recognize members on the floor during debate. The Senate majority leader, currently George Mitchell (D., Maine), has a *passive* right to be first recognized by the chair when he stands during debate.

Two Kinds of Democracy?

All of these contrasts amount to two very different articulations of democracy. Political historian Ross Baker suggests that the House reflects "adversary democracy," while the more consensual Senate embodies the principle of "unitary democracy."[3] Stated differently, members of the House tend toward the agent or advocate role, while senators have more leeway for playing the trustee of the common good. The Founders designed the House to be more responsive to electoral pressures and the Senate to be more responsible in resisting such pressures. As we shall see in discussing congressional elections, the Founders' intentions may have been turned on their head in recent years.

Environmental Analysis

Congress as an institution operates within a larger political system which in turn influences how it functions. Elements in the environment of Congress include the president, the executive bureaucracy, voters and constituents, interest groups, the media, and public opinion. The constitutional separation of powers is key to understanding the system within which Congress operates. As discussed above, the president is a key component in the environment of Congress, but more important for Congress may be the relationship between members of Congress and the voters.

Elections

Voter discontent with Washington in recent years may be tied to the problem of "permanent incumbency," especially in the House of Representatives. During the 1980s, partisan control of the Senate changed twice. During the past *forty* years, partisan control of the House has not changed at all. Democrats have controlled the House since 1954. The plight of House Republicans is unique in the history of Congress. Never has one party been in the minority in either chamber of Congress for nearly so long. No sitting House Republican has ever served in the majority, and only a few House Democrats have ever been in the minority. Many of the youngest House Republicans were not even born when their party last held majority status in the House. As a consequence of the "permanent" majority and minority status of House Democrats and Republicans, partisan strife in that chamber may be at an all-time high. Republicans accuse Democrats of arrogance, while Democrats point to the self-defeating frustration of "permanent minority" Republicans.

Such partisan gridlock is perhaps surprising in a legislative chamber designed by the Founders to be closer to the people and more likely to shift with changing electoral fortunes. What explains this electoral obstruction? Are House Democrats knaves or House Republicans fools?

Political scientists and politicians offer a variety of explanations for the permanent minority status of House Republicans. One argument holds that because Democrats have majorities in most state legislatures, Republican "farm teams" are thin. According to this argument Republicans tend to nominate weak candidates lacking campaign and government experience. Another argument is that voters choose Democrats because Democrats are usually correct on the issues, especially domestic issues, the sort congressmen confront more commonly than presidents. A related explanation suggests that the Republican party's supposed antigovernment philosophy hinders recruitment and promotes retirement among Republicans. A third answer insists that GOP success with winning the White House in recent decades has hurt congressional Republicans. Statistically speaking, the longer a party has held the White House during the twentieth century, the worse it has fared in House elections. According to this calculation, in order to regain the House, Republicans should begin by losing the White House, a feat they accomplished in the 1992 election.

While there may be an element of truth in all the above answers, a full explanation for Democrats' lock on the House must also consider the phenomenon of permanent incumbency. In recent election cycles House incumbents of both parties have been returned to office at record rates approximating 98 percent. Even in the 1992 election in which 110 new members of Congress won office, 93 percent of all incumbents seeking reelection succeeded. The irony may be that permanent incumbency and the resulting gridlock exist precisely because members are too much in touch with constituents. Congressional careerism may result from members being *too* professional at running for office.

The typical incumbent congressman has tremendous advantages over any challenger. With congressional reforms in the early 1970s came a dramatic increase in staff and travel allotments for members' personal offices and an enormous increase in use of the franking privilege. The frank allows members to mail letters to constituents at taxpayers' expense, and in the past two decades members have increasingly used the frank for mass mailings. Such mass mailings sometimes amount to little more than taxpayer-subsidized campaign literature. Congress spends *one billion dollars* a year on mailings, the equivalent of $5,000 per member per day. Estimates of the campaign dollar value of a House incumbent's office perquisites, including staff, travel, and franking, range from $500,000 to $750,000 during any two-year term, a sizable advantage few challengers can match.

To make matters worse for challengers, the existing campaign finance system, created in part by the 1970s reforms, overwhelmingly favors incumbents over challengers. PAC contributions, for example, favor incumbents 8 to 1. The average challenger cannot compete on such an unlevel playing field, and many potential challengers choose not to run given the daunting advantages of incumbents. But the biggest advantage for incumbents may be the role congressmen have assigned themselves and government.

Artificial permanent incumbency may ultimately be due to the growth of government. Indeed, the major incumbency perk may be the modern equivalent of patronage, namely the increased entitlement spending and constituent service members now focus on as ombudsmen. According to political scientist Morris Fiorina, the growth of activist government has changed the role of Congress from policy-making to pork-barreling, and changed the congressional office into a permanent campaign and constituent service office. As part of a self-perpetuating cycle of congressional support for unnecessary spending and bigger bureaucracies, members have become super-spoilsmen and errand boys for the special interests in their districts, thus ensuring their own reelection and a continuation of the status quo. If big government is an advantage for incumbents, big deficits may be even better. But if permanent incumbency feeds on budget deficits and promotes gridlock, there may be a limit to the patience of the American people.

Congress and the Political Culture

Congress is a creature of the surrounding political culture. According to Samuel Huntington in *American Politics: The Promise of Disharmony*, a mainstay of American political culture has always been the conflict between our ideals and our institutions, between the theory and practice of our politics. This conflict or dissonance is at once our defect and our virtue. Congress lives this conflict every day; Congress is this conflict. Again, Americans love to hate Congress.

Americans have traditionally been skeptical of politics. A healthy skepticism helps maintain limited government. But in recent years this healthy skepticism has become a corrosive cynicism as government and our expectations of government have grown. The increased scope of government and raised expectations have in turn allowed harsh critics of Congress like H. Ross Perot to foster and feed on the growing cynicism.

Critics like Perot may in part be justified in their concern about the role of special interests, money, self-interest, and ambition in politics. Unlike contemporary critics, however, the Founding Fathers did not seek to ban self-interest and ambition in politics. They did not expect "enlightened statesmen" (or political saints) always to be at the helm. Rather Madison sought to channel self-interest and ambition by means of a carefully structured, well-balanced constitutional order. The Founders' "institutional" regulation of self-interest does not threaten, indeed it promotes, the exercise of First Amendment freedoms, such as the right to petition government, otherwise known as lobbying. Self-righteous critics are too often willing to compromise such liberties by means of a "legal" regulation (e.g., ethics and lobbying laws, campaign finance laws) designed to cleanse politics of human nature.

Populist or Elitist?

Is Perot a democratic reformer or an autocratic despot? Is the solution to our national problems "just that simple," as he insists? Or can the diversity and complexity of America only be comprehended—and accommodated—institutionally, as Richard Fenno suggests?

Commentator George F. Will argues that the Perot phenomenon, including our newfound infatuation with electronic town halls, reflects "the decay of deliberative democracy into plebiscitary, answering-machine democracy." Perotism is reminiscent of earlier good-government reformers' desires to take the politics out of politics. The *Washington Post*'s Dan Balz called Perot the "candidate of non-politics" and one who promotes "the politics of no politics." Perot offered himself as the proverbial "man on a white horse" who would solve our problems without resorting to politics.

But the Framers embraced what Perot and other reformers deride as mere "politics," meaning the struggle among competing interests and ambitious politicians. They did this in the name of protecting the greatest amount of liberty. Unfortunately, the demagoguery of those who wish for, and promise, a politics above politics undermines any appreciation for the role of republican institutions and augments the level of what Madison called a corrosive "political jealousy." In *Federalist* 55 Madison notes:

> As there is a degree of depravity in mankind which requires a certain degree of circumspection and distrust, so there are other qualities in human nature which justify a certain portion of esteem and confidence. Republican government presupposes the existence of these qualities in a higher degree than any other form. Were the pictures which have been drawn by the political jealousy of some among us faithful likenesses of the human character, the inference would be that there is not sufficient virtue among men for self-government; and that nothing less than the chains of despotism can restrain them from destroying and devouring one another.

The false standard of good-government reform over the past two decades has helped undermine respect for republicanism and representative government. While the world was beating a path to democratic pluralism during the 1980s, self-proclaimed reformers and congressional critics were busy beating to death the very institutions designed to uphold democratic pluralism. Today Americans call out for leadership, but our institutions are no longer able to support and promote the kind of leadership we need. We need to restore an appreciation for republican government as the necessary foundation for effective leadership.

The point of reform should not be to make special interests weaker, or simply to make Congress "more open and more democratic." Rather, the point of reform should be to make elected representatives and institutions stronger and more capable of providing leadership. As George Will argues in *Restoration*, we need to restore an appreciation for deliberative democracy. We need a return to republicanism.

Notes

1. Herbert J. Storing, *What the Anti-Federalists Were For* (Chicago: University of Chicago Press, 1981), p. 60.

2. Richard F. Fenno Jr., *Watching Politicians* (Berkeley, Calif.: IGS Press, 1990), p. 93.

3. Ross Baker, *House and Senate* (New York: Norton, 1989), pp. 86–89.

Suggested Reading

Baker, Ross. *House and Senate*. New York: Norton, 1989.

Deering, Christopher J. *Congressional Politics*. Chicago: Dorsey Press, 1989.

Dionne, E. J. *Why Americans Hate Politics*. New York: Simon and Schuster, 1991.

Fenno, Richard. *Homestyle*. Boston: Little, Brown, 1978.

Huntington, Samuel. *American Politics: The Promise of Disharmony*. Cambridge: Harvard University Press, 1981.

Matthews, Christopher. *Hardball*. New York: Summit Books, 1988.

Mayhew, David. *Congress: The Electoral Connection*. New Haven: Yale University Press, 1974.

Will, George F. *Restoration*. New York: Free Press, 1992.

11

The Presidency and the Constitution

Richard J. Dougherty

Mr. [James] Wilson moved that the Executive consist of a single person.

A considerable pause ensuing and the Chairman asking if he should put the question [to a vote], Docr. Franklin observed that it was a point of great importance and wished that the gentlemen would deliver their sentiments on it before the question was put.[1]

So begins James Madison's account of the deliberations of the Constitutional Convention over the formation of the executive within the newly constructed Constitution. There was good reason for such a pause among the delegates. Had not monarchy just suffered perhaps its fatal blow through the proclamation of the Declaration of Independence? How could a country so permeated with opposition to unified, national rule—illuminated most dramatically by the complete absence of an executive power from the Articles of Confederation—now resurrect the idea and adopt a single executive?

In this essay I address some of the fundamental concerns of the executive office, including its origins and structure, the development of the electoral process, and some particular questions of executive power, including the exercise of the veto power and executive "prerogative." I conclude with a discussion of contemporary congressional–executive relations, showing how they reflect a new understanding of the role of the presidency in the American constitutional order. I begin with a consideration of the role of the executive in the Constitution's scheme of the separation of powers.

Separation of Powers and Executive Energy

The Articles of Confederation, under which the states operated from 1781 to 1787, contained no provision for an executive branch or department. The Articles did provide for a Committee of States, which was empowered to execute the powers of the Congress, but it was to meet only when the Congress was not in session. Eventually Congress did establish standing committees, then departments, to oversee particular activities, but these departments answered separately to Congress and had no independent powers. The absence of a proper executive was one of the critical causes of the instability that marked the tenure of the Articles.

The Framers of the Constitution recognized that what the new government needed was a strong central authority, characterized by the energy so critical to its success. This principal defect of the Articles, the complete absence of such an authority, was precisely the weakness that was to be addressed by the formation of the national executive. The absence of such a power was certainly one of the factors that led Publius to the recognition of the truth that "energy in the executive is a leading character in the definition of good government" (*Federalist* 70).

The Constitution's executive was to provide that absent energy. Its essential component is *unity*, meaning its direction by a single person. In *Federalist* 37, Publius notes that among the concerns of the delegates at the convention must have been the difficulty of reconciling seemingly opposing principles, incorporating into the Constitution some measure of energy, stability, liberty, and republican form. The delicate balance that had to be struck in this matter was achieved, Publius claimed, through the formation of the various branches, or departments, of the federal government. *Stability* is found in the Senate, which is relatively small, and whose members serve a long term of office. *Liberty* is secured through the House of Representatives, a large body characterized by frequent elections, and thus close to the people. *Energy*, though, requires at least a moderate term of office, with power exercised by a single hand. The Constitution, in order to produce a free and competent government, must intertwine these apparently antithetical precepts. (*Republican form*, we later discover, is preserved most especially by the judiciary.) These characteristics of good government point to the essential distinctions between and among the branches.

Federalist 51 lays out the groundwork for the successful operation of the separation of powers. The critical concern for the delegates at the convention, according to Publius, was to find a common ground between the establishment of specific constitutional powers and the personal motives of the members of the various branches to use and defend those powers. As he describes it, "Ambition must be made to counteract ambition." Experience has taught us that the members of the legislature would be ambitious. They will, by their nature, attempt to usurp the powers of the executive, and the separation of powers will function properly only if that danger is stifled. The remedy for this "defect" of character is to provide for an ambitious executive, who will counteract the "inconveniency" of having a powerful legislature. The only way for the executive to be successful, and for the separation of powers to work, is if he is also ambitious, and so has the motive to exercise the powers given him by the Constitution. The main concern of *Federalist* 51 is to strengthen the executive against the legislature.

An example of the strong president is Theodore Roosevelt, who remarked that "While President, I have *been* President, emphatically."[2] He described his understanding of the presidency in the following manner:

> I have a definite philosophy about the Presidency. I think it should be a very powerful office, and I think the President should be a very strong man who uses without hesitation every power that the position yields; but because of this very fact I believe that he should be sharply watched by the people, held to a strict accountability by them, and that he should not keep the office too long.[3]

But it is important to note that Roosevelt says he has been the president, not a member of Congress, not a judge, not a despot or tyrant.

The ambition that drives the executive must be an ambition to be president, not to go beyond the powers of the presidency as delineated in the Constitution. That ambition is employed by using his constitutional powers to thwart the attempts of the legislature to "encroach" upon the powers of the other branches. This ambition is in the service of the powers that make up the executive office. The proper functioning of the separation of powers occurs only when the president has legitimate constitutional powers (veto power, treaty-making power, appointment power, and powers of the commander-in-chief), and is willing to exercise those powers, sometimes in opposition to the demands of Congress. Those presidents who are generally regarded as among the best do seem to have been those who were willing to exercise vigorously the powers of the office.

The Electoral System(s)

The electoral system that was finally incorporated into Article II of the Constitution not only answered the desire for an admirable arrangement, but also responded to the various necessities of the day. It arranged for an independent body, the electors, to be chosen in each state, according to the discretion of the state legislature. The electors would then meet, each in their own state, on the same day, and cast their votes for president and vice president. In the event that no one received a majority of electoral votes, the election would then be decided by the House of Representatives, which would choose from among the top five candidates with the highest number of votes.[4]

This system recommended itself, according to Publius, for even if "the manner of it be not perfect, it is at least excellent" (*Federalist* 68). Its merits included the identification of a body of qualified electors, encouragement of dispassionate debate, avoidance of corruption, and ultimately, an independent executive who would not serve at the forbearance of any sitting body.[5] The selection system provided, in the words of Publius, a "moral certainty" that the election will "seldom fall to the lot of any man who is not in an eminent degree endowed with the requisite qualifications."

The Electoral College solved many of the problems the Framers encountered in establishing a formal process of election. The critical issues involved in selecting the executive (following the agreement that there would in fact be a unitary executive) were deciding who would comprise the electoral body, whether the president would be eligible for reelection, and the tenure of office. The first two matters were intimately connected. If the national legislature were to choose the president, the consensus was that he ought not to be allowed to seek reelection, so as not to be beholden to Congress during his term of office. But if an independent body did the selecting, there was less reason to rule out reeligibility. And if reeligibility was to be an option, then the term of office could be shorter, so as to reap the benefits of superior executives, and remove those who had proved to be inferior.

A further difficulty the Framers had to address was the demand by the states that they not be excluded from the electoral process. All of these concerns, we can see, were addressed through the establishment of the Electoral College. The final design, when presented to the convention, was described as having been "perfectly novel, and therefore [it] occasioned a pause; but when explained and fully considered was universally admired, and viewed as the most pleasing feature in the Constitution."[6]

Yet for all of its merits in the eyes of the Framers, the original design of the Electoral College was soon altered, with the rise of political parties in the United States. In the Framers' design, the electors were not limited in their search for worthy candidates by questions of party loyalty or popularity. But by the election of 1800, when Thomas Jefferson defeated John Adams, the distinction between party positions was beginning to create a system wherein the electors, prior to the November general election, were pledged to vote for particular parties and their candidates, and thus lost the independence which they previously had. The electors were now bound to vote for candidates of particular parties. The concern of the elector became loyalty to a person selected by the party, not the character of the prospective candidate. Under this remodeled system, the voters in the general election were left to choose between and among the candidates put forward by the parties themselves, but had little or no say in how those candidates were nominated.

This change in the electoral system, coupled as it was with the organization of political parties, was defended on the grounds that it was harmonious with the designs of the Framers. In this view the party conventions acted in a manner similar to the Electoral College, deliberating about the relative merits of various potential candidates before eventually putting forth their nominee for the general election. This restricted the field of candidates for the electors to consider, but still provided a generally well-qualified body to do the selecting. In addition, given the fact that the candidate would then have to run in the general election, the modified system typically provided for an absence of corruption while maintaining the independence of the executive. In keeping with the principles of the Framers, the executive was likely to be a respected national figure of good character, and not to be beholden to Congress or any other governmental body. The party system also gave the voters some sense of the policy direction that would be pursued by their candidate, providing them with an increased awareness of the consequences of their vote.

There have been numerous attempts made over the years at reforming this electoral system, on the principle that the process should be made more "democratic," or popular. But these efforts met with little success until the 1960s, when they culminated in the advent of the contemporary state primary and caucus system. In the previous system the party officials decided who would be put forward as the party nominee. Now the candidates, in attempting to garner the nomination of the national party, decide for themselves, without deferring to party leadership, whether to seek their party's nomination and how to conduct their campaign. The primaries and caucuses as presently conducted are virtually open elections run in the individual states over several months, with the party exercising limited control over the process. Under this current system, the electorate ostensibly controls the nomination process through these primaries and caucuses, in the spring, and then chooses the eventual victor in the general election in November.

There are, on the surface, many advantages to the new system. The process is more directly democratic. It allows "outsiders"—those who are not a part of the official national party structure—a chance at garnering the party nomination when they could not have done so under the old system (Jimmy Carter is an especially good example here). The public also gets a longer look at each of the candidates, so as to make it more likely that they could select the most qualified candidate, or the one whose views are most like their own.

But there are also some serious drawbacks to the new system. There is an increased focus on the candidate's "image," as opposed to his character or experience, witnessed by the rapidly growing influence of pollsters and advertisers in the campaigns. The proliferation of primaries and caucuses has, in one sense, diminished the influence of the public at large, for it has lent greater power to interest groups which can rally supporters around particular issues. In elections with a relatively light turnout, such as most primaries, these groups can have a disproportionate impact. The longer process is also much more expensive than in the past, and those who do not want to expend the time and effort to raise funds for such a campaign may decide against pursuing the office. Increasingly we see many of the most qualified potential candidates refusing to go through the arduous campaign. Many with good reputations do not want to endure the ordeal, as it may threaten their standing.

The great advantage of the new system, that it allows for the emergence of those leaders the party would otherwise refuse to nominate, must be rethought when considering the difficulty such individuals face when entering office as president. Because the nominee runs what is essentially an individual campaign, outside the boundaries of traditional party politics, he may then find it difficult to convince the members of his party in Congress to follow his policies once he is in office.

The electoral system, in Publius's view, is a distinctive characteristic of the executive under the constitutional arrangement. The system's capacity to produce an effective executive can be gauged by how ambitious and energetic the executive is, how capable he is of fulfilling his role in the separation of powers. But that ambition and energy must be directed toward the exercise of the constitutional powers of the executive. The specific power Publius points to as a check against legislative "predominance" is the veto power, and it is to that which we now turn.

Veto Power

Article I, Section 7 of the Constitution contains the passage dealing most directly with the "legislative" powers of the executive, in particular the veto power (though it is not called that). The section requires that all bills, having passed both houses of Congress, shall "be presented to the President of the United States." If the president signs the bill, it becomes law. If he does not, it is then returned for reconsideration, at which time the legislature can attempt to override the president's negative. A two-thirds vote of *both* houses of Congress is required to override the president's veto. The Constitution does not say why the president might exercise the veto power, although it does require him to state his "objections" to the bill as proposed. The power has most often been exercised on the basis of policy differences, when the president desires to pursue a course of affairs different from that suggested by the legislation.

Another significant reason why the president may exercise the veto power is on constitutional grounds, when he thinks the proposed bill violates particular provisions or principles of the Constitution. Perhaps the most famous example of a president employing this stratagem is Andrew Jackson's decision in 1832 to veto a bill rechartering the National Bank. The establishment of the Second National Bank, in 1816, had been a matter of great controversy, but had been sanctioned by the Supreme Court in *McCulloch v. Maryland* (1819).

By vetoing the bill, Jackson established the executive as a coordinate power with the Court in constitutional interpretation. In his view, the president, in fulfilling his obligations under the Constitution, must judge the legality of any proposition, as do Congress and the Supreme Court. The Court cannot settle the matter by itself:

> The authority of the Supreme Court must not, therefore, be permitted to control the Congress or the Executive when acting in their legislative capacities, but to have only such influence as the force of their reasoning deserve.[7]

Perhaps the most notable elaboration of Jackson's view is that made by Abraham Lincoln in his First Inaugural Address, commenting on whether he is strictly bound by the Court's 1857 decision in *Dred Scott v. Sandford:*

> [T]he candid citizen must confess that if the policy of the government, upon vital questions, affecting the whole people, is to be irrevocably fixed by decisions of the Supreme Court, the instant they are made, in ordinary litigation between parties, in personal actions, the people will have ceased to be their own rulers, having, to that extent, practically resigned their government, into the hands of that eminent tribunal.[8]

In Lincoln's view, the executive may be compelled to enforce the judgment of the Supreme Court in a particular case, but on a broader level may not be obliged to adopt and enforce the general principle laid down by the Court. In this case, the executive would be forced to apply the *Dred Scott* ruling against Dred Scott himself, but not necessarily against everyone similarly situated. It is not enough, according to Lincoln, for an executive to proceed with questions of administration and enforcement, and neglect constitutional concerns.

The decision to veto an act passed by both houses may be made wholly on principle, but may also be guided in part by political considerations—for instance, by whether the veto will be sustained in Congress. Presidents do not govern in a vacuum, and so are generally aware of the level of support they have in Congress; they have a perception of whether a particular veto will be a source of conflict with the legislature.

The decision to employ the veto, in part, is based on the calculus of political costs the president will have to bear for having exercised his power. Yet the veto power can also be a powerful tool for the president, as the legislature may alter or reject its own proposals when it knows that they are destined for defeat.[9] Consider the lengthy and complicated negotiations between Congress and the White House concerning the Civil Rights Act of 1991, precipitated by President George Bush's rejection of the proposed civil rights bill in 1990. Having clearly outlined his objections to the bill as originally proposed, and having already vetoed one version of the civil rights bill in 1990, Bush was able to force Congress to alter some of the provisions of the act which he found most problematic. In this case, it was not the exercise of the veto, but the threat to use it, coupled with a prior instance of having done so, that illustrated the executive's energy.

The veto power is even more valuable for the executive in securing the constitutional powers granted him under Article II. The Framers understood that the great threat to the effective working of the separation of powers was the tendency of the legislature to encroach on the other branches. The executive had to be given the means by which to avoid that difficulty. The veto power, or qualified negative, enables the executive to secure his position within the constitutional design, refusing his assent to measures that are either contrary to the public good or injurious to the legitimate powers of the executive department.

The knowledge that legislation can be reconsidered by Congress, and perhaps improved as a result of executive criticism, also makes it more likely that the veto will actually be employed by the executive and thus produce positive results. As Publius puts it in *Federalist* 51, one of the problems with an absolute veto is that "on ordinary occasions it might not be exerted with the requisite firmness." In a different system, an executive aware of the fact that he has the final say in any legislative considerations may be less likely to use the veto power, aware of the fact that there is no further appeal. He may allow harmful legislation to pass uninhibited if there is no provision for reconsidering it in whole or in part, not wishing to prevent the beneficial provisions of the bill from taking effect.

Consideration of the veto power invites us to reflect on further connections between the executive and Congress, particularly in terms of legislation. In Article II, Section 3, the president is compelled, "from time to time," to "give to the Congress information of the state of the union, and recommend to their Consideration such measures as he shall judge necessary and expedient." The first part of this clause has become the annual State of the Union Address, but the second part is often overlooked.

This second part imposes an obligation on the president to involve himself in the legislative process—in fact, to initiate the process when he deems it necessary or beneficial to the country. This provision points to the conclusion that the president's legislative power is not merely passive. The veto power is a negative, but the duty to recommend legislation gives the executive, in theory if not in practice, substantial legislative authority. The success that presidents will have in getting their proposals approved by Congress will obviously vary and will be affected by circumstances such as the party control of the various branches.

One cannot take it for granted that the president will be able to get his legislative proposals through a Congress dominated by the opposition party. But it is a further mark of executive leadership that he be able to muster congressional support for his policies and programs. One can think here of the success Ronald Reagan had in 1981 in getting his tax-cut program through a Congress divided along party lines. By using his energy and powers as president, he was able to persuade enough Democrats to provide the support he needed in the House of Representatives.

Executive Prerogative Power

Is there, in all republics, this inherent, and fatal weakness? Must a government, of necessity, be too *strong* for the liberties of its own people, or too *weak* to maintain its own existence?[10]

This quotation from Abraham Lincoln points to a common concern about executive power—whether the president is powerful enough to maintain the Constitution he is sworn to "preserve, protect, and defend." Or is he legally too weak to address real threats to the permanence of the American political order? This question requires a consideration of the nature of executive power and, in particular, whether the executive possesses anything like prerogative power.

Prerogative power, according to John Locke, is the power to act according to one's discretion, for the sake of the public good, "without the prescription of the Law, and sometimes even *against* it."[11] The issue at stake here is whether the president has the authority to act outside of or against the Constitution in the name of the public good. Prerogative power is not explicitly acknowledged in the Constitution.

Lincoln faced this issue at the outset of the Civil War. His actions, including the blockade of southern ports, the calling up of military troops, and the suspension of the writ of habeas corpus, are often used as the primary examples of executive power overreaching its constitutional boundaries. Lincoln's justification for his actions was twofold. On the one hand, he argued that he had not overstepped the boundaries of executive power in any of the actions he had undertaken. On the other hand, he suggests that even if he had, he would have been warranted in doing so, for they were pursued for the sake of the public good. In regard to the suspension of the writ of habeas corpus, for example, he noted that the Constitution does provide for such a step (in Article I, Section 9), but does not say what body has the power to suspend.

The second line of defense is more complicated, though, and certainly more contested. He defended his actions before Congress in the following terms:

> These measures, whether strictly legal or not, were ventured upon, under what appeared to be a popular demand, and a public necessity; trusting, then as now, that Congress would easily ratify them. It is believed that nothing has been done beyond the constitutional competency *of Congress.*[12]

Note here that Lincoln appears to be suggesting that his acts are constitutional acts, or are within the confines of governmental powers under the Constitution, though they are congressional powers. But in a later letter, his interpretation of those powers and their limits is more broadly circumscribed:

> By general law life *and* limb must be protected; yet often a limb must be amputated to save a life; but a life is never wisely given to save a limb. I felt that measures, otherwise unconstitutional, might become lawful, by becoming indispensable to the preservation of the constitution, through the preservation of the nation.[13]

Here Lincoln does not explicitly state that his actions were in any way unconstitutional, but he clearly suggests that even if they were, the principle of the preservation of the Constitution would have obviated any concern about the legality of the act. Does the Constitution provide all the powers necessary for its preservation? Or is the executive called upon, at times, to act beyond the Constitution in order to preserve the Constitution, or the Union? Two earlier instances of executive action may illuminate these questions. The first is Washington's Neutrality Proclamation of 1793 (concerning the war between France and England), promulgated without the prior approval of Congress. The controversy over the constitutionality of such a declaration was carried on most notably between Alexander Hamilton and James Madison. Their debate focused on the degree of power vested in the executive by the Constitution.

Hamilton, writing as Pacificus, defended Washington on the grounds that the broad wording of Article II allows for an expansive interpretation of executive powers. In this case, the proclamation was to be understood as falling within the power to regulate foreign affairs. Madison (Helvidius), on the other hand, considered the issuance of the proclamation to be an unconstitutional limitation on the power of Congress, because it foreclosed the possibility of Congress exercising its unquestioned power to declare war. So the essential difference between the two positions came down to distinct understandings of the nature of constitutional law, and the rules of construction one should employ in interpreting the document.

But the lesson learned from the proclamation controversy was somewhat limited, given the variant claims of constitutionality. The final example to be considered here, the Louisiana Purchase, puts the issue in starker terms. Thomas Jefferson himself asserted that he was clearly acting outside the boundaries of the Constitution in adding the territory to the United States. What makes this case most striking is that Jefferson, prior to his ascendancy to the office, had argued for a restrictive understanding of the powers of the government. For instance, he opposed the establishment of a national bank as a too expansive reading of the "necessary and proper" clause. As president, though, Jefferson approved the purchase of the Louisiana Territory, with full knowledge of the fact that the Constitution gave him no explicit power to undertake such a deed.

> The constitution has made no provision for our holding foreign territory, still less for incorporating foreign nations into our Union. The Executive in seizing the fugitive occurrence which so much

advances the good of their country, have done an act *beyond the Constitution*.[14]

The legislature, Jefferson goes on to note, must approve the appropriations for the purchase, and so it must appeal ultimately to the people for their sanction. A later remark by Jefferson expresses more fully his understanding of the connection between necessity and the law:

> A strict observance of written laws is doubtless *one* of the high duties of a good citizen, but it is not *the highest*. The laws of necessity, of self-preservation, of saving our country when in danger, are of higher obligation. To lose our country by a scrupulous adherence to the written law, would be to lose the law itself, with life, liberty, property and all those who are enjoying them with us; thus absurdly sacrificing the end to the means.[15]

It may very well be that his years in office taught Jefferson the lessons of executive power, and drove him to expand that authority. This decision, in Jefferson's view, was not justified merely on the basis of self-interest, but was grounded in the most fundamental duties of the executive. The principle set forth here is the same principle which Lincoln claimed was available to him in preserving the Union.

Jefferson's justification for his actions is the protection of "life, liberty, and property" as the ends of the law. The protection of these rights, put forth by the Declaration of Independence as the reason for which "Governments are instituted among Men," is what Jefferson takes as his guide in interpreting the powers of the executive under the Constitution. He looks beyond those powers to the ends of government itself. But such power seems to undermine the claim that the Constitution establishes a government of limited powers, and that any fundamental alterations in the constitutional arrangement can be undertaken only by the people, through the amendment process.

The critical question that arises concerning the exercise of prerogative power is whether there are any limits on the use of the power, and whether those limits can be effective. Critics of prerogative power would argue that its use constitutes a violation of the principles of the Constitution, and that there can be no effective controls over an executive who does not subordinate himself to the constitutional design. Defenders of executive prerogative contend that it is used only in extreme circumstances, it does not become the *principle* of executive power, and there are always remedies available to the people if they wish to employ them. Dissatisfaction with the executive's actions in any particular instance can be registered through impeachment by the Congress, defeat in the ensuing presidential election, or ultimately, by revolution, if the people conclude that their rights and liberties have been denied them.

Alexis de Tocqueville's assessment of the American presidency captures well the nature of the executive power:

> [It is] clear that we should not judge the practice of the government by the theory. The President of the United States possesses almost royal prerogative which he has no occasion to use, and the rights of which he has been able to make use so far are very circumscribed; the laws allow him to be strong, but circumstances have made him weak.[16]

The political and military prominence of the United States in the 1990s has clearly expanded the practical demands on the executive, and Tocqueville seems to have understood the latent powers of the office. The president is now called on to conduct policies that are broad-reaching and that affect relations with countries throughout the world. In the military and economic spheres the United States has become perhaps the most influential power, and the executive has been given the responsibility for the conduct of the country's affairs in almost every quarter. Along with that responsibility, though, has come an expansion in the powers of the executive, powers that Tocqueville saw as inherent in the nature of the office. Whether those powers extend beyond the limits of the Constitution is a matter that demands careful scrutiny. Attempts to limit the authority of the executive are a prominent part of the contemporary struggle between Congress and the president.

The Contemporary Presidency

The contemporary presidency has been most notably affected by the marked hostility between Congress and the president himself. The primary illustration of this tension can be found in the legislation passed in the 1970s (often over executive vetoes) aimed at restricting the authority of what came to be known as the "imperial presidency." Chief among those acts were the War Powers Resolution (1973), the Budget Control and Impoundment Act (1974), and the Ethics in Government Act (1978). What these acts all shared was the clear intent to legalize the relationship between the two branches, to turn policy differences into potentially indictable offenses. Here we will consider the War Powers Resolution, focusing on how this statute affects executive–congressional relations.

The War Powers Resolution, passed over Richard Nixon's veto in the fall of 1973, claims to be a delineation of the military powers of the president according to the Constitution. The resolution encompasses a comprehensive view toward the exercise of those powers. It restricts the number of instances in which the executive can introduce military troops. It requires that the president consult with Congress prior to the introduction of those troops, and report on their intended use. It limits the use of the troops to a sixty- or ninety-day period. And it allows for the possibility of Congress passing a resolution requiring the removal of the forces at any time.

The curious aspect of the War Powers Resolution is that, though it has been violated by every president since it was enacted, neither the resolution nor the president has ever been challenged in court.[17] The executive seems to have little incentive to challenge the constitutionality of the law, because it has been so regularly violated without serious repercussions. Congress, on the other hand, apparently finds it useful to have the law on the books, but not to test the executive's authority in a trial. Members of Congress can criticize the president for having violated it—and thereby undermine his authority—but never have to prove their case.

Criticism of the War Powers Resolution can be found among both defenders and detractors of an energetic executive. Defenders of a strong presidency see various provisions of the act as being unconstitutional restrictions on executive authority and as being unwise limitations on the foreign policy negotiations of the president. Critics of broad executive power, on the other hand, have argued that the resolution grants the president too much leeway. Because prior consultation is not an absolute necessity, the president can commit troops without Congress's approval. He then essentially has sixty—or ninety—days to do as he wishes, with little or no interference from Congress.

George Bush's handling of the Persian Gulf War is instructive on this matter. Bush introduced troops into Saudi Arabia in apparent contradiction of the requirements of the resolution (none of the conditions for committing troops had been met), though he did "consult" with Congress. He began ordering the troops out on August 8, 1990, but did not get full congressional approval until January 1991, well beyond the sixty-day limit imposed by the resolution. His actions at the outset of the involvement give an indication of what an effective president can do in the face of congressional opposition. But if the outcome had not been favorable, the assessment of his actions might also have been different.

The role of the "legislative veto," which the War Powers Resolution contains, must also be a significant factor in any assessment of the contemporary presidency. It serves as an indication of the interdepartmental struggles which have characterized recent administrations. The legislative veto, struck down as unconstitutional in *Immigration and Naturalization Service v. Chadha* (1983), is a tool used by Congress to exercise oversight of executive agencies (or, sometimes, of the president himself). The veto is generally contained in a bill through which Congress grants certain general powers to the executive, but retains for itself the authority to alter the decisions that are subsequently made within the executive branch. It is a relatively recent invention, and is especially connected with the modern proliferation of federal agencies carrying out the broad grants of power imparted to them by Congress.

The *Chadha* decision could have been quite dramatic, for some form of a legislative veto was to be found in more than two hundred acts dating back to the 1930s. But the ruling was disregarded by the legislature (and, in many instances, the executive). Since 1983 more than two hundred laws have been passed containing a legislative veto.

The significance of the legislative veto is found precisely in its ubiquitous nature. It has become an all-purpose instrument Congress can use to direct particular actions of particular agencies within the executive branch (the Immigration and Naturalization Service, for instance, is directly responsible to the attorney general). That direction is generally done in a nonpublic manner, so that policy changes are brought about without anyone taking responsibility for the alteration, and often without the change becoming a matter of public knowledge, as happened in the *Chadha* case. In this way, members of Congress can intervene in executive decisions, but without being held directly accountable for their actions. The result of these activities is that members of Congress are not forced to legislate by casting public votes on policy questions, because they can always exercise the authority they wish over specific policies or programs when they desire to do so.

One of the striking facts about the legislative veto is that Congress uses it to defend itself or to extend its powers. But the executive rarely, if ever, uses the veto for that purpose: to ward off incursions of the legislature into executive authority. It is the duty of the executive, as Publius has pointed out, to restrain the legislature in such matters by exercising his own authority in defiance of such "encroachments." The failure to do so results, inevitably, in a breakdown of the separation of powers, the consequences of which are a loss of the independence of the executive and an enfeebling of the rights of citizens. Evidence in support of this claim can be found in the refusal of President Reagan to veto the reauthorization of the Ethics in Government Act in both 1983 and 1987, though he was opposed to it on constitutional grounds. Reagan considered the act to be a violation of executive independence, especially in its provisions for the appointment of special prosecutors (or independent counsels), but *twice* signed the bill into law.

The failure to provide a vigorous defense of executive power served, in the end, to undermine Reagan's capacity to govern, for the independent counsel became a powerful congressional weapon, wielded against numerous executive branch officials in the latter years of the Reagan administration.[18] By contrast, Bush's threat to veto the bill in 1992 was partially responsible for its expiration.

Conclusion

Much attention has been given in recent years to the question of what has been called "divided government," because of the fact that the contemporary Congress has been controlled by the Democratic party, while the presidency has, for the past twenty-five years, been dominated by the Republicans.[19] Even when the Democratic party controlled both branches, there was anything but harmony between the two. This was particularly true of the Carter administration, and there were reminders of this in the early months of the Clinton administration. This situation suggests that there is more to the question of congressional–presidential relations than a simple consideration of party affiliation would explain.

The analysis of this issue would necessarily have to include an appraisal of the loss of party unity and influence over the past thirty years, an issue discussed above in connection with presidential elections. As the parties have lost much of their direct influence over the election process, so have they lost much of their authority over individual members of Congress. Congress itself has been characterized by a vast decentralization of authority, so that power is now in the hands not only of the top party leaders, but is dispersed also to committees and subcommittees and to committee staffs. There are still important ways in which the party can influence its members, such as through committee assignments, but they cannot command the kind of loyalty that they were able to in the past.

The fact that much of the legislation forwarded by contemporary presidents often does not garner the approval of Congress cannot be seen, then, as simply the result of party differences. There are, in addition to policy disagreements, important institutional struggles at the heart of the contemporary gridlock. These struggles have intensified with the increasing size and complexity of the modern administrative state, and with the increased federal spending and federal regulation that have characterized the U.S. government at least since the Great Society programs of the 1960s.

The fact the federal government is now involved in regulatory details unbeknown to past generations must certainly have an effect on the way that the branches operate, and particularly on the relations between the two. For instance, there is much more to be gained, or lost, in negotiations between the branches, or in compromise legislation, and that, coupled with the decline of the party influences on individual legislators, leads to the balkanization of American politics. The struggle between the branches is a struggle that involves the control of powerful policy-making agencies, interpretation and enforcement of an imposing array of statutes and regulations, a budget of over one and a half trillion dollars, and about two million employees.

Notes

1. Max Farrand, ed., *The Records of the Federal Convention of 1787* (New Haven: Yale University Press, 1966), I:65.
2. Theodore Roosevelt, *Letters*, Elting E. Morison, ed. (Cambridge: Harvard University Press, 1951–1954), 1:1087.
3. Letter to Henry Cabot Lodge, July 19, 1908, in *Selections from the Correspondence of Theodore Roosevelt and Henry Cabot Lodge, 1884–1918,*

Henry Cabot Lodge and Charles F. Redmond, eds. (New York: Scribner's, 1925), 2:304.

4. In choosing the president in this manner, each state delegation would be allowed one vote. The election process was altered by the Twelfth Amendment.

The House of Representatives has chosen the president twice, in 1800 and 1824. There have been three occasions in which the plurality winner in the popular election has lost the Electoral College vote—1824, 1876, and 1888.

5. The Electorial College, once it casts its votes, is immediately dissolved.

6. This is the account given by John Pickering of the report of Abraham Baldwin, a delegate from Georgia (in *Records*, Max Farrand, ed., 3:403).

7. J. D. Richardson, ed., *Compilation of the Messages and Papers of the Presidents*, (Washington, D.C.: 1908), 2:1144–45; quoted in Robert Remini, *Andrew Jackson and the Course of American Freedom* (New York: Harper and Row, 1981), 2:368.

8. Roy P. Basler, ed., *The Collected Works of Abraham Lincoln* (New Brunswick, N.J.: Rutgers University Press, 1953), 4:268. Consider, in this context, the following remark by Hamilton: "He who is to execute the laws must first *judge for himself* of their meaning" ("Pacificus No. 1," in *The Papers of Alexander Hamilton*, Harold C. Syrett, ed. [New York: Columbia University Press, 1969], 15:43; emphasis added).

9. Publius describes the utility of the veto in the following terms: "A power of this nature in the executive will often have a silent and unperceived, though forcible, operation. When men, engaged in unjustifiable pursuits, are aware that obstructions may come from a quarter which they cannot control, they will often be restrained by the bare apprehension of opposition from doing what they would with eagerness rush into if no such external impediments were to be feared" (*Federalist* 73).

Consider the similar remarks on the role of the judiciary in affecting potentially corruptive legislation: "It not only serves to moderate the immediate mischiefs of those which may have been passed but it operates as a check upon the legislative body in passing them; who, perceiving that obstacles to the success of an iniquitous intention are to be expected from the scruples of the courts, are in a manner compelled, by the very motives of the injustice they meditate, to qualify their attempts" (*Federalist* 78).

10. "Message to Congress in Special Session," July 4, 1861 (*Collected Works*, 4:426).

11. *Second Treatise*, Section 160; emphasis added.

12. "Message to Congress in Special Session" (*Collected Works*, 4:429; emphasis added).

13. Letter to Albert G. Hodges, April 4, 1864 (*Collected Works*, 7:281).

14. Letter to John C. Breckinridge, August 12, 1803 in *Thomas Jefferson: Writings*, Merrill D. Peterson, ed. (New York: Literary Classics of the United States, Inc., Library of America, 1984), 1138–39; emphasis added.

15. Letter to John B. Colvin, September 20, 1810 *(Writings,* 1231).

16. *Democracy in America,* trans. George Lawrence (New York: Doubleday, 1969), p. 126.

17. There was an abortive attempt at challenging the authority of George Bush during the troop buildup prior to Desert Storm.

18. The Supreme Court upheld the constitutionality of the Ethics in Government Act in *Morrison v. Olson,* 487 U.S. 654 (1988).

19. See, for example, Morris Fiorina, *Divided Government* (New York: Macmillan, 1992).

Suggested Reading

Ceaser, James W. *Presidential Selection.* Princeton: Princeton University Press, 1979.

Eastland, Terry. *Energy in the Executive: The Case for the Strong Presidency.* New York: Free Press, 1992.

Mansfield, Harvey C., Jr. *Taming the Prince: The Ambivalence of Modern Executive Power.* New York: Free Press, 1989.

Neustadt, Richard. *Presidential Power and the Modern Presidents: The Politics of Leadership.* New York: Free Press, 1990.

Thach, Charles C., Jr. *The Creation of the Presidency, 1775–1789: A Study in Constitutional History.* Baltimore: Johns Hopkins University Press, 1923.

12

War Power and the Constitution:
Chaining the Dog of War

L. Peter Schultz

I have chosen to discuss the war power for a couple of reasons, which I will sum up as follows: It seems relevant and timely given recent events, for example, Desert Storm in 1991. The war power is, I think, one of the most interesting parts of the Constitution and one that requires reconsideration. It is all too common for those who claim to practice a jurisprudence of "original intent" to co-opt this field, to occupy the "high ground," as it were, and to carry the battle that often rages over the meaning of the war power clauses in the Constitution.

But before we can consider the war power directly, it is necessary to say a few words about interpreting and understanding the Constitution. Interpreting and understanding the Constitution is deceptively difficult, a fact too often overlooked by both sides of the current debate about the meaning of the Constitution. On the one hand, there are those like Justice William Brennan who believe that interpreting the Constitution requires little more than determining current notions of "dignity" and using them to fill in the "blank spaces" or the "great generalities" in the Constitution. On the other hand, there are those like former Attorney General Edwin Meese who believe that we need only read the Constitution as the Framers wrote and intended it in order to properly interpret and understand the Constitution.

But there are a couple of reasons why interpreting and understanding the Constitution is not as easy as either of these camps suggests. First, the Constitution is more than two hundred years old and, second, it is "ours." With regard to the age of the Constitution, because it has been around for so long we tend to think that we should be able to understand it easily. After all, it was written in simpler times, so we like to think. Second, we think we can understand it as easily as we understand baseball, football, or any other activity considered to be an American pastime. Nonetheless, it is often more difficult to understand the Constitution than we imagine.

Let me give you a couple of examples by way of questions to illustrate what I mean. First, under the Constitution as written, in how many ways could a person become president? Second, when was the phrase "judicial review" first used? Now let me tell you the answers before continuing with a discussion of the war power. Under the original Constitution there was only one way to become president—to be selected for that office by what we call the Electoral College (although it was never called that by its creators) in a presidential election. If you do not believe me, just look at the first sentence of the Twenty-fifth Amendment which specifically amends the Constitution to provide that upon the death, resignation, or removal of the president, the vice president shall *become* president. It says: "In case of the removal of the President from office or his death or resignation, the Vice President shall *become* President" [emphasis added]. If the original Constitution had provided for the vice president to become president, why would this part of the Twenty-fifth Amendment have been necessary?

Second, the phrase "judicial review" was first used, contrary to all expectations, in the early part of the twentieth century by Edward S. Corwin. Surprisingly for many, Chief Justice John Marshall, the man credited with creating or at least with implementing judicial review, never used that phrase in *Marbury v. Madison* or in other places where you might expect to find it.

My examples are intended to illustrate two phenomena that adversely influence our ability to understand the Constitution. First, our thinking about the Constitution is influenced by practices long continued, even though these practices are constitutionally suspect. From the language of the Constitution, as well as from James Madison's notes from the Constitutional Convention, there can be little doubt that the Framers did not intend the vice president to legally succeed to the presidency when that office became vacant because of death, resignation, or removal. But because vice presidents have succeeded to that office ever since John Tyler succeeded to the presidency upon the death of President William Henry Harrison, we think this is what the Constitution says. Of course,

this influences how we understand that document and the government it creates. Let this fact—that the only way to become president was to be selected for that office—rattle around in your head
for a while and you will, I think, see what I mean.

Second, we often use words not used by the Constitution's Framers
and with significant impact. Take, for example, the phrase "judicial review," which may be distinguished from the phrase "constitutional interpretation." I often ask my constitutional law students:
"Who can do 'judicial review'?" And they know: "The courts." But
who can do "constitutional interpretation"? Anyone can—legislators, presidents, and even you and I. By speaking of judicial review, we imply that because only courts should interpret and determine the meaning of the Constitution, the courts, and especially
the Supreme Court, are the *sole* guardians of the Constitution. But
it is far from clear that the Framers of the Constitution, or even
Chief Justice John Marshall, thought about the Constitution this way.

Today, we use terminology that the Framers of the Constitution
never used. This terminology should alert us to the possibility that
we have a different understanding of the document than its Framers had. It is then necessary—but not easy—to get back to the original
Constitution or, as Jim Morrison of the Doors might say, "break on
through to the other side."

One more example relevant to my topic: In the midst of a heated
discussion about the Desert Storm operation with a colleague, I
asserted that Alexander Hamilton argued in his "Pacificus" papers
that it was the responsibility of the president to preserve the peace
of the nation and that only Congress could take the nation to war.
My assertion was met, as I expected, with disbelief. After all, I
had cited Hamilton, not Madison, Thomas Jefferson, or even William Howard Taft. As everyone knows, Hamilton was pro-executive. So we tend to think that, like many pro-executive types today,
Hamilton could not and would not have held such a view. I later
produced the passage I had in mind from Pacificus:

> While, therefore, the legislature alone can declare war, can alone
> actually transfer the nation from a state of peace to a state of hos-
> tilities, it belongs to the "executive power" to do whatever else the
> laws of nations, cooperating with the treaties of the country, enjoin
> in the intercourse of the United States with foreign powers.
>
> In this distribution of authority, the wisdom of the our Constitu-
> tion is manifested. It is the province and duty of the executive to
> preserve to the nation the blessings of peace. The legislature alone
> can interrupt them by placing the nation in a state of war.

It is fair to say that my colleague's surprise was not, in itself, surprising. Many familiar with *The Federalist* and Hamilton's arguments therein on the executive power would share that surprise. Because Hamilton was pro-executive, he may be said to have defended executive prerogative, and he was clearly a proponent of a vigorous and energetic executive. The first paragraph in *Federalist* 70, where Hamilton calls our attention to the similarities between the executive power and the Roman practice of relying on dictators, is one of *The Federalist*'s most interesting passages.

But our understanding of the executive power is, I think, different from Hamilton's, a fact that often escapes our attention because we have different concerns than Hamilton had. In other words, the contemporary debate about executive power is simply not the same debate that took place in 1787 during George Washington's administration. For example, the debate in 1787 was more often about the "executive power" whereas today it is about "presidential power," a subtle but important difference which owes much to the writings of Woodrow Wilson and the presidential politics of Theodore Roosevelt. However, the "executive department" is composed of two different parts, the presidency and the bureaucracy, as we call it today.

The Framers of the Constitution, and certainly Hamilton, were more aware of this fact than we are when the presidency is called "the executive." So when we enlist Hamilton as an ally in *our* debate, we should be careful not to overlook the differences between his understanding of the Constitution and our own. All too often, when we rely on Hamilton to settle issues that concern us today, we distort his arguments just as we distort the jurisprudence of Marshall by labeling him either an "activist" or a "restraintist." Although Marshall didn't use the phrase "judicial review," notions of "activism" and "restraint" are intimately connected with judicial review. And just as Marshall was neither an activist nor a restraintist, so too Hamilton should not be made into an advocate of the modern presidency, the imperial presidency, or the rhetorical presidency, just as surely as he should not be made into an advocate of a narrow or legalistic understanding of executive power.

The War Power and the Constitution

How can we make sense of Hamilton's argument in his Pacificus essays? More broadly, how can we make sense of the war power clauses in the Constitution in order to square them with the interpretation offered by Hamilton in those essays?

That Hamilton signed himself Pacificus is a fact of some importance because it alerts us to the possibility that he was as concerned with "chaining the dog of war" as he was with empowering the new government to wage war. Of course, many today emphasize, and correctly, that Hamilton and the Framers more generally were proponents of a powerful government, of a government that could protect national security. This is all too true. As Hamilton wrote in *Federalist* 23:

> The authorities essential to the common defense are these: to raise armies; to build and equip fleets; to prescribe rules for the government of both; to direct their operations; to provide for their support. These powers ought to exist without limitation, *because it is impossible to foresee or to define the extent and variety of national exigencies, and to the correspondent extent and variety of the means which may be necessary to satisfy them.* The circumstances that endanger the safety of nations are infinite, and for this reason no constitutional shackles can wisely be imposed on the power to which the care of it is committed.

On the other hand, it also needs emphasis that the Framers were concerned with "pacifying" political life even while they equipped their new government with the power needed to meet unforeseen exigencies. Pacification was necessary because the Framers were aware of a tendency in human affairs toward war, an awareness seen throughout *The Federalist*. For example, it is evident in *Federalist* 9, where Hamilton paints the gloomiest of pictures of the ancient republics of Greece and Italy. In *Federalist* 6, Hamilton also tells us that "The causes of hostility among nations are innumerable," that even commercial nations are and will be prone to war. As he wrote there:

> Sparta, Athens, Rome, and Carthage were all republics; two of them, Athens and Carthage, of the commercial kind. Yet were they as often engaged in wars, offensive and defensive, as the neighboring monarchies of the same times. Sparta was little better than a well-regulated camp; and Rome was never sated of carnage and conquest.

Of course, Hamilton even argued that modern commercial nations would often engage in war, a view at odds with Montesquieu's more sanguine view that commerce alone could pacify the world. And that this tendency toward war might affect the new republic is evident also from Madison's defense of a "well-constructed Senate," which would provide, among other qualities, "a due sense of national character." As he wrote in *Federalist* 63:

> Without a select and stable member of the government, the esteem of foreign powers will not only be forfeited by an unenlightened and variable policy, proceeding from causes already mentioned, but the national councils will not possess that sensibility to the opinion of the world which is perhaps not less necessary in order to merit than it is to obtain its respect and confidence.

Madison sought then to make the new republic "sensitive" to "the opinion of the world." A world, I remind you, that was overwhelmingly monarchical *and* hostile to the new republic. Despite this monarchical and hostile environment, nonetheless, he feared a republic blind to world opinion, one that might adopt a hostile stance toward that world. A parochial republicanism, perhaps eventuating in a spirited and warlike foreign policy, was not then beyond the parameters of Madison's and Hamilton's concerns. "Chaining the dog of war" may be taken then as one important concern of those who framed the Constitution, even of men like Hamilton who were quite willing to invest the new government with enough power to meet unforeseen circumstances.

Institutional Checks and Balances

If we can accept this argument, the question then is: How did the Framers try to chain the dog of war? First, it should be evident that they did *not* do so by withholding a part of the war power or granting this power in a narrow or niggardly fashion. The war power, like the commerce power, is broad and comprehensive. It is, as Chief Justice Charles Evans Hughes once said, not only the power to wage war but the power to wage war successfully. As such, it is difficult to establish any constitutional limitations on this power, as the case of *Korematsu v. United States* (1944) aptly illustrates.

In *Korematsu*, the Supreme Court upheld the constitutionality of the government's policy of interring all persons of Japanese descent long after the attack on Pearl Harbor. The case has earned the opprobrium of most scholars and lawyers and with good reason. For if the government could inter those who did nothing criminal just because they were of Japanese ancestry—including, I remind you, American citizens of such ancestry (Korematsu's first name was "Fred")—then is there anything the government could not do to win a war? It is difficult to imagine a greater invasion of the rights and privileges of persons and citizens residing within the United States than the policy the government used to deal with persons of Japanese descent during World War II. And yet I must say that on the question of constitutionality of the government's policy, as opposed to its necessity, I find it difficult not to agree with the majority in *Korematsu*. As Hamilton wrote in *Federalist* 23, "This power [over the common defense] ought to be coextensive with all possible combinations of such circumstances. . . ."

So without withholding power, in order to chain the dog of war the Framers relied, I think, on the separation of powers. By virtue of the separation of powers, the Constitution divides the war power between Congress and the executive. Whatever the exact terms of this division—and we will never decide them once and for all— by virtue of this separation neither department can claim the war power as its own. Neither Congress nor the president can take the nation to war without defending to the other department the necessity for going to war. This separation means, then, that going to war will be treated as a prudential and not as a formal question. Neither the president nor the Congress can claim the war power as its own, to be used unilaterally as it thinks best. And as a result, each decision must be made as "necessity" dictates, and each war must be justified as necessary. When a president or a Congress claims the right to take the nation to war unilaterally, the prudence required by the Constitution is short-circuited.

To be sure, the president possesses important prerogatives with regard to war, as recent events illustrate. But in order to understand these prerogatives and the purposes they were intended to serve, it is crucial to remember that the Senate under the original constitutional scheme was part of the executive. For example, the Senate's advice and consent were necessary for the president to make appointments and treaties. Indeed, in *Federalist* 77, Hamilton argued that the Senate's approval would be necessary for removing executive officials as well as for appointing them. Hamilton's language in that context bears quoting:

The consent of [the Senate] would be necessary to displace as well as to appoint. A change of the chief magistrate therefore would not occasion so violent or so general a revolution in the officers of the government, as might be expected if [the president] were the sole dispenser of offices.

Of course, Hamilton's argument was rejected by the First Congress. But obviously Hamilton prized stability in government, particularly bureaucratic stability. "Stability" is not necessarily "pacification," but it certainly points in that direction with regard to foreign affairs, as we noticed in Madison's argument in *Federalist* 63. Thus, by making the Senate a part of the executive, the Framers sought to give ballast to the new republic—to give it, in Hamilton's words, "greater permanency" and to make it "less subject to inconstancy." So when it is said that the executive department possesses certain prerogatives regarding foreign affairs and war, it should be remembered that these prerogatives were granted to "stabilize," as well as to "energize," the new government. And to say that the executive department has important prerogatives is not, or was not, the same as saying that the president can take the nation to war unilaterally, without the consent of Congress or of the Senate.

Civilian Supremacy

Second, the Constitution relies on the principle of civilian supremacy to chain the dog of war. By making the president the commander-in-chief of the nation's armed forces, the Constitution does more than "unify" military command. It subjects or subordinates the military to the command of a civilian who is not "in" the military, but who is "outside of" and "apart from" the military. The president's office of commander-in-chief requires him to govern the military, not be governed by it. At the very least, this means that the president must act on more than mere military considerations. He should assess each war and each military action from a perspective that transcends a simply military perspective. General Norman Schwarzkopf was reminded of this fact during Desert Storm when he publicly suggested, and was just as publicly rebuked for suggesting, that President Bush had erred in not letting him "finish the job" in Iraq. Under the principle of civilian supremacy, it is not the function of the military to define the objectives of any given military action. This is left to civilians, most especially to the president who is expected to act and think like a civilian even while commanding the military.

Taming the War Power

So while the Constitution grants the government a broad and comprehensive war power, it also tries to tame the war power to ensure that it will be used with restraint. As we have seen, the use of this power should be governed by "necessity" as determined by civilians consulting our interests, including our interest in meriting the good opinion of other nations and other peoples. The war power granted by the Constitution is indeed great, but it also is constrained, or tamed, in order to prevent the possibility that like other republics, both ancient and modern, the new republic would be led to war by "The love of power or the desire of pre-eminence and dominion," or by "the jealousy of power, or the desire of equality and safety" (Hamilton, *Federalist* 6). The Constitution equips the new republic to wage war successfully. But, unlike ancient republics and more revolutionary modern republics, it would wage war only when it had to. Although the new republic was not "pacifistic," it would be "pacified."

Assessing the Constitution's Institutional Arrangements

What can be said of the Constitution's attempt to chain the dog of war? Has its institutional arrangements proved adequate in practice, or has practice proved them insufficient? Without intending to argue that the Constitution is radically defective, I suggest that practice has proved the document's institutional arrangements to be insufficient for restraining the dog of war. As evidence that such a view might be held by reasonable and eminently respectable people, I offer two speeches given by two different presidents, separated by more than a hundred years, both of whom were famous generals, George Washington and Dwight David Eisenhower.

George Washington's Farewell Address is generally agreed to be one of the most justly celebrated speeches ever given by a president. In it he spoke against two dangers. First, he warned of a turbulent kind of republicanism that reflected and fostered a virulent party spirit inconsistent with "domestic tranquillity." Second, he warned of a foreign policy that would unduly and unwisely "entangle" the new republic in world affairs. Now it is reasonable to argue that these two dangers were linked in Washington's mind because he feared that some forms of republicanism, for example, that advocated by Jefferson and his followers, would unnecessarily and dangerously entangle the new republic in world affairs.

A spirited republicanism, driven by a desire to universalize republican principles or to "energize" republicanism at home, would lead the new nation into an unduly warlike foreign policy, without giving due consideration to the "interests" of the new republic. Most generally put, Washington's Farewell Address may reflect his fear that the institutional arrangements of the Constitution would be insufficient to chain the dog of war in the face of what he perceived to be a spirited and warlike republicanism. In this light the Farewell Address can be understood as Washington's attempt to supplement the Constitution's institutional arrangements by lending his name and stature to a foreign policy of "detachment." As Washington said there: "'Tis our true policy to steer clear of permanent alliances, with any portion of the world" and "to keep ourselves, by suitable establishments, in a respectable defensive posture. . . ."

The second speech I have in mind is Dwight David Eisenhower's Farewell Address, in which he warned the nation of "the military-industrial complex." As Eisenhower said then:

> This conjunction of an immense military establishment and a large arms industry is new in the American experience. The total influence—economic, political, even spiritual—is felt in every city, every state house, every office of the federal government. We recognize the imperative need for this development. Yet we must not fail to comprehend its grave implications. Our total resources and livelihood are all involved; so is the very structure of our society. In the councils of government we must guard against the acquisition of unwarranted influence, whether sought or unsought, by the military-industrial complex. The potential for the disastrous rise of misplaced power exists and will persist . . . We should take nothing for granted. Only an alert and knowledgeable citizenry can compel the proper meshing of the huge industrial and military machinery of defense with our peaceful methods and goals, so that security and liberty may prosper together.

Of course, to warn the nation of the power of the military-industrial complex is different from arguing that republicanism is likely to become rabid, virulent, and warlike, as Washington argued. Apparently, though, like Washington before him, Eisenhower thought that this republic was not immune to the virus of militarism even though he traced that virus to twentieth-century sources that were different from those in Washington's eighteenth century.

Need we have similar concerns today? Ultimately, you will have to decide this for yourself. Let me only point out that throughout American history, doctrines have been enunciated whose purposes or results were to animate, if not militarize, U.S. foreign policy. There was, in the 1830s and 1840s, the doctrine of Manifest Destiny, which held that it was the destiny of the United States to expand and fill the continent.

After the Civil War, there were arguments that wars should be fought to develop patriotism and civic spiritedness, as well as to advance the cause of European civilization (Theodore Roosevelt and others). Woodrow Wilson defended our participation in World War I as a noble attempt to "make the world safe for democracy," while most presidents after World War II sought to contain communism, and, most recently, George Bush declared his desire to "create a new world order." The presidency and American foreign policy today have been greatly influenced by what might be called progressive liberalism, a liberalism that values leadership of a popular variety and that expects this leadership to remake the world in the image of the United States. In sum, we might say that the danger perceived by the Framers of the Constitution and by George Washington—that republics, even commercial republics, too often pursue a warlike foreign policy—is not a danger to which the United States has always been immune.

In the aftermath of Desert Storm, the military-industrial complex looks much different than it did in the 1960s and 1970s, especially after the debacle in Vietnam. And there is a resurgent patriotism abroad in the land, a Top Gun kind of mentality, which coincides with the idea that we are at a "pivotal moment in history," that a "window of opportunity" has opened through which we can see a new world order. Indeed, it seemed that we might reach this new world order, if only we were suitably "impetuous" and "bold."

In light of these circumstances, I find it gratifying that the Framers, in constructing their new republic, sought to tame that spiritedness that too often afflicts republican governments. Spiritedness is dangerous insofar as it is not tamed or ruled by prudence. A spirited politics, although often presented to us as noble, is dangerous insofar as it rules and is not ruled by prudence. To put this in contemporary terms, it is not clear that a republicanism which seeks to remake the world, reinforced by an apparently invincible military-industrial complex, is compatible with that "kinder and gentler nation" which President Bush spoke of at the Republican National Convention in 1988. In their own way, the Framers were aware of this problem. So even if we cannot say that the institutions they designed to chain the dog of war have been unqualifiedly successful, even if we still must look for ways to reinforce the work of the Framers, we should surely start with them and make use of their counsels and "the wisdom of our Constitution" in assessing where we are and where we would like to be.

Suggested Reading

George Washington, The Farewell Address.
Dwight David Eisenhower, The Farewell Address.
The Federalist, 6, 9, 63, 70, 77.

13

Presidential Elections and Voting

Sidney A. Pearson Jr.

Presidential elections are usually the most visible, often the most amusing, frequently the most puzzling, and occasionally among the more important domestic political events in the life of the nation. Trying to interpret them has become a full-time occupation for journalists, professors, theologians, and other assorted pundits in recent years. The American electoral system is complex, perhaps the most complex of any democratic regime, but it is not a random, irrational system. Presidential elections are part of the logic of the original constitutional design.

The complexity of presidential elections derives largely from the Founders' understanding of a representative democracy. One of the purposes of government was, and is, to protect the natural rights of its citizens. But all forms of government, democracy included, have a natural tendency to usurp their rightful function and become tyrannies. To guard against this danger required the interaction of two fundamental principles of free government: the separation of powers and periodic elections. Both of these devices were essential. As James Madison argued, the separation of powers was a necessary auxiliary precaution, but elections were to be the primary control on the abuses of government (*Federalist* 51).

In order for elections to perform their proper institutional function, they would have to accomplish six distinct but interrelated goals: (1) promote able leadership, (2) maintain the separation of powers, (3) provide a reasonable amount of choice among candidates, (4) decisively choose a single candidate, (5) control the natural, but potentially dangerous, ambition of candidates for the office, and (6) provide a legitimate succession to the office of president. Any one of these goals would be difficult enough to accomplish. Holding all six together simultaneously required extraordinary political balance.

While the Founders were sensitive to formal institutional arrangements of presidential selection, the act of voting itself was thought to be comparatively simple. They assumed that citizens would vote their passions, interests, and opinions (*Federalist* 10 and 51). Beyond a few cursory remarks, they did not have very much to say about the vote as an independent part of the process. They worried about factions, demagoguery, and private ambition overwhelming constitutional liberties. But they generally took it for granted that periodic elections, combined with the rest of the constitutional order, would be sufficient to preserve a free government.

The procedural aspects of voting proved to be more complex than many of the Founders originally imagined. The reason was that the act of voting itself has often been more important to the general strategic environment of presidential selection than they first thought. That environment includes the formal constitutional rules, but also includes the behavior of the voters themselves that may be independent of formal institutions. How the popular vote is organized and directed before the election has proved to be as important as the way the vote is formally recorded on election day. But whereas the constitutional rules of presidential elections have remained fairly constant, the strategic environment in which voters are mobilized has been subject to continual change almost since the founding itself.

The Constitutional Rules
for Presidential Selection

The president is elected to a four-year term of office by an *electoral college*, not by a direct popular vote. The electoral votes in each state are cast by electors who are selected by the state under provisions of Article II, Section 1 of the Constitution. The electoral vote of a state is determined by adding the number of representatives to the number of senators. Because each state is guaranteed two senators and at least one representative, each state will have a minimum of three electoral votes, regardless of population. The only exception is the District of Columbia, which acquired the right to vote in presidential elections with the ratification of the Twenty-third Amendment in 1961. The combined electoral vote in a presidential election is 538—435 representatives, 100 senators, and 3 votes from the District of Columbia.

In forty-eight of the fifty states, the electoral vote of the state is determined by a *plurality* of the popular vote. The state electors are chosen on a statewide ballot. The candidate who receives the most votes, even if less than a majority, receives *all* of the electoral vote of that state. So the Electoral College vote is for the most part a *winner-take-all* system. There is no reward for placing second in the popular vote.

The exceptions to this pattern are Maine and Nebraska. Since 1967 for Maine and 1991 for Nebraska, both states choose one elector from each congressional district on a district by district ballot. In addition, two electors are chosen on a statewide ballot and would presumably vote for the plurality winner in the state.

The consequences of this winner-take-all system are reflected in the 1992 election returns. Democratic candidate Bill Clinton received about 43 percent of the popular vote but carried a plurality or majority of 32 states and received 370 electoral votes. He received 50 percent or more of the vote in only three states plus the District of Columbia. Republican incumbent George Bush received about 38 percent of the popular vote and 168 electoral votes. He received 50 percent of the vote in only one state. Independent candidate H. Ross Perot received about 19 percent of the popular vote. But because he did not carry a plurality of the popular vote in any state, he failed to receive any electoral votes.

The Constitution allows each state to decide independently how it will select its electors. Electors may not be persons holding an office of trust or confidence under the United States. The electors are formally chosen on election day, the first Tuesday after the first Monday in November, by the voters in each state. About six weeks later the electors assemble in their respective state capitals and cast one vote each for president and vice president. In casting their ballot the electors are not necessarily bound to vote the way the voters instructed them to vote. Twenty-six states have no requirements of any sort that bind the vote of the electors. Nineteen states have laws requiring electors to vote as instructed by the voters, but have no penalties for enforcing the law. Five states stipulate modest fines for the *faithless* elector. To date, however, none of the penalties has ever been invoked.

There is no constitutional requirement that the electors vote for someone who is officially on the ballot or in any particular order in which names appear on the ballot. In 1988 Democratic presidential candidate Michael Dukakis and vice presidential candidate Lloyd Bentsen carried the state of West Virginia. But when the West Virginia electors met to cast their six electoral votes, one elector voted for Bentsen for president and Dukakis for vice president. From 1789 through 1992 there were only nine electors out of more than 17,000 chosen who violated their pledge. No election outcome has ever been changed by the vote of a faithless elector.

The electoral votes are officially counted by the president of the Senate before a joint session of Congress in January. Then, according to the Twelfth Amendment (1804), "The person having the greatest number of votes for President, shall be President, *if such number be a majority of the whole number of Electors appointed*" (italics mine). The vice president is also chosen by the greatest number of electoral votes, if such number be a majority. But what happens if no one receives a majority of the electoral vote?

If the Electoral College vote does not produce a winner, the president and vice president are elected by Congress. The top *three* candidates in electoral votes are placed before the House. The House then chooses the president with *each state* having a single vote. How each state delegation will determine its single vote is unspecified. A *majority* of states, 26 votes, are necessary to choose the president. The vice president is chosen by majority vote in the Senate with *each senator* having a single vote. There have been only two disputed elections since the adoption of the Twelfth Amendment that could have resulted in the House deciding the presidential election. It is unclear how much precedent they set if the Congress should again be called upon to choose a president.

Following the 1824 election, in which no candidate received a majority of the electoral vote, the House chose John Quincy Adams as president. The 1876 election between Republican candidate Rutherford B. Hayes and Democratic candidate Samuel J. Tilden was also disputed, but was not resolved in the House. Rather, a special Electoral Commission was established to decide how to count state electoral votes that were being disputed by the opposing candidates. In the compromise that resulted from the Electoral Commission, Hayes won the disputed electoral votes and became president even though he lost the popular vote and initially lost the electoral vote as well. In 1887, Congress changed the procedure for counting disputed electoral votes and the specific problems of 1876 are unlikely to be repeated. Final authority for determining the validity of electoral votes now resides with each state. Congress can overturn a state certification of electoral votes only with a concurrent majority in both houses.

Problems with the Electoral College System

There are few aspects of the American constitutional system that have been as frequently criticized as the Electoral College. Yet for the founding generation, Federalists and Anti-Federalists alike, the Electoral College seemed to be one of the least controversial features of the proposed constitution. Alexander Hamilton wrote in defense of the Electoral College that "This process of election affords a moral certainty, that the office of President will never fall to the lot of any man who is not in an eminent degree endowed with the requisite qualifications" (*Federalist* 68).

The Founders designed the Electoral College for what we would today call a *nonpartisan* system of presidential selection. The idea behind it was that the president would be "above parties" and chosen not because of partisan politics, which implied a potentially dangerous ambition, but because of a demonstrated record of public service: The office would seek the man rather than the man seek the office. The Electoral College would function more or less as a deliberative body, much like Congress, to elect the best man to the office. Independent electors would vote for the most able candidate among the numerous choices that were expected to be available in each election.

The Electoral College was originally designed to choose a president only. The vice president was to be the presidential candidate who received the second highest electoral vote total. Each elector would cast *two* votes for two different presidential candidates: in effect, a first and second choice from among able candidates. The presidential candidate who came in second would get the second-place prize—the vice presidency (a prize more than one vice president has regarded as akin to a booby prize). But partisanship changed the significance of these informal calculations. The idea of a president above party factions proved to be unrealistic in the real world of democratic politics.

In the election of 1796, both John Adams and Thomas Jefferson tried to craft a strategy that would have amounted to a partisan competition for the offices of both president and vice president simultaneously. The idea of the president as an initiator of public policy, latent during the ratification debates, emerged as a dominant issue of presidential elections before the end of Washington's second term. It was evident that the question of able leadership was more than one of administrative competence alone. It was also associated with specific policy choices. Contrary to both their strategies, Jefferson finished second to Adams in the Electoral College and subsequently chaffed for four years as vice president in an administration whose policies he deplored. A combination of policy and personalities quickly undermined the notion that presidential selection would, somehow, be "above politics."

As a consequence of this bitter experience, both Jefferson and Adams repeated the strategy of 1796 the second time they faced each other for the presidency (1800), but this time with more success. They each presented a party ticket for president and vice president. Jefferson paired with Aaron Burr of New York and Adams paired with Charles Cotesworth Pinckney of South Carolina. The success of this strategy required that electors commit in advance to one ticket or another. The notion of the independent elector voting for "the best man" was one of the first political casualties of partisan competition for the presidency.

The Jefferson–Adams strategy in the election of 1800 was logical given the original rules of the Electoral College. Each elector would cast *two* votes for both the president and the vice president. Because both votes would be known in advance and would be for a unified "ticket," a single party would control the office of both president and vice president. The opposition would come in third in the Electoral College and return home, possibly to write their long-awaited memoirs, while the winners got to be president and vice president respectively. The executive branch would no longer be divided by partisan bickering between two men who had been candidates for the same office, such as that of Adams and Jefferson after the election of 1796. The plan was only almost flawless.

The Jeffersonian half of the plan worked in the sense that he and Burr got most of the electoral votes. Adams came in third with 65 electoral votes. Pinckney was fourth with 64 electoral votes because one elector cast an odd vote for yet another candidate. But Jefferson and Burr tied with 73 electoral votes each. In such cases the House was to select the president from among the three candidates with the highest number of electoral votes. What complicated the matter was Burr's own personal ambitions. Under the formal rules of the Electoral College, Burr had the same legitimate claim to be president as did Jefferson and he pressed those claims in the House voting. After 36 ballots the deadlock was broken when Hamilton used his influence to persuade the opponents of Jefferson to abstain from voting, thus giving Jefferson the election.

This practical compromise did not, however, entirely resolve all of the issues to the satisfaction of each party involved. The separation of powers doctrine had been breached on the question of presidential selection. And the personal ambition of contending candidates reached alarming proportions. Burr never forgave Hamilton, his longtime foe in New York politics: in 1804 he shot and killed Hamilton in a duel in New Jersey. Fortunately for future presidential candidates who were less than crack shots, the formal rules of presidential selection were altered with the adoption of the Twelfth Amendment in 1804.

Under the provisions of the Twelfth Amendment electors would cast a *single* vote for president and a separate *single* vote for vice president. The intention was to eliminate confusion in the Electoral College over who was supposed to hold which office and thus resolve the problems of decisiveness and legitimacy. They succeeded in solving the problem of legitimacy. After the election of 1800 the question of which candidate has been elected to which office has never been in doubt. But the Amendment did not resolve problems that might arise if no one received a majority of electoral votes in the first place. The election in 1824 remains the only one decided under the provisions of the Twelfth Amendment.

In 1824 four major candidates split the electoral vote with no one receiving the necessary majority to win in the Electoral College. All of the electoral votes and most of the popular votes were divided among Andrew Jackson (99 electoral votes, 44 percent popular vote), John Quincy Adams (84 electoral votes, 30 percent popular vote), William H. Crawford (41 electoral votes, 12.5 percent popular vote), and Henry Clay (37 electoral votes, 13.2 percent popular vote). And because only the top three *electoral* vote winners could be considered, Clay was eliminated at the outset even though he received the third highest *popular* vote total. As speaker of the House, Clay had every reason to believe that in a House-decided election, such as 1800, he would be elected president in a three-way vote among himself, Jackson, and Adams. But the Twelfth

Amendment precluded his consideration in the first place. In the backroom dealing that took place, Adams emerged as president, and Clay got to be secretary of state (a post he thought was the sure route to the presidency).

For a second time since the adoption of the Constitution, the Electoral College had failed to produce a decisive winner. It seemed at the time as if House-decided elections would be more commonplace than was originally thought prudent. And with House-decided elections of the president, the entire logic of the constitutional separation of powers was in jeopardy of being undermined. Candidates for the presidency would be dependent on legislative opinion rather than on public opinion for election.

The formal rules had been changed in the Twelfth Amendment. But these rules did not deal with the problem of decisiveness in the event of multiple candidates who split the electoral vote between them. The Electoral College could be decisive only if the choice of presidential candidates was narrowed down to *two* major candidates prior to the election. A solution had to be crafted that understood the institutional problems as well as the candidate-centered problems that were involved in 1824.

The Founders had designed a system whereby "ambition would check ambition," but now ambition was helping to wreck the formal institutional arrangements. A way out of this dilemma had to be found that could (1) preserve the constitutional architecture of the Founders and (2) control the effects of ambitious politicians seeking the office of chief executive. The way out was a change in the extraconstitutional rules of presidential selection.

Extraconstitutional Rules in Presidential Elections

The most important variables in the strategic environment of the electoral process are the effects of the two-party system. Since the "invention" of modern political parties in the era of Andrew Jackson, parties have provided the basic means by which voters are linked to elected officials. Parties have, at least until recently, helped to preserve the original constitutional architecture and to control the ambition of presidential candidates. They have also had the effect of narrowing the effective choice of candidates to two.

One of the most important functions of parties in the electoral process is to help build coalitions of voters *before* election day. Only if a majority coalition is formed before election day can we be reasonably assured that the Electoral College will function decisively to chose a president. If such a coalition is not built before the election, the experience of 1824 could easily have become the common electoral experience rather than a single historical footnote. The constitutional rules of presidential selection—in particular, winner-take-all presidential elections promoted by the logic of the Twelfth Amendment—encouraged two-party competition. But the logic merely encouraged, it did not require party development. Two-party electoral competition did not just happen. It had to be invented.

The formation of the Democratic party, under the tutelage of Martin Van Buren, changed the politics of electoral competition more than any other extraconstitutional development. Partisan competition was designed, in part, to replace exclusively personal competition for the presidency. Candidates would typically be nominated by party conventions dominated by party "regulars." The personal ambition of candidates would be checked by the organizational interests of a party. One of the primary organizational interests of any party would be to prevent the destruction of the constitutional system by excessive ambition.

The heart of this party system was the way it structured competition for the office of president. One of its central tenets was the notion that voters would vote on the basis of party identification as well as issues and candidate appeal. Because the electoral process rewarded parties as well as candidates on a winner-take-all basis, the party system has tended to discourage multiple candidates from seeking the presidency and has discouraged the formation of a multiparty democracy. Since the election of Democratic candidate Franklin Pierce in 1852, every president has been either a Democrat or a Republican. Third parties have little chance of electoral success and typically enter the competition for reasons other than winning.

How the two-party system dictates electoral strategy can be seen in part by the way it affects third-party and independent candidates. In the twentieth century there have been several elections in which serious candidates and alternative parties have challenged the two-party monopoly on presidential elections. None has succeeded in electing a president. The reasons lie in the interaction of the formal and informal rules in the electoral process.

In 1912 the Republican party split between incumbent President William Howard Taft and former President Theodore Roosevelt. Taft won the party nomination, but the politically ambitious Roosevelt led a breakaway movement of dissident Republicans under the label of the Progressive (Bull Moose) party. The split in the Republican party proved fatal in the fall elections to both Taft and Roosevelt. Taft won 23 percent of the popular vote but only 8 electoral votes. Roosevelt won 35 percent of the popular vote and 88 electoral votes. The Democratic candidate, Woodrow Wilson, won the election with 42 percent of the popular vote but 435 electoral votes. The combined popular vote totals for Taft and Roosevelt would have easily meant a Republican party victory in 1912, but a breakdown in the preelection party coalition cost Republicans a victory they should have won.

In 1968 it was the Democratic party that split apart, this time over a combination of civil rights and the war in Vietnam. The breakaway movement was led by Alabama Governor George Wallace who formed the American Independent party. The Democrats nominated Hubert Humphrey who had been vice president under Lyndon Johnson. In the 1968 election, George Wallace received 13.5 percent of the popular vote and 46 electoral votes, Humphrey received 42.7 percent of the popular vote and 191 electoral votes, and Republican candidate Richard Nixon won 43.4 percent of the popular vote but 301 electoral votes. Nixon won the election with a decisive majority of the electoral vote.

Wallace's strategy seems to have been to keep either of the two major party candidates from receiving a majority of the Electoral College vote and thus forcing the election into the House. There each state would have had a single vote and Wallace could expect to control those votes in the states he carried in the Electoral College. He then could have played the role of Henry Clay in 1824. Although Wallace's percentage of the popular vote was about half that of Taft in 1912, his electoral vote total was considerably higher because it was geographically concentrated. His strategy came close to succeeding.

In 1992 it was the independent candidacy of H. Ross Perot that threatened to upset the electoral strategy of the two major parties. On election day he received about 19 percent of the popular vote but no electoral votes. His popularity was considerably greater than that of Wallace, but the votes he received were not as geographically concentrated and so he was at a more serious disadvantage in the Electoral College. Because Perot did not win a plurality in any state, the two major parties divided all of the electoral vote between them and the Electoral College was the decisive institution of electoral choice.

The Perot candidacy in 1992 does not easily fit into the traditional pattern of third-party candidates. He was not the product of a dissident movement within one of the two major parties. And unlike Wallace in 1968, his strategy was not deliberately designed to force the final election for president by the House. Even if Perot had pursued a Clay or Wallace strategy of trying to force the decisive vote by the House, it is not clear that it could have worked. In 1992 the chairman of the Democratic party, Ron Brown, publicly stated that if the election were to be decided in the House, he expected Democrats to vote the party line.

Nevertheless, Perot's independent candidacy may foretell other changes in the strategic environment of modern elections. What made his campaign for the White House feasible was both his personal wealth and the way the political party has been replaced by the news media as an "organization" capable of screening and promoting candidates. His candidacy reinforces the perception that the parties may have lost some of their traditional ability to structure the electorate.

A growing body of research argues that political parties are in fact losing their hold on voter loyalty. For the most part it has been interpreted to mean that contemporary elections are more likely to be decided by the personal appeals of the candidate or a dominant issue than by party loyalty in voting. In order to assess the basis of this argument we need to consider voting behavior as a separate category of "rules" that influence the strategic environment of presidential elections.

Why Do Voters Vote the Way They Do?

The act of voting itself was relatively uncomplicated for the Founders. They were more concerned with institutional questions. But when the mobilization of voters came to be part of the strategic environment of the electoral process as a whole, the motivation of voters also became a matter of prime concern to candidates. The Founders' interest in the individual vote for "the best man" above partisan politics has remained a viable part of the American political culture. But political parties have complicated the original conception of presidential voting.

How and why certain groups are likely to vote in any given election is usually treated by the media as the key to an election. Journalists often tend to treat the electorate as up for grabs in each election, voting solely on the basis of issues. But if that really were the case, it would be extraordinarily difficult for candidates to conduct an organized campaign for the presidency. Most political scientists tend to think that probably 70 to 80 percent of the voters have made up their mind almost before the candidates are nominated and that the real campaign is aimed at the 20 to 30 percent who make up their mind during the campaign.

Most contemporary voting studies analyze the presidential vote in terms of the interaction of three basic reasons why people vote the way they do: (1) *party identification*, (2) *candidate appeal*, and (3) *issues*. A fourth factor, incumbency, is generally thought to be more important in congressional elections than in presidential elections and is typically studied apart from presidential voting. The arguments about voting behavior have centered on the relative importance of each of these three factors.

The serious search for a theory of voting in modern political science owes much to the work of V. O. Key Jr. He was a leader in the 1940s and 1950s in what was called the "behavioral revolution" in political science. Generations of political scientists have routinely acknowledged their debt to him even as they have just as routinely taken issue with major points of his analysis.

Key's major contribution to a theory of voting was his identification of what he called *critical elections* as the mainspring of American politics. What he meant by critical elections was that certain elections were so important that they signaled major changes in the direction of public policy and with it the consensus of democratic politics. The careful study of the voting patterns in those elections would provide not only a snapshot of a particular election. The patterns traced over time would provide a moving picture of American politics. The study of voting should be able to tell us something about the political center of gravity in American politics.

For Key the crucial linkage in elections was the political party. When certain critical issues became especially salient, there was a tendency for the parties to move toward polar positions. Slavery was one such issue in the election of 1860. The New Deal and the establishment of the welfare state was one in the election of 1936. These elections were the basis of political realignments along policy lines when the two major parties provided the voters with reasonably clear policy choices. The role of the electorate in this process was a dynamic one—to affirm one choice as the new "consensus" of the American polity.

The choices made during the 1936 election helped to cement party loyalties in later elections that persisted, as Key demonstrated in his *Southern Politics in State and Nation*, across generations. This powerful argument in explaining voting behavior began with the idea, in Key's own words, that "the voters are not fools." Elections were about public policy choices and the voters understood those policies. The vote was rational enough to choose candidates who represent their choices. The Founders probably would not have wanted elections to turn on critical issues such as Key described, but they would generally have agreed that the voters know what they are doing when they vote.

But challenges to Key's arguments were not long in coming, and voting studies have not been the same ever since. The single most influential study of modern presidential elections, and the study that has more or less set the agenda for subsequent analysis, was *The American Voter*, by Angus Campbell, Philip Converse, Warren Miller, and Donald Stokes. After acknowledging their genuine debt to Key, the authors then proceeded to a thoroughgoing critique of his proposition that "the voters are not fools." In effect, *The American Voter* seemed to say, somewhat contra Abraham Lincoln's oft-quoted aphorism, politicians and parties *can* fool most of the voters most of the time. But given the high levels of misinformation and ignorance combined with widespread political apathy in large segments of the public, it was not really necessary to go to the trouble of trying to fool the public on issues. Ignoring the public had about the same practical consequences and with far less bother.

The most important finding to come out of *The American Voter* was its analysis of the ideological or issue orientation of the individual voter. Voters did not vote for reasons that could properly be labeled "issue voting." According to *The American Voter*, party identification was the major explanation of voting behavior. But it was a party identification not rationally linked to candidates or issues or even the voter's own passions, interests, and opinions. Party identification was so overwhelming that both candidate appeal and issues mattered only at the margins. The new role of the voters was more "passive" than "dynamic."

In *The American Voter* parties and candidates emerged as virtually independent players in the political arena. They were neither accountable nor particularly responsive, at least not in any ordinary sense of the way these terms had been used in democratic theory. Voters voted party identification regardless of whether they agreed with the party on issues, and often in near total ignorance of where either party or candidate stood on specific issues. Party voting thus emerged as basically "irrational." Only elites voted issues, candidates, or party in a more or less rational way. The paradoxical implication was that "elites" were more "democratic" than most voters. Democratic theory seemed to be turned upside down.

This finding led to a typology of presidential elections based on party identification as the dominant factor in interpreting elections. Presidential elections were classified as (1) *maintaining* elections, where the majority party wins, (2) *deviating* elections, where the minority party wins, and (3) *realigning* elections, where a critical issue, such as slavery or the Great Depression, reverses the prior majority/minority party status. In the context of this classification, party identification was seen as the long-term factor that influenced the vote, while the candidates and issues were short-term factors. Maintaining elections were primarily about long-term factors in politics whereas deviating elections reflected short-term forces at work.

The permanent, and irrational, structure of party identification dictated the strategy each party should follow to win normally issueless elections. In the twentieth century, only the election of 1932 seemed to qualify as a realigning election, that is, an election that turned on "issue voting." Thereafter, the strategy of the Democratic party was to campaign on the basis of party identification and make the election turn on that long-term factor. With more party identifiers than the Republican party, Democrats should expect to win most elections.

Republicans, on the other hand, had to base their electoral strategy on the dynamics of deviating elections. Any election that turned on party identification was to their disadvantage. So they had to design a campaign strategy based on issues and candidate appeal. The issues had to be important enough to peel away weak Democratic party identifiers. A particularly strong candidate might also attract enough support to overcome the normal Democratic advantage. For Republicans, the elections of Dwight Eisenhower in 1952 and 1956 were textbook examples of deviating elections. The Democratic party remained the majority party, but a candidate with attractive personal qualities, having little to do with party politics, and a few salient issues were sufficient for Republicans to win the general election.

The American Voter's interpretation of election outcomes based on party identification was not entirely unreasonable for the 1932–1964 electoral era. The New Deal did realign majoritarian issues of that time in favor of the Democratic party. And the popularity of Franklin Roosevelt welded the three major components of voting behavior—party identification, issues, and candidate appeal—into a formidable bloc. But the model depended for its logic on the stability of party identification in the electorate and the power of party identification to predict which party was likely to win any given election independently of issues. As Martin Van Buren well understood, party identification was not entirely natural. Ambitious candidates could overwhelm party identification in any given election, and issues could overwhelm the system itself.

Beginning with the 1968 election, *The American Voter* model of elections began to break down. The majority of subsequent elections seemed to be deviating elections. And if deviating elections become the norm, they really cease to be deviating. There were at least three obvious explanations for why *The American Voter* model of electoral behavior seemed to break down: (1) the strategic environment had radically changed, making the party-based typology itself obsolete, (2) the original typology itself was somehow flawed, meaning that perhaps issues and candidates mattered more than the study suggested, or (3) a "realignment" had occurred.

Realignment and American Elections

It would be difficult to overemphasize the influence that the realigning election has had on voting studies. The concept has tended to dominate voting studies for more than thirty years despite some increasingly obvious flaws. However much Key's argument may have been weakened by various studies, it has never lost its fundamental appeal. If Key was right, if issues, however vaguely transmitted through the electoral system, are the driving force in elections, then *The American Voter* typology is considerably weakened. Elections since 1968 certainly suggest that *something* is going on with the American electorate that *The American Voter* model is inadequate to explain.

We may start by asking to what extent the New Deal electoral coalition put together by Franklin Roosevelt was a Democratic party coalition and to what extent it may have been primarily a Roosevelt coalition, or an issue coalition, or some unique combination of these factors. The answer seems far less obvious today than it did when *The American Voter* first appeared. Since the last Roosevelt election, in 1944, the Democratic party has won a majority of the popular vote for president only twice in twelve elections, in 1964 and 1976. Under such circumstances we are hardly entitled to regard a "normal" election as a "maintaining" election in which the Democratic party receives a majority of the popular vote. Has a "realignment" occurred? If so, how did it occur apparently unnoticed by specialists in voting behavior?

Voting studies have taken several approaches. Perhaps the dominant approach has been to look at the stability of partisan identification. *The American Voter* analysis made party appeals the most salient motivational factors in voting behavior. Most people do identify with one of the two major parties. There is evidence that even so-called independent voters are, beneath the surface, more committed to one or the other party than their self-identification as independents might suggest. Changes in the partisan composition of the electorate seems to take place within fairly narrow statistical margins. These factors tend to support key elements of *The American Voter* thesis, though not in its entirety. Has the model masked a contemporary realignment?

A modified realignment theory has stressed that realignment may take place *within* the two-party system by a fundamental change in the coalitions that make up the two parties. For example, after the New Deal realignment, northern Catholic ethnic voters and southern white voters were solidly Democratic party identifiers. As late as 1960 the Republican party could routinely count on about 25 percent of the black vote. Since the mid-1960s, however, each of these coalitions has shifted. Beginning in 1964, the black Republican vote dropped to about 10 percent while Catholics vote pretty much like the rest of the country and southern white voters are increasingly Republican. And beginning in the mid-1970s, Republican candidates have done a better job attracting first-time voters than has been the case since the New Deal patterns were established.

Some Republican party strategists have argued that these patterns suggest a new partisan realignment in favor of Republicans.

Others are more skeptical. If there has been a partisan realignment, public opinion polls that probe partisan identification have not provided the evidence. Democrats are still the majority party in terms of voter identification. If this is the decisive element, there would seem to have been no general realignment.

A strong case can be made that significant rules changes in the Democratic party following the 1968 election altered the strategic environment in which parties, issues, and candidates interact. The proliferation of preferential primaries beginning in 1972 changed the informal rules of presidential selection, which, in turn, affected how electoral coalitions were formed *before* the general election and, as a consequence, *who* won at the Electoral College buzzer.

What Difference(s) Have Primaries Made in Election Results?

Reformers argued that the system of presidential selection would be more democratic if the voters could nominate the candidates for president directly rather than have the parties act as an intermediary institution in the process. More candidates would present themselves to the voters and the result would be to broaden the range of choice among potentially able candidates. But parties as intermediary institutions would no longer be a primary control on the political ambition of the candidates. Either the voters would have to exercise that function directly or there might be no effective control on ambition beyond the candidate's personal sense of responsibilities—always a frail reed under these circumstances.

Beginning with the election of 1912, *preferential primaries* were introduced into the presidential nomination process. Most states did not adopt primaries and most delegates were not chosen by primaries. But from 1912 until 1968 the system of delegate selection consisted of a mixture of preferential primaries and traditional party systems of delegate selection. The mix, however, was dominated by the traditional party or state convention system begun by Van Buren.

The mixed system of delegate selection changed in the Democratic and Republican parties after 1968. Following the defeat of Democratic candidate Hubert Humphrey in 1968, the Democratic party's McGovern-Fraser Commission recommended greater participation by voters in the delegate selection process. The recommendation was translated by state parties and state legislatures into an increase in the number of states that used the preferential primary as a means of selecting delegates to the national party conventions. In 1972, delegates were selected by either state preferential primaries or "participatory caucuses" which are quite similar to primaries. A candidate seeking the nomination for president found that the route to the White House lay through victories in primaries and not necessarily through the political party as an organization. The change had some unintended consequences.

The proliferation of primaries after 1968 might not have mattered as much as it did if voting behavior in the primaries were the same as voting behavior in the general election. But it is not the same. Primary voters tend to be stronger party identifiers. But because all of the candidates are in the same party the effects of party identification are muted. The Democratic party also adopted a system of proportional delegate selection rather than the winner-take-all system that the Republicans adopted until 1992. Proportional delegate selection meant that a primary candidate could expect to receive a percentage of delegates roughly proportional to the votes received in a particular state's primary. The rules encouraged candidates to differentiate among themselves on issues and personal qualities, thereby fragmenting party unity.

The delegate selection process encouraged multiple candidates. It also encouraged those candidates to stay in the primaries longer than their strength might warrant. It even encouraged intraparty challenges to incumbent presidents because there was no party discipline to check these challenges. When Eugene McCarthy challenged President Johnson in the 1968 primaries he could not hope to actually wrest the nomination from him. Johnson still could control the delegates. But in 1980 Senator Ted Kennedy could challenge President Jimmy Carter in the primaries with a reasonable expectation that the incumbent president might be defeated that way.

Primary voters, liberal and conservative, are generally more knowledgeable about political issues and more active in pursuit of those issues that interest them. Because proportional delegate selection discourages preconvention coalition building, candidates are tempted to appeal to single-issue constituencies that may, by both their knowledge and their activism, be unrepresentative of the general electorate. The strategy used to win the primaries often weakens the candidate in the November election. In 1988, George Bush branded Democrat Michael Dukakis as an out of the mainstream "liberal" on the basis of Dukakis's campaign statements in states with liberal primary electorates.

Interpreting Presidential Elections

The notion that presidential elections *should* be occasions for critical public policy choices, whether "liberal" or "conservative," is often implicit in what is said about presidential elections. There is also the assumption that the president ought to be the dominant branch of government in deciding these policy questions. But this was not how the Founders originally understood presidential elections. Elections were not supposed to alter the constitutional distribution of powers. Congress, by its power to "make" laws, was understood to be the dominant branch of government. The idea that ordinary elections are acts that empower the president to "make policy" is unsettling to constitutional design.

The focus on voting behavior in presidential elections has had the effect of diverting attention away from a systematic analysis of how elections fit into the constitutional architecture as a whole. To protect free government, the Founders relied on both elections *and* institutional arrangements such as the separation of powers.

Changes in the rules are normally designed to change who wins the election. Democratic party reformers after 1968 really thought the rules changes they advocated would make the process more democratic, and that their party would win in a more democratic system. What they did in fact was to reward participation and penalize nonparticipation. In the process they gained increased representation for their own views and, in effect, disenfranchised the views of those Democrats who disagreed with them. Voters who participated in the primaries had very different opinions from those who did not participate. The differences showed up in the policy positions of delegates selected to attend the party convention, which in turn were reflected in the presidential candidates nominated.

In the end we are again reminded that the electoral process is complex because a liberal democratic regime is the most complex form of government yet devised. We should not expect it to be otherwise. Reform arguments aimed at simplifying the electoral process are too often based on the unwarranted assumption that at its heart democracy is a simple form of government.

Modern technology has made a direct democracy possible in a territory as large as the United States—a possibility that the Founders could not have foreseen. But technology does not make it any more desirable. We ought not to lose sight of what presidential elections are supposed to accomplish: to elect able persons to the presidency of a regime founded on the principles of democratic liberty. It is a system both fragile and complex.

Suggested Reading

Berns, Walter. *After the People Vote: A Guide to the Electoral College*, revised and enlarged edition. Washington, D.C.: AEI Press, 1992.

Ceaser, James W. *Presidential Selection: Theory and Development.* Princeton: Princeton University Press, 1979.

——— and Andrew Busch. *Upside Down and Inside Out: The 1992 Elections and American Politics*. Lanham, Md: Rowman and Littlefield, 1993.

Key, V. O. *Southern Politics in State and Nation*. Knoxville: University of Tennessee Press, 1984.

Niemi, Richard G., and Herbert F. Weisberg, eds. *Classics in Voting Behavior*. Washington, D.C.: Congressional Quarterly Press, 1993.

———. *Controversies in Voting Behavior*, 3rd ed. Washington, D.C.: Congressional Quarterly Press, 1993.

Polsby, Nelson W., and Aaron Wildavsky. *Presidential Elections: Contemporary Strategies of American Electoral Politics*, 8th ed. New York: Free Press, 1991.

14

The Least Dangerous Branch?

Ralph A. Rossum

"What do you do when the Supreme Court is wrong?" This question was posed by Senator Daniel Patrick Moynihan in *The Public Interest*. For the Framers of the American Constitution, one obvious answer to this question was for the Congress to correct judicial error and curb judicial excesses by employing its powers under Article III, Section 2 to curtail the appellate jurisdiction of the Court. In *Federalist* 80, for example, Alexander Hamilton reviewed in detail the "particular powers of the federal judiciary" and observed that

> if some partial inconveniences should appear to be connected with the incorporation of any of them into the plan, it ought to be recollected that the national legislature will have ample authority to make such exceptions and to prescribe such regulations as will be calculated to obviate or remove these inconveniences.

For the Framers, the federal judiciary was the least dangerous branch. Having neither the power of the sword nor the power of the purse and possessing only power of judgment, it was, in the words of *Federalist* 78, "the least dangerous to the political rights of the constitution, because it will be least in a capacity to annoy or injure them." Although the judiciary had the least capacity to be dangerous, the Framers still recognized that any power, even "mere judgment," was potentially arbitrary and oppressive. And while they expected that the "arbitrary discretion" of the courts could be "bound down by strict rules and precedents which [could] serve to define

241

and point out their duty in every particular case that comes before them," they also provided the other branches with various powers to check judicial error and encroachments.

Accordingly, the Framers provided for presidential appointment and senatorial confirmation of judges and for congressional determination of the size, shape, and composition of the federal courts. They also provided for the impeachment of judges (*Federalist* 81 called it a "complete security" against "judiciary encroachments on the legislative authority"). They also supplied the Congress with "ample authority" under Article III, Section 2, so that if "some partial inconveniences" were to arise as a result of the Supreme Court's exercise of its powers, Congress could use the exceptions clause to "obviate or remove" them. Under the separation of powers they provided in the Constitution, they never intended the judicial power, any more than the legislative or executive powers, to be absolute, or for the judiciary to be completely independent. Just as they provided means whereby the legislative and executive branches were to be kept, in the words of *Federalist* 51, "in their proper places," so, too, they included mechanisms to restrain the judiciary—the exceptions clause being one such mechanism.

Today, however, most legal scholars, substantial majorities in Congress, and many judges would find the Framers' answer to Moynihan's question unacceptable. They fear that any use of the exceptions clause will destroy the Court's power of judicial review and therewith its ability to play its proper role. So they join with Moynihan, who insisted that the only appropriate responses to judicial error are to "debate" the Court's decision, "litigate" the same issue in another case and hope for a better result, or "legislate" remedial measures (if the Court's error involved statutory construction). Elaborating on this theme three years later in an address to the graduating class of St. John's University School of Law, Moynihan deplored the fact that "the concept of debate, legislate, litigate" seemed to have given way to an "emerging triumvirate" of "convene, overrule, and restrict." He found especially troubling "attempts to restrict federal jurisdiction," pronouncing them to be "profoundly at odds with our nation's customs and political philosophy."[1]

Moynihan's analysis was badly flawed. His understanding of "our nation's customs and political philosophy" is embarrassingly superficial because he describes the United States as a "pure democracy," a patently false characterization which, if true, would surely rule out judicial independence of the kind he was attempting to preserve. So, too, is his assertion that "our Constitution vests majority rule in the legislative and executive branches, while the judiciary protects the rights of the minority." But his observations on the nature of our democratic republic and the role of the Supreme Court in it are rock-solid compared to the thinking of most law school faculty members who specialize in what is commonly referred to as constitutional theory.[2]

Contemporary Theory versus the Constitution

Contemporary constitutional theorists consider the Supreme Court to be "the ultimate arbiter of social ethics in the nation" whose responsibility it is to "articulate the public good as . . . [the justices] understand it." They urge the Court to go beyond the Constitution, "invent" new constitutional rights, and acknowledge openly "that the source of those rights is not the constitutional text but the enhanced seriousness of certain values in American society."[3] They view the Court as a "Council of Elders" and its justices as "High Priests." They argue that the Court must assume a "prophetic stance" and oppose itself to established conventions by submitting governmental actions to a moral critique and striking down such actions if they violate any human rights that the Court believes individuals ought to have. They contend that by institutionalizing prophecy in this manner, the Court provides the public with the occasion for "moral reevaluation and possible moral growth" in a way that the popular branches—guided by what constitutional theorists such as Michael J. Perry consider to be "a stagnant or even repressive morality"—cannot.

The justices, therefore, must not be "wedded to a closed morality." Quite the contrary, they must be "committed to the notion of moral evolution and be open to the possibility of moral growth." They must therefore shake themselves free from the constraining influence of the Constitution. It is, according to Perry, nothing more than the "sediment of old moralities," weighing them down and impeding their efforts to move American society to a higher moral plane. In fact, the justices must model themselves after Chief Justice Earl Warren, whom Anthony Lewis describes as "the closest thing the United States has had to a Platonic Guardian, dispensing law from a throne without any sensed limits of power except what was seen as the good of society."[4]

According to his biographer, University of Virginia Law Professor G. Edward White:

Most of Warren's energy on the Court was directed toward achieving the "right" results. He did not often agonize, as did Frankfurter, over an outcome in a case, nor did he despair of finding an adequate constitutional basis for justifying his intuitions, nor did he worry about being overly activist. He spent his time on discerning results that seemed just and on marshalling support for those results by attempting to convince others of their inherent justice."[5]

Today's theorists invite the entire Supreme Court to emulate Warren. By doing so it would more effectively protect human rights and foster "moral growth" and "human dignity" among the citizenry.

The Court, for the most part, has not frustrated those constitutional theorists who flatter it. Through its creative reading of four words in the Constitution—due process and equal protection—even the Rehnquist Court (with eight of the nine justices having been appointed by Republican presidents, and six of those eight by Ronald Reagan and George Bush) has "advanced" the cause of "human dignity" by substituting its morally superior views for the morally stagnant and repressive views of the benighted popular branches.

In *Lee v. Weisman* (1992), for example, the Court banished completely all traces of religion from the public schools, including the recitation of a nonsectarian prayer by a member of the clergy at a commencement ceremony. In *Simon & Schuster, Inc. v. New York Crime Victims Board* (1992), it invalidated a law that transferred to their victims the royalty payments that criminals earned from books they wrote that highlighted their criminal exploits. In *Texas v. Johnson* (1989) and *United States v. Eichman* (1990), it struck down both state and federal laws that prohibited the burning of the American flag.

In *Jacobson v. United States* (1992), it overturned the conviction of a defendant who was found guilty of receiving child pornography through the mails on the grounds that he had been entrapped. Simply because he collected child pornography before federal law made it illegal was, the Court held, no reason to suspect that he would wish to collect it once it was illegal, so using a sting operation to mail him "kiddy porn" catalogs and invite his patronage was an excessive inducement for him to violate the law. In *Georgia v. McCollum* (1992), the Court struck down the practice common in both state and federal courts of allowing criminal defendants unqualified use of their peremptory challenges, because in the instant case, the defendant used them to remove all blacks from his jury panel. The Court turned the "state action doctrine" on its head and held that the criminal defendant, in the process of defending himself against the state, was as much an agent of the state as the prosecutor. In *Lucas v. South Carolina Coastal Council* (1992), it invalidated a state environmental regulation on the implausible grounds that it had totally destroyed the value of the plaintiff's beachfront property.

Finally, in *Planned Parenthood v. Casey* (1992), the Court struck down key provisions of Pennsylvania's antiabortion statute because it violated a right to privacy that the Warren Court, in *Griswold v. Connecticut* (1965), had found to exist in a "penumbra" formed by emanations of the First, Third, Fourth, Fifth, and Ninth Amendments and that the Burger Court, in *Roe v. Wade* (1973), asserted included the right to an abortion. While a majority of the Rehnquist Court held that *Roe* had been wrongly decided, they concluded that *Roe* should not be overturned, arguing that such an action would create the impression that the justices were not guided in their decision-making by the constitutional text, and that it would also result in "both profound and unnecessary damage to the Court's legitimacy, and to the Nation's commitment to the rule of law."

The Creation of the Judicial Article

This contemporary understanding of the proper role of the Supreme Court would have truly astonished the Framers, who had far more modest designs for the federal judiciary. Just how modest their designs were can be appreciated by simply noting the placement, brevity, and generality of the judicial article. To begin with, Article III, establishing the federal judiciary, follows the articles that establish the legislative branch and the executive branch. By so arranging these articles, the Framers addressed each branch, in the words of James Wilson, a member of the Constitutional Convention and an original justice on the Supreme Court, "as its greatness deserves to be considered."[6] Further, Article III is only about a sixth as long as the legislative article, and only about a third as long as the executive article.

Article I specifies in great detail the qualifications of representatives and senators (including age and citizenship requirements), the size of the two houses of Congress, the procedures they must follow, and the powers they are authorized or prohibited to exercise. Article II is likewise quite detailed in its discussion of the president's qualifications, mode of appointment, powers, and responsibilities. By contrast, Article III merely vests the judicial power of the United States in one Supreme Court (its size is unspecified) and in "such inferior Courts as the Congress may from time to time ordain and establish." Article III outlines no procedures the courts are obliged to follow, and it imposes no qualifications on the judges, not even the requirement of citizenship.

Article III is as brief and general as it is because the Framers spent almost no time considering the judiciary. Discussion of the judicial branch consumed, in total, only about two days of the seventeen-week Constitutional Convention. Resolution 9 of the Virginia Plan provided for a federal judiciary. It proposed that

> a National Judiciary be established to consist of one or more supreme tribunals, and of inferior tribunals to be chosen by the National Legislature, to hold their offices during good behavior; and to receive punctually at stated times fixed compensation for their services, in which no increase or diminution shall be made so as to affect the persons actually in office at the time of such increase or diminution.

It further proposed that

> the jurisdiction of the inferior tribunals shall be to hear and determine in the first instance, and of the supreme tribunal to hear and determine in the dernier resort, all piracies and felonies on the high seas, captures from any enemy; cases in which foreigners or citizens of other States applying to such jurisdictions may be interested, or which respect the collection of the National revenue; impeachments of any National officers, and questions which may involve the national peace and harmony.

This resolution generated almost no controversy or debate. To begin with, the delegates quickly agreed to the creation of one "supreme tribunal" on June 4. Likewise, while the delegates differed among themselves concerning the mode of appointing judges, with a majority voting repeatedly from early June through late August for appointment by the Senate, they nonetheless accepted, unanimously and without debate, language supplied in early September by the Committee of Eleven that changed the mode to appointment by the executive. They accepted from the outset that the judges should serve during good behavior and that their compensation should be free from political interference. They also accepted without controversy and with little discussion the substituted language from the Committee of Detail specifying the Supreme Court's original jurisdiction and subjecting the Court's appellate jurisdiction to such exceptions and regulations as the Congress shall make.

The only part of Resolution 9 to generate any sustained debate was its language mandating the creation of "inferior tribunals." John Rutledge was representative of a majority of the delegates. He insisted "that the State Tribunals might and ought to be left in all cases to decide in the first instance, the right to appeal to the supreme national tribunal being sufficient to secure the national rights and uniformity of judgments." James Madison made the case for Resolution 9 as presented. He pleaded that "an effective Judiciary establishment commensurate to the legislative authority was essential. A Government without a proper Executive and Judiciary would be a mere trunk of a body without arms or legs to act or move." But his plea was unavailing. All he could eventually secure was the delegates' consent to provide the national legislature with the option "to institute inferior tribunals" if it should choose to do so.

While not directly implicated, the federal judiciary figured in one other controversy during the convention: the desire of the authors of the Virginia Plan to create a Council of Revision. Resolution 8 of the Virginia Plan proposed the establishment of a "council of revision" composed of "the Executive and a convenient number of the National Judiciary" which would have the "authority to examine every act of the National Legislature before it shall operate" and to negative any act unless the national legislature were to pass it again. This resolution received the sustained and eloquent endorsement of both Madison and Wilson. Madison insisted in a speech on July 21 that "the object of the motion was of great importance to the mediated Constitution."

It would be useful to the Judiciary department by giving it an additional opportunity of defending itself against Legislative encroachments; It would be useful to the Executive, by inspiring additional confidence and firmness in exerting the revisionary power; It would be useful to the Legislature by the valuable assistance it would give in preserving a consistency, conciseness, perspicuity, and technical propriety in the laws, qualities peculiarly necessary and yet shamefully wanting in our Republican Codes. It would moreover be useful to the Community at large as an additional check against a pursuit of those unwise and unjust measures which constituted so great a portion of our calamities.[7]

But Madison argued in vain. The Council of Revision was decisively rejected by the delegates, and the capacity to review and negative acts of the national legislature was confined solely to the executive, who was provided with a qualified veto power. While the delegates felt obligated to strengthen the executive in its conflicts with the legislative branch, and did so by explicitly providing it with a qualified power to negative legislative acts, the delegates apparently felt less of a need to defend the judicial branch from the dangers of legislative encroachment (or, for that matter, the "Community at large" from "unwise and unjust measures"); consequently they failed to provide protection for the judiciary (and the "Community at large") as explicitly as they provided for a qualified veto for the executive.

A protection they could have provided the judiciary (but, in fact, did not provide) was an explicit authorization for the Court to exercise a general power of judicial review—the power to expound the Constitution and to invalidate those actions of the Congress and the president that the Court finds to be contrary to the Constitution. Does the Framers' failure to make explicit reference to judicial review mean that they did not intend for the Court to have this power? Or are we free to conclude that they intended it nonetheless?

Those who contend that the Court legitimately has the power of judicial review argue inferentially. They argue that the way in which the Constitution provides for a separation of powers that, in the words of *Federalist* 48, so "connects" and "blends" the three departments of government "as to give to each a constitutional control over the others" implies the appropriateness, nay the necessity, of judicial review. This power simply gives the Court a means of checking and restraining the popular branches and thereby of protecting itself from their encroachments, much as the popular branches—through such constitutional controls as impeachment and congressional appropriation of money for the judicial branch—have means at their disposal for restraining the courts.[8]

This inference is further supported, claim those who argue for judicial review, by (1) statements made by several delegates during the convention explicitly favoring judicial review; (2) the contention that judicial review was so well known and normal a function of the courts that the Framers took it for granted and saw no need to make explicit provision for it in the Constitution; and (3) the specific acknowledgment of judicial review made by Alexander Hamilton in *Federalist* 78. These three specific arguments need to be considered before addressing the more general claim that the separation of powers present in the Constitution implies judicial review.

Several delegates to the convention clearly believed that the Court should have the power of judicial review. Gouverneur Morris, for one, observed that the judiciary should not "be bound to say that a direct violation of the Constitution was law." Luther Martin, for another, argued against the Council of Revision on the grounds that "the constitutionality of laws . . . will come before the judges in their official character. In this character, they have a negative on the laws." Similar observations were made by Elbridge Gerry, Caleb Strong, John Rutledge, and Rufus King.

The problem with these statements, however, is that they imply neither a general power to expound the Constitution nor an obligation on the part of the other branches to regard a judicial decision on the constitutionality of their actions as binding. Statements were also made by other convention delegates unequivocally rejecting judicial review. For example, John Mercer "disapproved of the doctrine that the judges as expositors of the Constitution should have authority to declare a law void. He thought laws ought to be well and cautiously made, and then to be uncontrollable." So, too, did John Dickinson, who argued that, "as to the power of the Judges to set aside the law, . . . no such power ought to exist."[9]

The contention that judicial review was so normal a judicial function at the time of the convention that no explicit provision had to be made for it in the Constitution likewise cannot withstand close scrutiny. Leonard W. Levy has shown that prior to the drafting of the Constitution in 1787, there were only two legitimate instances where state courts actually invalidated state laws: the "Ten Pound Case" in New Hampshire and *Bayard v. Singleton* in North Carolina. In the former case, the court's action resulted in an abortive attempt to impeach the offending judges (the motion to impeach was defeated by a vote of 35 to 21). In the *Bayard*, the North Carolina legislature angrily summoned the judges before it to explain their disregard for its authority; a legislative committee that included William R. Davie and Richard Dobbs Spaight—later both delegates to the federal convention—found the judges guilty as charged.

Other, but spurious, instances of state courts exercising the power of judicial review prior to 1787 have also been identified. What is significant about these spurious precedents is that they involve instances where court decisions were either deliberatively or mistakenly misinterpreted for the purpose of discrediting the judges, and where the state legislatures, protective of their powers, condemned the courts in the mistaken belief that they had invalidated an act. If the Framers had intended judicial review, it is highly unlikely that they would have allowed it to rest on so precarious a foundation or have failed to make specific provision for it.

Hamilton's arguments in *Federalist* 78 also fail to provide much support for the inference that the Framers intended judicial review. His arguments there were primarily in response to a series of Anti-Federalist essays written by Brutus. Brutus sought to discredit the Constitution by, among other things, magnifying the power of the federal judiciary and presenting it as an instrument for consolidating national powers at the expense of the states. In his response in *Federalist* 78, Hamilton was not so much advocating judicial review as attempting to turn Brutus's arguments against himself. He suggested that the Court's power was intended to hold Congress in check and thereby safeguard the states against national aggrandizement by a Congress seeking consolidation. If the Congress were to act "contrary to the manifest tenor of the Constitution" and were to attempt to scuttle the federal structure that the Framers had established, Hamilton argued, the Court could be trusted to invalidate those congressional efforts.

But Hamilton really knew that the Court would never hold the Congress's consolidationist tendencies in check, and for the very reason that Brutus had already identified in an essay he penned four months before Hamilton drafted *Federalist* 78. The judges, Brutus predicted, will "lean strongly in favor of the general government" and will rule in such a way as "will favor an extension of its jurisdiction," because by so doing, they will "enlarge the sphere of their own authority." As Brutus was at pains to point out, "every extension of the power of the general legislature, as well as of the judicial powers, will increase the powers of the courts; and the dignity and importance of the judges, will be in proportion to the extent and magnitude of the powers they exercise."[10] Hamilton's remarks in *Federalist* 78 have been accurately characterized by Levy as "evidence of shrewd political tactics, not of the framers' intention to vest judicial review in the Supreme Court over acts of Congress."[11]

Hamilton's personal views toward the Court and its exercise of judicial review were quite different and are apparent elsewhere. For example, during the Constitutional Convention when he introduced his own plan for a new constitution as a substitute for both the Virginia and New Jersey plans, Hamilton made no provision for any kind of judicial review. In fact, he limited the jurisdiction of "the Supreme Judicial authority" he was proposing to "original jurisdiction in all causes of capture, and an appellative jurisdiction in all causes in which the revenues of the general Government or the citizens of foreign nations are concerned."[12]

In *Federalist* 33, when Hamilton discussed the necessary and proper clause, regarded by many Anti-Federalists as a source of unlimited power for Congress, he did not so much as allude to the Supreme Court when he answered his own question of "who is to judge the necessity and propriety of the laws to be passed for executing the powers of the Union?" For him, the Congress was to judge "in the first instance the proper exercise of its powers; and its constituents in the last." If the Congress were to use the necessary and proper clause "to overpass the just bounds of its authority and make a tyrannical use of its powers," Hamilton argued that "the people whose creature it is must appeal to the standard they have formed, and take such measures to redress the injury done to the constitution, as the exigency may suggest and prudence justify." Again, he made no reference to the Supreme Court exercising judicial review to negative such congressional actions.

Finally, in *Federalist* 84, Hamilton made no mention of judicial review as a means of securing the guarantees of a bill of rights. Again he insisted that "whatever fine declarations may be inserted in any constitution" respecting these rights, they "must altogether depend on public opinion, and on the general spirit of the people and the government" for their enforcement. These, he continued, are the "only solid basis of all our rights."

The Separation of Powers and Judicial Review

It is now possible to return to the more general claim that the separation of powers present in the Constitution implies that the Court has final authority to pass judgment on the constitutionality of the acts of its coequal branches. As with the more specific arguments, this more general claim cannot be sustained. While it is possible to argue that the separation of powers present in the Constitution implies the existence of judicial review as a means by which the Court can check and balance the popular branches, just as Congress and the president have means by which to check and balance the judiciary, this line of reasoning is, in Justice Oliver Wendell Holmes's words, a "spider's web inadequate to control the dominant facts."[13]

The Constitution simply does not make explicit provision for judicial review. But it does explicitly provide for impeachment, congressional control of the Court's appellate jurisdiction, congressional determination of the size, shape, and composition of the entire federal judiciary, presidential appointment of judges subject to Senate confirmation, congressional appropriations for the courts, etc. Separation of powers, from which judicial review is inferred, is itself never explicitly mentioned in the Constitution. Rather it is inferred from the specific powers that the Constitution assigns to the branches. Judicial review is no more than an inference drawn from an inference.

That judicial review can be reasonably inferred from the separation of powers present in the Constitution is also contradicted by the fact that Madison, whose contributions to the delegates' emerging understanding of separation of powers was second to none, flatly denied that the Supreme Court had a general power to interpret the Constitution. So, when it was proposed on August 27 that the Court's jurisdiction extend to "all cases arising under this Constitution," Madison "doubted whether it was not going too far to extend the jurisdiction of the Court generally to cases arising under the Constitution and whether it ought not to be limited to cases of a Judiciary Nature. The right of expounding the Constitution in cases not of this nature . . . ought not to be given to that Department." Only when he was assured by his fellow delegates "that the jurisdiction given was constructively limited to cases of a Judiciary Nature" did Madison acquiesce.

For Madison, the Court is not to pass on constitutional questions because it has vested in it a special function to enforce the Constitution or police the other branches of government. It does so only because it must decide a litigated issue that is otherwise within its jurisdiction and in doing so must give effect to the supreme law of the land. Such an issue would present a "case of a Judiciary Nature." Article III, Section 2 can be used to restrict even this limited power of judicial review, for it grants Congress, in the words of *Federalist* 80, the power "to obviate or remove" all inconveniences that a particular litigated issue may pose, by excepting it from the Court's appellate jurisdiction.[14]

Madison's belief that the judiciary did not possess a general power of expounding the Constitution did not end with the adjournment of the convention. He reiterated this belief on October 15, 1788, in his "Observations on Mr. Jefferson's Draft of a Constitution for Virginia":

> In the State Constitutions and indeed in the Federal one also, no provision is made for the case of a disagreement in expounding them; and as the Courts are generally the last in making their decision, it results to them, by refusing or not refusing to execute a law, to stamp it with its final character. This makes the Judiciary Department paramount in fact to the Legislature, which was never intended and can never be proper.[15]

He argued similarly on the floor of the House of Representatives during a June 16, 1789 debate on the president's removal power. While he acknowledged the duty of the judiciary to expound the laws and Constitution, he demanded to know "upon what principle it can be contended that any one department draws from the Constitution greater powers than another, in marking out the limits on the powers of the several departments." He insisted that the Constitution provided the courts with no "particular authority to determine the limits of the constitutional division of power between the branches of government."[16]

The Judiciary Act of 1789

The creation of the federal judiciary was not concluded with the adjournment of the federal convention. The bare bones provided in the Constitution by the Framers were fleshed out in the Judiciary Act of 1789 by the members of the First Congress, who would have been as astonished as the Framers themselves by the contemporary thinking on the proper role of the Supreme Court. In the Judiciary Act, the Congress constituted the Supreme Court, consisting of a chief justice and five associate justices. Congress also exercised its constitutional option to establish a system of inferior federal courts. It believed that an effective maritime commerce (essential to the new nation) needed a dependable body of maritime law and that the most reliable method to assure its development would be to entrust it to a new set of courts. So it established thirteen federal district courts with one judge each—one district for each of the eleven states that had, by that time, ratified the Constitution and two additional districts, in Virginia and Massachusetts for, respectively, Kentucky and Maine. It also provided for three circuit courts, each composed of two justices of the Supreme Court sitting in conjunction with one district court judge.

Federalist 39 had described the new Constitution as neither wholly national nor wholly federal but a composition of both. The members of the First Congress acted in conformity with this statement as they drafted the Judiciary Act of 1789. Parts of the act were unquestionably national in character. So in addition to establishing inferior federal tribunals rather than simply relying on state courts, the Congress also included Section 25, which brought the state courts directly under federal appellate jurisdiction by providing for appeals from state courts to the federal judiciary. Under Section 25, appeals could be taken to the U.S. Supreme Court whenever the highest state court having jurisdiction of the case ruled against the constitutionality of a federal law or treaty, ruled in favor of the validity of a state act that had been challenged as contrary to the Constitution or federal law, or ruled against a right or privilege claimed under the Constitution or federal law.

While the creation of inferior federal courts and Section 25 were national in character, other provisions of the Judiciary Act of 1789 were federal. Thus, it granted state courts concurrent original jurisdiction in all civil suits at common law and equity, conferring upon the federal courts exclusive jurisdiction only in admiralty and maritime cases and in cases involving the few crimes and offenses cognizable under the authority of the United States. It withheld from the federal trial courts jurisdiction over cases "arising under" the Constitution and laws of the United States, leaving these to be adjudicated in the state courts. (Congress did not provide the federal courts with federal question jurisdiction until the Judiciary Act of 1875.)

The Judiciary Act of 1789 also subjected to a jurisdictional amount Supreme Court review of civil cases, a requirement that Congress did not eliminate for all cases involving constitutional issues until 1891 and did not abolish with respect to Supreme Court review of all federal questions until 1925. It also withheld Supreme Court review of federal criminal cases, something Congress did not provide until 1891. Still another provision that was definitely federal in character was Section 34, called the Rules of Decision Act. It provided that "the laws of the several States, except where the Constitution, treaties, or statutes of the United States shall otherwise require or provide, shall be regarded as rules of decision in trials at common law in the courts of the United States in cases where they apply."[17]

The Contemporary Court
versus the Rule of Law

In light of the facts surrounding the creation of the least dangerous branch in the federal convention of 1787 and its implementation in the Judiciary Act of 1789, Justice Sandra Day O'Connor's language in *Planned Parenthood v. Casey*—that the American people's aspiration "to live according to the rule of law" is inseparable from the Court's authority to "speak before all others for their constitutional ideals"—is exposed as arrogant and self-serving. O'Connor and her contemporaries, encouraged by the flatteries of the constitutional theorists, equate their sense of the public good with the Constitution's ideals and, hence, with the rule of law. They even assert that their judicial opinions are as much the "Supreme Law of the Land" as the Constitution itself.[18] Failure on the part of the people and their representatives in Congress to accept the Court's sense of the public good is evidence of the presence of "stagnant and repressive morality" and of the absence of the rule of law, which is, of course, further evidence of the need for a prophetic court.

For students of the Constitution (as opposed to constitutional theory), the Court's equation of the rule of law with acceptance of its efforts to invent new rights and thereby foster "moral growth" is evidence of something quite different. It establishes dramatically how far the federal judiciary has shifted off its constitutional foundation. In the words of John Marshall, a member of the Virginia Ratifying Convention and later the Supreme Court's great chief justice: "The framers of the Constitution contemplated that instrument as a rule for the courts, as well as of the legislature."[19]

To the contemporary Court and those theorists who defend and encourage it, the Constitution is not a rule for the Court, and for a good reason. The Constitution is only what the judges say it is.

Efforts to correct judicial error are wrong in principle (for the Constitution means only what the Court says it means), unconstitutionally motivated, and therefore "tawdry" and "lewd."[20] Not even explicitly granted constitutional powers, such as the power to make exceptions to the Court's appellate jurisdiction, can be legitimately employed if their use in any way restricts judicial review, nowhere even hinted at in the Constitution. The letter of the Constitution must yield to the spirit of a prophetic court, inventing new rights and urging the people to undergo "moral reevaluation." Like the Prophets of the Old Testament, the Supreme Court is to speak out on behalf of justice and the public good. Unlike their biblical brethren, however, the justices are to be spared any retaliation from the people and their representatives for having done so.

Senator Moynihan posed the right question when he asked: "What do you do when the Supreme Court is wrong?" He was clearly convinced that the Court had been wrong—on many occasions and on important issues. Regrettably, while he asked the right question, he gave the wrong answer. He said, in effect, "You do nothing." To do more than debate, litigate, or legislate is at odds with our custom (or at least the Court's custom) of treating judicial opinions as the Supreme Law of the Land. With enemies like Moynihan, the Court doesn't need any friends.

Notes

1. Daniel Patrick Moynihan, "What Do You Do When the Supreme Court is Wrong?" *The Public Interest*, No. 57 (Fall 1979), p. 8; and "Constitutional Crisis," 27 *Catholic Lawyer* 271, 277 (1982).

2. "Law-office philosophy" is to philosophy what "law-office history" is to history. See Alfred H. Kelly, "Clio and the Court: An Illicit Love Affair," in Philip B. Kurland, ed., *The Supreme Court Review: 1965* (Chicago: University of Chicago Press, 1965), pp. 119–58.

3. See Arthur S. Miller, *Toward Increased Judicial Activism: The Political Role of the Supreme Court* (Westport, Conn.: Greenwood Press, 1982); G. Edward White, "Reflections on the Role of the Supreme Court: The Contemporary Debate and the 'Lessons' of History," 63 *Judicature* 168 (1979); Michael J. Perry, *The Constitution, the Courts, and Human Rights* (New Haven: Yale University Press, 1982), and *Morality, Politics, and Law* (New York: Oxford University Press, 1990); and Sanford Levinson, *Constitutional Faith* (Princeton: Princeton University Press, 1990).

4. Anthony Lewis, "Earl Warren," in L. Friedman and F. Israel eds., *The Justices of the United States Supreme Court*, 4 vols. (New York: Chelsea, 1969), 4:2726.

5. G. Edward White, *Earl Warren: A Public Life* (New York: Oxford University Press, 1982), p. 190.

6. Robert Green McCloskey, ed., *The Works of James Wilson* (Cambridge: Belknap Press of Harvard University Press, 1967), p. 290.

7. Max Farrand ed., *The Records of the Federal Convention of 1787*, 4 vols. (New Haven: Yale University Press, 1937), 2:74.

8. See John Agresto, *The Supreme Court and Constitutional Democracy* (Ithaca: Cornell University Press, 1984).

9. See Farrand, II:299; II:76; II:298; and II:299.

10. "The Essays of Brutus," in Herbert J. Storing, ed., *The Complete Anti-Federalist*, 7 vols. (Chicago: University of Chicago Press, 1981), Essay 11, II:421.

11. Levy, "Judicial Review, History, and Democracy," in Leonard W. Levy, ed., *Judical Review and the Supreme Court* (New York: Harper and Row, 1967), pp. 6, 10.

12. Farrand, I:292.

13. *Myers v. United States*, 272 U.S. 52, 177 (1926). Mr. Justice Holmes dissenting.

14. In addition to *Federalist* 80, Hamilton makes the following argument in *Federalist* 81: "To avoid all inconvenience, it will be safest to declare generally that the Supreme Court shall possess appellate jurisdiction both as to law and fact, and that this jurisdiction shall be subject to such exceptions and regulations as the national legislature shall prescribe. This will enable the government to modify it in such a manner as will best answer the ends of public justice and security." In the Virginia Ratifying Convention, John Marshall, later the author of *Marbury v. Madison* (1803), made very much the same argument: "Congress is empowered to make exceptions to the appellate jurisdiction, as to law and fact, of the Supreme Court. These exceptions certainly go as far as the legislature may think proper for the interest of liberty and the people" (Jonathan Elliot, *Debates on the Adoption of the Federal Convention*, 5 vols. [2nd ed., 1888] III:560). In the Pennsylvania Ratifying Convention, the only other convention that specifically discussed the exceptions clause, James Wilson, chairman of the federal convention's Committee of Detail, likewise noted that if the Court's powers under its appellate jurisdiction "shall be attended with inconvenience, the Congress can alter them as soon as discovered" (John Bach McMaster and Frederick D. Stone, eds., *Pennsylvania and the Federal Constitution* [Philadelphia: Historical Society of Pennsylvania, 1888], p. 359).

15. Gaillard Hunt, ed., *The Writings of James Madison*, 9 vols. (New York: Putnam, 1904), V:294.

16. James Madison, "Speech in the House of Representatives," June 16, 1789, in *The Debates and Proceedings of the Congress of The United States* (Washington, D.C.: 1834), I:500.

17. Act of September 24, 1789, I *Statutes at Large* 73.

18. See *Cooper v. Aaron*, 358 U.S. 1 (1958), a unanimous opinion signed by all nine justices in which the Warren Court explicitly proclaimed that its

opinion in *Brown v. Board of Education*, 347 U.S. 483 (1954), was "the Supreme Law of the Land."

19. *Marbury v. Madison*, 1 Cranch 137, 179–80 (1803).

20. Lawrence Gene Sager, "Foreword: Constitutional Limitations on Congress' Authority to Regulate the Jurisdiction of Federal Courts," 95 *Harvard Law Review* 17–89, 41, 74, 89 (November 1981).

Suggested Reading

Agresto, John. *The Supreme Court and Constitutional Democracy.* Ithaca: Cornell University Press, 1984.

Berger, Raoul. *Congress v. The Supreme Court.* Cambridge: Harvard University Press, 1969.

Ely, John Hart. *Democracy and Distrust: A Theory of Judicial Review.* Cambridge: Harvard University Press, 1980.

McDowell, Gary L. *Curbing the Courts: The Constitution and the Limits of Judicial Power.* Baton Rouge: Louisiana State University Press, 1988.

Rossum, Ralph A. *Congressional Control of the Judiciary: The Article III Option.* Washington, D.C.: Center for Judicial Studies, 1988.

15

The Anti-Federalist View
of Judicial Review

Peter Augustine Lawler and Jennifer D. Siebels

The United States is a liberal democracy. The majority rules, but not at the expense of minority rights. One way the Constitution seems to provide for the protection of rights is judicial review. The purpose and the extent of judicial review have always been controversial. The main reason for this controversy is that judicial review seems to be the least democratic feature of a mostly democratic government. Another reason is that judicial review is not actually mentioned in the Constitution. There is even some doubt that the Framers intended it.

Maybe the most solid evidence we have that the Framers intended judicial review is that the best spokesmen on both sides of the struggle over the Constitution's ratification assumed its existence. The Anti-Federalist author writing under the pseudonym Brutus urged Americans to vote against the proposed Constitution because judicial review was implied. In response *Federalist* 78 argued that judicial review will be of great use in protecting rights and ensuring good government against majorities aroused by unscrupulous demagogues.

Our intention is to consider Brutus's warning as an accurate and detailed prediction of how the Court would function. He argued that the Court would undermine the authority of the states. He thought that this was reason enough for the Constitution to be defeated by the state ratifying conventions. We do not necessarily share Brutus's desire to defend the states. But he does show that the states were giving up much more than they knew. He also explains better than most contemporary analysts how and why the Court functions as it does today.

Brutus's Warning

Brutus viewed the Constitution as the product of a conspiracy to destroy the states. Its most nationalizing features were hidden from view, and their very existence was denied by the Framers in public. This destructive power was meant not to be noticed, much less felt, until after ratification. Brutus wrote to oppose ratification by exposing hidden dangers:

> It is, moreover, of great importance, to examine with care the nature and extent of the judicial power, because those who are to be vested it, are to be placed in a situation altogether unprecedented in a free country. They are to be rendered totally independent, both of the people and the legislature, both with respect to their offices and salaries. No errors they may commit can be corrected by any power above them, if any such power there be, nor can they be removed from office for making ever so many erroneous adjudications. (Letters of Brutus, XI)

The reason for this unprecedented independence is the purpose of the written Constitution. It exists primarily to control the legislature, which means that the legislature cannot have the final say over its meaning. The Constitution must control the legislature, not the legislature controlling the Constitution. So the Court must have the final power of interpretation. But there seems to be no way of correcting the Court. Its errors go unchecked.

Here Brutus seems to go too far. The Constitution does provide for legislative and executive checks on the Courts. Congress can, for example, alter the Court's size and even take away most of its jurisdiction. But Brutus might respond by reminding us of how ineffective those checks have usually been.

The Court will use its independence, Brutus goes on, mainly to restrict the power of state government. "Every adjudication of the supreme court," he wrote, "on any question that may arise upon the nature and extent of the general government, will affect the limits of state jurisdiction." In determining those limits, the Court will have great latitude. In "giving the sense of every article of the Constitution," the justices "will not confine themselves to any fixed or established rules, but will determine, according to what appears to them, the reason and *spirit* of the Constitution" (emphasis added).

The Constitution is often vague, ambiguous, or lacking in necessary detail. The Court will have to "unfold" its meaning, which means interpreting the parts in light of the "reason and *spirit*" or purposes of the whole. The spirit will be what it appears to be to the Court. So the justices will be able "to mould the government into almost any shape they please." The Constitution will be whatever the Court says it is.

The justices are merely human. For them, as for us, reason cannot be separated from self-love. So, Brutus concludes, they will tend to rule to "enlarge the sphere of their own authority," which means enlarging the power of the national government. The Court will work over time to "mould" the states almost out of existence. Constitutional controversies will not be resolved by an impartial umpire, but by members of the national government.

Brutus later gave what he believed to be the only effective remedy to this judicial imperialism. The power of final interpretation of the Constitution's meaning should be given explicitly to the legislative branch. The legislators are not more trustworthy, but they are more readily checked:

> [I]f they exceed their powers, or sought to find, in the spirit of the Constitution, more than was expressed in the letter, the people from whom they derived their power could remove them, and do themselves right . . . A constitution is a compact of a people with their rulers; if the rulers break the compact, the people have a right to remove them and do themselves justice. (Letters of Brutus, XV)

The people can correct the legislature's expansive misinterpretations of the Constitution through the ordinary means of election. But, if the Court breaks the "compact," the only remedy the people have is revolution. The people, finally, must be the judges of the Constitution's meaning, because it is a compact they have made with their rulers. They must be ready to "do themselves justice" or act decisively if their rights are threatened.

Brutus's belief that the Constitution was a conspiracy against the states was not without foundation. Many of the leading Framers thought that the compromise that produced the federal system was necessary, but not desirable. *Federalist* 10's argument in favor of the large republic is based on the opinion that state government is characteristically bad government. It is too easily dominated by the passion or interest of a majority faction, and so the rights of minorities are insecure.

With this thought in mind, James Madison proposed at the Constitutional Convention that Congress have a veto on state laws. He later tried to use the enthusiasm for the Bill of Rights to amend the Constitution so that "no state shall violate the equal rights of conscience, or freedom of press or trial by jury in criminal cases." He regarded this proposal as substantially improving a defective Constitution, one that left rights too much at the mercy of state legislatures. But it was not adopted, because most of the proponents of the Bill of Rights were animated by the perception that the states and individuals needed further protection from the national government.

Brutus, as an Anti-Federalist, wanted to protect the states because he did not share the view of the leading Framers concerning the best way to protect liberty. He put greater faith in the state governments because they are closer, and so more responsive, to the people. He was more suspicious of the national government, because of its size and its distance from the people. In his view, judicial review threatened both liberty and democracy by threatening the power and vitality of the states.

This hostility to judicial review on behalf of the states was not limited to the Anti-Federalists. Thomas Jefferson was a cautious supporter of the Constitution. But he had his reservations, because he was quite suspicious of the power of the new national government. His view was that its power should be minimal. Most matters should be decided at the local level, where a vigilant and educated people could be able more effectively to protect their rights.

Jefferson saw in the judiciary's exercise of its power a particular threat to effective rule by the people. His fear was Brutus's. The Court might well make the Constitution "a mere thing of wax . . . which they may twist and shape into any form they please." For Jefferson, only "the people themselves" could be trusted to protect their own rights. He added that "if we think them not enlightened enough to exercise their control with wholesome discretion, the remedy is not to take it from them, but to inform their discretion with education." The remedy for bad democratic government is not the surrender of the people's power to the judiciary, but the education of the people to govern well. No matter how wise and virtuous the judges may claim to be, they should not be trusted (Letter to William Charles Jarvis, September 28, 1820).

Judicial Review and the
Fourteenth Amendment

Almost from the beginning, the Court used the Constitution's "spirit" to resolve disputes over interpretation in favor of the national government. Chief Justice John Marshall (1801–35) used his great intelligence to promote the leading Framers' nationalism, sometimes almost against the letter of the Constitution. But there were limits to what the pre-Civil War Court could accomplish. Despite the Constitution's original silence on race and its antislavery spirit, the Court could not root slavery or racism out of state law. Nor could it use the Bill of Rights to compel the states to protect minority rights, because those first ten amendments were directed exclusively against the national government.

The constitutional balance between the states and the national government was decisively altered by the Fourteenth Amendment (1868). Section 1 states:

> All persons born or naturalized in the United States, and subject to the jurisdiction thereof, are citizens of the United States and of the States wherein they reside. No State shall make or enforce any law which shall abridge the privileges or immunities of the citizens of the United States, nor shall any State deprive any person of life, liberty, or property, without due process of law, nor deny to any person within its jurisdiction the equal protection of the laws.

In Section 5, Congress is given power "to enforce, by appropriate legislation, the provisions of this article." The extent to which this amendment empowers the national government has been a matter of controversy since the time of its ratification. The differences of opinion depend in great measure on differing perceptions of the amendment's purpose. The narrowest view is that it was enacted simply to prevent unequal treatment of black citizens, mostly recently freed slaves, by the states. The most expansive view is that it means to empower the nation's government to apply the whole spirit of the unamended Constitution, with its opposition to all racial, gender-based, and religious distinctions in the law, along with the Bill of Rights, to state law. In this view, the Fourteenth Amendment becomes the tool that the national government, including the Court, uses to eradicate all rule by majority faction in the states.

The Supreme Court, over the years, has put forth an astounding array of interpretations of the various provisions of the Fourteenth Amendment. It gradually worked its way to the conclusion that the amendment "incorporates" at least some of the Bill of Rights and so empowers the Court to use those statements protecting "fundamental rights" to declare state laws unconstitutional.

Brutus would no doubt say that the incorporation doctrine was clearly not intended by the framers of the Fourteenth Amendment. It was a clever usurpation of power by the Court for the national government and itself. We can say that the doctrine is not completely implausible, but it is surely the most expansive available interpretation of the "spirit" of a vague amendment. The extent of the Court's cleverness is clear in the fact that the incorporation doctrine is no longer questioned, although it deserves to be. There is almost no appreciation of the irony that the Bill of Rights, conceived and ratified mainly as a way of protecting the states from the national government, has been used by the Court to undermine, if not destroy, the states.

The Court has used the incorporation doctrine in recent decades to alter fundamentally and sometimes dramatically the character of state law. It has greatly increased its own power at the expense of that of the majority. In its view, it has done so to make the protection of rights more secure. In the view of its critics, the Court has gone far beyond any reasonable interpretation of the rights the Constitution actually protects in the service of its power and the justices' personal opinions. These critics say, in effect, that Brutus was right.

We think there is some truth in both of these views. But we will let you judge for yourself by considering two examples of the Court's use of the Fourteenth Amendment to strike down state law. The first concerns religious liberty, the second the right to privacy, especially in the choice of abortion.

The Establishment Clause

"Congress," says the First Amendment, "shall make no law respecting an establishment of religion, or prohibiting the free exercise thereof." We will be concerned only with the first part of this guarantee of religious liberty, the establishment clause. Its original purpose was to prevent the national government from establishing a religion, from making one religion the official religion, the special favorite of government. There was nothing in the Constitution or Bill of Rights to keep the states from establishing religions, and a number of them did.

The extent to which the establishment clause limits government is unclear, because there is a difference of opinion concerning the intentions of the amendment's Framers. One view is that the clause absolutely separates religion and government. Government can give no aid or encouragement to religion at all. This view was held by Jefferson and Madison, the two most sophisticated and extreme thinkers on religious liberty among the American Founders.

But Jefferson was not involved with the drafting of the First Amendment. Madison was, but his language and intention were modified by Congress. The state legislatures that ratified the amendment also had a less radical understanding of the establishment clause's purpose. If the legislative intention is viewed as a whole, the clause must be understood to keep government from preferring one religion over another, but also to allow some government aid to religion in general. The intention was not to banish religion from public life altogether. This more limited view of the establishment clause's purpose is sometimes called *nonpreferentialism*.

The Supreme Court did not "incorporate" the establishment clause into the Fourteenth Amendment until 1947, bringing state law accommodating religion under its scrutiny for the first time. The case was *Everson v. Board of Education*. It concerned a New Jersey statute which permitted the state to reimburse parents' money used to transport their children to parochial schools. Everson, a New Jersey taxpayer, charged that New Jersey had established a religion by using tax money to support religious schools.

The Court took the extreme view, Jefferson's and Madison's, of the meaning of the establishment clause, quoting a letter by Jefferson saying that the Constitution meant to erect a "wall of separation between church and state." It put forth a doctrine which has guided its constitutional interpretation to this day:

> The "establishment of religion" clause means at least this. Neither a state nor the Federal Government . . . can pass laws which aid one religion, aid all religions, or prefer one religion over another.

Even with this doctrine in mind, the Court managed to find a way to uphold the New Jersey law. But the doctrine, much more than the decision, turned out to be the precedent that guided future decisions.

The most controversial or unpopular of the establishment clause cases were *Engel v. Vitale* (1962), which invalidated the use of a government-composed prayer for voluntary recitation in the New

York public schools, and *School District of Abington Township v. Schempp* (1963), which struck down a Pennsylvania law that required daily Bible reading in the public schools. Students could be excused from the latter religious exercise with a note from their parents.

With these two cases, the Court aimed to eliminate the long-standing religious practices of the public schools in most of the states. These practices were sanctioned by the majority, and their constitutionality was not widely questioned. They were not regarded as threatening significantly the rights of any minority. Still, it is difficult to argue that once the Court decided to take these cases, it could have decided them any other way. Official prayer and Bible reading are preferences for one form of religion over another. They clearly fail even the more moderate nonpreferentialist test. One argument given against these decisions was that they inhibit the free exercise of religion. The Court responded forcefully in *Abington*: "While the Free Exercise Clause clearly prohibits the use of state action to deny the right of free exercise to *anyone*, it has never meant that a majority could use the machinery of the State to practice its beliefs." The free exercise clause cannot be used as an excuse for a majority faction to establish a religion.

These antiprayer decisions were opposed, and still are, by a large majority of Americans. But Congress never passed legislation depriving the Court of jurisdiction over such cases. Nor was it able to pass a constitutional amendment. President Ronald Reagan repeatedly endorsed an amendment that would restore voluntary prayer to the public schools, partly because he knew that such a stand was quite popular. But such an amendment never had a high or even serious place on his legislative agenda. Reagan and President George Bush were able to appoint six (out of nine) justices, but even they did not lead the Court to give the states significantly greater latitude. Brutus would seem to be right. The majority does not have an effective way of correcting what it believed to be an important error by the Court.

Some of the states continued to resist the Court's decisions. One method they used was to pass statutes testing their limits. An Alabama law said that "a period of silence not to exceed one minute in duration shall be observed for meditation or voluntary prayer." The Court, in *Wallace v. Jaffree* (1985), struck the law down, ruling that "the addition of 'or voluntary prayer' indicates that the State intended to characterize prayer as a favored practice. Such an endorsement is not consistent with the established principle that the government must pursue a course of complete neutrality toward religion." The Court justified its decision the same way it did the earlier ones on school prayer, as an obvious violation of the *Everson* principle.

But the *Wallace* decision was considerably more extreme than the earlier ones. *Engel* and *Abington* dealt with exercises that would not pass either the nonpreferentialist test or the "wall of separation" test. But a provision for voluntary, silent prayer gives religion no content, and so prefers no particular religion over others. Nor does the Alabama law seem even to favor religion over nonreligion. Students may choose prayer or meditation, with no guidance as to which choice is better.

Most importantly, no particular minority's rights are violated in any significant way by the law. No one will know whether a particular student prayed or not, and there seems to be no way to pressure conformity in some subtle way. The Court's opinion was not written with the protection of some minority's rights in mind.

The Court's view was that the mere mention of the word prayer makes the law unconstitutional, because it is presented as one of two possible favored practices. The law may do absolutely nothing that might be interpreted as encouraging religion. The Court's quest for extreme consistency on this point, Brutus would say, seems simply to be an attempt to maximize its own power by minimizing state discretion. The Court, in fact, seemed to be more animated by anger directed against the idea that Alabama would challenge the extent of its authority than anything else.

The Court has not always applied the "wall of separation" principle consistently. In *Marsh v. Chambers* (1983), for example, the Court upheld government payment of chaplains to open state legislative sessions with prayers, on the basis that such practices had a long, settled place in our history. Justice William Brennan argued quite reasonably in his dissenting opinion that the Court had not hesitated in other decisions to use the *Everson* principle to negate settled practices. The cause of this and other, similar inconsistencies seems to be mainly the Court's fear of angry public opinion. Brutus is not completely right. The Court knows there are limits to how completely it can apply its view of the Constitution's "spirit."

Justices William Rehnquist and Antonin Scalia in dissenting opinions have argued that the "wall of separation" principle is historically unsound and too extreme to be applied consistently. They call for doing away with the *Everson* precedent and replacing it with a prudent nonpreferentialism. Perhaps the best statement of this prudent nonpreferentialism is Scalia's dissent in *Lee v. Weisman* (1992). The first thing worth noting is that his dissent had to be a dissent because three Reagan–Bush appointees voted to uphold the "wall of separation" doctrine.

The opinion of the Court was written by Justice Anthony Kennedy, a Reagan appointee. The Court struck down a Rhode Island practice of inviting members of the clergy to give invocations and benedictions at the graduation ceremonies of public high schools. In an effort to make sure that the prayers were inoffensively nonsectarian, local government officials gave out pamphlets with guidelines for the composition of prayers. The Court noted this government involvement which made the prayer official. The "pressure from their peers toward conformity" also produced "social pressure" to seem to participate in the prayer by "the act of standing or remaining silent."

Scalia argued in dissent that this violation of minority rights is negligible. Standing or silence need not mean participation, only respect. Scalia "would deny that the dissenter's interest in avoiding *even the false appearance of participation* constitutionally trumps the government's interest in fostering respect for prayer generally." An "important unifying mechanism" that gives spirit or life to the community ought to prevail over a "minimal inconvenience." That order of priorities may be sensible, but the Court would have to abandon the "wall of separation" doctrine to affirm it.

Abortion and the Right to Privacy

The "right to privacy" has a rather convoluted history. Insofar as it applies to personal decisions having to do with sex and reproduction, it appears for the first time in *Griswold v. Connecticut* (1965). In that case, the Court invalidated a Connecticut law prohibiting the use of contraceptives.

The five justices who held that the law was unconstitutional could not agree on which part of the Constitution made it so. Justice William Douglas, in the opinion for the Court, used the incorporation doctrine to apply the Bill of Rights against the states. But he pointed not to a particular amendment, but to "penumbras [or shadows], formed by emanations from those guarantees [of the Bill of Rights] that help give them life and substance." He found a number of "zones of privacy" in the various amendments, and from them come the penumbras, formed by emanations that constitute the right to privacy.

Justice Arthur Goldberg, in his concurring opinion, focused on the Ninth Amendment to show that the Court "is not confined to the specific terms of the Bill of Rights." According to that amendment: "The enumeration in the Constitution, of certain rights, shall not be construed to deny or disparage others retained by the people." Goldberg seemed to see in this amendment an opportunity for the Court to protect rights the Constitution does not mention explicitly. Justice John Marshall Harlan, in his concurring opinion, held that the due process clause of the Fourteenth Amendment was sufficient authority to protect the liberty to use contraceptives.

This remarkable difference of opinion concerning the location of the constitutional foundation for a decision, together with the sheer vagueness of Douglas's and Goldberg's opinions, suggest that the Court is molding the Constitution in terms of its view of its spirit, as Brutus predicted. The justices did clearly agree that a religiously inspired majority faction is violating rights with a meddlesome law.

Douglas's opinion for the Court in *Griswold* emphasized that the right to privacy being protected is that of the marital relationship. He would not have the police "search[ing] the sacred precincts of the marital bedroom." He describes marriage as "a coming together for better or worse . . . and intimate to the degree of being sacred." Both the most lucid and the most poetic parts of Douglas's opinion say that the Connecticut law is unconstitutional because the privacy in marriage is sacred.

But in *Eisenstadt v. Baird* (1972) the Court used the *Griswold* precedent to invalidate a Massachusetts law that made it a felony to give unmarried persons contraceptives. While acknowledging that "in *Griswold* the right to privacy in question inhered in the marital relationship," the Court added: "If the right to privacy means anything, it is the right of the individual, married or single, to be free from unwarranted government intrusion into matters so fundamentally affecting a person as the decision whether to bear or beget a child." The Court's power expanded dramatically with this movement from marital to individual privacy. Gone is any reference to the sacred character of the reproductive relationship. How *Eisenstadt* flows from *Griswold* was not properly explained.

But this conclusion that the Constitution protects individual sexual and reproductive privacy from majority faction laid the foundation for *Roe v. Wade* (1973), the decision which invalidated nearly all state law restricting abortion. This decision had an extraordinarily sweeping and profound effect, because almost all the states had such laws. What made and still makes *Roe* controversial is not only this effect, but the looseness and even the arrogance of the Court's constitutional argument.

The Court's opinion begins with an acknowledgment of "the sensitive and emotional nature of the abortion controversy, of the vigorous opposing views, even among physicians, and of the deep and seemingly absolute convictions the subject inspires." But that acknowledgment was not a prelude to a cautious or modest opinion. The Court went on to show with confidence that it could perform its self-designated task, which was "to resolve the issue by constitutional measurement, free of emotion and predilection." It was able to do so without even addressing *the* controversial question: When does human life begin?

The Court waffled a bit, following precedent, on where the right to privacy is found in the Constitution, but finally claimed that it is "founded in the Fourteenth Amendment's conception of personal liberty and restriction on state action" and "is broad enough to encompass a woman's decision whether or not to terminate her pregnancy." The Court added that this "personal liberty" might be limited by a "compelling state interest." It, through "constitutional measurement," decided how weighty each of the relevant state interests were, the protection of the mother's health and the protection of potential life.

Using the idea of "constitutional measurement" quite precisely, the Court divided a pregnancy into three trimesters. For the first three months, there can be no limitations on the woman's freedom to choose. During the second trimester, health regulations are permissible, because abortion has become more dangerous than carrying the fetus to term. After this trimester, it can be assumed that the fetus has reached "viability," or a capacity to exist independently of the mother. So for the last three months the state "may go so far as to proscribe abortion during this period, except when it is necessary to protect the life of the mother."

Justice Rehnquist complained in dissent:

> The decision here to break pregnancy into three distinct terms and to outline the permissible restrictions the State may impose on each

one . . . partakes more of judicial legislation than it does a determination of the intent of the drafters of the Fourteenth Amendment.

Brutus would say that the Court has used the Constitution's spirit willfully to expand its own power beyond anything the letter of the Constitution allows. It has done so in a way which fundamentally constrains the flexibility of the majorities in the states to legislate on a matter of fundamental moral importance. But the issue here, as Brutus himself implies, is not simply a matter of power. The Court is clearly animated by the conviction that laws that restrict abortion are an imposition by a majority faction on minority rights. Many Americans agree. The Court cleverly expanded its power to make the Constitution's protection of rights more effective.

But, in this case, the Court's argument was not particularly persuasive. The trimester approach really does seem like legislation, not constitutional interpretation, and many critics have shown that it is not even solid or stable legislation. The Court's claim that the issue can be resolved without considering when human life begins is equally unpersuasive. The division of opinion in America concerning the constitutionality and the rightness of laws restricting abortion still centers on divergent and, as the Court says, probably irreconcilable answers to that question. Many pro-choice legal scholars, such as President Bill Clinton's first appointee to the Court, Ruth Bader Ginsburg, acknowledge that *Roe* is bad constitutional law.

The intent of *Roe* was to remove abortion for controversy, and there is evidence in subsequent opinions that the Court was surprised, even angered, that it was unable to do so. Its effect was to make the abortion controversy in America immediately much more intense and extreme. In the liberal and democratic nations of Western Europe, abortion policy is not made by the courts, but by the legislature. So compromise is usually reached, and policy is a mixture of extreme views.

As Justice Ginsburg has pointed out, the American states were in the process of liberalizing their abortion laws in the years immediately preceding *Roe*. Compromise was occurring, and Americans were showing a readiness to curb their strongly held views by accepting the principle of majority rule. The Court's extreme imposition destroyed this spirit of compromise and aroused almost unprecedented animosity in American political life.

Consider how this animosity polarized America's two major

political parties. The Democrats became strongly pro-*Roe*, and it soon became impossible to express doubts about the Court's decision and be a national figure in the party. The Republicans quickly became more than anti-*Roe*. They endorsed in their party platform a constitutional amendment that would prohibit abortion almost altogether. Many or most of the American people, ambivalent about public policy on abortion, are dissatisfied with the positions of both of the parties.

Roe has distorted American political life in other ways. It has, for example, made the selection of justices too political. Democrats view anti-*Roe* appointees as outside the mainstream of responsible constitutional opinion. Republicans view pro-*Roe* appointees in the same way. When the Democrats control the Senate, and the Republicans the presidency, as was the case for part of Reagan's and all of Bush's administrations, the result has been confirmation processes full of distortions and dirty tricks on both sides.

The Court also has not been wholly consistent in its application of its right to privacy doctrine to the choice of abortion. It upheld laws passed by Congress and by a state legislature to prohibit public funding for abortion, although it was made available for other medical procedures. In *Bowers v. Hardwick* (1986), it also upheld a Georgia law prohibiting sodomy, on the basis that there is no constitutional right to homosexual sodomy. Its decision not to find such a right just because there was no precedent for it was out of keeping with the spirit of *Roe*.

Consensual sodomy also would seem to be less ambiguously a private act than the decision to have an abortion. The Court's reluctance always to follow the logic of the *Roe* precedent can be attributed almost exclusively to fear of public anger, which might arouse Congress actually to use its checks. Once again, Brutus is not completely right. The Court does perceive limits, although only very broad ones.

Despite much talk and some action on legislation and amendments, Congress has never acted to curb the Court's abortion authority. Again, President Reagan used anti-*Roe* sentiment to win votes, but he did not really push hard for congressional action. Still, he might be viewed as having worked effectively toward the decision's reversal. He and Bush won confirmation for six presumably anti-*Roe* justices, and for several years the imminent reversal of the decision was expected.

The Court did come very close to reversing *Roe* in 1989. But in

Planned Parenthood v. Casey (1992), two Reagan and one Bush appointees unexpectedly joined the majority to uphold the ruling of *Roe* on a new foundation designed by Justice Sandra Day O'Connor. She tried to provide the argument for the Constitution's special protection of the abortion right missing from the *Roe* opinion:

> Abortion is a unique act . . . Though abortion is conduct, it does not follow that the State is entitled to proscribe it in all instances. This is because the liberty of the woman is at stake in a sense unique to the human condition and so unique to the law.

Whether or not this argument is satisfactory, we leave to you to judge. It depends far more on what seems to be a new view of the Constitution's spirit than its letter. But it is undeniably an improvement on *Roe*, and perhaps the right to privacy to an abortion has been set on better foundation. But O'Connor and her two "centrist" Republican colleagues, Anthony Kennedy and David Souter, were also very candid in saying that another reason why they could not vote to reverse *Roe* was that such a reversal would diminish public confidence in the Court. O'Connor argued that "overruling *Roe*'s central holding . . . would seriously weaken the Court's capacity to exercise judicial power and to function as the Supreme Court of a Nation dedicated to the rule of law." The Court, it seems, should never do anything to undercut its power and dignity, even if it means not admitting to an error. It is clearly in the Court's self-interest almost never to correct itself by reversing a precedent.

Brutus was right in two senses. The Court will act to maximize its own power, and it will strongly tend not to surrender what it has acquired. It is also extremely difficult, if not quite impossible, for the other branches or the majority to correct a judicial error, even one as important as *Roe*.

Scalia, in his dissenting opinion in *Planned Parenthood*, vigorously called for *Roe*'s reversal in words reminiscent of Brutus:

> The States may, if they wish, permit abortion-on-demand, but the Constitution does not require them to do so. The permissibility of abortion, and the limitations upon it, are to be resolved like most important questions in our democracy: by citizens trying to persuade one another and then voting.

The Constitution, in truth, says nothing that prevents the majority from resolving the abortion question as it thinks best. The question is left to the state legislatures. If the legislators abuse the rights and interests of citizens, it is the right of citizens to vote them out.

That abortion is properly a political, not a constitutional, issue is clear to Scalia in the scandalous politicization of confirmation hearings for new justices since *Roe*. "Senators," he observes, "go through a list of their constituents' most favored and disfavored constitutional rights, and seek the nominee's commitment to support or oppose them." The fiasco involving Clarence Thomas and Anita Hill in 1991 was primarily not the fault of the president or Congress, but of the Court.

A reasonable objection here, perhaps, is that abortion policy is too important and sensitive to be left to state legislatures, where the danger of majority faction is too great. But another possibility is legislation by Congress to protect a woman's choice of an abortion, one favored by Democratic congressional leaders and the Clinton administration. Congress, in passing such a law, might be usurping some state power under the Constitution, but it is doubtful that the Court would declare such a law unconstitutional. In any case, Congress will be easier for the people to correct than the Court. If the people don't like the law, they can vote the bums out.

Conclusion

We have said enough to show that Brutus's warning about the Court was accurate and astute. It has functioned to maximize its own power, in the name of protecting individuals from state majority factions. Its errors have proved to be very difficult to correct. Even angry majorities usually fail. Because there is a connection between reason and self-love, the Court has sometimes pushed its authority to extremes, and it has been extremely reluctant to admit its own errors.

But many thoughtful Americans will acknowledge all this and still praise the Court. They believe that the Court, by empowering the national government, works to strengthen good government against bad. They share *The Federalist*'s distrust of the states, and they look to Washington for ways to protect the individual against unjust majorities.

But others worry because the states have become too weak and our political life has become corrupted by excessive judicial power. State and local governments are an indispensable source of our political vitality, and the Court has gone farther than is reasonable in demoralizing them. The people themselves have become habituated to looking too readily to the Courts, rather than themselves, for protection of their rights and the resolution of controversial political questions.

Suggested Reading

Allen, W. B., and Gordon Lloyd, eds. The Letters of Brutus, IV, XI, XII, XV, in *The Essential Anti-Federalist*. Lanham, Md.: University Press of America, 1985.

Craig, Barbara Hinkson, and David M. O'Brien. *Abortion and American Politics*. Chatham, N.J.: Chatham House, 1993.

Eastland, Terry. *Religious Liberty in the Supreme Court*. Washington, D.C.: Ethics and Public Policy Center, 1993.

Everson v. Board of Education 330 U.S. 1 (1947).

Planned Parenthood v. Casey 112 S.Ct. 2791 (1992).

Roe v. Wade 410 U.S. 113 (1973).

Wallace v. Jaffree 469 U.S. 1102 (1985).

16

The Two Executives: The President and the Supreme Court

Robert Scigliano

We do not usually think of the presidency and the judiciary as having anything in common. The one takes care that the laws are faithfully executed (in addition to other tasks bestowed on it by the Constitution) and the other decides cases and controversies arising under the laws and the Constitution. But, as I shall try to show, the two branches can be said to share a common power under different names and to perform similar tasks in different ways. The Framers arranged matters so that the two branches might act from a common interest in restraining Congress. But some of their sharpest differences have been with each other and the connection between them has been weakening.

The Common Power

The American Framers borrowed from the writings of the English philosopher John Locke and the French philosopher Montesquieu in devising a government based on separated powers. Writing in the late seventeenth century, Locke seems to have been the first person to speak of executive power as that of carrying out laws made by the legislative authority. There was no separate judicial power in his scheme; judging was considered to be part of executive power. For example, Locke includes "the administration of justice" within the execution of the laws. He does consider judging to be a distinct activity, if not a distinct power, and insists on the need for "indifferent [impartial] and upright" judges.[1]

277

Montesquieu is the bridge between Locke and the American Framers. Writing in the first part of the eighteenth century, he was "the oracle who is always consulted and cited" on the subject of separation of powers, according to *Federalist* 47. Adopting Locke's view that judges are engaged in executive activity, Montesquieu placed that activity within the executive power, calling it the power of judging.[2]

Apparently influenced by Locke and Montesquieu, many Americans at the time of the founding thought judges were to engage in the execution of the laws. In the Constitutional Convention, for example, Gouverneur Morris observed that "the judiciary . . . was part of the executive," and James Madison saw "an analogy between the executive and judicial departments [branches] in several respects." He mentioned that both the executive and the judges executed, interpreted, and applied the laws.[3]

A presidential cabinet containing the chief justice and the heads of the executive departments was proposed by several delegates at the Constitutional Convention. In one version, called a council of state, the president could "submit any matter to the discussion" of his council and could "require the written opinions" of its members. The chief justice, who would preside over the body in the president's absence, had the specific duty to "recommend such alterations of and additions to the laws of the U.S. as may in his opinion be necessary to the due administration of justice, and such as may promote useful learning and inculcate sound morality throughout the nation."[4] These proposals failed because most of the Framers were opposed to saddling the president with a cabinet, not because they were opposed to a Supreme Court justice's membership in it. The final draft of the Constitution did not prohibit judges from also serving in the executive branch, even though they did not allow members of Congress or the executive to serve in each other's ranks, or members of Congress to be judges. So a Supreme Court justice could be an ambassador and a secretary of state could be a member of the Supreme Court, but neither official could be a senator or representative.

The idea of a close relationship between the executive and the judiciary was carried into practice under the Constitution. President George Washington saw nothing wrong in asking Chief Justice John Jay, along with his department secretaries, to suggest legislation that he might recommend to Congress. On a number of occasions Washington and his secretary of the treasury, Alexander

Hamilton, consulted the chief justice on matters of foreign policy and national security, including the constitutionality of Washington's Neutrality and Whiskey Rebellion proclamations. The president asked the Supreme Court as a whole for its written opinion on questions related to American neutrality in the war that broke out in Europe at the end of 1792. When Jay, as Washington's special ambassador to Great Britain, negotiated that treaty, he was a member of the Supreme Court. A few years later, Oliver Ellsworth, in a similar appointment by President John Adams, negotiated a settlement of differences between the United States and France while serving on the Court.

Nor did Congress, at first, see anything wrong with using judges to assist the executive. When it enacted Hamilton's plan for funding the public debt in 1790, it accepted the treasury secretary's recommendation that the chief justice be a member of the commission to manage the fund for paying off the debt. A pension law that was passed in 1791 to handle the claims of Revolutionary War veterans made federal judges, in effect, aides to the secretary of war. They were to examine pension claims and submit their reports to the secretary, who would approve or correct the reports and forward them to Congress. Supreme Court justices were included in the task because in those days they "rode circuit"; that is, they periodically conducted court with district judges in the territorial circuits to which they were assigned.

So in the earliest years of the republic, presidents and Congress alike engaged judges in the business of the executive branch with hardly a thought that they might be violating the principle of separation of powers. Washington, most members of Congress, and the justices of the Supreme Court, including John Jay, Oliver Ellsworth, and John Marshall, had been delegates to the national or state ratifying conventions, and so we can assume that they acted with some notion of what the Constitution allowed.

But a stricter notion of separation of powers, one that placed the judiciary at a greater distance from the presidency, emerged in the course of the 1790s. No serious objections were made to the departmental caretaker duties performed by Chief Justices Jay and Marshall. But the appointments of Jay and Ellsworth as ambassadors did draw criticism, especially within the Senate, when those nominations were approved. The Supreme Court itself decided that formal advice-giving to the president was improper, and in 1793 it politely declined Washington's request for answers to questions. By this time, the chief justice's name had been dropped from circulars that the president sent to his department secretaries. Not long after, the practice of informal advice-giving by individual members of the Court declined sharply.

The presidency and the judiciary further adjusted their relations after the 1790s, moving toward clearer institutional separation and a clearer differentiation of the common power they exercised. Thomas Jefferson's eight years in the presidency hastened the separation. Little common ground existed between the judiciary and a president who regarded it as "the stronghold" of his defeated Federalist enemy. Before he gave up the presidency to Jefferson in early 1801, John Adams had appointed a number of members of his party to the court, the most important of whom was Jefferson's political adversary, John Marshall.

In the view of separation of powers that has prevailed since the early nineteenth century, Supreme Court justices are supposed to have little to do with the executive branch—or the legislative branch, for that matter. For a justice to enter into executive service, as Jay and Ellsworth did, would be considered improper. In fact, only Justice Robert H. Jackson has done it since then, acting as the chief American prosecutor at the trials of the defeated Nazi leaders at Nuremberg, Germany. Many people today would probably disapprove of a justice serving even in a quasi-judicial capacity off the Court, as Chief Justice Earl Warren did in chairing the commission that investigated the assassination of President John F. Kennedy, and as a number of justices had done previously, usually without a murmur of criticism. It still seems acceptable for justices to speak out in a nonpartisan way on matters that directly affect the court system. Chief Justice Warren E. Burger made it a practice to give the president and Congress his views on judicial workloads, the need for more judges, and reforms in the Court's jurisdiction. Perhaps most Americans would not object to the long-standing, though intermittent, practice of justices giving the president their views on appointments to the Supreme Court or lower federal courts. Still, this kind of advice-giving has always taken place privately.

Public sentiment is strongly opposed to judges acting as informal presidential advisers. Such activities have not been an issue until recently, partly because they were not generally known until long after they had occurred but mostly because they seem not to have taken place often. Apart from Chief Justice Jay's assistance to the Washington administration, which was conducted before the protocol between justices and the executive had been established, not many justices have been involved in significant ways with the executive branch. Such involvement appears to be mainly a phenomenon of this century (or perhaps judicial secrets have been harder to keep in modern America) and seems to have taken place mostly between justices and the presidents who appointed them. In each instance, the parties were continuing a previous political relationship. The issue came to a head in 1968 when President Lyndon B. Johnson nominated Justice Abe Fortas, an old friend whom he had appointed to the Court three years earlier, to succeed Earl Warren as chief justice. Fortas's activities as a presidential adviser already had been widely reported in the press, and these reports were offered in the Senate as a major reason why Fortas's appointment should not be approved. (It was not.)

No executive position has been held by a Supreme Court justice since Robert Jackson in 1946. No justice has performed judicial functions outside the Court since Earl Warren in 1964. None seems to have lent his services as a White House adviser since Fortas in 1968. Practice has brought about this situation. Today we hardly ever think of judges and executive officers as sharing the common task of executing the laws.

The Hard and Soft Executives

In their execution of the laws, the president and the judiciary play complementary parts. As a federal court described the relationship in an 1837 decision: "the judicial and executive powers are closely allied; they are necessary to each other in the discharge of the duties of both departments."[5] The differences between the two branches are important, to be sure. The president is an active agent in law enforcement with an energy—sometimes referred to as "force" by the Framers—that pervades the entire government. He is an Argus with hundreds of thousands of eyes. His subordinates in the executive branch ceaselessly watch over the laws and those to whom they apply. As the Framers intended, he can do many things, do them quickly and with decision, and when necessary, do them secretly. Those who are slow in yielding to him are prodded, and those who might think of violating his orders are admonished. And when prods and threats fail, the president's minions take the recalcitrant and disobedient to court to be coerced into compliance, punished for their disobedience, or if they are fortunate, told that they have not offended the laws after all.

Judges, on the other hand, are (or were intended to be) passive in their enforcement of the laws. They "can take no active resolution whatever," according to *Federalist* 78. Theirs is the power of judgment, really not a power at all. To overcome their "natural feebleness," the Constitution gave them their offices during good behavior (practically speaking, for life) and prohibited legislative reductions in their salaries. But, although judges act only on the specific parties in cases brought to them, they also serve law enforcement generally, for many people take note of what happens in court and govern themselves accordingly.

Like the president, the Supreme Court primarily supervises the work of others. Several hundred judges in the federal district (trial) courts and, above them, in the federal courts of appeals handle nearly all judicial business before it gets to the Supreme Court, which few cases do. The thousands of state court judges also act under the Court's supervision when their business involves "federal questions," which under today's expanded notion of federal authority covers a great deal of their litigation. The Supreme Court alone decides about two hundred fifty cases a year on their merits nowadays, less than a handful of which come into the Court without having first passed through other tribunals.[6]

The executive assists the judiciary in several ways. It assigns marshals to the judges to serve their writs and other orders, to make arrests, to guard prisoners, and to transport the convicted to prisons it maintains. It also sends the judges much of their business. The executive arm of government institutes all criminal cases and a large portion of the civil ones that are tried in courts, and the government is often the defendant in other civil suits. In a typical recent term, the government has been a party, one way or another, in about two-fifths of the cases that have been filed in federal district courts and courts of appeals (which take their appeals laterally from decisions of administrative agencies as well as vertically from the district courts). It has also been a party in nearly all of the minor matters tried before U.S. magistrates (who are appointed by federal district judges). Further, it has participated in about a third of the appeals (from lower federal and state courts) that the Court has considered accepting for decision and in about two-thirds of the cases that it accepted and decided on their merits after having heard argument on them.

These figures only partly tell the story of the relationship between the executive and the judiciary. Consider the Supreme Court's appellate caseload, which runs to more than 4,000 cases a year. The Court has a great deal of discretion in deciding which appeals to accept, and it needs help in doing so. The executive, through the solicitor general and his staff, who are located in the Justice Department but exercise considerable autonomy, provides a good measure of this help. The solicitor general almost always decides whether the government will appeal its defeats in lower courts to the Supreme Court, and the Court relies on him to appeal only the most deserving cases. In a recent term, for example, the government appealed only 43 of its 637 lower court defeats, compared with 1,430 defeats that were appealed by its adversaries.

The solicitor general helps out in other ways. He sometimes tells the Court which appeals by the government's adversaries are worth hearing. Increasingly over the past few decades, he has entered into other people's litigation in his capacity as *amicus curiae*, or friend of the court. He might suggest two dozen or more cases for review to the justices and, when cases are to be decided on their merits, may just as often throw the government's support to one side or the other. Quite often, the Court will invite the solicitor general to enter other people's fights, as it has done in such important controversies as those concerning school integration and abortion. What seems still more remarkable, the solicitor general will on rare occasion come into Court to say that the government did not deserve to win a case in district court or the court of appeals.

What does the executive ask of the Supreme Court justices in return? Only that they do their jobs in administering justice. Of course, the executive has its own idea of what justice requires: it would not have gone to trial, appealed its defeats, defended its victories in appellate court, or offered its friendly advice to the Court if it did not believe it was in the right. So in wishing that the Supreme Court should do what is right, the executive wants the Court to decide its way. And the Court usually does. In a typical term, it will accept for decision between two-thirds and three-fourths of the government's appeals and 90 percent of the appeals supported by the government as *amicus curiae*. In comparison, it will accept only two or three percent of the appeals of the executive's defeated opponents.

The executive branch does very well, too, in cases decided by the Supreme Court on their merits. It is usually on the winning side as party and *amicus* in perhaps three-fourths of the Court's decisions, with its success rate having fallen some in recent years. Clearly, the executive branch is very active and persuasive in the Supreme Court, whether in getting into Court and keeping its adversaries out or in winning cases for itself and its friends.

What we have been describing is "tough" and "soft" law enforcement. The president is a tough executive and judges are soft executives. Unlike the president, whose hand grasps a sword in his capacity as commander of the armed forces, or Congress, whose hand clutches a purse, the judiciary, exercising judgment, holds the scales of justice.

The tough executive, keeping his sword in its scabbard and out of view, sometimes presents himself as softer than he is. What he executes, he or his defenders will say, are laws passed by Congress—neglecting to mention that these laws in all likelihood were approved or even recommended by him. The Constitution, a president might add, imposes law enforcement as a duty, and yet he and his subordinates seem to enjoy their work. He certainly resents interference with it, for he not only threatens and arrests but also calls out the military power of the nation to overcome resistance. He cites his duty to execute the laws to justify some unusual actions: for example, George Washington's issuance of a Neutrality Proclamation in time of foreign war, Abraham Lincoln's proclamation of a blockade of southern ports during the Civil War, and Harry Truman's seizure of the steel industry during the Korean War. And when the tough executive really has his spirits aroused, he speaks of the duty imposed by his constitutional oath "to execute the Office of President," not simply the laws of Congress, and "to preserve, protect, and defend the Constitution of the United States." Whatever the tough executive may say about his power, ordinary citizens recognize it for what it is in the vast array of law enforcers, administrators, investigators, prosecutors, and jailers—all of them backed by the military might of the commander-in-chief.

The exercise of judicial power looks quite different from the exercise of executive power. Wearing robes, sitting singly or collegially, judges seem to be onlookers above the fray, usually saying little and almost never in harsh tones. If it is a trial court, the judge will carefully explain to the criminal defendant his rights against the government or assure the plaintiff and the defendant in a civil trial of his neutrality in their contest. Occasionally, he will dismiss a case or find a statute unconstitutional. It is true that most persons accused of crime are convicted, and nearly all civil suits end in a victory for one side or the other. But, as the trial judge may inform the parties, this is not because it is his hand that has come down harshly but that of the law or the Constitution itself. "Don't blame me," his tone implies, "if things have gone badly with you, or if you must find fault with somebody, blame the jury—for they rendered the verdict." With this, the soft executive moves to the next case, turning over the criminally convicted to agents of the tough executive. The loser may appeal his case to a higher court, where again he will be treated with courtesy and perhaps sympathy—but probably no better result.

In this view of things, it is hard to think of judges as being in law enforcement, or even as being part of government. They sometimes speak as though they are not. This is the secret of their power, for the work of judges is best done when it is thought to be different from that of busy administrators and busybody legislators. It is most effective when kept out of sight, when its actions are supported by judgments and the source of judgment is seen to be the will of the lawmaker. Judges forget the advantage that comes from being regarded as "the living oracles" of the law when they exercise "raw judicial power," that is, when they move into the domains of lawmaking and tough, exposed execution of the law.

Harmony and Conflict

The Framers expected that the president and judges would usually share a common outlook on matters that came to them. Congress would be the discordant member of their system of separated powers. In their experience under the early state governments, it was the legislative branch that was "everywhere extending the sphere of its activity and drawing all power into its impetuous vortex" (*Federalist* 48). The Framers feared it would be like this under their government if preventive measures were not taken. And they thought the House of Representatives, with its numerous members elected directly by the people for limited terms, would be the main embodiment of the legislative power in their Constitution. The president and judges would lack the House's claim to popular support, for they would be more distant from the people. The president would be elected for four years by special electors who themselves would be chosen as the state legislatures devised and the judges would be appointed during good behavior by the president and Senate.

More specifically, the Framers seemed to expect that the presidency and the judiciary, as the weaker branches of government, would form a limited defensive alliance against an encroaching Congress. In addition, these two branches would protect the rights of the people, especially property rights, against oppressive legislation. In what follows I will be concerned with the alliance's operation as a mutual defense against congressional encroachments.

I begin with the observation that the alliance has not worked out quite as the Framers seem to have expected. It is true that the presidency and the judiciary have supported each other against Congress more often than not or, at least, have not often joined in legislative actions against the other, but the exceptions have been fairly numerous and have sometimes been of major significance.

Presidents have certainly had reason to be gratified by certain decisions of the Supreme Court that supported their claims to authority against those of Congress. In *Myers v. United States* (1926) for instance, the Court struck down, on the broadest grounds, a legislative provision that limited the president's right to remove postmasters appointed with senatorial consent. The president, the Court said, could remove all executive officers—not just postmasters—for any reason whatsoever.[7] In *Immigration and Naturalization Service v. Chadha* (1983) it ruled, also on the broadest grounds, that Congress could not delegate authority to the executive conditionally, reserving the right to "veto" legislative actions taken pursuant to that authority or to "veto" entire laws. Here the House of Representatives had overridden the decision of the attorney general allowing a Kenyan national to remain in the United States.[8] In one swoop, veto provisions in about two hundred laws were rendered useless. Also, federal courts have in recent years refused in a number of instances to decide cases brought by individual members of Congress challenging actions that presidents have taken in the realm of foreign affairs. A recent example was President George Bush's claim in late 1990 and early 1991 (not acted upon) that he could engage the nation in war against Iraq without the prior authorization of Congress.

The judiciary has also benefited on a number of occasions from the position taken by the president when efforts have been made within Congress to take action against judges or their authority. Most threats, I should mention, have not been seriously pursued, for Congress has been more often irritated by the judiciary than resolved to take action against it. In 1869, it sought to deprive the Supreme Court of jurisdiction to decide a case, *Ex parte McCardle*, which the Court had accepted but not yet decided.[9] President

Andrew Johnson vetoed the act, Congress overrode the veto, and the Court gave up the case. The issue at stake was an important one, for the *McCardle* case challenged the constitutionality of the congressional program for reconstructing the South after the Civil War. In the 1950s the Justice Department under President Dwight Eisenhower opposed legislation that would have deprived the Supreme Court of jurisdiction in matters related to internal security.

But let us turn to some important instances in which the two "allies" did not support each other. Less than a decade after the Supreme Court upheld the president's unrestricted right to remove executive officials, it began to cut back on it, significantly in the case of *Humphrey's Executor* (*Rathbun*) *v. United States* (1935). Here the Court said the president had no such power if the executive officials exercised functions of a legislative or judicial nature and if Congress limited the reasons for which they might be removed. The case involved President Franklin Roosevelt's removal of a member of the Federal Trade Commission.[10] In *Morrison v. Olson* (1988), the Court upheld congressional power to provide for the appointment by judges of special counsel to investigate executive wrongdoing and to prosecute those persons whom they succeeded in having grand juries indict.[11] Not only did the law give the president no say in the appointment or budgets of these special counsels, but it assigned their removal to the attorney general and empowered him or her to act only under stringent restrictions. Here we have a case of legislative–judicial cooperation to limit presidential power!

Whether intentionally or not, the judiciary also cooperated with Congress in *United States v. Nixon* (1974), the so-called Watergate tapes case. A federal court of appeals had decided in another case that a congressional committee could not compel the president to furnish it with records it demanded. But the Supreme Court said in *Nixon* that the records could be ordered by a federal court for use in a criminal proceeding—the trial of some of those involved in the break-in at the Democratic party headquarters at the Watergate Hotel in Washington, D.C.[12] Solid evidence of President Richard Nixon's complicity in covering up the break-in came into the possession of Congress and furnished the basis for the president's impeachment (which he avoided by resigning his office).

In recent years, federal judges have moved more directly to curtail the president's authority in relation to Congress. Lower courts have limited his use of the pocket veto, which the Constitution allows

when Congress has adjourned within ten days of his receiving legislation, by telling him that this applies only to adjournments at the
end of Congress's biennial sessions and not to intra- and interses-
sional adjournments. They have told executive officials they had
to produce testimony or documents demanded by committees of
Congress.

The purported alliance between the presidency and the judiciary
has broken down fairly often on the other side as well. In fact, the
president was the instigator in three important moves that Congress
has made against the courts. Jefferson was behind Congress's repeal of the Judiciary Act of 1801. The act, enacted by the Federalists just before they gave up their control of the government, had,
by establishing a system of circuit courts, relieved Supreme Court
justices of the duty of conducting trials in their circuits. The repeal, enacted the following year, abolished the new judgeships and
returned the justices to circuit duty. The Supreme Court accepted
the repeal, although some of its members had private doubts as to
its constitutionality.

And it was at Jefferson's suggestion that the House of Representatives impeached Justice Samuel Chase of the Supreme Court.
Chase was able but intemperate. He had offended the Jeffersonians
by the political views he expressed from the bench and still others
by his conduct of trials under the sedition and revenue laws. But
he had committed no "high crimes or misdemeanors," as the Constitution requires for impeachment. It was Jefferson's view that
Congress could impeach judges for political reasons, to bring the
judiciary into line with the other branches of government. The
Senate's refusal to convict Chase, in 1805, probably saved other
justices of the Supreme Court from the impeachment blade, at least
for a long time.

The most celebrated action ever taken against the Supreme Court
was the court-reform bill of 1937. The legislation was inspired and
pressed by President Roosevelt, who wanted Congress to allow him
to appoint an additional Supreme Court justice for every sitting
member over the age of seventy, up to a total of six justices. (Six
of the justices were over that age.) The constitutionality of the
measure, strictly speaking, was clear, for the document does not
fix the size of the Supreme Court, which had been changed several
times in the past.

But only once before had the Court's size been changed for a
clearly political reason. In 1866, when Congress provided that no

appointments were to be made to the Court until its membership
fell to six justices, and that was for the limited purpose of preventing President Andrew Johnson from making any Supreme Court
appointments. (When Johnson left office, Congress set the Court's
size at nine justices.) Furthermore, Roosevelt's action seemed aimed
at the integrity of the Court, for his purpose was to bring about a
reversal of decisions that had voided New Deal legislation and social
legislation enacted by some of the states. Despite the president's
urging, Congress did not give him the authority he sought.

Presidents and judges have occasionally regarded each other, rather
than Congress, as the encroacher upon their constitutional rights.
Much more often than judges, presidents have had reason to think
that their constitutional powers have been encroached upon. Sometimes judges have earned this disfavor by telling presidents that
the Constitution required them to perform acts that they thought
they had a right not to perform. In *Marbury v. Madison* (1803), the
Supreme Court informed Jefferson that he was obligated to deliver
William Marbury's commission to a minor judicial office to him
(although it did not order the commission to be delivered).[13] Jefferson was involved also in the trial of Aaron Burr for treason,
when John Marshall, holding circuit court in Richmond, summoned
him to appear as a witness and to bring along certain documents,
unless he could satisfy the court that he should be excused.

Sometimes the unwelcome news from judges has been that presidents must stop doing something they thought they had a right to
do. Several federal and state judges told Lincoln during the Civil
War that he had no right to suspend the writ of habeas corpus and
keep under military arrest persons suspected of disloyalty or draft
evasion. In *Youngstown Sheet and Tube Company v. Sawyer* (1952),
the Supreme Court told President Truman that he lacked constitutional authority to seize most of the nation's steel mills when a
strike threatened that industry during the Korean War.[14] And in *New
York Times v. United States* (1971), it rejected the Nixon administration's argument that the executive had a constitutional right "to
protect the nation against publication of information whose disclo-
sure would endanger the national security."[15] This decision led to
the release of a purloined documentary history of the Vietnam War,
the Pentagon Papers, which had been prepared within the Defense
Department.

Sometimes presidents have refused to do as the courts ordered.
Jefferson refused to show up at Burr's trial, furnish the requested

documents to the court, or even answer the court's subpoena. (He did send some papers to the government's attorney with permission to make them available as he saw fit.) Lincoln refused to acknowledge several judicial decisions ordering him or his commanders to release persons from military custody, the most famous of which concerned the case of *Ex parte Merryman*, decided at the start of the Civil War in early 1861.[16]

Presidents also have threatened that they would disregard judicial commands, anticipating confrontations that never happened. Jefferson would not have had William Marbury's commission for a judicial office delivered to him if the Supreme Court had ordered it in the case of *Marbury v. Madison*—or so he said privately several years later. Lincoln informed Congress in 1863 that he would not "return to slavery any person who is free by the terms of [the Emancipation] Proclamation or by any of the acts of Congress," and he confided in a rather enigmatic note to himself that "[if] such return shall be held to be a legal duty by the proper court of final resort . . . I will promptly act as may then appear to be my personal duty."[17] Roosevelt twice threatened—also privately—to disobey the Supreme Court. The first time was when it was considering cases that challenged Roosevelt's authority to take the country off the gold standard. But, as it happened, the Court's decision in *Norman v. Baltimore & Ohio Railroad Company* (1935) left his action intact.[18] The second instance occurred when the Court, to Roosevelt's annoyance, agreed to decide whether he could appoint a special military tribunal to try Nazi saboteurs landed from submarines on the American coast during World War II. The Court affirmed his authority in *Ex parte Quirin* (1942).[19]

More recently, in the Watergate tapes case, President Nixon hinted that he might not give over the tapes, if the Supreme Court ordered him to do so. As his counsel said in oral argument before the justices: "This matter is being submitted to this Court for its guidance and judgment with respect to the law. The president, on the other hand, has his obligations under the Constitution."[20] Because Nixon realized, as he has stated in his *Memoirs*, that defiance of a clear ruling against him would have brought about his impeachment, he considered "abiding" by an unfavorable ruling without actually "complying" with it, that is, providing only excerpts of the tapes in his possession. Nixon required at least a month to carry out his plan and, to stall that long, he needed a division of opinion on the Court—perhaps, he thought, only a single dissent. But the Court held against him unanimously.[21]

Taking American history as a whole, the courts have not been very hard on the office of president. For example, a study of the subject reveals that between 1789 and 1956, the courts have struck down only "an infinitesimal fragment" of the total number of orders issued by presidents.[22] But once again, I must qualify what I have said by adding that in recent years there has been a very noticeable quickening of the tempo of judicial disapproval of executive actions.

Conclusion

How do we explain the circumstance that the presidency and the judiciary—our two executives—have been so often in conflict with each other, sometimes in alignment with Congress and sometimes with the legislative branch on the sidelines? I might begin my explanation by reminding you that the early ties between the executive and judicial branches began to loosen quickly, by the end of the 1790s, as a stricter notion of the proper relationship between them gained ground. Also, the limited alliance between them, of which I have spoken, was based on the idea that the weaker parts of government—the presidency and the judiciary—would have a common interest in resisting encroachments on each other by the stronger part, Congress. But it has been a long time since the presidency could be considered a weak institution. Intermittently in earlier American history—for example, in the presidencies of Jefferson, Jackson, Lincoln, and Theodore Roosevelt—it has loomed as quite strong. Since the time of Franklin Roosevelt, the office could be called imperial. It is worth noting that all of those presidents I have mentioned and several of those who came after Franklin Roosevelt have been in conflict or at least in tension with the judiciary as a result of the latter's decisions. Some of their troubles have been recounted in these pages. To add examples from the near-present, Ronald Reagan supported constitutional amendments to reverse the Supreme Court's decisions outlawing prayers in public schools and allowing abortions and George Bush supported one to reverse its decision permitting desecrations of the national flag.

The executive has two ways of doing well in the courts. One is to choose carefully the cases it will take to court and which it will appeal to the Supreme Court. The great success of the solicitor general's office in Supreme Court litigation is due in good part to its selectivity in choosing appeals there and also to the expertise that comes from appearing frequently before that Court. The other way for the executive to do well in the courts is to chose with care the persons to be appointed as judges and especially as justices of the Supreme Court. The success of presidents in this respect can be seen in the fact that about three out of four justices have met the expectations which their appointers had in choosing them. But, as this estimate also reveals, presidents cannot be sure of getting the justices they want and their record in the past generation has fallen somewhat.

Our two executives have never been as close as the Constitution's Framers seem to have supposed they would. In fact, they seem to be moving farther apart.

Notes

1. John Locke, *Two Treatises of Government*, Peter Laslett, ed. (New York: New American Library, 1965), Second Treatise, paragraphs 87–88, 125, 131, 219.

2. Montesquieu, *The Spirit of Laws*, trans. Thomas Nugent (New York: Hafner, 1949), book 11, chap. 6, pp. 151–56.

3. See *The Records of the Federal Convention of 1987*, Max Farrand, ed. (New Haven: Yale University Press, 1937), vol. 2, p. 299 (Morris), p. 34 (Madison).

4. Proposal of G. Morris and C. Pinckney, *Records of Federal Convention*, p. 342; see also Ellsworth's proposal, ibid., p. 328.

5. *U.S. v. Kendall*, 26 Fed. Cas. 702 (1837), at 749–50, Circ. Ct. Dist. of Col., No. 15,517.

6. Data on judicial cases contained in this and the paragraphs that immediately follow have been taken from the *Annual Reports of the Director of the Administrative Offfice of the United States Courts* (Washington, D.C.) and the *Annual Reports of the Attorney General of the United States* (Washington, D.C.).

7. *Myers v. U.S.*, 222 U.S. 52 (1926).

8. *Immigration and Naturalization Service v. Chadha*, 462 U.S. 919 (1983).

9. *Ex parte McCardle*, 7 Wall. 506 (1869).

10. *Humphrey's Executor (Rathbun) v. U.S.*, 295 U.S. 602 (1935).

11. *Morrison v. Olson*, 487 U.S. 654 (1988).

12. *U.S. v. Nixon*, 418 U.S. 618 (1974).

13. *Marbury v. Madison*, 1 Cr. 137 (1803).

14. *Youngstown Sheet and Tube Co. v. Sawyer*, 343 U.S. 579 (1952).

15. *New York Times v. U.S.*, 403 U.S. 713 (1971).

16. *Ex parte Merryman*, 17 F. Cas. 144 (1861), Cir. Ct. Md., No. 9487.

17. Lincoln, Annual Message to Congress, Dec. 8, 1863, in Abraham Lincoln, *Collected Works*, Roy P. Basler et al., eds. (New Brunswick, N.J.: Rutgers University Press, 1953), vol. 7, p. 51; and fragment [c. Aug. 26, 1863], vol. 6, p. 41.

18. *Norman v. Baltimore & Ohio Railroad Co.*, 294 U.S. 240 (1935).

19. *Ex parte Quirin*, 317 U.S. 1 (1942).

20. James D. St. Clair, *U.S. Law Week*, July 16, 1974, p. 3012.

21. Richard Nixon, *Memoirs* (New York: Grosset and Dunlap, 1978), p. 444.

22. Glendon A. Schubert Jr., *The Presidency in the Courts* (Minneapolis: University of Minnesota Press, 1957), p. 355 and app. A, pp. 361–65.

Suggested Reading

Genovese, Michael A. *The Supreme Court, the Constitution, and Presidential Power.* Lanham, Md.: University Press of America, 1980.

Murphy, Walter F. *Congress and the Court: A Case Study in the American Political Process.* Chicago: University of Chicago Press, 1962.

Salokar, Rebecca M. *The Solicitor General: The Politics of Law.* Philadelphia: Temple University Press, 1992.

Schubert, Glendon A., Jr., *The Presidency in the Courts.* Minneapolis: University of Minnesota Press, 1957.

Scigliano, Robert. *The Supreme Court and the Presidency.* New York: Free Press, 1971.

17

The "Fourth" Branch
of Government

Robert Martin Schaefer

We are, it seems, moving away from constitutional government and steadily becoming a bureaucratic society. Many functions of life, including health, business, civil rights, elections, environment, and education, are now controlled by the federal government through its regulatory apparatus, the bureaucracy. To comprehend the significance of these changes, we must reflect upon the traditional understanding of American government, specifically the separation of powers, to see how the regulatory revolution has altered our political order.

The term "bureaucracy" itself is somewhat confusing. Politicians, scholars, and the media interchangeably use the terms "public administration" and "regulation" when referring to bureaucracy. Bureaucracy, in this essay, is understood to be the creation and implementation of regulations by public administrative agencies. These agencies, created by Congress, issue broad commands, including, for example, cleaning up the environment and overcoming discrimination.

The first regulatory agency was the Steamboat Inspection Service in 1837. But this agency, and those few that followed over the next one hundred years, tended to be specific in goals and controlled primarily by the president. Even by 1900 only five regulatory agencies were in existence. In the early 1930s there were only fifteen such agencies. Today there are more than eighty major regulatory agencies which compete and sometimes conflict with each other.

Many people argue that the transformation of American constitutionalism into bureaucratic government is not only inevitable but good. Today the traditional view of constitutionalism is being countered by their view that constitutionalism is no longer legitimate. Our current form of government, they claim, does not yet eliminate poverty, guarantee health care, or prevent racism. They see the new postconstitutional state as a comprehensive entity which can function more justly, more efficiently. The state should control, through bureaucracy, the "details of everyday life," details normally left to private associations such as the local community and family.

Some scholars and commentators, on the other hand, suggest that the growth of public administration has perverted the nature of American constitutionalism and points to the destruction of the American regime. Those who argue against bureaucratization suggest that liberty is being replaced by government that is not only expensive but also aimless, arbitrary, and despotic.

The contemporary bureaucratization that is occurring is not simply an enlargement of constitutional government. Rather, modern public administration is the result of a radically new theoretical assumption: that the state is not only capable of, but responsible for, reforming the nature of the American political order.

In the past, "state" meant the national government that was concerned with public things, for example, foreign policy, economic policy, and other issues that pertain to the general citizenry. Separate from the state is the private sphere, the family and social relations. As a result, bureaucratic agencies normally regulated public things. To this end, bureaucracy has always been viewed as necessary for good government.

Since the founding, bureaucracy was also considered to be the regulatory element of the executive branch. For example, the military establishment is a bureaucracy. The president, as commander-in-chief, gives specific orders which his chief of staff, and all those down the line, must follow. Publius suggests that the administration of government is naturally under the control of the executive, for the president's purpose is to carry out the duties assigned to him by the Constitution or Congress. *Federalist* 72 argues that bureaucracy, including the budget, foreign affairs, execution of war, and

> other matters of a like nature, [should] constitute what seems to be most properly understood by the administration of government. The

persons, therefore, to whose immediate management these different matters are committed, ought to be considered as the assistants or deputies of the chief magistrate. . . .

In recent years, however, we have witnessed the growth of many new bureaucracies as part of the national government. These agencies were conceived in the belief that America is not truly "just." In order to achieve justice, goods must be redistributed and the lives of American citizens regulated, ensuring fairness and equality. President Lyndon Johnson articulated this belief when he declared, in 1964, that the new purpose of federal government was to eradicate the trap of poverty.

Although there has never been complete agreement as to the function and purpose of modern bureaucratic government, there was a burst of regulatory growth during the 1960s and 1970s. Not only did the number of agencies increase, but the quantity of "regulations" also increased dramatically. As Theodore J. Lowi points out, "the number of pages in the *Federal Register* increased from 14,479 in 1960 . . . to 86,000" by 1979.[1] The "major" regulatory agencies increased from twenty-eight in 1960 to fifty-six by 1980. Numerous other regulatory programs (well over 150) have also been created. Consider Table 17-1 on the following page, which lists only a few of the programs passed by Congress in recent years.[2]

Proponents of modern bureaucracy often insist that bureaucrats are guided by scientific principles and therefore can be professionally trained, nonpartisan experts. Hence their authority could never constitute a threat to liberty and justice. But *science* cannot dictate what values (or rights) should be defended and promoted. Science, by its very nature, is neutral to moral and political questions. Bureaucrats can, and sometimes do, impose their values on a particular policy, or interpret the values current in society. But their understanding of values is not uniformly grounded in any fixed set of principles. The principles articulated in the Declaration and implied in the Constitution are more often than not ignored, or negated, or at least disputed.

The Intellectual Founding of Bureaucracy

The root of modern bureaucracy's dissatisfaction with constitutionalism can be found as early as 1885 in the writings of Woodrow Wilson. He insisted that the separation of powers and the com-

Table 17-1
Federal Regulatory Laws and Programs
Enacted from 1970 to 1976

Year Enacted	Title of Statute
1969–70	Child Protection and Toy Safety Act
	Economic Stabilization Act
	Egg Products Inspection Act
	Fair Credit Reporting Act
	Occupational Safety and Health Act
	Poison Prevention Packaging Act
	Securities Investor Protection Act
1970	Economic Stabilization Act Amendments
	Federal Boat Safety Act
	Lead-Based Paint Elimination Act
	Wholesale Fish and Fisheries Act
1972	Consumer Product Safety Act
	Equal Employment Opportunity Act
	Federal Election Campaign Act
	Federal Environmental Pesticide Control Act
	Federal Water Pollution Control Act Amendments
	Motor Vehicle Information and Cost Savings Act
	Noise Control Act
	Port and Waterways Safety Act
1973	Agriculture and Consumer Protection Act
	Economic Stabilization Act Amendments
	Emergency Petroleum Allocation Act
	Flood Disaster Protection Act
1974	Atomic Energy Act
	Commodity Futures Trading Commission Act
	Consumer Product Warranties Act
	Council on Wage and Price Stability Act
	Employee Retirement Income Security Act
	Federal Energy Administration Act
	Hazardous Materials Transportation Act
	Housing and Community Development Act
	Pension Reform Act
	Privacy Act
	Safe Drinking Water Act
1975	Energy Policy and Conservation Act
	Equal Credit Opportunity Act
1976	Consumer Leasing Act
	Medical Device Safety Act
	Toxic Substances Control Act

mittee system debilitated "good" government. As a result, the American president does not act as efficiently as, for example, the British prime minister, who is much more powerful than his American counterpart. The prime minister is often single-handedly capable of creating and executing laws. The American executive, on the other hand, must always deal with an often intransigent Congress filled with factious committees.

Wilson believed that the executive's power should be based on popular opinion—and the emotions that animate popular opinion—and not principles enumerated by the Constitution. Wilson thus found it necessary to go beyond constitutionalism in order to achieve his goals. Wilson's vision saw "the meaning of life" as being constantly reinterpreted by the executive. He hoped to see the day when the executive/bureaucracy could rule in accordance with the people's will unhampered by the Constitution. The executive would interpret the will of the people and then instruct the bureaucracy to implement his policy. The bureaucracy, though powerful, would be subject to a "higher authority."

Wilson held an evolutionary view of government and, therefore, human nature. Wilson argued that American government

> is accountable to Darwin, not to Newton. It is modified by its environment, necessitated by its tasks, shaped to its functions by the sheer pressure of life.[3]

The president, under stress of contemporary times, must take unusual measures to bring about justice in society. The American Constitution is outdated and inadequate. A truly active executive must seize the day and reinvent government.

To understand the implications of Wilson's thought more clearly, one must consider the arguments presented by the Founders in defense of the Constitution. They claimed that an effective government requires a separation of powers if it is to avoid tyranny. So the three branches of government are delineated in the Constitution. The intense desire to prevent tyranny was itself grounded in the belief that equality and liberty are fundamental principles which could be understood only coterminously; in other words, liberty can be understood only in light of equality, and vice versa. Political equality, that is, government based on consent as described in the Declaration of Independence, can be preserved only if liberty is also preserved through constitutional means. If liberty is destroyed, then equality becomes meaningless. Indeed, Alexis de Tocqueville admonishes that a healthy democracy requires a proper mixture of equality and liberty. Otherwise an intense desire for equality will necessarily undermine liberty. Tocqueville warns:

> I think democratic peoples have a natural taste for liberty; left to themselves, they will seek it, cherish it, and be sad if it is taken from them. But their passion for equality is ardent, insatiable, eternal, and invincible. They want equality in freedom, and if they cannot have that, they still want equality in slavery.[4]

The Federalist indicates the nature and severity of this problem: human beings are attached to their own interests and, if unchecked, are capable of acting in a beastlike fashion. But, through reason, they are capable of determining what is just. Human reason, though, is imperfect. Imperfect reason, when added to our natural self-interest, can easily result in unjust actions. The Founders argued that a rule of law should be created to form and guide the people. "We the People" create law which in turn rules us. The best process by which to make decent law, so the Founders argued, is reflected in the constitutional separation of powers and checks and balances.

Yet, this paradigm is rejected wholeheartedly by modern scholars who, echoing Wilson, claim that the Constitution is based upon eighteenth-century "truths." Publius's view that political institutions are required because men are not angels is replaced with the belief that modern politics has evolved to such a degree that bureaucratic government, not constitutionalism, can resolve man's problems. According to Wilson and other modern scholars, the eighteenth-century truths do not apply to us today. In fact, these "ancient verities" lead only to "an enfeebled, even nonexistent state" which does not deal with twentieth-century problems.

The end result promised by Wilson's reforms is the complete cleansing and separation of politics from administration. Politics, which is disorderly and full of conflict, is replaced by administration, which is rational, orderly, and efficient. To enable this to occur, technical administrators are needed. But it was immediately clear to the early proponents of public administration that a true separation of politics and administration requires some control over the administrators. Who, though, would control the bureaucrats? The executive? the courts? Congress? or the people?

For many years scholars debated the difficulties presented by this new branch of government. If the executive controlled the bureaucracy, the power of Congress would be diminished. But Congress is too large to adequately control the bureaucracy. Nor does it have the overall vision or unity of the executive. The courts, it was argued, are not or should not be concerned with the implementation of policy. Still, without some control, the agencies would soon be captured by "powerful interest groups. So who rules the bureaucracy? This question has yet to be adequately answered.

Although the intellectual basis of modern bureaucracy is found in the writings of Wilson and fellow Progressives, such thoughts did not formally enter American government until President Franklin D. Roosevelt's New Deal. At that point public administration was promoted at the national level. The famous 1937 Brownlow report, a product of the New Deal, set the stage for the bureaucratization of America.

The Brownlow Report

The Brownlow report was first submitted to FDR and then presented to Congress. The primary finding of the report is that a need for reorganization at the federal level exists in order to facilitate the workings of government. Government, as FDR and the report tell us, is inefficient, awkward, and incapable of "action." Constitutionally speaking, FDR claims that he is not asking for more power, but simply the "tools of management."

The two overriding themes within the report are the need for a stronger executive branch, and a greater responsibility of government to foster and implement social change. The report states that "There is room for vast increase in our national productivity and there is much bitter wrong to set right in neglected ways of human life."[5] Louis Brownlow argues that the problems of modern government can be solved by good management. Traditional political solutions—the separation of powers—have faded into history. The goal, now, is to increase the managerial skills of government, with the president as the primary manager.

For this to occur, Brownlow asserts, the "fourth branch" must become more responsive to the executive who, in turn, is responding to the will of the people. Brownlow's concern is that the creation of an *independent* fourth branch would not result in a unified and stable organization. Therefore he wanted a more powerful bureaucracy that remains in the service of the executive. The president would become more powerful but his increased authority would always be under the scrutiny of Congress. Congress would review the executive department periodically via its budgetary controls. If, according to Brownlow, Congress did not approve of the actions of the executive branch, then Congress may penalize the executive by denying appropriations. In such a system, then, Congress becomes an overseer, and its main focus is the prevention of executive tyranny. As a result, Congress becomes less of a lawmaking body in the traditional sense.

Brownlow's report also indicates the need for "new major fields of activity of the National Government." These include "five great categories: public welfare, public works, public lending, conservation, and business controls." Congress is to pass sweeping laws (e.g., the Federal Trade Commission) and the executive is to carry out these laws ("fair trade"). These laws will be general in nature, allowing for great latitude and interpretation by the executive.

The goal of "making democracy work" forces Congress into actually supporting an increase in regulatory lawmaking. Indeed, Congress must allow regulatory lawmaking on a grand scale. The report, though, suggests that "rulemaking" has in fact been occurring since the beginning of the republic. For example, President George Washington was authorized by Congress to delegate authority to various officers to carry out an embargo. Based on this ostensible tradition of rulemaking, the report defends an extensive broadening of executive powers to address the "modern" problems of government.

Brownlow and FDR promise to stay within the bounds created by the Constitution. Yet they know that their quest necessitates the transformation of the social and moral fabric of America. The report states:

> Public service is the service of the common good in peace or war and will be judged by this standard. Not merely lower unit costs but higher human happiness and values are the supreme ends of our national life . . . Good Management will promote in the fullest measure the conservation and utilization of our national resources, and spell this out plainly in social justice, security, order, liberty, prosperity, in material benefits, and in higher values of life.[6]

This instrumental vision of government is a radical departure from the traditional goals of American constitutionalism. It would result in the national government's taking on those responsibilities normally controlled by state and local governments. The national government must necessarily expand to encompass almost all aspects of life.

The Brownlow report, as well as many of the other New Deal proposals, was rejected by Congress. Nonetheless, the thoughts and ideas which underlie the report soon became entrenched in the American polity and promoted the enlargement of bureaucracy. Today's more powerful bureaucracy now has two masters, Congress and the executive. These two masters, with their bureaucratic servants, produce what many postwar commentators have reported to be a disastrously ineffectual public administration.

Contemporary Bureaucracy

In the mid-1960s, the federal government began to turn from lawmaking to the administration of bureaucracy. Congress, under the influence of President Johnson, accepted the notion that it was responsible for social health. Johnson argued that

> The Great Society rests on abundance and liberty for all. It demands an end to poverty and racial injustice, to which we are totally committed . . . There are those timid souls who say this battle cannot be won; that we are condemned to a soulless wealth. I do not agree. We have the power to shape the civilization that we want.[7]

This new government actively created numerous agencies with broad powers. The bureaucracies would be responsible for eliminating racism and poverty; creating better insurance programs and more hospitals; improving education, housing, mass transit and libraries; rebuilding cities; preserving the environment; and even overcoming "loneliness and boredom."

As a result of the Great Society Congress turned from lawmaking to administration. Modern American government is now clearly composed of four branches of government. But this fourth branch is difficult to understand. Simply put, it is composed of regulatory agencies, many of which are insulated from the political realm normally associated with the other three branches of government.

An examination of a few contemporary bureaucratic agencies will illuminate this point. Agencies such as the National Labor Relations Board and Equal Employment Opportunity Commission have as their aim the regulation of the "public interest." These agencies are given free rein to determine who gets what, when, and how. Many businesses and scholars claim, though, that the outcome of much of this regulation is the imposition of extensive requirements that impede the entry of new businesses into the marketplace. It has been shown time and again that through regulation, established businesses become a protected class because of the cost of regulation, the complexity of rules, and other biases favoring existing companies. New companies thus find it difficult, if not impossible, to enter the market. Although large established firms would prefer not to deal with the regulatory agencies, they find that once a relationship is begun with an agency, they benefit.

Large firms quickly learn that competition can be prevented through numerous regulations that limit the creation of new businesses or shut down smaller, less competitive firms. The agencies themselves benefit from this arrangement. Lawsuits or public outcry is limited when the larger corporations are willing to work with the agencies. Ironically, then, "big business" actually benefits from administrative government. The regulatory agencies befriend big business even though on the surface agencies like the Federal Trade Commission and Environmental Protection Agency appear antibusiness.

In 1914, the Federal Trade Commission Act and the Clayton Act were both passed with the intent of preventing "unfair methods of competition in commerce and unfair or deceptive acts or practices in commerce." The purpose of the FTC was originally to limit unfair competition, prevent monopolies from controlling the economy, and ensure that the markets remain competitive. Robert Katzmann argues that the unclear language and lack of goals made the FTC Act a shoo-in for congressional support. "In short, the advocates of the FTC Act and the Clayton Act represented different interests: the consumer, large corporations, and the small businessman."[8]

The FTC was not created to please just one interest group. Because of this, the goals of the FTC are unclear. Unfortunately, no one has attempted to articulate a mission for the FTC from a legislative or moral perspective. The mission of the FTC seems to depend in great part on what party is in office, the mood of the American people, and the commissioners themselves. Some FTC officials may define "unfair" as those who have more property compared to those who have less. Or unfair might be interpreted as a monopoly, for example, the oil industry. As such, the FTC attempts to rearrange a whole industry to make it more competitive. Yet the definition of "competition" remains unclear. Certain industries are by nature big, others small. Other industries require extensive technical competence which prevents easy market entry. A further problem is the question of consumer costs. Should the consumer pay more or less because of the FTC's activities? In many instances, the FTC purposely causes the market price of goods to rise, fostering a kind of upward "competition."

Within the FTC itself there is little agreement as to its purpose. The Bureau of Competition of the FTC is concerned with the legal aspects of antitrust, determining if an infraction of the law has occurred and by whom. The Bureau of Economics assists the Bureau of Competition by offering advice as to whether a particular business's activities are anticompetitive. Understanding what is anticompetitive is a difficult task, particularly in an open market where economic activities are in constant flux. In many instances, there will be tension between these administrative tasks.

The purpose of the FTC's action remains open. Ought it be pro-business? antibusiness? Should it promote small business? promote social stability? or keep consumer costs down . . . or up? These responses are all part of the question, what is the public interest? In addition, in many instances the Bureau of Competition is animated by a desire to win cases. The lawyers who run this bureau desire to gain prestige, to grow professionally and move up the bureaucratic ladder. Yet promotion rarely occurs without courtroom experience and/or successful suits. Many times politicians seek to influence the FTC officials for political reasons. Corporations also make attempts at influencing the FTC for obvious reasons, and the FTC often succumbs to one or many of its suitors.

Accountability

The scope of rulemaking in recent years has changed. For example, the Consumer Product Safety Commission (CPSC) was instructed by Congress in 1981 to "analyze the costs and benefits of its [own] proposals." Those who will bear the brunt of the costs and those who receive benefits must be clearly outlined by the commission. The CPSC must also determine how its rulemaking will affect both the environment and small businesses. Consequently, the commission is limited in what it may do, at least regarding rulemaking.

As a result of being held accountable the CPSC and numerous other agencies have resorted to adjudication. They simply settle a complaint through a process that avoids an official complaint. What is curious about this process is that "Adjudication is also, by nature, retrospective—that is, it penalizes a firm for its conduct during a period before the agency acted, conduct that in many cases was legal at the time."[9] In other words, if an agency such as CPSC decides to prosecute a company, the company will lose one way or another. The threat of legal fees and bad press force companies to negotiate with the agency more than 98 percent of the time. Interestingly, Justice Antonin Scalia points out that Congress and the White House are "squeezing the balloon of bureaucratic arbitrariness at one point, only to have it pop out somewhere else."[10] Once an agency is created, it must be held responsible by Congress or the executive. So far neither of these two branches, or even the courts, rule the bureaucracy. Congress refuses to give more authority to the president (particularly if the president is of another party), yet Congress does not have the time, inclination, or ability to regulate the regulators.

It would seem that Congress prefers writing vague laws inasmuch as their vagueness requires further interpretation by designated administrators who will issue the appropriate "rules." Congress has little time for the tedious task of regulatory rulemaking. To ensure that the thousands of rules passed each year are just, Congress has created oversight committees which monitor the agencies. Prior to 1983, one or both houses of Congress could overrule any rule created by an agency. However, the Supreme Court decision in *Immigration and Naturalization Service v. Chadha* (1983) declared "legislative vetoes" unconstitutional. As a result, Congress has learned to make informal agreements with the White House— agreements that have the same force as a legislative veto. Congress has also learned that it could reap numerous benefits by strengthening the bureaucracy and directing benefits to particular interest groups. By offering benefits or regulatory relief, or by limiting competition, Congress could garner the support of many pleased voters.

President Ronald Reagan made some initial headway in regulatory reform. Executive Order 12291 (1981) allowed the Office of Information and Regulatory Affairs to benefit those burdened by regulations and to make administrative rulemakers accountable to the executive branch. Although the OIRA had some success, it eventually incurred the wrath of Congress, which threatened to withhold OIRA funding. Ultimately, the OIRA succumbed to the wishes of the Congress and the bureaucracy. Reagan, it seems, overestimated the power of his rhetoric and underestimated both the people's desires and Congress's persistence. At first Reagan seemed determined to fight and cajole Congress into waging the battle against bureaucracy, but he also succumbed to the demands of popularity and an image of how history would record his efforts.

Reagan seemed destined to fail: More than half the American population benefits directly at the hands of "big government," and rarely do people reject those programs or agencies that benefit them. Those receiving federally funded benefits are from all areas of the political spectrum, not merely the poor. Frankly, Americans enjoy receiving these benefits. Why should they view their benefactor as evil? Small programs such as Aid to Families with Dependent Children were easy targets for Reagan's rhetoric. However, such programs make up only a small portion of the budget. But in the end, Reagan cannot be criticized for failing to bring the bureaucracy under control. Once in office, he was faced with the discovery that the ultimate responsibility for the bureaucracy lies with Congress. Even the "Republican Establishment" is opposed to true regulatory relief. Although it is expensive, the regulatory bureaucracy protects many businesses from competition.

Curiously, Congress understands clearly what it is doing. Representative Gillis Long (D., Louisiana) noted:

> It appeared to me that with the application of an extreme type of legislative veto . . . we were turning ours from an institution that was supposed to be a broad policymaking institution with respect to the problems of the country and its relationship to the world, into merely a city council that overlooks the running of the store every-day.[11]

The true issue is not whether politics can be separated from administration, or even whether democracy needs centralized administration. Rather, the issue turns on whether constitutionalism is worthy of perpetuation and preservation.

Conclusion

The issue can be restated as follows: Can bureaucratic government, at the national level, properly rule the nation? In light of the natural tendency for bureaucracies to "grow" and protect their own interests, we may reasonably wonder if bureaucracies could ever rule for the common good. Whether in regard to education, environment, or race relations, or whatever, it is difficult for many agencies to know what is best for local communities. These agencies do not know, and cannot know, the circumstances or people involved. Bureaucracies, in and of themselves, appear harmless. After all, they distribute goods, dictate policy, and enforce rules very efficiently. But once separated from the local communities, agencies cannot adequately rule. Recall that Congress, as created by the Founders, was supposed to deliberate and pass *general* laws that benefit the entire country. The Founders never envisioned a time when Congress would rule the details of everyday life. The nature of human beings, they believed, made that impossible.

Perhaps Congress ought to limit its activities and not attempt to regulate all aspects of society. For two reasons, such an expectation is hardly realistic. First, the majority of Americans now enjoy these benefits from the federal government. These benefits include Social Security, welfare, health care, subsidies, and numerous other entitlements. It is primarily the *middle class* that is most attached to these programs. All recent presidents, Democrat and Republican, have learned that these "sacred cows" cannot be touched. To do so would be political suicide. Second, other nonentitlement programs, such as the Environmental Protection Agency, are too far removed from everyday Americans (and most congressmen) to be understood. The EPA's policies often affect many other areas of life, including the economy, housing, and employment. Most of us cannot properly judge the efficacy of the EPA from an overall view.

So, what is to be done? Perhaps it would be wise to reconsider the thoughts and ideas of the Founders. Their understanding of good government is fundamental to comprehending the character of American society, constitutionalism, and human nature. Perhaps the Founders can offer to us, their heirs, an understanding of the *limits* of this, our "more perfect Union."

Notes

1. Theodore J. Lowi, "Liberal and Conservative Theories of Regulation," in *The Constitution and the Regulation of Society*, Gary C. Bryner and Dennis L. Thompson, eds. (Provo, Utah: Brigham Young University Press, 1988), pp. 11–13.

2. Lowi, p. 12.

3. Woodrow Wilson, *Constitutional Government in the United States*, quoted in *American Political Rhetoric*, 2nd ed., Peter Augustine Lawler and Robert Martin Schaefer, eds. (Lanham, Md.): Rowman and Littlefield, 1990), p. 106.

4. Alexis de Tocqueville, *Democracy in America*, trans. George Lawrence (New York: Anchor Books, 1969), vol. II, part II, Chapter 1, p. 506.

5. *Report of the President's Committee on Administrative Management* (Brownlow Report), 74th Congress, 2d session (Washington, D.C.: Government Printing Office, 1937), p. 2.

6. Brownlow, p. 53.

7. Lyndon Johnson, "Commencement Address at the University of Michigan" (1964), *American Political Rhetoric*, pp. 121–24.

8. Robert A. Katzmann, "Federal Trade Commission," in *The Politics of Regulation*, James Q. Wilson, ed. (New York: Basic Books, 1980), p. 155.

9. Terrence M. Scanlon and Robert A. Rogowsky, "Back-Door Rulemaking: A View from the CPSC," *Antitrust and Trade Regulation*, 2nd ed., Thomas W. Dunfee and Frank F. Gibson, eds. (New York: Wiley, 1985), p. 317.

10. Scanlon, p. 314.

11. Quoted in John Adams Wettergreen, "Bureaucratizing the American Government," in *The Imperial Congress*, Gordon S. Jones and John A. Marini, eds. (New York: Pharos Books, 1988), p. 85.

Acknowledgment

I would like to thank the Earhart Foundation for kind assistance which aided me in the completion of this essay.

Suggested Reading

Harris, Richard A., and Sidney M. Milkis. *The Politics of Regulatory Change*. New York: Oxford University Press, 1989.

Marini, John. *The Politics of Budget Control: Congress, the Presidency and Growth of the Administrative State*. Washington, D.C.: Crane, Russak, 1992.

Ostrom, Vincent. *The Intellectual Crisis in American Public Administration*. Tuscaloosa: University of Alabama Press, 1973.

Shafritz, Jay M., and Albert C. Hyde, eds. *Classics of Public Administration*, 2nd ed. Chicago: Dorsey Press, 1987.

Wilson, Woodrow. "The Study of Administration," in *The Papers of Woodrow Wilson*, Vol. 5, 1885–1888, pp. 357-80. Princeton: Princeton University Press, 1968.

18

Understanding America's
Two-Party System

Donald V. Weatherman

After two hundred years' existence, America's party system is still a mystery to most voters. Are political parties a blessing or a curse on the American political system? Even our political leaders have trouble deciding whether campaign laws should encourage or discourage the role that parties play in our electoral process. With such confusion on the part of our political leaders, it is little wonder that the average American voter is often puzzled by the role parties play or should play in his own political activities.

Few students of American politics have a clear understanding of the true origins and purpose of the American party system. There are many reasons for this. One of the best, or at least most obvious, reasons is that it is very hard to determine exactly when and how political parties developed in America. Unlike the Declaration of Independence or the Constitution, there is no precise date or even a general time period that we can point to as signaling the origin of political parties in America.

Once we have a better understanding of the true origins of the American party system, we will see that political parties were developed to strengthen and complement our constitutional system of government. We will never comprehend the true nature of American political parties if we do not accept them as an extension of our constitutional order.

Much of the confusion surrounding American political parties has to do with some rather important misunderstandings about the founding generation. Most students of American history or politics are familiar with the statements many of the Founders made decrying the baneful effects party divisions would have on our young republic. Two of the most often cited are George Washington's Farewell Address and James Madison's *Federalist* 10. But both of these are warnings against a kind of party structure that is unlike what we recognize today as formal political parties.

There is now and always has been a wide variety of party divisions in American society. Some of these are religious, economic, geographical, ideological, racial, or even educational. While all of these divisions are, or certainly can be, important components of a formal political party, they are not the same thing. Herein lies the first and most fundamental distinction that one must make to understand the difference between formal political parties and those other types of parties. Clearly not all party divisions are created equally.

How Did Political Parties Develop in America?

America's party system developed in two distinct stages. Congressional parties emerged as something more than factional alliances in the mid-1790s. Madison played a major role in the development of congressional parties to oppose Alexander Hamilton's executive initiatives. Madison defended this role in a series of editorials in the *National Gazette*.

The second stage of America's party development occurred in the late 1820s and early 1830s. Our presidential parties became something more than a mere extension of the congressional party system. A key advocate and creator of America's presidential party system was Martin Van Buren. Senator Van Buren took to Washington, D.C. the organizational skills he had developed and refined in New York State as the leader of the Albany Regency.

Party machinery had existed in most, if not all, of the states prior to the development of national parties. Many of these state parties were organized around individuals. Others were more issue- or interest-oriented. Our first national parties were little more than loose coalitions of these more deeply rooted state organizations. But such coalitions required a common thread to hold them together, which forced them to rise above their narrow personal or issue orientations. The most often cited glue for these coalitions has been constitutional interpretation. Not surprisingly, each side claimed that its constitutional vision was the one most closely tied to the true intentions of the Founders.

Because our earliest party battle was fought while the founding generation was still leading the nation, both sides could claim first-hand knowledge of the Founders' intentions. The partisan battle that developed during Washington's second administration placed the two major contributors to *The Federalist Papers*, Hamilton and Madison, in conflicting camps. What distinguished these national parties from their predecessors was described quite ably by a French visitor to America in the 1830s. Alexis de Tocqueville provided one of the earliest and most basic understandings of our party structure in *Democracy in America*. He distinguished between them:

> The political parties that I style great are those which cling to principles rather than to their consequences; to general and not to special cases; to ideas and not to men. These parties are usually distinguished by nobler features, more generous passions, more genuine convictions, and a more bold and open conduct than the others.[1]

Tocqueville added that minor parties are never dignified by "lofty purposes" and that they "display the selfishness of their character in their actions." What he identified as minor parties are usually called interest groups today.

Madison's warning against parties in *Federalist* 10 was quite obviously a warning against Tocqueville's minor parties. That is why Madison used the terms party and faction interchangeably in that essay. Tocqueville's discussion of great parties focused exclusively on the Federalist and Republican parties that developed during Washington's second term as president. These he considered to be the great parties of America. There is no inconsistency in Madison's warning against the danger of minor parties in the 1780s and his defense of great parties in the 1790s. Quite the contrary, he shows an understanding of parties and the differences among them that few of his critics have been able to comprehend.[2]

The Federalists and Republicans of the 1790s were guided by profoundly different political principles. Many issues separated the two political parties, but they were all related to the central issue of how much power the states transferred to the national government under the new Constitution. In one sense or another, this issue has continued to confront America's party leaders.

There is another aspect of this first partisan division that must not be overlooked. The Republican party was every bit as concerned with the location of the new government's power as it was with the extent of that power. Republican rhetoric, at least in the early years, wanted the lion's share of the federal government's power to be lodged in the legislative branch, not the executive branch.

Madison's efforts to build a party structure were motivated by a desire to maintain the proper constitutional balance between the popular branches of government. We must credit Madison with practicing in the 1790s what he preached in the 1780s. An organized congressional party was the best way to protect that institution from executive encroachment.

Madison's efforts proved to be so successful that the national legislature became the nominating vehicle for the executive branch. The Congressional or King Caucus was the presidential nominating vehicle for more than twenty years (1800–1824). But Madison's success in shifting the political balance to the legislature's advantage was precisely what worried the next generation of party developers. Martin Van Buren viewed legislative domination of national politics with the same suspicion that Madison held for executive domination. For this reason, Van Buren channeled his efforts into building an executive party structure.

The emergence of a presidential party system can most easily be tied to the demise of King Caucus and its replacement by national party conventions. While Van Buren may not deserve full credit for the development of national party conventions, it was his work with Thomas Ritchie in reviving national parties and building one around the personality of Andrew Jackson that helped move the nation toward the convention system. The new party organization that was built around Jackson was America's first successful presidential party. National party conventions gave the presidential parties an identity and political base independent of the Congress.

With the development of national nominating conventions, presidential candidates exchanged a process dominated by Congress for one dominated by state party leaders and political machines. This change accomplished two things, both of which strengthened important aspects of the constitutional system of checks and balances. First, by making the presidential nominating process less dependent on Congress, the president became more independent and freer to exercise his important check on the legislative branch. Second, the new link between the president and state party organizations enhanced federalism by developing a new avenue through which states could influence national affairs. The stronger state voice in the national conventions made the nominating process more closely resemble the selection process used in the Electoral College.

This two-stage development of America's party system is what is often overlooked by students of party politics. The oversight is what enables many scholars to ignore the fact that America's party founders desired a party system that was perfectly compatible with the new science of politics described in *Federalist* 9. By giving each popular branch of government the organizational strength of a party system, they enhanced our national government's ability to permit "ambition to counteract ambition."

When state parties are added to this party formula, the question of what constitutes the American party system becomes more complex. Party theorists who desire neatness and order have never been happy with the American party system because it defies their theoretical models. This is probably why many American party scholars have managed to build entire careers on assailing the American party system.

One of the most common arguments is that the American party system has failed because it does not function like the British party system. The British model (often called the responsible model) is a more centralized party system. It is more centralized because party leaders, not voters, select the parties' candidates for public office. By controlling access to public offices the parties are in a better position to control how public officials vote in key policy issues.

How Do American Parties Function?

In reality the American party system has been a wonderful success because it has permitted a high degree of political organization within a constitutional system that mandates a bicameral legislature, separation of powers, and federalism. It was never the purpose of our party system to overcome these democratic "inconveniences." Critics of the American party system, beginning with Woodrow Wilson, have disliked American parties because they work so well within our constitutional system.

But it is not just the American Constitution that has made America's party system less centralized than its British counterpart. Equally important is our use of party primaries, which are unique to the

American political system. They are what permit voters at the grass-roots level of our political system to determine who will be the Democratic and Republican candidates for public office. For this reason, Arkansas Democrats and Massachusetts Democrats may not always adhere to the same policies; the same is true of Arizona Republicans and Wisconsin Republicans.

Primaries are what make the American party system a decentralized system. Primaries permit voters, not party officials, to select the parties' candidates for office. There are a variety of different types of primaries but the most common and basic are open primaries, closed primaries, blanket primaries, and presidential primaries. Generally it is up to the states to determine what types of primaries they will have.

Open primaries permit registered voters to select which party primary they will vote in when they arrive at the polls. Voters can participate in only one primary but do not need to decide which one until they arrive at the polling place. In contrast, *closed primaries* require some test of party loyalty or commitment prior to letting a person vote in a primary. Some states require voters to list their party affiliation on their voter registration form. Only those people who have identified themselves as party members on the registration form will be permitted to vote in that party's primary. In some closed primary states, one must swear or affirm allegiance to a party before being permitted to vote in the primary.

Blanket primaries place all candidates for office on a single ballot. They permit a voter to cast a vote for a Democrat in one race and a Republican in another. So, while voters can vote for only one person for any particular office, they can freely move from one party to the other as they move down their ballots.

Presidential primaries are used by political parties to select delegates to attend their national convention. Each presidential candidate has a slate of delegates committed to backing his candidacy. When voters cast a vote in presidential primaries, they are actually voting for a slate of party delegates. Generally the ballot lists only the name of the candidate to whom the group of delegates is committed, but in fact, the vote is for a particular group of delegates. It has been argued in recent years that primary elections may actually be rendering national conventions meaningless, because primaries have generally settled the issue of the party's nominee long before the convention takes place.

The candidate who has secured the party's presidential nomination prior to the convention certainly has control of the convention. But conventions still perform important party functions such as creating a platform, confirming the presidential nominee's choice for vice president, and helping reunite the party after a series of divisive primary elections. Conventions continue to be extremely important occasions for party faithfuls to meet, settle differences, organize for the general election, and introduce their presidential slate to the nation's voters.

Television has clearly changed the makeup of American elections in general and party conventions in particular. The role conventions perform in an age dominated by mass media is radically different from what it was in the nineteenth century. But conventions still provide an important foundation for presidential elections.

Conventions continue to be the national parties' singular opportunity to articulate the themes and principles they hope will unite the diverse state organizations. To understand how this is accomplished requires that we look first at the different elements that make up a political party. Party membership is usually divided into three categories: the party in office, the party in the organization, and the party in the electorate.

The party in office consists of the most obvious, and in many ways the most influential, members of any political party. These are the people who become the standard-bearers of the party. Many voters cannot separate the party from these public figures. These people articulate a party's policies and determine whether the stated policies of that party are ever enacted into law. Understandably, it is presidents and governors who become the true leaders of their party in the nation and states.

The party in the organization consists of all those people who organize party activities. With the exceptions of the leaders of the two national organizations, these are usually people who staff obscure party commissions and organize local party functions. The leaders of the two national parties are most visible during the parties' quadrennial national conventions. Each state has a party leader and numerous other staff members as well. Most of these are volunteer positions. The organizational structure varies from state to state but generally there is a state chair, some sort of county leader, a city leader, and precinct captains. The parties have a number of affiliate groups as well; youth organizations, college clubs, and women's groups are just a few examples. The purpose of these local groups is to do the legwork of the campaigns. Mainly, they distribute literature and provide transportation to the polls on election day.

The affiliate groups also try to bring a sense of belonging and identity to the party in the electorate. How clearly defined this group is depends to a large extent on state registration laws. In some states voters are required to list party preference or affiliation on their registration forms. In other states affiliation is determined by which party primary one chooses to vote in. Some states have absolutely no way of determining party preference outside of election results.

One becomes a member of the party in the electorate simply by voting for the party's candidates. Because many people do not vote a straight party line, the party in the electorate is very difficult to quantify. With the exception of the 1992 election, most American voters have been presidential Republicans and congressional Democrats in recent years.

The breakdown in party loyalty among the electorate has caused great concern among many professional students of American politics. But party trends are, and ever have been, little more than a reflection of trends that are more deeply rooted in our overall society. The function that parties must perform within our democratic system has altered considerably over the decades, but this does not mean their purpose has changed. Parties still recruit candidates for public office, they still try to mobilize the electorate on election days, and they still organize our government.

The electoral function of parties is where we have seen the greatest changes. Technology—primarily the electronic media—has been the major driving force behind these changes. Advances in transportation have played a part in these changes as well. Modern presidential candidates are less dependent on the party organization than they were before radio and television. Air travel makes it possible for candidates to visit many more cities and states than they ever could in stagecoaches or trains. But the need to develop a message and communicate it to the voters has not changed.

Mass communication has provided candidates much more direct access to voters. While this has clearly weakened the role political parties play in communication between the candidates and voters, it has by no means eliminated it. Party symbols are still an important means of association for candidates and voters alike. Despite the generalities of their party platforms and the emphasis on campaign rhetoric, the two major parties in America still provide different approaches to government.

While political parties' campaign functions have diminished in recent years, their organizational and educational functions have not. Political parties continue to be the organizational units of the American legislature just as Madison intended. All leadership positions within our legislative branches are determined by party affiliation. Congressional caucuses make committee assignments at the start of each legislative session and provide orientation for new members.

The party caucuses in both houses of Congress not only make committee assignments and select the leadership for each party, they also become the bargaining and organizational groups for every piece of legislation steered through the legislative process. The party leaders are the main strategists for their party, and the party whips make sure individual legislators are on the floor of the legislative chamber when key votes occur. To function effectively within the legislature one must work with the party leadership.

Each congressional party in each house of Congress has its own campaign organization. One of the key factors in determining how much support a party will give an individual member of Congress is the extent of that member's loyalty to the party over the years. A member who votes with the party on key legislation 90 percent of the time is going to get more support than one who backs the party 70 percent of the time. This support takes many different forms. Important committee appointments can provide legislators with extensive media exposure. The amount of money the federal government spends within a congressional district may be directly tied to the extent of one's party loyalty. Presidents, for instance, have used such things as highway funds and new postal facilities as rewards for supporting their policy initiatives.

At election time, the party not only controls large sums of money, it also controls which candidates receive campaign visits by the key party leaders. The amount of money a fund-raising dinner generates is often related to the prestige of the speaker who visits on a candidate's behalf. The party leadership has some control over whose district will receive visits by the most popular speakers. While the role political parties play in elections has diminished over the years, parties still control some valuable resources for candidates.

A major job of the party leadership in Congress is to keep records on each party member so the party can calculate the individual member's worth. Whether a legislator's name appears on a key piece of legislation may be determined by the party's loyalty test. One's effectiveness as a legislator may rest on such associations. The effectiveness of a congressional party is closely tied to its ability to use these inducements to persuade legislators to vote with the party on a regular basis. Individual legislators find it easier to campaign as a member of a political party that has a distinct record of accomplishments than to campaign as a member of an organization that has accomplished nothing in recent years. If the same political party controls both the Congress and the presidency, the pressure to run on its record of accomplishments is even greater.

For the executive, organization usually refers to how well the president works with Congress and how effectively the president deals with foreign policy. The opinion many voters have of a party's effectiveness is more directly related to executive performance than to anything the legislature does.

The president is always the symbolic leader of his party and becomes the most important mobilizing force within the party. Presidential rhetoric is the focal point of the party's educational function. Presidential campaigns are what define the parties in the eyes of most voters. So while the link between presidential elections and congressional elections has been weakened in recent years, there is still an important association between the two for American voters.[3] A strong and popular presidential candidate can still influence some congressional races.

Parties Are Essential to Civic Education

The role presidential elections have performed in the education of the American public has varied considerably, yet one should never doubt their potential to be a catalyst for sweeping reforms. Every watershed or critical election in American history has been built around a presidential campaign, and as Jefferson learned in 1796 and Jackson learned in 1824, an organized party was an essential ingredient in their educational endeavors. Party leaders proved vital to their efforts to sell the American people on a new approach to government. The unified front parties present reinforce the candidate's message. Presidential candidates who want to champion the kind of intellectual revolutions these elections have produced must never lose sight of the role political parties have played in these historic elections.

The role of political parties in leading realignments of the American electorate may be their greatest contribution to the American political system. These are the bloodless revolutions that have transformed our entire political horizon. Jefferson argued that the electoral revolution of 1800 was the intellectual culmination of what had begun in 1776. Similar rhetoric surrounded John Quincy Adams and Andrew Jackson's 1828 election.

Abraham Lincoln's renewal of the American spirit in 1860 is probably the clearest example of what political parties can accomplish with a strong leader and an appeal to fundamental principles. In each of these cases we witnessed a new party movement guided by a statesman who recognized that the issues of the day needed to be tied to the fundamental principles of the American regime. Critical elections, as the birth of the Republican party reveals, can bring an entirely new party into national prominence. Tocqueville understood this phenomenon when he argued:

> All the skill of the actors in the political world lies in the art of creating parties. A political aspirant in the United States begins by discerning his own interest, and discovering those other interests which may be collected around and amalgamated with it. He then contrives to find out some doctrine or principle that may suit the purposes of this new association, which he adopts in order to bring forward his party and secure its popularity.[4]

When these new parties have been successfully created, the tendency is for them to dominate America's national political machinery for many years thereafter.

A convincing case can be made for these critical elections being the only periods in America's political history when we have had true two-party competition. Between these electoral realignments we have had periods of one-party domination with the minority party providing a critique of the governing party's policies and waiting for an opportunity to wage a serious challenge. It can also be argued that the past half-century has been an exception to this rule, because most American voters no longer vote a party line. Everett Carll Ladd makes a strong case for presidential parties being divorced from other party activities since the 1950s.[5]

Critical elections have historically occurred at those moments when America's parties have most closely resembled Tocqueville's great parties. When an election is over and a new majority party is clearly in control of our national government, the two major parties seem to degenerate into organizations that more closely resemble minor parties. During this time, the parties appear to be more concerned with the spoils of government than with the principles of government. This indifference continues until there is some major political crisis that returns the nation's attention to salient constitutional issues and forces the major parties to reexamine the positions and principles that divide them. These reexaminations generally elevate the level of political discourse and present the American voters with a clearer set of alternatives than they routinely have.

The central task of statesmanship in America has been to raise the political vision of the nation by clarifying how the transient issues of a particular election are linked to the permanent principles that guided the founding generation. Making the link between current issues and the perennial principles that should guide republican governments is no easy task. For that reason such critical elections have been few and far between in American history: 1800, 1828, 1860, 1896, and 1936 are those generally recognized.

These partisan renewals have been the lifeblood of American political parties. So far, there has been only one of these elections in the twentieth century, which probably accounts for the weakened condition of political parties in recent decades. Speculation about the demise of the American two-party system has been credited to many factors—mass communications, a better educated electorate, voter apathy, and failure of the system, to name a few—but American history would point more specifically to the absence of the kind of statesmanship that has renewed our parties while ennobling and reviving our national purpose.

America's party history has been neither neat nor predictable. This is another reason for some of the confusion of students of America's party system. The American party system is generally considered a two-party system. There is ample historical proof for making such a claim, but there is a fair amount of literature that supports other classifications as well.

The case for a two-party system is firmly rooted in America's party history. Since 1860 we have had two major parties competing for control of our national political machinery. Since that time, our national government has been under the control of either the Democratic or Republican party. While there have been times when these two parties have shared power, it is common for one to be the dominant force in our political system. When this occurs, it falls to the other party to provide an ongoing critique of the party in power and to present the American electorate with an alternative.

During this time most Americans have identified with either the Democratic or Republican party. Research data are mixed, but the dominant view is that genuine independents are rare among American voters. Even in recent years, when ticket-splitting has become more common, voters still tend to identify with one of the two major parties. Such identification may be due to family ties, single issues, or attachment to key party figures. Whatever the source of party loyalty, it remains an important force among voters.

Among those who serve the party in government, party ties are rooted in a different orientation toward government's role and responsibilities. Parties differ over how active a part the government should take in our daily lives. In recent decades, the Democratic party has been more inclined to look to the government for solutions to problems related to such matters as unemployment, child care, and medical expenses. Republicans tend to prefer programs that aid the private sector in addressing these problems. In many areas the difference between the two parties is a matter of degree.

Regardless of the extent of the parties' differences, it is elections that permit them to take their case to the American voters. Elections provide an opportunity for each party to redefine what it is that distinguishes it from the opposition. On many occasions, the genuine issues that separate the two parties seem to become secondary to questions of a more personal nature about the candidates and their records. But even when this happens, the questions of party preferences and leanings are not totally abandoned.

Party loyalty and preference can vary with the level of a campaign as well. The South is a good illustration of this point. In most southern states the Democratic party maintains its dominion over state and local offices. Yet the South has been a fairly secure region for Republican presidential candidates over the past two decades. While there are many conflicting theories that attempt to explain this phenomenon, one seems to be rooted in the dual nature of the American party founding. Recognizing that America's congressional and presidential parties were founded at separate times helps explain many of the characteristics of the party system.

James MacGregor Burns's book, *The Deadlock of Democracy: Four-Party Politics in America*, represents this theoretical position. The four-party system he described divides each of the two major parties into a presidential party and a congressional party. While such a breakdown is consistent with the dual founding, Burns failed to recognize that such a party structure may have actually been by design.

Burns, like other advocates of a British party system, thought that the educational role of America's party system is a poor substitute for the coercive powers enjoyed by centralized parties. Yet this is consistent with the Founders' desire to produce a political system that aimed at "refining and enlarging the public's views." The decentralized American party system relies on rhetorical skills to mobilize its vast populace. But statesmen with the necessary rhetorical skills and clear political vision needed to guide our diverse nation are extremely rare, so rare that many would prefer to see institutional arrangements that could force compliance to their political schemes. Fortunately, the American public has never been receptive to such centralizing programs.

Still other scholars have argued that the American party system is really a hundred-party system. By their lights, the two major political parties are in reality state organizations. Because there are fifty states with two-party systems, we have, in effect, a hundred-party system. Carrying such logic to extremes, we could apply the four-party argument that claims executive and legislative parties are different to the fifty states and define a two hundred-party system. But the more we fragment the American party system, the harder it is to defend as a legitimate political system. This is an increasingly difficult position to maintain given the greater centralization created by national party policies and court rulings.

Conclusion

In certain ways, the two major parties have altered their positions on some issues and even some principles, yet they remain the two prime contenders for control of our national government. So we can legitimately consider ourselves to be a two-party system. But it must not be forgotten that America's two major parties continue to be decentralized parties, which means, among other things, that they remain loose confederations of many different party organizations. Every two years, these loose confederations organize both houses of Congress, and every four years, they meet at national conventions to select candidates for president and vice president of the United States.

America's national parties may not meet as national parties very often, but when they do they are involved in settling some of the nation's most important political business. So far, we have found no better alternative for accomplishing these essential democratic tasks.

Notes

1. Alexis de Tocqueville, *Democracy in America*, Phillip Bradley, ed., 2 vols. (New York: Vintage Books, 1945) I:182.
2. E. E. Schattschneider's critique of Madison revealed no understanding of or appreciation for the distinction between great and minor parties. See *Party Government* (New York: Rineholt, 1942), especially Chapter 1.
3. Campaign reform legislation has been the single greatest contributor to this growing independence of presidential elections.
4. *Democracy in America*, I:185.
5. See "Like Waiting for Godot," in *The End of Realignment? Interpreting American Electoral Eras*, Byron Shafer, ed. (Madison: University of Wisconsin Press, 1991).

Suggested Reading

Hofstadter, Richard. *The Idea of a Party System: The Rise of Legitimate Opposition in the United States, 1780-1840.* Berkeley: University of California Press, 1969.

Tocqueville, Alexis de. "Parties in the United States," *Democracy in America*, Vol. 1, Phillip Bradley, ed. New York: Vintage Books, 1945.

Van Buren, Martin. *The Origin and Course of Political Parties in the United States.* New York: Hurd and Houghton, 1867.

Weatherman, Donald. *Endangered Guardians: Party Reform Within a Constitutional System.* Lanham, Md.: Rowman and Littlefield, 1994.

Zvesper, John. *Political Philosophy and Rhetoric: A Study of the Origins of American Party Politics.* New York: Cambridge University Press, 1977.

19

The Future of American Foreign Policy

Daniel J. Mahoney

The end of the Cold War was a victory for liberal or constitutional democracy over its principal ideological opponent of the twentieth century, communist totalitarianism. The communist efforts to create a wholly new man and society and the accompanying ideological justification of that effort in the name of "history" or "socialism" have revealed themselves to be a political and human nightmare. The liberal democracies, with their prosaic defense of individual and political liberties and their historically unprecedented combination of wealth creation, personal opportunity, and technological dynamism, do not seem so ordinary or unexceptional when seen in contrast to the human devastation wrought by ideological tyranny.

The liberal regimes recover some of their "lustre and youth," as Raymond Aron recognized, "in the experience of revolutions." In the "revolutionary" struggle to establish regimes of political liberty, the nobility of democracy is most evident. Human beings willingly risk their lives for the sake of truth and liberty. In the process, human liberty is revealed to be more than the self-interested search for security and aggrandizement—it is shown to entail the necessity for participation in public life and the defense of personal honor and self-respect. The antitotalitarian revolution of 1989–1991, which put an end to the one-party socialist regimes in Eastern Europe and the Soviet Union, ought to contribute to a renewed and heightened appreciation of the dignity of our liberal regimes.

The defeat of communism, or rather its self-destruction, also signaled a victory for the Western policy of containment. This policy entailed the "long term, patient but firm and vigilant containment" of an expansive Soviet empire and ideology by the use of "unalter-able counter-force at every point where they show[ed] signs of encroaching upon the interests of a peaceful and stable world."[1] Most comprehensively sketched by George F. Kennan in his famous 1947 Mr. X. article, "The Sources of Soviet Conduct," in *Foreign Affairs*, this policy was carried out by a series of American presidents of both parties from Harry Truman to George Bush. This policy demanded sustained Western responsibility, including the ability to carry out a strategic design, over the long haul.

Containment was not, of course, an uncontroversial strategic design. Some left-leaning politicians and intellectuals questioned the need for containment and sometimes blamed Western imperialism for the continuation of the Cold War. The dogmatic application of containment in questionable circumstances such as Vietnam also weakened the widespread consensus behind an anticommunist foreign policy which existed in this country in the first two decades after 1945. Many on the political left in the 1970s and 1980s came to fear a repetition of another Vietnam, of American involvement in a protracted conflict of questionable justice.

Despite such fears, containment remained the basic core of American foreign policy until the collapse of the Soviet empire. Alexis de Tocqueville, the best student of democracy's strengths and weaknesses, questioned the capacity of democracies to carry out prudent, sustained, and settled foreign policies and statecraft. But the United States and its allies were able to carry out such a sustained and responsible policy until the implosion of communism finally occurred. The success of this policy proves that a consistent strategic design and morally serious statesmanship are compatible with the unavoidable fluctuations and petty selfishness inherent in democratic political life.

In 1947, Kennan welcomed the Cold War as a "providential" challenge, an opportunity for democracies and democratic statesmen to exercise their virtue.[2] Facing the communist challenge was a coalition of often divided democracies, each characterized by a volatile domestic public opinion, by an intellectual class that was deeply ambivalent about the justice of liberal society and states, and by a widespread yearning on the part of ordinary citizens for peace and commercial prosperity. That such a coalition was able to see through the communist episode with a considerable constancy of purpose is an achievement of high order, and worthy of serious reflection and justifiable pride.

The End of Ideological Politics?

Ideological revolution, the comprehensive effort to embody utopia in power through a politics of revolutionary transformation, seems to have come to an end. Of course, the fundamental movements of societies and politics can change in dramatically unforeseen ways. But the bankruptcy of the "ideologies" or "secular religions"[3] which have served to legitimize the various projects of coercive revolutionary world transformation is now obvious for all to see.

While some "progressive" intellectuals retain illusions concerning the original "good intentions" of Vladimir Lenin and his Bolshevik revolutionaries, they have been forced to admit that communism's "coercive utopianism," to quote Zbigniew Brzezinski, necessarily ends in the negation of human rights and the throttling of the human spirit. To put the point as directly as possible, *really existing socialism* is inextricably linked to its most horrifying yet revealing product, the Gulag Archipelago, the massive system of political repression and concentration camps which enveloped the Soviet Union under the rule of Lenin and Joseph Stalin and which persisted, in a much attenuated form, until Mikhail Gorbachev's ascension to power in 1985. The Gulag reveals communism in the way that Auschwitz and the other Nazi death camps show what national socialist totalitarianism is. This massive testimonial by itself makes any complete revival of such secular religion impossible. But the discontents beneath the seemingly peaceful surface of modern, secular democratic societies should not be ignored or underestimated. Liberal or bourgeois society, with its relentless pursuit of happiness, is not and can never be fully satisfying to humanity. Neither it nor any other social order can satisfy the powerful democratic passion for equality in all things.

There is also the problem of instituting and maintaining democratic constitutionalist practices in those parts of the world where one-party ideological regimes have fallen or lost their legitimacy. Nationalist and other powerful social passions still oppose liberal democratic ideas and practices. In the former communist bloc, some expressions of ethnic nationalisms are openly antiliberal and antidemocratic while other "moderate" national movements attempt to synthesize national and liberal sentiments and principles. In both cases there is a tension between the particularist tendencies of nationalism and the universalism of liberal democratic aspirations and politics.

There is also the problem of historical "memory" so vividly brought out by thinker-writers from East–Central Europe such as the Russian Alexander Solzhenitsyn and the Czech Václav Havel. A society can never forget its most fundamental and soul-shaping experiences without losing its vitality. In the ideological tyrannies of the East, the party-state forcibly imposed the big "Lie." Those tyrannies attempted to create a new man and a new society based on an official ideology and a philosophy of history proclaiming the historically preordained victory of "socialism."

As George Orwell revealed with characteristic brilliance in his novel *1984*, these regimes radically transformed the memory of the past and obscured the realities of the present in the name of a fictive and unachievable future. In the West, the danger is different but related. Will our dynamic and fundamentally future-oriented commercial societies remember the powerful civic and philosophical lessons to be drawn from the communist experience? Will our intellectuals modify their sometimes merely "negative" and often utopian criticisms of the liberal, commercial regimes? Will the experience of totalitarianism and ideological tyranny teach intellectuals the antihuman character and results of such projects? No one can answer these questions with anything approaching certainty. But so far there is disappointingly little evidence that these lessons from the failure of ideology have been recognized, acknowledged, and assimilated by citizens, politicians, or intellectuals in the West. And if these lessons are not learned now, it is difficult to see how they will be learned later when the vivid experience of totalitarianism is clouded by the inevitable erosion of memory.

The End of History?

The "end" of the ideological revolution is quite distinct from, and does not necessarily entail, the "end of history." What is frequently spoken of today as the end of history derives from the philosophy of history of the nineteenth-century German G. W. F. Hegel, as interpreted by the twentieth-century French philosopher Alexander Kojève, and recently popularized by Francis Fukuyama in his best-selling *The End of History and the Last Man*.[4]

Kojève's Hegel is the wise man who has fully understood the rationality of the historical process because he stands at its end. Hegel, we are told, understood that the driving force of human history—the dialectic of masters and slaves—had resulted in the definitive victory of the democratic slave who rejects all efforts or pretensions of aristocratic mastery in the name of the "universal recognition" of man by man.

Let us briefly explain this dialectic which is at the heart of theories about the end of history. According to this Hegelian view, in the primordial beginning of human history, domineering and glory-seeking masters had gained "recognition" by subduing "slaves" who subordinated their desire for "recognition" to their own preservation. But in accommodating themselves to physical work and to the mastery of nature, these "slaves" mastered their own passions and revealed the possibilities of genuinely human desires and genuine human self-mastery. The master class of aristocrats and feudal warriors continued to seek recognition by dominating other glory-seekers. The recognition received by such masters is finally socially destructive and fleeting in character. It is the "bourgeois" and "Christian" slave, in contrast, who reveals the possibility of rational human freedom, of a society of free and equal individuals who are worthy of recognition precisely because they are human beings capable of exercising human freedom for the sake of the rational mastery of nature and oneself. The constitutional or liberal state is for Hegel the "rational" state precisely because it makes democratic, universal, and rational the primordial human desire for recognition.

With the completion of the French Revolution in the person of Napoleon, the "universal and homogenous state" of "democratic" and egalitarian modernity emerges. This achievement is *rational* in character. It is the satisfaction of the deepest needs of human beings, and it is the political embodiment of "human dignity." At one time Kojève located the apex of human dignity in the form of mutual recognition and the universal and homogenous state in the tyrannical "wisdom" of Stalin. At another time he found the most fully rational and pacific embodiment of that state in the European Community being built by posthistorical West Europeans after 1958.

Fukuyama "Americanizes" Kojève, finding the political embodiment of the end of history for the capitalist liberal democracies of Western Europe and North America. He revises Hegel's and Kojève's "universal history" in the light of the collapse of the ideological revolution, of the collapse of both totalitarianism and authoritarian "strong states" in the world. Fukuyama sees the victory of the principle of universal recognition of man in the formal or political equality of liberal democratic politics and in the competitive prosperity of domestic and international markets.

Fukuyama sees no credible or widely accepted challenge to liberal democracy left in the world. Liberal democracy and the social market economy are, in his view, the undisputed institutional-political expression of the regime grounded in the modern and "rational" experience of mutual human recognition.

But Fukuyama adds a series of reservations to his initial argument. What if human spiritedness (the desire to have things our way and to be humanly "recognized") is too powerful and robust in some men to be satisfied by merely "democratic" recognition? What if the smug self-satisfied selves of victorious liberal democracies reveal themselves as the "last men" feared by the philosopher Friedrich Nietzsche—the equal herd of individuals who are without any serious human longings or aspirations, who conform to the sentiments of the many and who can not appreciate genuine human individuality or spiritual independence? What if democratic "equality" culminates in philistinism and creeping conformism? Fukuyama, in the end, seems to side with Nietzsche against Hegel. No rational human order, certainly one based simply on principles of equality and mutual recognition, can fulfill all human longings and possibilities.

Fukuyama's work—both his thesis and his reservations about it—calls attention to our political situation at the end of the ideological revolution. His questions can be restated for American foreign policy debate in the following terms: Are we at a moment when global democratization is unfolding in principle and practice? And is it the proper task of American foreign policy to promote this moment by working to "make the world safe for democracy"?

Realism and Global Democratization

In taking up the issue of global democratization and the place that "democratic idealism" ought to play in American foreign policy, two fundamental questions have to be addressed. (1) Is the global promotion of democratic values and institutions a possible, reasonable, and realistic goal? (2) Is it a desirable goal or end of American foreign policy?

A varied collection of writers from the left to the right of the political spectrum oppose active, democratic internationalism as incompatible with a realistic American foreign policy. Some on the left question the exportability of America's political institutions and practices and are often sympathetic with radical political experiments in the underdeveloped part of the world. They doubt or deny the democratic character of America's representative institutions and capitalist economy.

A more influential group of academics and publicists, representing a fairly broad spectrum of political opinion but often called "realists," criticize what it takes to be the implied moralism of a democratic, internationalist stance in foreign policy. These writers, indebted to the realist critique of idealism pioneered by Hans J. Morgenthau and Kennan in the 1940s and 1950s, assert the primacy of the "national interest" as the standard that ought to guide American statecraft.

The realists believe that American foreign policy has been prone historically to a naive belief in American "exceptionalism." As the first truly self-governing or republican polity, Americans believed that they stood outside the course of traditional history, with its clash of national interests and its power political games, a politics which really served the partisan interests of oligarchs and autocrats. Lamenting the ahistorical and immature character of American statecraft, the realists looked for guidance to the older diplomatic practices of Europe, with their emphasis on political realism and the maintenance of the balance of power.

The realists appealed to the thought and practice of those few men of the founding generation, such as Alexander Hamilton, who recognized that nations have only enduring interests and no permanent friends. Despite the few Founders in whom they sought support, the realists recognized the largely "un-American" character of their reflection about foreign policy and doubted the possibility of reorienting American foreign policy around the twin notions of the national interest and "interest defined as power." But they persisted in their efforts to instill a more "realistic" element in American foreign policy.

The realists attacked the "idealism" of President Woodrow Wilson as the most dangerous and utopian version of American exceptionalism. Wilson's emphasis on "open diplomacy openly arrived at," his desire to replace the ancient principle of international order, the balance of power, with a new role for international organization (the League of Nations), his deemphasis if not contempt for "national interests," and his attraction to abstract notions and causes ("making the world safe for democracy") were evidence, to the realists, of antipolitical and antihistorical thinking.

But Morgenthau and the other realists were remarkably vague about the meaning or content of the national interest. The national interest was related to something abstractly called "power politics" and was distinguished from a "legalistic-moralistic" approach to international relations. For the realist, the national interest is closely linked to the nation's permanent geographic or geostrategic constants. From this perspective, regimes or ideologies are seen as relatively unimportant developments. Morgenthau stressed this point in his 1948 classic *Politics Among Nations*:

[There is] astounding continuity in foreign policy which makes American, British, or Russian foreign policy appear as an intelligible, rational continuum, by and large consistent within itself, regardless of the different motives, preferences and intellectual and moral qualities of successive statesmen.[5]

Nobel Prizewinner Solzhenitsyn offers almost the opposite understanding from Morgenthau's of the relation of national interest to regime. Solzhenitsyn emphasized the ways Leninist *ideology* had essentially *transformed* the understanding of the national interest held by the rulers of Russia. He sometimes wrote as if no important domestic or foreign policy continuities existed between the Soviet regimes and Czarist predecessors. But his work has the great advantage of reminding us of the *fundamental* importance of the regime as the organizing principle of political life, and of the profound impact that "secular religions" have had on modern political life and the conduct and character of international politics.

Morgenthau and the realists abstract from the political regime as well as ideas and ideologies as determinants of the national interest. Such an abstraction from the *content* of the nation's principles and self-definition is particularly a problem in America's case. The United States explicitly defines itself as a nation by its dedication to certain "self-evident" political truths. The nation derives its identity from its dedication to certain universal truths about man and by its recognition of the fact that legitimate politics must respect the fundamental and natural "liberties" and "rights" delineated in the Declaration of Independence. So America's "national interest" is inseparable from its adherence to universal and natural principles of justice and liberty, from its character as a liberal democratic or democratic republican polity or regime. In some real sense, realism is a "European" imposition on America, and it attempts to separate too radically American foreign and domestic policy.

Today, Morgenthau's and Kennan's disciples, mostly conservatives, warn against a foreign policy which is tempted by excessive idealism and by calls for humanitarian intervention. They oppose an excessively or dogmatically "legalistic" and "multilateralist" foreign policy and are wary of attempts to promote global democratization as a precondition of a new world order. Some conservatives, such as Irving Kristol and Charles Krauthammer, used to criticize realists for downplaying the ideological dimensions of Cold War politics. But now they have joined moderate realists such as Robert Tucker in asserting the contemporary necessity of a modest foreign policy guided mostly by considerations of the national interest.

This new center-right "realist" coalition is skeptical, for instance, of intervention in faraway places for merely or primarily humanitarian reasons. It is also skeptical of a multilateralism that makes American sovereignty and foreign policy subordinate to international organizations or of efforts to settle long-standing conflicts where American "interests" are not clearly at stake. Above all, the new realists reject the claim that American power and statecraft can readily contribute to the democratization of peoples and cultures who have no long-standing experience of liberal democratic institutions, practices, or principles.

Realists generally believe that "democratic capitalism," although the best practicable regime in the contemporary world, depends on preconditions which rarely exist outside the "civic cultures" of Western Europe and North America. Some realists are cultural relativists, but others who believe in the intrinsic superiority of the liberal regime are deeply skeptical of its likely or immediate universalizability. For both groups, Wilsonian idealism, with its desire to "make the world safe for democracy" is a naive, moralistic temptation to be avoided. At best, such idealism will lead to disappointment, and at worst to a dangerously immoderate and interventionist foreign policy. Such a policy, they think, does not serve recognizable American national interests and is unlikely to promote rooted or sustained experiences of democratic self-government in non-Western parts of the world.

On the far right wing, and standing on the outskirts of the realist camp, the 1992 Republican presidential candidate Patrick Buchanan asserted the need for a new "America First" foreign policy. For Buchanan, internationalism was only temporarily mandated by the comprehensive threat that communism posed to Western civilization. With the collapse of the "Soviet threat," Buchanan has become the advocate of a semi-isolationist foreign policy. If left-isolationists such as George McGovern, the Democratic party's candidate for president in 1972, believed that America must "come home" in order to avoid oppressing the Third World with its imperialist and capitalist presence, Buchanan and his supporters believe that America is too good or too pure to be contaminated by ongoing contact with the rest of the world. Buchanan is too moralistic to be a simple realist. But he shares with the realists a disdain for democratic internationalism or any variant of a neo-Wilsonian foreign policy.

The Neo-Wilsonian Perspective

The most thoughtful and sober presentation of a neo-Wilsonian position has been made by Joshua Muravchik in his recent book *Exporting Democracy: Fulfilling America's Duty*.[6] Muravchik was the author of an impressive and nuanced criticism of Jimmy Carter's human rights policy entitled *The Uncertain Crusade: Jimmy Carter and the Dilemmas of Human Rights Policy*. Muravchik admired the democratic idealism which seemed genuinely to inspire Carter's human rights policy, but he criticized its naive and unrealistic application. He also criticized the Carter administration for failing to understand that the struggle against communist totalitarianism was the most important dimension of any human rights policy during the Cold War period. This failure to grasp the specific evil and danger of totalitarianism contributed to the Carter administration "undermin[ing] undemocratic regimes because of their human rights violations, without regard to what kind of regime might follow."[7]

Muravchik believes that in Iran and Nicaragua the consequences were disastrous. The somewhat unsavory but relatively moderate authoritarian and pro-Western regimes of the Shah and the Somoza family were replaced by militantly ideological, proto-totalitarian Islamic and Marxist–Leninist regimes in the two nations. The dangerous consequences for America's strategic interests in two vitally important parts of the world were immeasurable. (Both revolutionary regimes actively supported terrorist movements and anti-American regimes and movements from Lebanon to El Salvador.)

So Muravchik is no doctrinaire democratic "universalist." His argument for a principled, democratic internationalist foreign policy recognizes the obstacles to an immediate or thoroughgoing democratization of the world. He also makes distinctions between better and worse, and more or less liberal and permanently nondemocratic regimes. But he is relatively optimistic about the long-term prospects for democracy and global democratization.

Muravchik even considers the possibility that Fukuyama's thesis is correct and that the end of history, in the sense of the absence of any credible ideological alternative to liberal democracy, may be in the process of occurring.[8] But Muravchik is sober enough to reject any confusion of a foreign policy infused by democratic idealism with a "crusade" to make the world safe for democracy. He recognizes that there are important social, economic, cultural, and political prerequisites for successful democratization.[9] He is aware that the recent collapse of communist totalitarian regimes in East–Central Europe and the Soviet Union and the weakening of authoritarian regimes in Latin America and Asia do not guarantee a permanent victory for democracy. As with the first two major historical waves of democratization, some reversals are to be expected. But Muravchik sees grounds for real hope.

The collapse of communism as a regime and ideology makes a return to the most virulent and "totalitarian" form of contemporary tyranny highly unlikely. Democratic ideas also have never before achieved such a degree of legitimacy and acceptance as they have in the contemporary international environment. With the spread of global markets and the increasing rejection of centrally planned, socialist economic models, prosperous middle and entrepreneurial classes are providing important social prerequisites for global democratization.

Finally, Muravchik rejects cultural relativism. He believes that the desire to govern oneself and to be free from the threat of arbitrary government is a sentiment rooted in human nature and increasingly supported by the spirit of modern times. He is a moderate proponent of the politics of progress—of a Wilsonianism sobered by the experiences of totalitarianism. If he is not sure that history has come to an end, he is fairly sure that the gradual advance of democracy will continue. He believes that American foreign policy has been vindicated in its struggle against totalitarianism and must continue the struggle against existing forms of totalitarianism (Cuba, Vietnam, North Korea) and authoritarianism in the world. His practical suggestions include continuing support for the National Endowment for Democracy, the use of radio services to promote democratic ideas, (such as Radio Martí and Radio Free Asia directed at Cuba and China) and the placing of economic and political pressure on remaining authoritarian regimes where genuine democratic alternatives are available. They are in general both sensible and tough-minded, and inspired by a thoughtful and principled adherence to democratic values.

Still, there are some reservations. In addition to the question of continuing obstacles to successful global democratization, one must ask the following troubling question, which the neo-Wilsonian Muravchik is not prone to ask. Is global democratization simply a good thing? The defects and limitations of democracy as a regime or way of life must also be addressed.

Tocquevillean Reservations

Muravchik and other defenders of a principled, neo-Wilsonian foreign policy are not sufficiently aware of the problem with democracy as a category of thought or a way of life. Tocqueville was. He suggests that the movement toward democracy, toward equality of conditions and of human relations, is a "revolution," a revolution for which there is no foreseeable end or final port of destination. Democracy unleashes new human possibilities but it also erodes the moral contents of life—the *substance* of human goods, relationships, and associations. The democratic revolution defends and promotes human rights and political liberties. The value of this achievement, as the experience of totalitarianism has taught us, must not be understated. We can agree that human beings need freedom, but we must also ask, what are they to do with their freedom? What is the content of freedom? But as we see today, the democractic state is largely silent about the ends that liberty is intended to serve.

Tocqueville suggests that the end result of the process which is the democratic revolution may in fact be a kind of "democratic despotism" where formal liberties and popular sovereignty coexist with an "individualist" withdrawal from both civic life and an active sense of personal responsibility. Tocqueville feared this enervation of the human spirit unless countered by an active and thoughtful "political science" and reinvigorated citizenship. "Democracy" needs an art of liberty in order to truly serve rather than negate human dignity and liberty.[10]

Brzezinski, a distinguished political scientist and former Carter administration National Security Council Adviser, echoes Tocqueville's concerns about "democratic despotism" in a work on the character of global politics in the twenty-first century entitled *Out of Control.*[11] Brzezinski sees that American power is largely unchallenged as a force for world order and human liberty in the coming decades. He also recognizes that America remains a model for many peoples struggling with the disorders of modernity. But Brzezinski is concerned that America is in the process of losing its appeal or stature as a global "model" and inspiration unless it makes a concerted effort to put its domestic house into some kind of effective and morally estimable order.

Brzezinski is concerned with such relatively "technical" problems as national indebtedness, continuing trade deficits, industrial noncompetitiveness, low productivity growth rates, etc., that preoccupy politicians and agitate foreign policy and public policy elites. But more deeply, he is concerned that America's moderate, resilient, and responsible democracy has degenerated into what he calls a "permissive cornucopia." His fear is that the American experiment in self government is threatened by our increasing incapacity to place moral restraints on the individual will or even to recognize an enduring and immutable human self. He writes:

> The global relevance of the West's political message could be vitiated by the growing tendency in the advanced world to infuse the inner content of liberal democracy with a life-style that I define as permissive cornucopia. The priority given to individual self-gratification, combined with the growing capacity of the human being to reshape itself through genetic and other forms of scientific self-alteration—with neither subject nor moral restraint—tend to create a condition in which little self-control is exercised over the dynamics of the desire to consume and to tinker with the self.[12]

Solzhenitsyn, the greatest critic of totalitarian thought and practice in our century, also renews the Tocquevillean perspective. Solzhenitsyn is obviously more critical in his moral and political judgments than Tocqueville or Brzezinski. Yet, in his recent open letter to the Russian nation on its postcommunist future, entitled *Rebuilding Russia*, Solzhenitsyn recognizes the inevitability of some kind of democracy for all modern peoples including his own:

> So that, if we disregard the complete absence of rule (i.e. anarchy, or the role of every strong individual over every weak one), and

avoid falling once more into the trap of totalitarianism, that twentieth-century invention, then we cannot be said to have much of a
choice: the whole flow of modern history will unquestionably pre-
dispose us to choose democracy.[13]

But Solzhenitsyn warns that democracy must be judged in a clear
light, with an honest and unflinching awareness of its virtues and
vices, and its strengths and weaknesses.

> But in opting for democracy, we must understand clearly just what
> we are choosing, what price we shall have to pay, and that we are
> choosing it as a means, not as an end in itself. The contemporary
> philosopher Karl Popper has said that one chooses democracy, not
> because it abounds in virtues, but only in order to avoid tyranny. We
> choose it in full awareness of its faults and with the intention of
> seeking ways to overcome them.[14]

Solzhenitsyn had first presented his analysis and evaluation of
the state of Western democracy in his controversial 1978 Harvard
Commencement Address, "A World Split Apart." There, he expressed
his unrelenting admiration for the liberties and opportunities available in the West. But he noted the decline of civic courage and
spirit in the West, its rampant legalism (as opposed to the rule of
law which he praises), and the degrading tendencies of its popular
culture. He links these tendencies to a mistake at the origin of modern
politics, an anthropocentric error which locates the origin and foundation of politics in the human body and its needs and which recognized no transcendent order or "Superior Spirit" that serves as a
foundation for human self-respect and self-limitation.[15] We need
not share all of Solzhenitsyn's sociological analysis or moral evaluation of the contemporary state of liberal democracy or all of his
reservations about the modern project to recognize the profound
challenge that he poses to a complacent acceptance of democracy.

Solzhenitsyn, like Tocqueville, poses a friendly challenge to
supporters of Western democratic "values." He also helps us to see
that the question of "exporting democracy" cannot be separated from
the "problem of democracy." Democracy is a necessary "solution"
to the political problem, the worst form of government except for
all the rest as Winston Churchill quipped, and yet is deeply and
profoundly problematic in itself.

Conclusion

As the democratic internationalists such as Muravchik rightly
recognize, it is important to promote a principled American for-

eign policy, based on America's political tradition, a foreign policy that does justice to the moral dimensions of political life. Americans must offer the world a proud and principled defense of human liberty. Given the universalist character of our nation's self-understanding (again, see the Declaration of Independence) and the absence of any serious superpower challenge to our international role, it is important for America to continue to play a global or great power role in international affairs.

But such a foreign policy must not make absolutes of either democracy or the free market. A major task for democratic statesmanship today is to show that the democracies really are what Abraham Lincoln called them, the "last best hope on earth," and this can only be done if the weaknesses of democracy are confronted with honest self-awareness. Democracy has triumphed over totalitarianism but it must confront its own internally generated pathologies: those summarized by Tocqueville's evocative notion of "democratic despotism." Of course, it is necessary to avoid a facile or cheap pathos and gloomy pessimism as well as a "reactionary" rejection of democratic politics and institutions. Here again, Tocqueville is a most helpful guide:

> Let us, then, look forward to the future with that salutary fear which makes men keep watch and ward for freedom, and not with the flabby, idle terror which makes men's hearts sink and enervates them.[16]

Notes

1. George F. Kennan, "The Sources of Soviet Conduct" in *Foreign Affairs*, July 1947, pp. 566–82.

2. Ibid., p. 582.

3. The term "secular" or "political" religion was first used by European students of totalitarianism such as Raymond Aron and Eric Voegelin to describe the efforts of modern "atheistic" revolutionaries to establish the perfect human community (the "kingdom of heaven" on earth) through the systematic eradication of evil and evildoers (who are located in an intrinsically evil class or race). The term suggests that fanaticism is not the prerogative of believers, and that "impious cruelty" can far surpass the pious variety in its ferocity and destructiveness.

4. Francis Fukuyama, *The End of History and the Last Man* (New York: Free Press, 1992).

5. Hans J. Morgenthau, *Politics Among Nations: The Struggle for Power and Peace*, 6th ed., revised by Kenneth W. Thompson (New York: Knopf, 1985), p. 5.

6. Joshua Muravchik, *Exporting Democracy : Fulfilling America's Destiny*, rev. ed. (Washington, D.C.: AEI Press, 1992).

7. Ibid., p. 36.

8. Ibid., p. 36.

9. Ibid., pp. 72–73.

10. The fullest expression of Tocqueville's concern can be found in the penultimate chapter of Volume II of *Democracy in America*, "What Sort of Despotism Democratic Nations Have to Fear" in Tocqueville, *Democracy in America*, J. P. Mayer, ed., Vol. II, Part 4, Chapter 6 (New York: Harper and Row, 1988), pp. 690–95.

11. Zbigniew Brzezinski, *Out of Control: Global Turmoil on the Eve of the Twenty-First Century* (New York: Scribner's, 1993).

12. Ibid., p. xxi.

13. Alexander Solzhenitsyn, *Rebuilding Russia: Reflections and Tentative Proposals* (New York: Farrar, Straus, and Giroux, 1992), p. 62.

14. Ibid., pp. 62–63.

15. Alexander Solzhenitsyn, *A World Split Apart* (New York: Harper and Row, 1980).

16. Alexis de Tocqueville, *Democracy in America*, Vol. II, Part 4, Chapter 7, p. 702.

Suggested Reading

Brzezinski, Zbigniew. *Out of Control: Global Turmoil on the Eve of the Twenty-First Century.* New York: Scribner's, 1993.

Fukuyama, Francis. *The End of History and the Last Man.* New York: Free Press, 1991.

Morgenthau, Hans J. *Politics Among Nations: The Struggle for Power and Peace*, 6th ed., revised by Kenneth W. Thompson. New York: Knopf, 1985.

Muravchik, Joshua. *Exporting Democracy: Fulfilling America's Destiny*, rev. ed. Washington, D.C.: AEI Press, 1992.

Solzhenitsyn, Alexander. *A World Split Apart.* New York: Harper and Row, 1980.

———. *Rebuilding Russia: Reflections and Tentative Proposals.* New York: Farrar, Straus, and Giroux, 1992.

Part Three

Issues

20

Interest Group Liberalism versus the Virtuous Statesman

Robert P. Hunt

When a congressman casts his vote in support of higher taxes, or for a federal death penalty statute, or against federal funding for abortion, what factors should contribute to his decision? Should he be guided by his own judgment of what constitutes good public policy? By the wishes of his constituents? By some combination of the two? These important questions have plagued a number of theorists of representative government for the past several hundred years. They lead to a larger question: What is the relationship between the legislator or representative and the constituency he seeks to represent?

The nineteenth-century American essayist Parke Godwin argues for what can be described as the "representative as delegate" position. "A representative," Godwin contends, "is but the mouthpiece and organ of his constituents. What we want in legislation as in other trusts, are honest fiduciaries, men who will perform their duties according to our wishes."[1] The "good" representative, according to Godwin, is the man who accurately "mirrors" or reflects the interests, goals, and wishes of the particular constituency that elected him. By extension, any good representative institution ought to be a mirror image of the various particular interests that make up the nation as a whole. Good public policy is whatever flows out of the process of balancing and compromising needed to reconcile these presumably divergent particular interests. And the good statesman is that figure who is the most adept at the fine art of balancing interests.

The eighteenth-century British statesman Edmund Burke, on the

345

other hand, argues for what can be described as the "representative as trustee" position. As a candidate for the House of Commons, Burke told his electors that "your representative owes you not his industry only, but his judgment; and he betrays, instead of serving you, if he sacrifices it to your opinion."[2] The good representative, Burke contends, is the man who, exercising his reasoned judgment and enlightened conscience, articulates the "true" interests of his constituency, as he perceives those interests.

So a good representative institution is comprised, for Burke, of sober, dispassionate, and mature persons who display an ability to deliberate, in light of the diversity of "legitimate" interests, about the best way to achieve the "common good" of the nation as a whole. The art of statesmanship, according to Burke, cannot be practiced effectively if the statesman himself lacks what Aristotle called practical wisdom or prudence. This virtue perfects man's reason, weighs ends and means within a complex realm of human choices and political possibilities, and determines whether the consequences of various possible public policies are conducive to the common good of society. Such an art requires something more than the mere ability to balance interests. It requires some general knowledge of what is "good" for man and an ability to articulate that knowledge clearly. It also requires particular knowledge of what is possible given the limitations of particular political circumstances.

It is often argued that the Framers of the American Constitution were fearful of governance by Burkean "virtuecrats" who believed that they were entitled to govern because of their superior understanding of the common good. And it is certainly true that in *Federalist* 51, Publius argued that within a constitutional system of separated powers, ambition must be made to counteract ambition. It is unrealistic to believe that outstanding leaders will be motivated only by virtue. The pursuit of self-interest will always be part of democratic self-government, but that pursuit can be turned to the public good.

But Publius also recognized, in *Federalist* 70 and elsewhere, that the essence of the legislative branch's legitimacy was its ability to conciliate the confidence of the people through its deliberative and sober reflections on what constitutes good public policy. The Burkean emphasis on reason and virtue should be supplemented by institutional restraints on power.

And yet modern critics of Burke seem to advance a more radical criticism of his position than that advanced by the Framers. These critics fault Burke not only for his imprudent reliance on virtue alone in constructing a theory of representation, but because he argues for a substantive conception of the good society. For those critics, Burke's argument seems to be anachronistic.

Burke offends our democratic sensibilities because we are, as Hannah Pitkin has pointed out in *The Concept of Representation*,

> individualists and democrats and relativists in our thinking, not quite content to tell a man what is in his interest without any regard to his wishes. We tend to think that, in the last analysis, each man has the right to define his own good, and, if he rejects something, no one has the right to insist that it is good for him.[3]

Given the individualistic and relativistic society in which we live, Pitkin contends, it is foolish to attempt to reinvigorate the Burkean conception of the "virtuous representative." Some variant of Godwin's position must invariably fill the theoretical and practical vacuum.

I will analyze those Godwinesque, pluralist theories of representation that emphasize the need for the representative to embody the will, or perceived interests, of the individuals or groups he represents. I will show that the "pluralist" emphasis on the need to reflect the "particular wills" of as many interests as possible runs two complementary dangers. First, it could paralyze the representative institution, making it incapable of governing. Second, such paralysis could lead directly to the call for a vigorous "chief executive" who receives a mandate for action because it is believed that only he embodies the "general will" of the people and can truly "represent" them and their interests. (This paradoxical situation was realized most recently, as we shall see, in the 1992 presidential candidacy of H. Ross Perot.)

The pluralist argument fails to provide a substantive role for the people's representative because of its emphasis on the source of political authority (the people) and the process of governance. The pluralist does not recognize that, in Burke's words, "government and legislation are matters of reason and judgment"[4] and not just of will. Perhaps we should dispel the ghosts of individualism and relativism that plague modern theories of representation, and return to the ideas of philosophic statesmen like Burke and Publius in order to restore a firm theory of representation within a constitutional society.

Representation versus Lawmaking:
A False Dichotomy?

David Vogler, in *The Politics of Congress*, aptly points out that "any list of universally accepted functions of [the U.S.] Congress is bound to gloss over important conflicts about what the proper legislative role is." Vogler contends that there is an inherent conflict between those who expect Congress to be "a forum where the interests and demands of all groups in society are expressed" (that is, a representative institution) and those who expect Congress to be "a decision-maker that translates popular mandates into law" (that is, a lawmaking body abiding by the principles of majority rule).[5]

Scholars who portray Congress as a representative, pluralistic institution tend, according to Vogler, "to deny that there is some substantive definition of the public interest apart from that which emerges by balancing group interests."[6] Each representative is expected to reflect the interests of his particular constituency (or group interest), and the public interest is defined as whatever emerges from the reconciliation of these competing group interests. If we adhere to the process of bargaining and compromise, the result will necessarily be "fair" to all conceivable groups.

Vogler adds that there is another group of scholars that takes issue with the "representative institution" position. These scholars see Congress as a legislative body and argue that "the public interest is defined in terms of electoral mandates."[7] True representation is achieved when legislators pass laws that reflect the types of programs desired by a majority of the people. The articulation of all conceivable interests or particular wills does not serve the public interest. It causes stalemate, deadlock, and an inability of the general will of the community to express itself through electoral mandates. So these scholars seek to reform Congress, to make it more efficient, to make it better able to respond to whatever the majority of the American people desire.

Vogler seems to believe that these two divergent views on the primary function of Congress exist at polar extremes and that the remedy for the extremism of each position is a middle ground that carefully balances the principles of representation and lawmaking. According to Vogler, there must be an attempt to reconcile the "general will" of the nation with the particular wills of the various interests that comprise the nation.

What Vogler fails to recognize, however, is that *both* theories place a heavy emphasis on the accurate reflection of will, either the will of each particular constituency or the will of a national majority. Once we recognize that these positions are *not* mutually exclusive—that they are two sides of the same Godwinesque coin— we begin to see that there may be a need for a shift in perspective away from the concept of will as the primary criterion for political legitimacy.

Interest Groups and the Pluralist Theory of Representation

The pluralist or interest group theory of representation is based on a value-free definition of what constitutes an interest in general and a political interest in particular. The political scientist David Truman defines "interest group" in *The Governmental Process*:

> Interest group refers to any group that, on the basis of one or more shared attitudes, makes certain claims upon other groups in the society for the establishment, maintenance, or enhancement of forms of behavior that are implied by the shared attitudes.[8]

An interest group, according to Truman, is formed whenever people who share certain attitudes about what is good for them unite in order to extract some concession from other groups in society. A political interest group is any group that makes certain claims on, and expects some response from, the governing apparatus.

For Truman, there are no substantive, objective criteria for judging the merits of any group's claims. There can be no appeal to some mystical "national interest" or "common good." He argues that there can be no "totally inclusive" national interest because there are no attitudes shared by all people within the nation. For example, even during wartime there are a number of people who dissent from what the government asserts is the national interest. How likely is it, then, that there will be unanimous agreement (or discoverable "national interest") when we talk about divisive social or economic issues? Where there is no unanimity of interest—that is, where there is no "willed" concurrence about what is "good" for society as a whole—there is no "common good." And there can be no such concurrence within a complex modern nation because "the differing experiences and perceptions of men not only encourage individuality but also . . . inevitably result in differing attitudes and conflicting group affiliations."[9] As a society becomes larger and more heterogeneous, talking about the "common good" of that society becomes less and less feasible. We may employ the phrase but it does not reflect reality.

There is, however, a notion of the "good society" implicit within Truman's supposedly value-free analysis of interest groups. The good (or fair) society allows all interests to be represented because there is no way that we can weigh the legitimacy of any group's claims. The good society establishes certain rules of the game with which all groups are expected to comply because those rules favor no particular interest or conception of what is good. Society becomes, in Truman's own words, "a protean complex of crisscrossing relationships that change in strength and direction with alterations in the power and standing of interests, organized and unorganized."[10] The potential for totalitarianism exists in any society where there is some predominant ideology or conception of the common good. The remedy for totalitarianism lies in the ability of a multiplicity of interest groups to have input into the public policy-making process.

For Truman, no substantive criteria can be used to determine the legitimacy of any group's perception of its own interest. An interest group might become stronger or weaker depending on such factors as its internal organization or how the general public perceives its goals. But there is no objective way of deciding whether that interest is good or bad.

The good society is not defined by its pursuit of certain objective ends or purposes because it is impossible to discover a set of objectively valid ends or purposes. Rather, the good society is the fair society, the society that gives all interests, whatever their conception of the good, an ability to have an impact on the making of public policy.

Truman's argument is open to some criticism. For example, he says that unanimous agreement is needed before it can be claimed that a collective interest exists. The absence of unanimity implies the absence of a common "interest." But if unanimity is the essential attribute of a collective interest, there can be no such thing as a group interest either. Every group is composed of individuals who by no means agree on every substantive political issue.

The absence of any standard for determining the substantive content of the "common good" also has disastrous consequences. If there is no objective definition of the common good, decisions must be made through the interaction of conflicting wills and interests. Public policy becomes little more than the triumph of the will of the more organized and socially respected groups. Justice becomes, as Thrasymachus argued in Plato's *Republic*, simply the interest of the strong imposed on the weak.

What happens when this pluralist or interest group theory of politics is applied to a representative body? Each legislator, it seems, represents a particular interest. The criterion for judging whether he is a "good" or "bad" representative is whether he accurately reflects the particular will of his constituents. His only obligation to the legislative body of which he is a part is to play by the rules of the legislative game.

The "good" representative assembly is the "open" representative assembly. Its members presuppose that no legislator can achieve the level of detachment required to be able to define the common good of society. In fact, the common good is nothing other than whatever policy is decided after each interest has had a fair opportunity to articulate its opinion. No legislator can define justice in substantive terms. All he can do is "represent" interests, and there can be no criticism of the "particular will" that he ostensibly represents. The Burkean "virtuous representative" has been replaced by the courteous skeptic. He must remain a skeptic if the legislature is to function smoothly.

John Hallowell, a critic of the pluralist view of representation, argues that this type of legislature, carried to its logical extreme, becomes "a field of combat ever ready to disintegrate into chaotic futility or into servile submission to the will of the stronger."[11] An unfortunate solution proposed to this problem of disintegration is that the nation's policies should be determined by translating popular mandates into law. This voluntarist solution to the problem of deadlock, to the possibility of chaotic futility, implicit in the pluralist theory of representation was originally enunciated by Woodrow Wilson in the late nineteenth century and later supported by presidential scholar James MacGregor Burns. It is also a solution advocated by H. Ross Perot.

Wilson, Burns, Perot, and the General Will of the People

For many years before he became president of the United States, Woodrow Wilson was a critic of the American experiment in self-

government and of the principle of separation of powers in particular. His analysis of the American constitutional scheme depended,
to a large extent, upon the work of Walter Bagehot, a British essayist and author of *The English Constitution* in the late 1860s.
Bagehot compared the British and American constitutions and found
the American constitution wanting. He concluded that "the splitting of sovereignty [in America] into many parts amounts to there
being no sovereign."[12] Bagehot's criticism of the American "splitting of sovereignty" between different branches and levels of the
federal government lies at the heart of what has come to be the
Wilsonian and Burnsian attack on the system of checks and balances.

Wilson, in his *Congressional Government: A Study in American
Politics* (1885), argued that a system of government in which important decisions are made by congressional committees is singu-
larly incapable of providing effective national leadership. He portrayed congressmen as glib sophists rather than as models of
exemplary statesmanship.

> Legislative leadership . . . is the leadership of orators; it is the as-
> cendancy of those who have a genius for talking. In the eyes of
> those who do not like it, it seems a leadership of artful dialecti-
> cians, the success of tricks of phrase, the victory of rushing decla-
> mation—government not by the advice of statesmanlike counselors,
> but by the wagging of ready tongues.[13]

The nation, in Wilson's view, could not prosper if congressional
committees of professional sophists governed it. He searched for a
remedy. In *Constitutional Government in the United States* (1908),
he thought he had found it. He contended that the American experiment in democracy would be successful only if a single figure (the
president) could capture the imagination of the people and turn his
election into a societal mandate for action and reform:

> His [the president's] is the only national voice in affairs. Let him
> once win the admiration and confidence of the country, and no other
> single force can withstand him, no combination of forces will easily
> overpower him. His position takes the imagination of the country.
> He is the representative of no constituency, but of the whole people.[14]

The president receives a mandate not to reason and deliberate
about the best means of promoting the common good, but to *act*.

And his ability to act is increased when he wins "the admiration and confidence of the country." Wilson undoubtedly believes that the president will have the political virtues needed to refine and enlarge public opinion (so resembling Burke's virtuous representative). But he also seems to believe that the president is justified in taking control of the levers of power in our constitutional system because he alone represents the "will of the people." For Wilson, "good" national policy is the enactment into law of the substantive mandate that the people give to the president when they elect him.

Presidential scholar and historian James MacGregor Burns echoes Wilson's preoccupation with the ability of the government to reflect the general will of the people. In *The Deadlock of Democracy*, Burns argues that progress under what he describes as a Madisonian regime is "snail-like." In describing the snail-like progress of America, Burns gives his readers a clear indication of the goals that a presidential activist ought to pursue:

> We have been captured by that model, which requires us to await a wide consensus before acting, while we have neglected, except furtively and sporadically, the Jeffersonian strategy of strong leadership, majority rule, party responsibility, and competitive elections. Hence, government action has been unduly delayed, whether measured by the progress of other comparable nations, such as Britain; or the ascertainable needs of people, such as the jobless of the 1930s or the civil rights of minorities today [*sic*]; or by what the voters wanted or would accept, as reflected in the national platforms of both major parties and in the campaign promises of their presidential candidates.[15]

The primary duty of a strong president is to ensure that the wishes of the majority of the people are realized. His job is made easier by the fact that voters have given tacit support to the national platform of his party in general and responded to his promises in particular. They have, in other words, given him a mandate to act on their behalf. He is their only true representative, and he must commit himself to effective and exuberant leadership. He must devote his energies to replacing the Madisonian model of government that has "thwarted and fragmentized leadership instead of allowing it free play."

The implication of Burns's argument is clear. The achievement of domestic priorities (that is, social and economic policy), which had for the authors of *The Federalist* been placed in the hands of "a numerous legislature [which was] best adapted to *deliberation* and *wisdom*, and best calculated to conciliate the confidence of the people and to secure their privileges and interests," is henceforth to be turned over to a Wilsonian chief executive (*Federalist* 70, italics mine). This true representative of the people must be able to control Congress in the latter's consideration of social and economic policy. What the country needs is a president who exemplifies the ideal of "heroic leadership"—one willing to bring pressure to bear on recalcitrant legislators who fail to share the people's vision of America as it is refracted through a single man's eyes.

In 1992, Independent presidential candidate. H. Ross Perot advanced an argument for presidential ascendancy remarkably similar to Burns's. He argued that the American system of checks and balances and separation of powers was bound to produce policy gridlock. Perot promised that if he were elected president, he would end gridlock by going over the heads of congressmen and holding national electronic town-hall meetings. At these "meetings," the public would have an opportunity to express its will on important public policy questions. Perot would then give effect to the people's will by echoing and implementing their concerns and desires.

It could be argued that Perot is the most recent embodiment of the pluralist theory of representation. He emphasizes will to the total neglect of reason, promising to be an empty vessel into which the American public will pour its dreams and aspirations. If Congress cannot be that vessel, then perhaps the president can be.

Against Burns's and Perot's argument, political scientist Willmoore Kendall argued some thirty years ago that theorists have become so preoccupied with the need for the president to reflect the "will of the people" that they are unable to differentiate between the just rule of the majority (that is, the deliberate sense of the community as it expresses itself through virtuous representatives) and the potentially unjust rule of the majority (that is, plebiscitary democracy).

The Wilsonian democrat, Kendall argues, makes a terrible mistake when he equates majoritarianism with the rule of a popularly elected president. He believes that "either the majority rules through the presidential elections . . . or it does not rule at all."[16] For Kendall, on the other hand, our Founding Fathers were not bent upon thwarting majoritarianism. But they were determined to see that the majority would govern justly. That was best assured in a polity where, according to Publius, civic-minded citizens returned to the legislative body men "whose merit may recommend [them] to the esteem and confidence of [their] country" and who "promise a sincere and scrupulous regard to the nature of their engagements" (*Federalist* 57). The Senate in particular commended itself because it would consist of "those men only who have become the most distinguished by their *abilities* and *virtue*, and in whom the people perceive just grounds for confidence" (*Federalist* 64, italics mine).

Kendall does tend to make the Framers too Burkean by deemphasizing their reliance on checks and balances, separation of powers, and so forth. But there is an important truth in his view: The Framers had no desire to turn representatives into moral ciphers, as does Truman. Nor did they think that a democratic experiment in self-government could survive without some consensus on the constituent elements of the public good.

The Recovery of Reason and Virtue

This analysis of interest group liberalism, and its theory of representation, leads us to ask several important questions: Is justice more substantially promoted in a regime that extols the notions of "virtue," of "deliberation," and of reasoning in pursuit of some substantive conception of the "good life?" Or is it more substantially promoted in a regime that emphasizes either the sovereign equality of all preferences, no matter how strange or perverse, or the sovereign strength of a simple national majority?

The Wilsonian or Perotean "presidentialist," like the Trumanite "pluralist," emphasizes the concept of will over reason. The "true representative," for Wilson, Burns, and Perot, is a single figure who reflects the will of a national majority as it expresses itself through a plebiscitary election. This triumph of will over reason runs counter to the classical and early modern notions of representation and statesmanship handed down to us by such men as Burke and the authors of *The Federalist*.

While Publius did not share Burke's faith in a natural aristocracy, he would have had an even greater problem with the pluralist emphasis on will alone as the foundation for an experiment in self-government. He would have been opposed to Ross Perot's call for the election of a "leader" who makes policy that "reflects" decisions made at national town-hall meetings.

For Burke and the authors of the *Federalist*, it makes little difference who governs if government is nothing more than the will of the strong imposed on the weak and the only sanction for law becomes the force behind it. What might be needed is a revival of some conception of virtue in discussing the role of legislators in a constitutional democracy. To revive such a conception is to question the argument of political scientist Elaine Spitz that "even if a case for the identification of 'real' interest can be constructed, political equality precludes its implementation. For practical purposes, no one in a democracy can substitute his or her allegedly wise judgment for another's allegedly unwise judgment."[17]

Perhaps the concept of civic virtue, of the desirability of rational deliberation among well-intentioned and prudent representatives about the best way to achieve morally justifiable political "goods," is not dead. The Founders recognized that such "materials" were the lifeblood of a successful democratic republic. Does the American body politic need a reinfusion of such ideas into its system, rather than those of Truman, Wilson, Burns, and Perot? This larger question will become increasingly important as issues such as legislative term limitations, congressional gridlock, and the still possible ascendancy of Wilsonian populist presidential candidates like Perot become part of the national public debate.

Notes

1. Parke Godwin, quoted in David J. Vogler, *The Politics of Congress*, 4th ed. (Newton, Mass.: Allyn and Bacon, 1983), p. 77.

2. Edmund Burke, "Speech to the Electors of Bristol," *The Works of the Right Hon. Edmund Burke*, Vol. III (London: Rivington, 1826), p. 19.

3. Hannah Fenichel Pitkin, *The Concept of Representation* (Berkeley: University of California Press, 1967), p. 159.

4. Burke, p. 19.

5. Vogler, pp. 17, 11, 18.

6. Ibid., p. 36.

7. Ibid., p. 31.

8. David B. Truman, *The Governmental Process* (New York: Knopf, 1951), p. 33.

9. Ibid., pp. 50–51.

10. Ibid., p. 508.

11. John H. Hallowell, *The Moral Foundation of Democracy* (Chicago: University of Chicago Press, 1954), p. 31.

12. Walter Bagehot, *The English Constitution*, introduction by R. H. S. Crossman (New York: Cornell University Press, 1976), p. 219.

13. Woodrow Wilson, *Congressional Government: A Study in American Politics*, Chapter 4, Saul K. Padover, ed., *Wilson's Ideals* (Washington, D.C.: American Council on Public Affairs, 1942), p. 26.

14. Woodrow Wilson, *Constitutional Government in the United States* (New York: Columbia University Press, 1908), p. 68.

15. James MacGregor Burns, *The Deadlock of Democracy: Four-Party Politics in America* (Englewood Cliffs, N.J.: Prentice-Hall, 1963), pp. 323–24, 340.

16. Willmoore Kendall, *The Conservative Affirmation* (Chicago: Regnery, 1963), Chapter 2, pp. 21–49. Kendall's argument is directed against Robert Dahl, *Preface to Democratic Theory* (Chicago: University of Chicago, 1956), but it applies also to the theories of Wilson and Burns.

17. Elaine Spitz, *Majority Rule* (Chatham, N.J.: Chatham House, 1984), p. 42.

Suggested Reading

Burke, Edmund. "Speech to the Electors of Bristol." *The Works of the Right Hon. Edmund Burke*, Vol. III. London: Rivington, 1826.

Burns, James MacGregor. *The Deadlock of Democracy: Four-Party Politics in America*. Englewood Cliffs, N.J.: Prentice-Hall, 1963.

Hallowell, John H. *The Moral Foundation of Democracy*. Chicago: University of Chicago Press, 1954.

Truman, David B. *The Governmental Process*. New York: Knopf, 1951.

Wilson, Woodrow. *Constitutional Government in the United States*. New York: Columbia University Press, 1908.

21

Public Opinion and American Democracy

Sidney A. Pearson Jr.

All regimes, but especially representative democracies such as the United States, rest precariously on public opinion. Democracies, more than any other form of government, are explicitly designed to be responsive, accountable, and responsible to the many. Both their form and their function reflect the power of public opinion. The study of public opinion in a representative democracy must focus on three interrelated issues: (1) the role of public opinion in regime *maintenance*,(2) the political *analysis* of public opinion, and (3) the *political effects* of public opinion. Each issue is dependent on the others for its political significance and interpretation.

Regime maintenance concerns the substantive character of public opinion necessary to support a representative democracy. How much conscious or active application of political knowledge and citizen virtue is actually needed to maintain a popular government based on liberal principles? If, as James Madison argued in *The Federalist*, a representative democracy is *the* most difficult of all regimes to maintain, then it cannot be, in the words of Michael Kammen, a "machine that will go of itself." Some opinions are fundamentally hostile to democracy, and their influence must be opposed in democracy's name.

The Founders argued that representative democracy would have to incorporate two principles if it wished to preserve itself with justice: properly ordered institutions and a virtuous citizenry. Neither, alone, is sufficient. How could a virtuous citizenry be cultivated and maintained? The answer has never been entirely clear.

So public opinion analysis is an inquiry into the political health

of the regime. Systematic public opinion analysis that is related to
the nature of the American regime should (1) enable us to continually measure and evaluate the substantive content of contemporary public opinion, (2) properly situate that evaluation within the
context of regime maintenance questions, and (3) make recommendations, where appropriate, for strengthening those qualities of public
opinion necessary for regime maintenance. Such analysis will always be guided, implicitly or explicitly, by an inquiry into the health
of our regime.

We also need to understand the effects of democratic opinion on
government and politics. Most students of contemporary politics
recognize this implicitly. There is a widespread consensus among
political scientists that public opinion polls have altered much of
the modern debate over democratic regimes. But there is less consensus on *how* polls have changed politics and what, if anything,
these changes may mean.

The results of polling are perhaps most conspicuous in the office of the presidency. Modern presidents have been especially
sensitive to poll results. Continuous polling on the president's popularity and its reciprocal effects on presidential decision-making
have raised concerns that the modern presidency may have become
too much of a "public relations presidency." Presidents seem to
succeed or fail in direct relation to their standing in the polls. So
presidents and their media advisers are obsessed with their standing.

In *The Rhetorical Presidency*, Jeffrey Tulis argues that the modern
presidency has gradually moved away from the institutional basis
of power and authority embodied in the Constitution and toward
the more informal and volatile basis for power always latent in public
opinion. And in a democracy, there is no power stronger than the
force of majority public opinion. In effect, presidential leadership
has come to more closely resemble the "pure" democracy most feared
by the Founders, and less like the presidency envisioned by Publius.

How Did the Founders Understand
Public Opinion in Democracy?

Support for popular government, or democracy in any form, was
rare among political philosophers until the American founding. A

common sticking point was the problem of public opinion that the Founders well understood. The classical definition of democracy stressed the direct operation of public opinion on government. The Constitution of the American Founders explicitly rejected the classical objection to democracy by reframing the problem of public opinion in new terms. The new definition of democracy stressed representation of public opinion. The Founders' "new science of politics" was largely built around the differences between direct democracy and representative democracy.

Plato and Aristotle made justice the end of government. They went on to say that it should be much easier to educate one or a few of the best citizens about the principles of justice than to educate the many. So they had a general preference for monarchical or aristocratic forms of government.

The classical choice was typically presented as either democracy or justice. Because the end of government (justice) was more important than the means (democracy, aristocracy, or monarchy), the rejection of democracy was understandable. A defense of democracy that did not sacrifice justice would have to be able also to defend the role of popular opinion in a democracy. The American Founders understood this problem and undertook to provide such a defense. They began their defense of democracy, as did Plato and Aristotle, with a conception of human nature.

The Founders did not think of men as either wholly depraved or wholly good. The assumption of total depravity would lead to tyranny just as surely as the assumption of natural virtue. As Madison put it in *Federalist* 55:

> As there is a degree of depravity in mankind which requires a certain degree of circumspection and distrust: So there are other qualities in human nature, which justify a certain portion of esteem and confidence. Republican government presupposes the existence of these qualities in a higher degree than any other form.

Publius held that public opinion could be "represented" and, in the process of representation, be "refined" into a more rational product. But he did not presuppose that the "enlightened" opinion of either citizens or their representatives was sufficient for a just regime. Even universal enlightenment in every democratic citizen would not prove adequate to the task of governing. To quote Madison again, "Had every Athenian citizen been a Socrates: every

Athenian assembly would still have been a mob" (*Federalist* 55). All opinion must be refined by representation to make good government possible.

Representation did not alter the power of public opinion in a democracy. *The Federalist* was explicit that all of the great questions of government would sooner or later be referred to the people, "that pure original fountain of all legitimate authority" (*Federalist* 22). The nature of the regime, the way it defines what is just and good, should ultimately be determined by the citizens' opinions on these subjects.

In a representative democracy public opinion would be shaped by its interaction with other institutions and the rule of law. As Madison understood it, the problem was to cultivate the "reason" of the public as an expression of "republican virtue," while also tempering its "passions." Passions were more likely to prevail in a pure democracy where public opinion operated directly on government officials. Publius said that ancient democracies had uniformly failed because mass opinion was more often guided by passion than by reason. This ancient experience showed the insufficiency of civic education. In the pure or participatory democracy, justice would be *entirely* dependent on the moral education of the citizenry because public opinion alone would determine the character of the regime. In a pure democracy the only restraint on public opinion would be moral education.

But the Founders did take for granted the basic virtue of American democratic opinion because there was no obvious rift between popular culture and the ends of government. By taking for granted that private sources of moral education would defend representative democracy, they obscured the regime maintenance issue concerned with the character of opinion. There was little need for them to address the problem more explicitly than they did. Madison, along with most of the other Founders, might best be described as a long-run optimist and a short-run pessimist with regard to democratic opinion. While reason would prevail in the long run, it needed institutional support in the short run.

Modern Political Science and Public Opinion

The understanding of public opinion analysis by contemporary political science is significantly different from that of the Founders.

The difference strikes us first in the way the study of public opinion is organized. It is presented in the form of statistical representations of public opinion in which the chief problem is a technical problem of measurement. But beneath those statistics and measurement issues, there also seem to be different assumptions about where and how public opinion ought to be situated in democratic theory and practice. Modern political science follows the Founders in assuming the importance of public opinion in a democracy at the outset. But it often rests atop a fundamentally different conception of democracy. The real message of most public opinion polls is the rupture between mass opinion and representative institutions.

We are presented with a mass of public opinion polls and political analysis that seems to endorse a pure or participatory democracy. The very logic of participatory democracy seems to imply that the primary problem of public opinion analysis will begin with the problem of measurement.

Measurement is the problem because most contemporary studies of public opinion recognize that elections alone are not always the best way to tell what the public thinks about issues. Elections tell us who wins, of course, but they do not necessarily tell us what the public thinks about a wide range of public policy issues. People vote for reasons other than issues. Students of public opinion very often find the connection between public opinion and public policy to be haphazard at best. Yet if we start with the notion that public opinion ought to direct at least the broad outlines of policy decisions, finding links and repairing breaks in that connection is important.

Most Americans tend to think of public opinion in terms of public opinion polls. This is neither surprising nor entirely mistaken. Public opinion polls often form the very core of much political reporting. Major newspapers' own polls, such as those of the *New York Times*, *Wall Street Journal*, and *Washington Post*, often become the news itself. Newspapers often no longer merely report the news. They actually manufacture what seems to be a hard, objective reality. For better or worse, public opinion polls have become the hard currency of political campaigns.

In government and in political campaigns, the representative or political candidate who does not have a pollster to keep him informed may find himself tactically disarmed. For scholars and other pundits it has become virtually impossible to engage in any systematic interpretation of modern American politics without sooner or later having some recourse to polls. Polls shape so much of the public debate over what government ought or ought not to do that they seem to have taken on the role of an autonomous actor on the political stage.

The Origin of Public Opinion Polls

Public opinion polling dates from the late nineteenth century. But what we call "scientific" polling dates primarily from the 1930s with the work of George Gallup and a few other pioneers. From its beginning, polling has conceptualized democracy differently than the Founders. Gallup wanted to "take the pulse of democracy" or help translate that pulse into public policy, and provide politicians with a more accurate means of actually "knowing" the substance of public opinion than anything else available. He and other pioneers in public opinion polling were convinced that all too often "real" public opinion was distorted by the ordinary working of the political process. *Represented* opinion was not the same thing as public opinion *measured* by polling. Gallup conceived scientific polling techniques that would bring the full weight of real public opinion to bear on politicians and policymakers and so contribute to the fuller realization of a democracy in America.

Gallup founded his American Institute of Public Opinion in 1935 and immediately began writing a weekly newspaper column— "America Speaks!"—based on the results of his polls. He claimed that his was the first scientific poll of public opinion and sold the column to newspapers on that basis. The *Washington Post*, among others, picked up his column in 1935, advertised it from a blimp cruising over the city, and made his reports a centerpiece of newspaper coverage of the 1936 presidential election between Franklin Roosevelt and Alf Landon.

The major competition in political polling at the time came from the far more famous Literary Digest Poll that had been around since 1916. *The Literary Digest* was a mass-circulation magazine that had hit upon the idea of conducting a "straw poll" of the presidential election in 1916 as a means of promoting magazine sales. Straw polls were unscientific polls of public attitudes that had previously been used by newspapers, sometimes with surprisingly accurate results. Most straw polls relied on the participants themselves to initiate the response, such as by having them mail postcards or clip newspapers ballots to register their opinion on some issue. The general belief was that the size of the mail-in would be the test of accuracy.

From 1916 through 1936 no other poll had more responses than *The Literary Digest*, which by 1924 was mailing out over twenty million postcards soliciting responses on who people thought would win the upcoming presidential election. By 1932 *The Literary Digest* mailed out over 350 million such postcards and the poll had taken on a life of its own. In 1932 the Literary Digest poll projected Roosevelt the winner with 59.85 percent of the popular vote. The actual vote total was 59.14 percent—a margin of error so small that the poll looked virtually unassailable.

In 1936 *The Literary Digest* announced the results of its latest straw poll on the presidential election. And the winner, with "in the neighborhood" of 56 percent of the vote, was none other than the Republican nominee, Alf Landon. When George Gallup, using his more scientific sampling techniques, predicted the Democratic incumbent Roosevelt as the winner, the stage was set for a dramatic confrontation between rival pollsters and competing theories of how to conduct public opinion polls.

Roosevelt won in one of the greatest landslide elections in American history—with 60.8 percent of the popular vote. Not only did Alf Landon go down to defeat, but so too did the Literary Digest poll. The magazine folded shortly thereafter, no doubt in part because of the unfavorable results of its 1936 presidential poll. The question that was asked was *why* did the Literary Digest Poll turn out wrong and how did Gallup get it right? On the answer to that fundamental question has turned much of the modern science of public opinion polling.

What Is Scientific Polling?

The bias in the Literary Digest Poll began, but did not end, with its method of selecting who would be polled. The magazine had sampled public opinion relying on lists taken from telephone numbers and automobile registrations. The sampling technique excluded lower socioeconomic groups, those without telephones or automobiles. It excluded those who were more disposed to vote Democratic. The vote in 1936 was unprecedentedly class-based. The poor tended to vote for FDR's welfare state, the rich against it.

The relative accuracy of earlier polls in turn suggests that through 1932 there was less of a class bias built into the sample techniques, and that class-based voting had been less pronounced than was the case in 1936.

The editors at *The Literary Digest* truly thought they were sampling the American public as a whole. But they were merely sampling people with telephones and automobiles and who were sufficiently motivated to return the postcard. In the 1930s, in the midst of the Great Depression, the poll sample and the American public as a whole were not the same thing.

Modern, scientific public opinion polls are built on what is called *probability theory*. On its basis, large generalizations about politics can be made with limited evidence. It is a mathematical concept similar to the mathematics of gambling: "What is the probability that you can break the bank in Las Vegas by rolling a seven twenty times in a row?" It can be done but casino owners in Las Vegas and around the world have gotten rich from gamblers who think they can beat the odds. Probability theory has had the effect of making technological precision one of the hallmarks of the new science of public opinion polling.

Polls are based on what are called *survey* data, which are always subject to probability error. Most commercial and academic polls commonly accept a 3 to 4 percent probability error as a reasonable compromise between mathematical perfection and practical reality. This means, for example, that when a poll says "A is preferred by 50 percent, and B is preferred by 50 percent," it may in reality mean that A is preferred by as few as 46 percent and B is preferred by as many as 54 percent, or some other configuration of plus or minus 3 to 4 percent. A preelection poll that shows two candidates tied in a dead heat may mean on election day as much as an 8 percent difference. In the context of probability theory, such a difference would not indicate an inaccurate poll.

The theoretical problem after the 1936 fiasco was devising a system to sample public opinion that eliminates biased responses. Because it is impossible to totally eliminate all biases through technique alone, what probability theory promises to do is to reduce biases to manageable proportions. It should be able to tell the pollster what is the probable range of error that is always built into every sample. So it must devise a method that gives each person whose opinion is being measured the same mathematical chance of being selected. In that way, a small sample can reflect with accuracy the opinion of a large population. But because no method is perfect, what the pollster needs to know is how much the sample may deviate from reality. The deviation is expressed in mathematical terms as the probability of error. The larger the error, the less reliable the survey.

What Do the Best Public
Opinion Polls Really Measure?

Scientific polling has come to recognize four major components of public opinion: direction, saliency, intensity, and stability.

The most common dimension or component of public opinion that is measured is *direction*. It is typically expressed as support or opposition for a particular issue. It is information along a "yes" or "no" dimension. For example: "Do you agree with the death penalty?" or "Do you support stricter gun control laws?" or "Do you approve of the way_____is handling his job as president?" This is the most often reported dimension of public opinion in commercial and newspaper polls.

Saliency, a second component of public opinion, is described as the importance of a particular issue in public opinion and is almost always expressed in terms of comparison to other issues. For example, after asking someone about their support for stricter gun control laws, we might show them a list of a number of other issues, such as inflation, unemployment, civil rights, abortion, and so on, and ask them to rank gun control in relation to them.

Saliency may be quite unrelated to the direction of opinion. We cannot assume from the answer to the directional question alone whether gun control is a salient issue. Confusing direction with saliency has proved to be politically fatal to more than one candidate for elective office. For example, in the 1984 election Democratic presidential candidate Walter Mondale thought until quite late in the campaign that he would win because his polls told him that most people agreed with him on most of the issues *he* thought were most salient. But while the voters may have agreed with him on *most* of the directional questions, they also agreed with President Ronald Reagan on those fewer issues that were most salient and they voted accordingly.

A third component of public opinion is *intensity*. It is the strength and depth with which people feel about an issue. As such it does not easily lend itself to "yes" or "no" measurement. It is a component that tends to be associated with *action* in the sense that citizens are often motivated to act as a result of the felt intensity. Salient issues are important, but intense issues are urgent. However much we may regard "world peace" as important, we cannot do much about it. But we may view a vote in a local school board election as urgent, because we can do something about the election's outcome.

The political significance of intensity may depend on whether it is linked to majority or minority opinions and to the form of the government itself. In a pure democracy, when intensity is linked to majority opinion, it can overwhelm minorities and place their rights in serious jeopardy.

When intensity is linked to a minority opinion, especially in representative democracies, it may have a wholly different effect. Minority opinions that are strongly felt may be more formidable in shaping public policy than majority opinions that are less intense. For example, a minority of people may oppose stronger gun control laws supported by a majority. But if the majority regards gun control as neither salient nor intense, we should not be surprised or upset if the minority view prevails in public policy. And we can reasonably explain why such minorities may prevail without recourse to various conspiracy theories, such as an unscrupulous National Rifle Association lobby. But the NRA has had a great deal to do with generating much of the saliency and intensity that surround the issue.

Stability, the fourth component in public opinion, is simply the tracing of direction, saliency, and/or intensity components of public opinion over time. For example, we might ask people a directional question regarding gun control at periodic intervals. If we trace these opinions yearly over the past forty years or so, we find that directional opinions have remained fairly stable, whereas at the same time we find that the saliency and intensity components have fluctuated considerably. Stability questions require us to compare various components of opinion across time.

Keep in mind, regarding the measurement of public opinion, that no one component can be inferred from another. Significant mistakes can be made if we try to impute saliency or intensity to public opinion on the basis of direction alone. Each component is linked but not with equal weight. Even with regard to well-formed opinions, not every opinion is equally weighted. We may vote for one candidate with whom we disagree on the issue of gun control because we regard that candidate's position on the economy to be the more important issue. Such trade-offs are neither irrational nor undemocratic.

It is a commonplace criticism of modern democracy that many directional components of public opinion that appear to have overwhelming support do not always get translated into public policy. This criticism may arise from placing too much reliance on public opinion polls alone to form an understanding of democratic government. It may also result from conceptual confusion about how direction, intensity, and saliency combine to form the structure of public opinion. But even in the most general terms of democratic theory, it is not at all obvious why direction should always take precedence over saliency and intensity. A healthy democracy may well want to give primacy to saliency or intensity of minority opinion, especially if majority opinion, as measured by direction alone, is relatively indifferent.

A more fundamental critique of the relationship of public opinion polls to democratic government might begin with the nature of the polls themselves. Do even the very best public opinion polls, the ones with the most scientific methodology, really give us a truthful picture of public opinion?

Have Public Opinion Polls Helped to Change the Way We Think About American Government and Politics?

Scientific polling initially promised to take the true pulse of popular opinion. The original idea of pioneers like George Gallup was to transmit a snapshot of public opinion directly to policymakers, unfiltered by mediating institutions and representative deliberation. Public opinion analysis was typically conducted outside of institutional structures and was conceived as independent of those structures. So it is not surprising that the role of institutions as the other support for representative democracy tended to be slighted.

In a sense Gallup and the others succeeded beyond their own initial enthusiasm. But if the polls did take the pulse of raw democracy, many of the self-appointed doctors and nurses of democracy quickly discovered that the patient was not as healthy as they would have liked. And in the intervening years since Gallup first began taking the pulse of democracy, each succeeding wave of pollsters seems to find the pulse to be getting weaker and weaker. The polls pointed toward a crisis in modern democratic theory—the bias of opinion polls in favor of direct democracy. The entire burden of maintaining a liberal democracy came to rest on public opinion, and the measurement of that opinion was not always encouraging.

Democratic Man, or at least the abstract democratic man whose portrait emerged in public opinion polls, was anything but "enlightened." How could democracy work without an enlightened citizenry? The question became even more pressing than it was for the Founders because the mediating role of institutions had tended to recede from the pollsters' theory of democracy. And the American citizenry, as reflected in polls, did not match what some pundits thought an enlightened citizenry should be. How could the public opinion as it was being measured possibly support a liberal democratic regime?

One of the earliest such studies that explored and profoundly affected later conceptions of the problem was Samuel Stouffer's *Communism, Conformity and Civil Liberties*. Public opinion in Stouffer's analysis seemed to reveal that the attitudes of most Americans were far less supportive of basic civil liberties than were the attitudes of certain elites. This was not merely a question of esoteric rights defined in terms of procedural due process of law, but fundamental rights thought to be explicit in the Bill of Rights: questions involving censorship, religious and racial tolerance, separation of Church and State, and the like. Liberal support for regime principles seemed to conflict with conservative popular hostility to those same principles. Yet there was no doubt that basic civil liberties were at least as well protected in the United States as elsewhere. How could this be so?

According to Stouffer democracy *could* work without mass support for certain principles *if* they had elite support. The two legs of democratic theory were not institutions and public opinion, but elite opinion and mass opinion. Mass-based opinion came to be seen as the weaker leg of support for democratic government, but elite-based opinion could compensate. The general argument that emerged from Stouffer's work became known as the "theory of democratic elitism." It has had a long life span among general theories of how American democracy actually works and what keeps the regime a liberal democracy. Its central thesis, despite occasional mutations, has remained intact.

Stouffer's analysis of mass opinion could be criticized from a number of perspectives. One might begin by noting his Whig interpretation of history—the tendency to identify support for civil liberties as clustered at the liberal end of the opinion spectrum and opposition as clustered at the conservative end. The measurement of the relative strength of liberals and conservatives was tantamount to taking the pulse of democracy. Presumably democracy will be healthier with an increase in liberal opinions and a decrease in conservative opinions.

If Stouffer's definition of the problem was accurate, the task of pollsters was clarified. The polling problem logically shifted to measuring the relative strength of liberals and conservatives. "How strong is democracy in America?" seemed to be the same thing as "How many liberals are there among elites and in the mass public as a whole?"

Shortly after Stouffer published his results on weak public support for civil liberties, Philip Converse at the University of Michigan Survey Research Center was challenging the very notion of a liberal–conservative structure to public opinion. In a controversial study entitled "The Nature of Belief Systems in Mass Publics," he found that very few people could define or explain with any internal consistency the idea of liberal or conservative. These results held true for even the loosest definitions of the terms. The very notion that public opinion could be categorized in ideological terms seemed to be a error of the first order.

Converse found that among the general public, ideas were often totally unrelated to each other along any meaningful liberal–conservative continuum. Many responses to questions seemed to be entirely random, and the same or similar questions at different places in the poll elicited opposite responses. For Converse it was not so much "bad" opinions that threatened regime maintenance as it was ignorance, as measured as "nonattitudes." Still, the clear conclusion of Converse's study was also that regime maintenance depended on elite opinion and not mass opinion.

But it is not clear that the purely technical sort of public opinion analysis provided by modern political science is capable of providing a basis for judging whether contemporary public opinion supports or is at odds with regime maintenance. Elite opinion is not the same thing as represented opinion refined and enlarged through institutional mechanisms. Further, if various elite opinions are wedded to higher levels of intensity than is public opinion as a whole on the same issues, as they often seem to be, the effect may be to place ordinary citizens on a collision course with certain government policies that are dominated by intense elites. This collision seems to have caused the conservative "populism" or anti-elitism that elected Reagan.

Public Opinion and the Maintenance of Representative Democracy

If the maintenance of a liberal regime such as the United States *requires* the cultivation of civic virtue in public opinion, then we are forced to conclude that it cannot be maintained on the basis of institutional procedures alone. Some social behavior is destructive of ordered liberty under a constitution such as our own, whereas other behavior supports such a system. Failure to recognize this relationship tends to create a gap between democratic institutions and democratic opinion formation. The erection of a rigid wall of separation between the institutions of the state and social institutions may have resulted in a liberal democracy that finds it virtually impossible to teach those virtues necessary for the maintenance of a liberal democracy. Even the Founders did not advocate the deliberate cultivation of a virtuous citizenry by the government. But they did alert us to the problem the distinction posed: they properly situated the role of public opinion in a representative democracy. They also understood the difference between public opinion and the public interest. And when we consider public opinion analysis from the Founders' perspective, we begin to call into question the concept of public opinion as something wholly distinct from institutional arrangements designed to support a democratic regime. It is not merely that the distinction itself is artificial—a satisfactory political science of representative democracy cannot be formulated unless both institutions and public opinion are considered together.

When the Constitution was adopted, the nation was too large for the national government to function as a direct democracy. In the "extended republic" envisioned in *The Federalist*, the idea of a pure democracy was presented as an ideal type against which the virtues of a representative democracy could be better understood. Federalist and Anti-Federalist alike conceded the practical necessity for some version of a representative system. The critique of public opinion in a direct democracy was therefore presented more as an abstraction than a practical model. How could you actually assemble several million people in the same spot where they could all simultaneously register their opinion?

But technology and modern political science have contrived to weaken this practical side of the founding arguments. Technology has made possible the means of measuring something we might call the simultaneous "public opinion" of millions of citizens. The technical possibility of such opinion measurement has created a bias that now supports direct democracy. Some politicians have been quick to seize the implications. In the 1992 presidential election, presidential candidate H. Ross Perot advocated what he called "an electronic town-hall meeting." While the specifics were perhaps deliberately vague, evidently he had something in mind that resembled a teleconference between the president and the American people. Whatever else one may think of the idea, few politicians, journalists, or scholars seriously questioned the technical feasibility of the project.

We can see now that a significant part of the Founders' political science, their critique of pure democracy, was decided in part by default. The Founders ruled out direct democracy for practical as well as philosophical reasons. But the practical side of their arguments has been overtaken by technology and the promise of modern political science to "take the pulse" of public opinion. Even if we make allowances for technical problems of measurement, modern public opinion polling can come closer to taking the pulse of raw opinion than the Founders could have imagined. But their objections to direct democracy remain valid.

The proper analysis of public opinion in American democracy must therefore be directed, or perhaps redirected, by a political science explicitly designed for a representative democracy. The issue is less likely to be decided by default this time around. So it is crucial that the philosophical and political issues be spelled out independently of the purely technical issues, such as the issues that drive debates over modern public opinion polling.

Here modern political science has its greatest difficulty. The preference for direct democracy is too often implicit. If a case is to be made for a form of pure or participatory democracy, the full range of implications needs to be spelled out. The problem of mass opinion and regime maintenance also needs to be explicitly addressed. It is not that polls ask the "wrong" questions, but rather that the pictures of public opinion that emerge from scientific analysis never quite get to the heart of political analysis. For that, a different political science may be necessary—one that understands measurement as only one leg of the problem of public opinion analysis. Such a political science must clarify the difference between public opinion and the public interest and the difference it makes. It must confront the problem of regime maintenance more seriously than it does at present.

A weakness in the democratic theory of the Founders may be the absence of a more specific discussion of what they meant by "republican virtue" or an "enlightened public." But they did know the political questions we need to ask regarding public opinion— ones which point to the first principles of the American regime in theory and practice. Addressing those questions is to place public opinion as measured by polls in its proper perspective: a perspective that begins with a political science appropriate to representative democracy.

Suggested Reading

Asher, Herbert. *Polling and the Public: What Every Citizen Should Know*, 2nd ed. Washington, D.C.: Congressional Quarterly Press, 1992.

Brace, Paul, and Barbara Hinkley. *Follow the Leader: Opinion Polls and the Modern Presidents*. New York: Basic Books, 1992.

Converse, Jean M. *Survey Research in the United States: Roots and Emergence 1890–1960*. Berkeley: University of California Press, 1987.

Converse, Phillip E. "The Nature of Belief Systems in Mass Publics," in David Apter, ed., *Ideology and Discontent*. New York: Free Press of Glencoe, 1964.

Mann, Thomas E., and Gary R. Orren, eds. *Media Polls in American Politics*. Washington, D.C.: The Brookings Institution, 1992.

Moore, David W. *The Super Pollsters: How They Measure and Manipulate Public Opinion in America*. New York: Four Walls Eight Windows, 1992.

22

The Mass Media and
American Democracy

Roger Barrus and John Eastby

The media of mass communication are more than big business in modern America, they are a ubiquitous social presence. It is difficult to go anywhere without being overcome by the screaming headlines of the newspapers, the titillating images of the television, and the pounding "music" of the boom box. The growth of the mass media to their present state of influence has been the result of the interplay of public and private purposes. The media have developed under the legal protection of First Amendment guarantees of freedom of speech and freedom of the press. These freedoms are expressly affirmed in the Constitution because they are indispensable to the functioning of the American political system. But individuals and corporations exploit these constitutional guarantees, sometimes shamelessly, in pursuit of their private interests.

Considered as means of information interchange rather than merely as technologies, the media of mass communication belong essentially to modern representative democracies such as the United States. Premodern democracies, in which the people ruled directly, without the forms of representative government, had no need for media of mass communication. Ancient Athens was so small, and the political involvement of its citizens so great, that individuals were sufficiently informed of public affairs without the operation of special media of communication. Citizens learned what they needed to know in face-to-face contact in the marketplace and in public debates in the assembly.

Rulers in some modern regimes use the technologies of the mass media for purposes of indoctrination, not real communication. They claim the right to rule based on their supposed understanding of the real interests of the people. Because they, and not the people, understand the people's real interests, they are under no constraint to seek the consent of the people for their rule. The Communist bosses of the former Soviet Union made use of the technologies of the mass media, but only for the spread of propaganda from the top down, not for the flow of information back and forth between rulers and ruled.

Only in modern representative democracies, where the people rule indirectly, by means of their elected representatives, are the media of mass communication really required. The people need some means for informing themselves both of their own goings-on and of the activities of their rulers. The rulers need some means for gauging the people's opinions and eliciting their consent, and not just at election time, but in the normal course of governing. The media fill the necessary functions of mediating among the people, in the private sphere of society, and between the people and their rulers, in the public sphere of government.

The need for media of mass communication is compounded in the large, commercial republic of the United States, with its multiplicity of racial, ethnic, religious, and economic interest groups. Here the progress of the media has closely paralleled the process of democratic political development. The expansion of the effective citizen-body, from the landowning elite in the eighteenth century to the universal electorate of the twentieth century, has been accompanied by the growth of the media, from the local papers of the early republic, to the great newspaper chains of the nineteenth century, to the radio and television networks of today. The ubiquitous influence of the mass media today raises the question of whether the media are on the way to displacing the formal institutions of government as the real ruling powers in the American regime.

Mediation and Representation

The media of mass communication are not the only, nor even the primary, mediating institutions in American society. The primary mediating institutions are the structures of representative government themselves. The people's elected representatives take the multiple interests of their various constituencies—the nation, the state, or the congressional district—to Washington, where these interests are refined and enlarged in the process of policy-making for the country as a whole. The bureaucracies that implement the policies so developed serve not only as means of enforcement, but also as conduits for the flow of information between government and people. But the forms of representative government cannot function without the operation of other mediating institutions. The First Amendment guarantees the freedoms of speech, press, and assembly, and fosters the development of these extragovernmental mediating institutions—among which are the mass media.

Representative government is essentially a means toward democratic self-rule. The framing of the Constitution, for the Founders, was the ultimate test of the practical viability of democratic government. The possibility of democracy was questionable because of the experience of the direct democracy of classical antiquity. The principal problem of direct democracy is its proclivity to factionalism. Direct democracy tends to break down into factional warfare between the many poor and the few rich. This tendency to factionalism, according to *Federalist* 9, "continually agitated" the "petty republics" of ancient Greece and Italy, and accounted for the "rapid succession of revolutions" that kept them "in a state of perpetual vibration between the extremes of tyranny and anarchy."

The American political system deals with the problem of faction by taming or civilizing the passions that fuel factional struggle. It follows a kind of divide and conquer strategy. Factionalism originates in the interaction between the passions of rule and material self-interest. It is the struggle of individuals and groups claiming the right to rule over the whole of society on behalf of their own particular needs, interests, or desires. Representative government institutionalizes political power—associating it with legally defined forms, which function directly or indirectly by popular consent— in order to prevent any person or persons from being able to claim a natural or divine right to rule.

The most important result of the institutionalization of government, and the consequent mediation of the political passions, is the transformation of the factions characteristic of ancient Athens or Rome into the interest groups characteristic of modern America. Both factions and interest groups are self-interested. The difference between the two has to do with the claim to rule.

Factions make a claim to rule. Interest groups are not even concerned with making such a claim and, as a result, are politically safe. They are not interested in taking over government, but only in "who gets what, when, how" from government. Neither the National Association of Manufacturers nor the American Medical Association, nor even the Teamsters Union, would ever try to cause a revolution. Politics is transformed, from the dangerous but exciting struggle for power among groups dedicated to radically different conceptions of who should rule and for what purposes, into the more or less peaceful and even humdrum competition of groups out for relative advantage within the given social and economic structure of representative democracy.

The American Framers clearly understood the principle of mediation as it related to the institutions of representative government. James Madison, in *Federalist* 51, argues that to maintain the constitutional division of powers necessary to the security of individual liberty from government tyranny, it is necessary to construct the offices of government in such a way as to make "ambition counteract ambition," connecting the "interests of the man" with the "constitutional rights of the place." Madison says it is a profound reflection on human nature that such devices must be used to make good government. But it is no more of a reflection than the necessity of government itself. If "men were angels" then "no government would be necessary." But men must govern men, and a means must be found to supply the "defect of better motives."

The constitutional system of representative democracy requires distance between governors and governed in order to function. So it also needs extragovernmental mediating institutions, including the media of mass communication. Government officials need the freedom that comes with distance, physical and psychological, to deliberate over policy, and so to refine the interests and passions of the people. In the exercise of their responsibilities they must be remote from the people and their most pressing problems. Otherwise they will be swept along by popular passion.

This remoteness might sound undemocratic. It is certainly inconsistent with much contemporary political rhetoric, which emphasizes the alleged need to bring government "back to the people." But such distance is necessary to the success of democracy, allowing for the achievement of the common good on the basis of popular consent. So the Framers adopted a number of devices for maintaining the required distance between the people and their rulers.

One such device was the indirect election of government officials. In the original Constitution only members of the House of Representatives were to be elected directly by the people. Senators were to be elected by state legislatures. The president was to be selected by a national Electoral College, and federal judges were to be appointed by the president, with the consent of the Senate. Another device was the establishment of long terms of office for government officials. Even the two-year term for members of the House was long in comparison with the terms of state government officers. The president was to have the extraordinarily long term of four years. Critics of the Constitution thought this term to be extremely dangerous. They saw the risk of tyrannical usurpation by the president. Members of the Senate were to serve even longer, with six-year terms, and federal judges were to enjoy life terms in office, subject to removal only for misbehavior.

But the most important device for achieving the required distance from the people was the extension of the bounds of the Union. Until the time of the American founding, it was the universal judgment of statesmen and political philosophers that democracies had to be small in size and population to be successful. Only in a small society could the intense patriotism or love of country develop that might control the selfish passions of the people. The Framers, while not denigrating such self-sacrificing virtue, thought that it was unreliable and too rare to be effective.

The Framers turned to the system of representative government to find a more reliable substitute. One of the advantages of representative government, as Madison points out in *Federalist* 14, is that it makes possible the enlargement of democratic society. A direct democracy, in which "the people meet and exercise the government in person," must necessarily "be confined to a small spot." A republic, however, in which the people govern "by their representatives and agents" can be "extended over a large region."

The enlargement of the Union, made possible by the principle of representation, is essential to the functioning of representative government. The necessarily small size of a direct democracy, Madison argues in *Federalist* 10, accounts for its political failures. In such a small society, "a common passion or interest will, in almost every case, be felt by a majority of the whole." This vulnerability to the passions of the people has made democracies "as short in their lives as they have been violent in their deaths."

The introduction of the forms of representative government, without what Alexander Hamilton in *Federalist* 9 calls the "enlargement of the orbit" of government, would not improve the situation. Representatives would be too much under the influence of local and transitory interests. Extending the bounds of the Union, in addition to impeding the formation of a passionately interested majority by the multiplication and diversification of factions, allows for the establishment of a proper numerical relationship between the people and their elected representatives. The purpose, according to Madison in *Federalist* 10, is to ensure that representatives are not "unduly attached" to local interests, nor "too little fit to comprehend and pursue great and national objects."

Extragovernmental mediating institutions are necessary in the American political system to compensate, in a way appropriate to the functioning of the institutions of representative democracy, for the required physical and psychological distance between governors and governed. Government officials need to inform themselves of the opinions and the interests of the people, without falling excessively under their influence. The same goes for the people in their relations with government officials. The essential purpose of the media of mass communication is to allow for the flow of vital information between the people and their rulers, without the breach of the formal separation between them.

With the representative district so large that interchange between governors and governed could not take place principally by face-to-face conversation, most people would have to obtain information about the activities of their representatives by way of secondhand reports. Secondhand reports would also be the principal means of communication from the people to their representatives. The development of political parties—which the Framers apparently did not foresee—and the development of the free press, which they most emphatically did, answer the need for channels of information and communication between governors and governed. So Hamilton argues, in *Federalist* 84, that it is inevitable in the constitutional system that the "public papers" will become "expeditious messengers of intelligence to the most remote inhabitants of the Union."

Once the necessity of the mass media for the functioning of representative government becomes clear, the political problem of the media appears. For the institutions of representative government to fulfill their purpose of mediating the passions of the people, other institutions must exist to mediate between the people and the government. But because they are involved in the same kind of activity, the mass media and the institutions of representative government are inherently in competition with one another. As mediating institutions, the media and the institutions of government occupy the same ground and must necessarily come into conflict. This turf war is the ultimate cause of the hostility so often shown by representatives of the media toward government officials, and vice versa. It is clear that representative government cannot work without the media. But it is not clear that it can work with them either.

Television, Popular Culture, and Representative Democracy

This problem is seen most clearly in influence of what has become the most pervasive and influential of the media of mass communication, television. Criticisms of television programming, typically that it is either infantile or morally corrupting, have of course become commonplace. Nobody today would claim that television has fulfilled the hopes that greeted its advent in the 1940s and 1950s. It has not become an instrument for universal education and cultural revival. Quite the contrary, its effect on education and culture has been disastrous. But such criticism does not touch on what is most politically problematic about television. The problem is not so much in the message television conveys as it is in the nature of the medium itself. To use the famous phrase of Marshall McLuhan, the "medium is the message."

This is not to deny, of course, the social and political consequences of television programming. Television from the very beginning has exploited sex and violence to attract and hold its audience. What shocks or titillates when first portrayed, however, becomes banal or boring the tenth or twentieth time. It is characteristic of television programming that it imitates what is successful. The new in television rapidly becomes old. So television must always be opening up new vistas in the graphic depiction of sex and violence. The effect is inevitably brutalizing.

It is difficult if not impossible to trace specific acts of pathological social behavior to specific television portrayals of sex and violence. Still, it must be true that the continuous and progressively more graphic depictions of such matters must have a coarsening effect on the moral sensibilities of those exposed to them. Generations whose moral tastes have been dulled by the crude diet served up on television are not likely to be attuned to the moral ambiguities—the subtle distinctions of intention and action—that are encountered in real life.

Television emphasizes the immediate gratification of the desires. Love is fulfilled in easy, no-commitment sex between consenting adults. The passion for justice is fulfilled by the good guys blowing away the bad guys. The emphasis is always on the release, as opposed to the restraint, of the passions. This artistic licensing of the passions must have a profound influence on individual behavior.

Television has other effects, less notable perhaps but no less profound, on the tastes of its audience. These effects are the result of the nature of the medium itself. Television is distinguished from other mass media—in particular the newspapers—in that it requires virtually no active involvement on the part of its audience. Effort must be expended to read a newspaper or magazine, or even to see a movie. But television is universally available. It only has to be turned on to be enjoyed.

Requiring no active involvement, television is the most purely entertaining of the mass media. It is even entertaining when it seeks to be informative or educational. The essentially entertaining character of television is the cause of its almost universal appeal. The problem is that television creates the taste for entertainment. People come to expect to be amused or diverted. Television creates passive consumers of entertainment—intellectual couch potatoes. It stifles whatever inclination there is in human nature toward active learning or understanding.

The effect of television in creating the taste for entertainment can be traced in the other media. They have had to adapt to the new expectations in order to keep their audiences. Newspapers and magazines have become more showy and glitzy, and more concerned with the passing fads and personal trivia of popular culture. They contain less in the way of social and political analysis, and more in the way of human-interest stories. No newspaper now would be without a "Style" section. Finally, the very language of most newspapers and magazines is "dumbed down," to appeal to an audience that finds reading to be much more of a chore than any kind of fulfillment.

It is still another of the effects on popular taste of television as a medium of communication, however, that constitutes the fundamental political problem of television. Television specializes in the creation of an illusion of intimacy among human beings. It brings its programming, dealing with the most intimate details of life and death, directly into the living rooms and bedrooms of its audience.

It seems to remove all distances—of time, place, or status—among human beings. Exposure to television undermines whatever there is in human nature that appreciates distance and whatever inclines human beings to be reserved in their relations with others of their kind.

The effect of television as a medium is to create, in another phrase coined by Marshall McLuhan, a "global village." The fundamental problem of television from the point of view of the system of representative government is in the way that it cultivates the taste for intimacy or immediacy. What representative government was invented to separate—the public and the private—television links together. Television exposes the private to public view, and brings the public into the private domain of the home. This publicizing of the private and privatizing of the public is most clearly reflected in the so-called "talk shows," in which individuals are induced to disclose before an audience of millions the intimate particular details of their private lives. Judging by the immense popularity of talk shows—inevitably leading to ever more such programs investigating ever more bizarre forms of behavior—people must find the mixing of the private and the public to be enormously entertaining and exciting.

The taste for intimacy encouraged by television is potentially fatal for the system of representative government. Television renders all distance among human beings distasteful. Representative government, however, requires physical and psychological distance, between the people and their representatives, if not among the people themselves. It cannot work in the village, as Madison points out in *Federalist* 10, and that goes as much for the global as the traditional village.

Television, in its cultivation of the taste for intimacy, exploits the greatest vulnerability of representative democracy. There is something aristocratic or elitist about the distance required for the functioning of representative government. It has been a source of irritation in American politics from the very beginning. It is the ultimate source of the waves of populism—the effort to "take power back to the people" by breaking down the formal or institutional separation between governors and governed—that periodically have swept through American political life.

An early consequence of the populist frustration with representative government was the organization, in the Jacksonian era, of modern mass political parties. The parties, relying in large part on face-to-face contact, were much more intimate as media of communication than their only rivals of the day, the newspapers. They were more appealing to the democratic inclinations of the American people than the newspapers, which, requiring a reading audience, were "elitist." The parties soon came to control the newspapers. The party press was a characteristic of mid-nineteenth-century America.

Despite their populism, however, the political parties continued to maintain a certain distance between the people and their elected representatives. Political demands were filtered through party platforms. Policy decisions, at least until the advent of antiparty civil service reform around the turn of the century, were filtered through party-run bureaucracies. The competition between the parties gave substance to the complicated issues that were debated by political leaders in Washington and the capitals of the various states. The people could connect policy with party, and deliver their judgment on the parties and their policies through the ballot box.

In the twentieth century, the political parties have themselves been the objects of populist attack that they are closed or elitist institutions. The demand has been to open up the processes of party politics. The principal result of these demands has been the nearly universal adoption of the primary as the means used for the nomination of party candidates. The attack on the parties has been associated with the rise of new and even more intimate modes of mass communication, radio and especially television. The new media allow candidates for public office to ignore or even attack the parties, by talking directly to the people. All that a candidate now needs is a sufficiently large media budget. Rather than serving as the arena for the development and grooming of potential leaders, the parties themselves have been captured, by self-promoting political entrepreneurs seeking individual advancement. Most successful politicians in recent years have run as outsiders or antiparty rebels.

Television, the telephone, and the computer have made possible the virtual elimination of the distance between governors and governed required by representative democracy. Candidates now have instant access to their constituents. Constituents—through the polls conducted by independent polling organizations, newspapers and wire services, television networks, and the candidates themselves— have the opportunity to give immediate feedback to candidates.

The prominence of polls and polling in contemporary politics is perhaps the clearest manifestation of the changes brought about in

American society by television. Polls represent the triumph of the immediate. They measure essentially volatile opinions, and even moods. They deprive elected leaders of the last vestige of distance from the electorate, the time fixed by law before their terms are up and they must present themselves before the people for reelection. No sooner have elected officials taken the oath of office but polls are being conducted to measure their public approval.

There is much more to the fascination with polls than curiosity about the next round of elections, which might be four or six years away. Polls affirm the immediate dependence of governors on the opinions or passions of the governed for their title to rule. They gratify the taste for the immediate that is the principal cultural consequence of the modern media. Scientific polling has gone a long way toward delegitimizing the very elections that it supposedly is to predict. Elections are already largely anticlimactic. They are rapidly becoming empty formalisms, useful only for confirming the popularity polls preceding them, their results interpretable only on the basis of the exit polls following them.

Politicians, of course, use polls to help them get elected. Properly understood, however, polls are not so much instruments in the struggle among would-be political leaders as they are instruments in the struggle between legally authorized government officials and the mass media as mediators of, to, and for the American people. Government officials seek to build up their authority by citing numbers indicating public support for their policies. The media undermine the authority of government officials by citing numbers showing public opposition to their policies, or public concern for matters not even on their agenda.

In this competition, polls are the natural weapon of the media. The media commission public opinion polls, and then report as news the results of the polls they previously commissioned. They choose the questions to be asked, referring only to allegedly unmet needs in the body politic. Because human needs and wants are infinite, this process can go on indefinitely. The result of the use of polls by the media is a continuous process of issue inflation—old issues being made more weighty and urgent, while new issues are being created—that must eventually overwhelm even the most successful and statesmanlike of political leaders.

There is a fundamental disproportion between elected representatives and the mass media in their efforts to define the issues of politics. Elected representatives must respond to the long-term expectations of the frequently intricate coalitions that put them in office in the first place and that they hope will maintain them there. At the same time, they wish to avoid any commitment that will take away the freedom of action necessary for governing. The result is an extremely delicate balancing act that might appear as nothing more than opportunism, but is, in reality, the very essence of political prudence.

The media do not have an electoral interest, or indeed any responsibility for actually governing. They present themselves as being concerned only with the general good, the "American Agenda" in the phrase of ABC News. They insist that political leaders respond to such abstractly defined political issues. From this point of view, political leaders—subject to all the constraints of running for office and governing once they have won election—must inevitably appear to be acting in bad faith. Politics is made into a crude morality play, with the public display of good faith or good will, always as defined and interpreted by the media, the key measure of statesmanship.

Transforming the extended republic into the global village, television undermines the whole system of representative government. The populist irritation at the elitism of representative government is exacerbated by the taste for intimacy that television cultivates. Deliberation is made difficult, if not impossible, by incessant demands for immediate action on an ever growing list of policy problems. Political leaders are judged by their personal empathy for the victims of society's ills.

What all this means in actual practice is reflected in the call by some politicians, led by the billionaire populist Ross Perot and supported enthusiastically by media figures, for the "electronic town hall." All three presidential candidates in the 1992 campaign adopted campaign methods that had much in common with the electronic town hall, such as frequent appearances on television and radio talk shows.

The electronic town hall, using television and other modern technologies to create a contemporary version of ancient direct democracy, would not abolish the institutions of representative government, but rather would render them superfluous. Simple majoritarianism would take the place of the cool and deliberate sense of the community that was to be elicited through the working of those institutions.

The electronic town hall represents the most immediate danger from the transformation of public tastes affected by television. Exactly like the assembly of ancient Athens, it would be an arena of popular passion, subject to manipulation by vulgar demagogues. The art of demagoguery is not so arcane, nor are unprincipled men of ambition who would stoop to its employment so rare, that it can be supposed that the electronic town hall would long be free of the influence of the demagogues.

The history of ancient Athens and Rome gives some indication of how the demagogues would operate. They would begin by attacking the rich and powerful, for not bearing their fair share of society's burdens and for taking more than their fair share of its benefits. The purpose of such attacks would be to set the rich against the poor, the few against the many.

Increasing conflict between the rich and the poor would exasperate and then frustrate those interested in law and order, particularly the middle class. The demagogues could then present themselves as the guarantors of law and order. Such subterfuges accounted for the disorders that were so characteristic of Athens and Rome. Against the experience of antiquity, Hamilton argues in *Federalist* 1, it is the mission of the people of the United States, implementing the political system of representative democracy, to demonstrate the capability of human beings of "establishing good government from reflection and choice."

Conclusion

Judging by the rhetoric and some of the methods of contemporary politics, the transformation of the American system of representative democracy under the influence of modern mass media is already well under way. But it is much easier to find the cause of the danger than to find a remedy for it. The danger is a direct result of the public tastes cultivated by modern mass media, particularly television. Television has become a permanent feature of American society, however, and there is no hope that its influence will be eliminated, or even very much curbed.

If there is a remedy for the present danger, it must come in the form of education, to counter the cultural and political consequences of television. Media figures might be brought to understand that their own interests are involved in the preservation of representative democracy. After all, it is only in such regimes that the mass media as such are necessary and legally protected. Political leaders might be brought to see that their real interests are not served by taking advantage of the opportunities presented in the global village created by television to play the demagogue. The demagogue ends up being the slave of the people and their passions. There is nothing dignified in the posture of the political leader who always has his ear to the ground.

It is perhaps naive, however, to hope for much in the way of the education of politicians and media figures. The temptations of wealth and power involved in the present situation are such that we cannot expect that any but the most rational and farsighted will be able to resist them. If so, the political education of the American people is the only real hope for a remedy. The question here, of course, is who will do the teaching? And who will teach the teachers?

Suggested Reading

Anastaplo, George. "Self-Government and the Mass Media: A Practical Man's Guide," in Harry M. Clor, ed., *The Mass Media and Modern Democracy.* Chicago: Rand McNally, 1974.

Ceaser, James W. *Presidential Selection: Theory and Development* Princeton: Princeton University Press, 1979.

Ceaser, James W., Glen E. Thurow, Jeffrey Tulis, and Joseph Bessette, "The Rise of the Rhetorical Presidency," in *Presidential Studies Quarterly* (Spring 1981).

Mansfield, Harvey C., Jr. *America's Constitutional Soul.* Baltimore: Johns Hopkins University Press, 1991.

23

Public Policy

Christina Jeffrey

Public policy is that which governments choose to do or not to do.[1] Traditionally, public policy included those issues considered by Congress and the executive that resulted in specific laws which benefited the entire country. Normally those issues were limited to topics such as warfare, treaties, and economic policy. Today, when we use the term "public policy," we are usually referring to matters which not too long ago would not have been considered by the national government.

Social Security and family policy, which are concerned with provisions for family members, were once largely the responsibility of families or local government. Education policy was a state and local matter. If a presidential candidate in the nineteenth century had announced that he wanted to be the Education President, nobody would have known what he was talking about. Welfare policy was the province of charitable individuals, groups, churches, and local governments. Economic policy meant preventing public debt, minting money, and encouraging economic growth, but prior to the 1930s the federal government was not considered to be responsible for employment. Health policy involved only the prevention of contagious diseases and was usually a concern of state and local governments. The preservation of national forests was about as far as the federal government went toward establishing any kind of environmental policy prior to the Clean Air Act of 1963.

Since the early 1930s, the federal government has become responsible for all of these things and more. Through the Social Security Act of 1935 and its numerous amendments the government has assumed responsibility for income and health of the elderly, widows, children who have lost working parents, and the disabled. After the election of Jimmy Carter in 1977, education got its own Cabinet secretary and today there is talk of national standards promulgated by this department. The Department of Education has also assumed responsibility for issuing guidelines on the education of the disabled and others with special problems.

All levels of government have been involved in improving the environment. Cities such as Nashville, Birmingham, and Tuscaloosa, once known for their odors, are now pleasant places to visit. Many polluted rivers, lakes, and bays have been cleaned up and people are swimming and fishing in places they wouldn't have waded fifteen years ago. Federal legislation in this area was crucial, because it forced the kind of cooperation between levels of government which had not been forthcoming. Air and water cross jurisdictional lines and one jurisdiction is usually not willing to assume the full burden of cleaning up pollution.

The big and easy gains in environmental improvement have been made. The remaining policy questions concern more costly and controversial efforts at producing great environmental purity, ones that may lead to higher taxes and fewer jobs. A blow to the environmental movement came in a June 1992 Supreme Court decision in *Lucas v. South Carolina Coastal Council*, in which the Court held that states could no longer pass environmental costs on to property owners without compensation. In this case, Lucas had purchased two oceanfront lots for nearly one million dollars, planning to build houses on them—one to live in and one to sell. After his purchase, the state of South Carolina issued guidelines for coastal preservation which prevented him from building on his lots.

Lucas brought a constitutional suit, saying that South Carolina's actions constituted a taking without just compensation, which is forbidden by the Fifth Amendment. After all, the building ban was to protect the coast for the benefit of all the citizens of South Carolina. Why, reasoned Lucas, should all the costs fall on a few property owners? The Supreme Court agreed with Lucas's argument and sent the case back to the lower courts. This case will have serious ramifications for environmental efforts at all levels because if it is followed as precedent, no longer will the few be forced to bear the costs for the many. The public will have to decide how much environmental protection is worth to them.

In the small-government days prior to Franklin Roosevelt's New

Deal, public policy debate was largely limited to such questions as slavery, hard currency versus inflationary currency, high levels of immigration versus low, high tariffs versus low, and whether to go to war. Except for slavery, these are still important public policy matters. To these we have added a host of new public policy questions to be debated and dealt with at the national level.

State and local governments could address most of the nation's new policy problems, with some exceptions such as the environment, without requiring much direction from the federal government. Obviously questions of currency, immigration, trade, the environment, and foreign policy require national attention. And given our national identity, one closely tied to liberty and justice for all, civil rights has received national attention for decades. But how did these other problems become national problems?

Answering this question requires a brief historical review. First, I will sketch the history of public policy in America and flesh it out with analysis. Once we get to Lyndon Johnson's Great Society, I will concentrate on recent developments—the nationalization of problems which were once individual, local, or state problems.

Prior to the New Deal, two concerns kept the national government from assuming new responsibilities: excessive government spending and the belief that the national government, if it became too big, could threaten individual liberty. Both concerns are to some extent related to economics. The liberty concern had to do with people's belief that property ennobled the individual, made family life possible, and ultimately made self-government possible. Early American leaders feared public debt. They knew that interest payments soaked up capital which would otherwise go to the payment of wages. If that happened, poor people would lose their jobs, or not be hired because businesses would not be able to afford them. We still hear this argument today when the national debt and its consequences are discussed. Another argument used against the debt was that it would further enrich the wealthy who could afford to loan money to the government and their increased wealth would come at the expense of poorer taxpayers.

The Founders also believed that a person who worked and earned money should enjoy the fruits of his labor and not have large amounts of it confiscated by government. The pursuit of happiness and the right to own and use property to one's advantage were closely linked in their minds.

But liberty and economy were not the only reasons for limiting national involvement, at least where welfare activities were concerned. People genuinely believed that charitable work needed to come from charitable sources. Turning such work over to impersonal bureaucracies made it ineffective. A coalition of charitable organizations, the Benevolent Societies of Boston, explored the question of government aid in an 1834 report and came to the conclusion that government assistance might "gratify the benevolent feelings of our hearts," but lay "the foundation of a greater moral evil." Private groups, the report said, could act with more discernment and could thus say "yes" when help would do good and "no" when it might do harm.[2]

Typical of the attitudes in the eighteenth and nineteenth centuries toward charitable work were the words of Reverend William Ruffner from his pulpit in 1853. "Idleness and improvidence" result from "large funds provided—and especially when provided by state taxation, and disbursed by state officers." According to Ruffner, charity requires the greatest tenderness and sympathy and paid agents cannot be trusted to minister to the poor. He wanted donors to involve themselves personally with good works and not simply to contribute money.[3]

Given the prevailing sentiment about welfare and the need to keep it a private matter, it is no surprise that when Congress, responding to Dorothea Dix's plea for funding for mental hospitals, passed legislation for building and maintaining such hospitals, President Franklin Pierce vetoed the legislation. He said, in part: "If Congress has the power to make provision for the indigent insane, it has the same power for the indigent who are not insane." Pierce added that such apparent charity would in fact be counterproductive because those who would normally support such institutions at the local level would no longer feel obliged to do so. His veto was sustained.[4]

Concerns for liberty, economy, and private charity meant that everything possible was done at the local level. Alexis de Tocqueville remarked at the amazing vigor of America's local organizations, both private and governmental. While the nation–states of Europe, such as his own France, were moving toward more and more centralized governments, the United States remained administratively decentralized.

Local control and limited national interest in most public policy issues lasted through the nineteenth century until the rise of the Progressive movement at the turn of the century. The Progressives wanted more rationality and efficiency in government. They opposed machine politics and the patronage it fostered. They opposed hard money which couldn't be inflated to serve government purposes. And they opposed the overemphasis on low taxes and balanced budgets which also limited government activities. The Progressives wanted government to improve society. They were joined by many hardheaded businessmen who liked the emphasis on rationality and efficiency in government and believed that the Progressive program would reduce corruption.

With the adoption of such "progressive" ideas as the national income tax (1913) and the executive budget—a budget prepared by the president and submitted to Congress (1921)—the federal government had set the stage for Franklin D. Roosevelt to do something about the one-third of the nation he found ill-clothed, ill-fed, and ill-housed during the Depression. All Roosevelt needed was justification to abandon the balanced budget. Economist John Maynard Keynes conveniently supplied that justification, arguing that public debt in times of recession or depression can provide a needed stimulus to the economy.

The New Deal is important in the history of American public policy because it marked the beginning of a national consensus that the federal government had a role to play in what until then had been local government or private-sector functions. Even though the role of the federal government remained relatively small, and many of the New Deal programs were in fact discontinued after the Depression, the fact is that the nation now began to look to Washington as the ultimate source of economic well-being.

When government began to assume responsibility for the well-being of every American, we then began to have national programs for managing the relations between the races, the sexes, employees and employers, electors and elected, state and local governments and their constituents, consumers and producers, husbands and wives, parents and children, and so on.[5] The purpose of government became the regulation of human relationships for the justice and well-being of all. With this ambitious goal in mind, so many new agencies with society-wide jurisdiction were established that a 1975 report by a House Government Operations subcommittee could say "In its broadest sense, everything the government does is regulation. . . ."[6]

Beginning with Lyndon Johnson's Great Society in 1964, such New Deal programs as Social Security and Aid to Families with

Dependent Children (AFDC) were greatly expanded. Johnson's Great Society, in part, was a War on Poverty. No longer would government merely aim at the effects of poverty, it would eradicate its causes.

Let us look at the transformation of a traditionally local function, education. Although 87 percent of the funding for education is still from state and local revenues, federal mandates influence every aspect of education. Federal grants encourage the use of certain kinds of teachers and curricula in schools. Affirmative action laws affect hiring and firing of teachers. Title IX of the Civil Rights Act of 1964 affects funding for extracurricular activities such as sports. School systems must be careful to spend nearly equal amounts of money on sports for both sexes. School lunch programs must abide by federal guidelines so that eligible students can get free or reduced lunches. And there are Department of Transportation guidelines with which the schools must comply.

Retirement programs generally are governed by the Employee Retirement and Insurance Systems Act (ERISA), which dictates how employers must treat employee benefits. This regulation has successfully caused many companies to eliminate their benefit packages entirely, or modify them to the employees' disadvantage. Unscrupulous employers, on the other hand, have used government-created guarantees to defund their pension plans and defraud the public.

Congress has become more agreeable to passing laws with expensive consequences because those costs are often less apparent to taxpayers than they would be if adopted at the state level. State governments must balance their budgets every year, and the costs of various programs cannot help but be quite controversial in the state legislatures. Only recently has the cost of government programs really been debated at the national level. In fact, during the 1970s, there were almost no downward pressures on spending at the national level. Because of the committee system in Congress, spending decisions were fragmented and each committee responsible for each type of spending had vested interests in keeping that type of spending high. The relationship between a congressional committee, the agency bureaucrats overseen by that committee, and the interest groups affected by or concerned with the agency's work came to be known as an iron triangle, so closely did the three work together and identify with the same causes.

James L. Payne has shown how easy it is for members of Congress to vote for increased spending and how difficult and unnatural it is for them to vote against spending proposals. Taxpayers opposed to increased spending do not routinely visit their congressmen and lobby them to vote against certain bills. They do not testify against increased spending at congressional hearings. Payne found that 95.7 percent of witnesses at congressional appropriations subcommittee hearings spoke in favor of proposed spending legislation and only 0.7 percent spoke in opposition. The remaining witnesses gave mixed or neutral testimony.[7] Oversight hearings are not efforts to find out the truth about government programs but normally cheering sessions for the agencies involved. Public policy analysis is not always carried out by truly neutral personnel. Rather, it is often conducted by experts who want to be hired again by the agencies they are analyzing.

Some of those public policies which have become law have had very noble intentions and some of those intentions have been accomplished. But many of the best-intentioned national policies have had unintended negative consequences. For example, it was never intended that Aid to Families with Dependent Children should have the effect of lowering the marriage rate among poor women. But the availability of AFDC, coupled with the decreasing security of marriage thanks to no-fault divorce, really has affected the marriage rate. Certainly, the establishment of a minimum wage was intended to help the working people of the United States. It was not intended to keep people from working, especially inner-city youth. The tax increases of 1990 were supposed to help lower the national debt, but in fact they led the United States into a recession and even more debt. In short, government policies do not always do what the policymakers intend for them to do.

But how do we find out what effects government policies have had? That should be the purpose of public policy analysis. Thomas Dye calls the effort to determine the consequences of public policy "policy impact" research. This is a kind of cause and effect analysis. The researcher is trying to find out how a particular program affects certain variables—such as the income of participants, the teenage pregnancy rate, or the employment rate—that were supposed to be affected by the program being analyzed. For example, to determine if increases in the minimum wage have had the desired effect of raising incomes, a policy analyst might study the income of minimum wage earners. He might find that there are unintended negative effects from even so popular a program as the minimum wage.

Economists found that employment rates showed little change immediately after an increase in minimum wage. Employers do not mind granting a reasonable increase in wages to an employee who has proven himself or herself and usually do so regardless of the minimum wage law. Old employees are not usually negatively affected by the minimum wage. So an increase in the minimum wage does not usually cause massive firings. What it affects is new hiring and that effect actually begins long before a new minimum wage goes into effect. Because employers must now figure in higher labor costs, new businesses may not be started, existing businesses may curtail expansion plans, and others may simply allow attrition to shrink their work forces.

In many states, public policy has been directed toward helping the working people by improving worker's compensation benefits and health insurance. But there have been unintended consequences here as well. Worker's compensation costs have actually driven some companies out of business. In the area of ordinary health insurance, new mandated health insurance benefits such as cancer screening have helped push up insurance costs to the point that employers have dropped insurance programs completely.

Health insurance in this country began as prepaid hospitalization. Hospitals began to proliferate after the turn of the century with the improvement of medical care. But nobody planned on going to the hospital and so it was difficult for hospitals to get paid. More important, hospitals had to be open all the time and needed a regular source of income. They first offered their prepaid plans to teachers organizations and the idea spread. Later people wanted doctor's fees included in their health care plans. Government policy to exempt these prepaid health plans from federal taxes encouraged their support, but the biggest spur came during World War II, when wages were frozen but companies needed to attract workers. Insurance, a tax-free benefit to both the company paying for it and the employee receiving it, became more common. Labor unions negotiated for increased insurance benefits which paid for every dollar of an employee's family medical care, with the exception of such luxuries as cosmetic surgery and orthodontics.

Health care costs went up as a result of insurance, but increases remained moderate. Then in 1965, Congress passed the Medicare Act, which has been enormously successful in covering nearly every elderly person. Medicaid, which was created at the same time, is a safety net which catches the small percentage of elderly not covered by Medicare. It also covers the health care expenses of the poor who qualify. Nearly 40 percent of all medical services today are paid for by the government.

Medical care costs have risen quickly since 1965. Most elderly people are grateful for Medicare and Medicaid when they receive huge bills from doctors and hospitals. And people believe that health care costs have increased because of forces over which we have and could have had no control, such as new technology and wonder drugs. In 1965 elderly Americans spent 10 percent of their income on health care. Today, they spend 17 percent. Is this increase due to new technologies or to the unintended consequences of public policy?

Third-party payment by the government seems to encourage overuse and overcharging. In those countries which have national health care systems, people visit the doctor twice as often as Americans do. Then there is the effect of cost-plus pricing which encourages costs to go up. If an insurance company will reimburse a hospital for its costs plus 8 percent profit, anyone can see that 8 percent of ten million dollars is more than 8 percent of one million. Until recently, there were very few incentives to holding down costs.

One effort to hold down costs is to limit the amount doctors can charge and the number of days hospitals can keep a patient with a certain diagnosis and expect reimbursement from Medicare. These caps on charges have helped to slow the rate of increase in Medicare costs. Some believe that medical costs can be controlled with caps, regulations, and price controls. But those nations which use these methods have seen their costs go up at the same or even a more rapid rate than ours.

I think change is needed, but change in the direction of allowing market forces to influence behavior of both providers and patients. Medicine is as much an art as a science. If health care professionals are greedy mercenaries who care nothing about their patients, all the government regulations in the world will not save us. If they are the caring professionals we must hope them to be, then perhaps we should let the marketplace provide them (and us) with incentives to be cost efficient and trust them more, with the help of a compassionate citizenry, to catch those who fall through the cracks.

Because today the budget deficit in Washington has reached such huge proportions, alternative ideas and sources of money for solving problems other than the national government are being sought. One option is for Congress to mandate spending by nonfederal institutions such as state and local governments and private businesses. Congress, for example, has broadened the eligibility of pregnant women and children for Medicaid, thus increasing the numbers of Americans able to participate. However, the states provide a large portion of the money for Medicaid and so are forced to increase their contributions to this program. But mandates, so popular with Congress in the 1980s, have brought bitter objections from state and local governments which find themselves badly pressed by these mandates, which take 25 percent or more of their budgets. Businesses, which have been mandated to provide family leave with insurance coverage, special provisions for the handicapped, and increased pollution-control efforts, blamed the recent recession on these regulations coupled with tax increases which have occurred at the same time.

Another option is to gradually back the government out of some programs in order to return to individual families and communities those responsibilities which can best be performed at the grass-roots level. Phasing out Social Security in favor of personally controlled Individual Retirement Accounts (IRAs) is this sort of proposal. While there will always be a necessary role for the federal government in such national public policy areas as defense, environmental regulations, civil rights, and immigration, there is much room for divestment of centralized control of those public policy areas which do not require national administration.

But today Washington is trying a third option, raising taxes to cover more federal spending. New taxes are being considered to fund more public policy programs. These include, among others, national health care, long-term care for the elderly, free college educations, jobs for the unemployed, and more environmental clean-up programs. If the United States follows this route, it will be moving in a different direction from the other Western democracies. They became heavily socialized in the 1960s and 1970s but are now trying to divest themselves of as much of this legacy as possible. Great Britain has privatized much of its nationalized industries, turned public housing into private housing, and tried to eliminate socialized medicine. France, too, has gone from a socialistic government to a conservative one. Sweden has reduced its tax rates drastically, and now is trying to privatize its industry.

In a democratic nation such as the United States, public policy reflects the will of the people. It may be possible for elites to dominate the formation of policy, and it is understandable that interest groups and policy people would prefer to have their policy preferences mandated by Washington. It is much easier to deal with one national government rather than fifty state governments. Furthermore, those who are dedicated to egalitarian principles worry about the differences which come about when fifty states adopt fifty different policies. But only those policies which enjoy widespread public support will endure. Lacking this support, programs will eventually be abolished. For example, Social Security, which enjoys this kind of support, is in no immediate danger of being abolished. But AFDC is in danger because a growing percentage of people, including a majority of poor people, now view it as encouraging irresponsible behavior.

As a result we must give consideration to the nature and goals of public policy. We must seriously study public policy—and the institutional methods by which it is created—and reflect more seriously upon the *effects* of such policies. We must learn to balance our desire to implement policies with the realization that the central government cannot attempt to resolve all social problems without endangering morality, liberty, the family, or the economy.

Notes

1. Thomas Dye, *Policy Analysis* (Tuscaloosa: University of Alabama Press, 1976), p. 1.

2. *Benevolent Societies of Boston, Report* (Boston: 1834), pp. 4–5, cited in Marvin Olasky, *The Tragedy of American Compassion* (Washington, D.C.: Regnery Gateway, 1992), p. 48.

3. William Ruffner, *Charity and the Clergy* (Philadelphia: Lippincott, 1853), pp. 138–41, cited in Olasky, p. 49.

4. *Congressional Globe* XVIII, 2 (1854), p. 1062, cited in Olasky, pp. 49–50.

5. "Bureaucratizing the American Government," in Gordon S. Jones and John A. Marini, eds., *The Imperial Congress* (New York: Pharos Books, 1988), p. 87.

6. Ibid.

7. James L. Payne, *The Culture of Spending* (San Francisco: Institute for Contemporary Studies, 1991), p. 12.

Suggested Reading

Dye, Thomas. *Policy Analysis*. Tuscaloosa: University of Alabama Press, 1976.

Ellwood, David T. *Poor Support: Poverty in the American Family*. New York: Basic Books, 1988.

Murray, Charles. *Losing Ground: American Social Policy, 1950–1980*. New York: Basic Books, 1984.

Payne, James L. *The Culture of Spending*. San Francisco: Institute for Contemporary Studies, 1991.

24

The End of the Family?

Bruce Frohnen

It is no longer shocking to point out that nearly one in two marriages in the United States ends in divorce. But many Americans would be surprised to learn how unusual and how recent such a divorce rate really is. We now have the highest rate of divorce in the Western world. The number of divorces here rose from 479,000 in 1965 to 1,215,000 in 1992. And the effects of divorce have not rested solely on adults. In 1985 alone, more than a million children in America were involved in divorces.[1]

One cause of our divorce rate's increase was legal reform. A powerful movement to allow couples to divorce without claiming any fault (such as adultery or cruelty) swept the nation beginning in 1970. Today in almost every state one spouse may obtain a no-fault divorce, even over the express objection of the other spouse. In 40 percent of the states no other method of divorce is even permitted.[2]

Judging by their rhetoric, reformers did not set out to increase the divorce rate. Instead they sought to reduce hostility between people whose marriages already had broken down, and get government out of the business of judging the reasons behind the "purely private" decision to divorce.[3] But recent studies have shown that legal reforms did in fact play a significant role in increasing divorce rates.[4] And whatever reformers may have claimed, it seems only logical that when laws are changed so that either party may void the marriage contract at will, without having to show cause or obtain the consent of the other party, the number of divorces will increase.

Mothers and children are the primary victims of high divorce rates. In California, when the average woman divorces, she and her minor children suffer an almost 75 percent drop in their standard of living. Meanwhile, the average former husband may *improve* his standard of living by over 40 percent. At least in part because "blame" is no longer an issue in divorce proceedings, alimony now is given less often and much less generously.[5]

Men now may profit economically by leaving their families. And such considerations loom large today. Where once the family was considered the center and fountain of moral life, it increasingly is seen solely as an *economic* unit. We need government to support the family, in this view, so that children will not grow up poor. But bonds of affection and commitment must be kept loose enough so that family members may realize their desires as *individuals*. And it is the notion that a family is a collection of individuals, rather than the very basis of society, that leads family members to see marriage as a disposable relationship.

Things were not always this way. When French philosopher and statesman Alexis de Tocqueville came to the United States in the 1830s, he commented on the great severity of moral habits in America. The stability and almost puritanical morality of Americans' private lives surprised and impressed him. It was this private discipline, according to Tocqueville, that allowed Americans to deal with one another decently and so maintain a well-ordered but meaningful liberty.

The liberty Tocqueville saw in the nineteenth-century American community was based on local affections fostered in family, church, and local voluntary association. The community was held together by mores, or "habits of the heart," taught to children first by their mother, then by their participation in the family, then in the relationships of social, political, and religious life. America was a good nation, according to Tocqueville, because its institutions and practices fostered good character. Americans taught their children to value the interests of their neighbors as their own and so tempered the democratic tendency to demand ever greater wealth and material equality, while refusing to participate in public life.

In the America of Tocqueville's time, the self-made man forged a successful life for himself and his family through hard work, intelligence, and perseverance. His career and worldly success were his own in that he was personally responsible for their achievement. But his *person* was not simply his own. He "belonged" to—

that is, had involuntary responsibilities to—his church, his family, and his community. His character itself had been formed through interaction with these institutions. He showed his good character by proving his willingness and ability to aid his family and community.

By participating in social institutions, especially the family, Americans learned how to participate in public life. They gained the character necessary to avoid the particular hell Tocqueville saw awaiting people who give up their public responsibilities in pursuit of private pleasure. Such a people would appear, according to Tocqueville, as

> an innumerable multitude of men, alike and equal, constantly circling around in pursuit of the petty and banal pleasures with which they glut their souls. Each one of them, withdrawn into himself, is almost unaware of the fate of the rest . . . He exists in and for himself, and though he still may have a family, one can at least say that he has not got a fatherland. Over this kind of man stands an immense, protective power which is alone responsible for securing their enjoyment and watching over their fate. That power is absolute, thoughtful of detail, orderly, provident, and gentle. It would resemble parental authority if, fatherlike, it tried to prepare its charges for a man's life, but on the contrary, it only tries to keep them in perpetual childhood.[6]

In explaining why Americans had not suffered this horrible fate, Tocqueville looked to their moral character. And he gave credit for Americans' "severe" morals to the family—even more directly than religion. Tocqueville states:

> [R]eligion is often powerless to restrain men in the midst of the innumerable temptations which fortune offers. It cannot moderate their eagerness to enrich themselves, which everything contributes to arouse, but it reigns supreme in the souls of the women, and it is women who shape mores. Certainly of all countries in the world America is the one in which the marriage tie is most respected and where the highest and truest conception of conjugal happiness has been conceived.[7]

The American woman's moral regularity allowed her to establish a tranquil, regular family life. Her strength of reason and character allowed her to civilize her husband and children—and through them a continent—by bringing literature, manners, religion, and morals to the frontier, or wherever the domestic hearth happened to be situated.

Things have changed since Tocqueville's time. The notion that women should control the private sphere by shaping their husbands' and children's character while men tend to business and politics has fallen into disrepute as sexist and unjust. But Tocqueville pointed out that the nineteenth-century American family actually was *more* democratic than its counterparts in aristocratic Europe. It was true, Tocqueville observed, that women in America paid for their control over moral habits by remaining within the narrow sphere of "domestic interests and duties." But, unlike their European counterparts, American women were taught to develop their own reason and were given the latitude to experience the world and, perhaps most importantly, to choose their own husbands.[8]

Americans' vision of a proper family has changed dramatically since Tocqueville's time—indeed, since a few decades ago. We now live in an era of two-income families, of a continuing battle for sexual equality, and of increasing calls for government-subsidized day care. But the key change has been more general and far-reaching even than the change in attitudes toward the family.

Tocqueville's great fear was that Americans would sink into a selfish individualism. He feared that we would abandon social and political life in favor of private pleasures—including the pleasures of family life. But while he recognized that this would destroy the family's ability to defend liberty, he never dreamed that it would destroy the traditional family itself. And, for good or ill, this is precisely what is happening.

The family depends for its very survival on the sacrifice of personal ambitions and the damping down of personal appetites. It cannot accommodate multiple sex partners or vast amounts of private time away from the children. But today's morality emphasizes each individual's right to choose almost any pursuit, and the duty of society to aid such pursuit.

The goal of public policy and much political thought over at least the past hundred years has been to free us from the ties that bind us. The assumption has been that each of us spontaneously would choose a rewarding life. Our choices also would spontaneously complement one another, producing a caring and functional society. We would use the state, but only to obtain the tools necessary for free choice. So even family policy debates have come to focus on how best to provide the money and leisure necessary for choice.

Pragmatism and the "Autonomous Self"

The present troubles with the family can be traced to supporters of industrial capitalism in the late nineteenth century. These supporters of free markets commonly are called "Social Darwinists." American followers of English sociologist Herbert Spenser, Social Darwinists dispensed with "sentimental" defenses of the traditional American way of life in favor of a materialistic defense of the free market. Open competition, they argued, rewarded "winners" in the race of life with material wealth and punished "losers" with poverty and eventual extinction. In this way competition promoted material progress and improvement to the human race.

Social Darwinists defended traditional institutions, not because they provided for liberty and good character, but because they promoted efficiency in material production. Thus the traditional view that the family's purpose is to produce children and adults of good character came into question. Intellectuals came to see the family as merely a convenient tool in the quest for material progress.

Ironically, this new vision was made more popular and powerful by Social Darwinism's main opponents—those American philosophers and policy analysts who called themselves "pragmatists." Pragmatism, according to its most prominent figure, William James, stands for "no special results." It is a method only. Pragmatism explicitly stands only for "autonomy"—for the freedom and ability to make one's own choices. In this spirit John Dewey, the pragmatic philosopher of education, argued that education's sole purpose is to give us the skills we need to pursue our own, self-chosen goals. Yet pragmatism intentionally destroys all fixed rules by defining truth itself as merely what is useful in a given situation.

While pragmatism supposedly has no ends of its own, it dictates that we judge all ideas and all institutions by their consequences. The seeming paradox of a philosophy with no ends which judges everything by its ends is settled by a lowest common denominator: "you must bring out of each word its practical cash value."[9]

For the pragmatist, everything is subjective. "Truth" is what is useful *for us* in our particular circumstances. "Useful" is what helps us achieve our self-chosen goals. And our goals should be defined in manageable, material terms. Nonmaterial goals, for instance religion, are reduced to their material components. Religion is "true" only to the extent that it provides psychological comfort.

Pragmatism aims to solve practical problems at the least cost while securing the greatest degree of profit from each situation. Institutions as well as words are reduced to their cash value so that we may calculate potential costs and profits. But while pragmatism aims only to solve *particular* problems, it ends up calling into question entire social institutions.

Pragmatists criticized the American way of life at the turn of the century because it allowed poverty to exist. That poverty existed everywhere was no excuse, for pragmatists, because we always should be striving to achieve the best practical results. And because only material results count, arguments that the pursuit of material wealth and equality might destroy the moral fabric of family and society constituted irrelevant sentimentalism.

This pragmatic critique of the American way of life was spread by the Social Gospel movement around the turn of the century. Social Gospellers linked religion to a call for "social justice" and freedom from want through the redistribution of wealth. Their platform was institutionalized by the social programs of Franklin Roosevelt's New Deal and Lyndon Johnson's Great Society—by the rise and growth of the welfare state. While these programs did not eliminate poverty, they did create among Americans the expectation that government would see to our material needs.

No existing social structure can meet the demand that it provide any good to everyone with perfect efficiency, let alone meet ever rising expectations of prosperity and equality. But the attempt to meet these demands has brought into question traditional notions of the purpose of government, the goals of life, and the makeup of good character. In doing so they also have called into question traditional notions of the purpose, form, and very legitimacy of the family.

The Children of Pragmatism

Most contemporary social policy analysts can fairly be called "social engineers." I use the term social engineer to refer to that extremely broad spectrum of public policy makers and analysts who wish to use government to promote social justice. "Social justice" today means a "fair" distribution of wealth, employment opportunities, and social recognition. Social engineers argue that they wish only to make possible each individual's pursuit of a good life. In the pragmatic tradition, they decline to make value judgments, except concerning each institution's capacity to produce a fair distribution of wealth and the other tools each of us need in order to construct our own lives.

Social engineers claim to be friendly toward the family. A fair distribution of wealth, social engineers argue, will allow families to stay together which otherwise would break up because of their poverty. They assume that families break up for lack of funds rather than for lack of recognized purpose.

During the 1960s, Daniel Patrick Moynihan achieved notoriety by claiming that the primary cause of ghetto poverty was the breakdown of the black family. Children in broken homes have no strong and law-abiding male authority figure with whom to identify and so do not learn to respect authority and to hope for a better life. They also do not acquire the skills and habits necessary to succeed in a market economy.[10] Written before the explosion of divorce and illegitimacy of the late 1960s and 1970s, Moynihan's article was prescient. The solution he prescribed (an increase in government social programs) and the goal he continues to urge (material equality) have become familiar.

Government social programs treat citizens as individuals rather than as members of families, Moynihan argues, and so produce material injustices. Our minimum wage laws do not take into account the number of children a wage earner must support. We lack a European-style family allowance which redistributes money to families based on how many children they have. We have not "adopted a wide range of social programs designed specifically to support the stability and viability of the family."[11]

Moynihan's solution to family breakdown, pragmatically enough, is a more equal distribution of wealth. Citing Nathan Glazer, he notes that "the demand for economic equality is now not the demand for equal opportunities for the equally qualified: it is now the demand for equality . . . of results, of outcomes." Without equal results, according to Moynihan, "it would be judged that there never had been equal opportunity or, alternatively, that equal opportunity did not work."[12]

The family's proper role is to produce material equality by training children in the ways of material advancement. And while respect for law is necessary for success, the demand for material equality is, according to Moynihan, both universal and just. So the family must be both supported and transformed through government policies in order that children will be brought up in conditions of equal wealth and comfort. Otherwise "just" rage will produce violence and chaos—including family breakdown.[13]

William Julius Wilson argues that it is the state's failure to provide income and work guarantees that has increased illegitimacy
and female-headed households. He argues that black ghetto wom-
en do not marry because there are too few "eligible" employed young
men for them to marry. Reasonably refusing to marry unemployed
men with no prospects, these women have no choice but to join the
welfare roles.[14] Families would form, according to Wilson, if government would do its job of seeing to it that young black males
earn enough money to support a family.

The family is necessary because its breakdown is largely at fault
for ghetto poverty. Welfare dependency itself, for Wilson, is undesirable because welfare payments are too low to provide for a decent life. Thus government must control the hiring, investment, and
production decisions of "private" companies to ensure everyone "good
jobs at good wages."

For social engineers, the traditional American ideal of the self-
made man, which is reflected in opposition to government social
programs, is inherently hypocritical. In America, according to
Moynihan, self-reliance has become a myth because "every other
American household [in 1984] had one or more members participating in one or more government social welfare or social insurance programs." Moynihan obtains this figure by including Social
Security retirement benefits. But his point is clear: none of us is
independent from government, so we should not demand such independence from poor people.[15]

Moynihan also is offended by recent calls for increased oversight of welfare recipients, particularly in their search for appropriate jobs and housing. To say that welfare recipients must be led
to regain habits of punctuality, politeness, and hard work is to say
that they have flawed habits to begin with. For the social engineer,
so long as government funding has no "strings," it is liberating.
But any attempt to instill good character enslaves. Government should
support the family by providing funds without "judging" the choices made by family members, such as whether to work, whether to
marry, or whether to divorce.

Can such a program "save" families? Charles Murray has argued that social engineering programs are counterproductive. Social engineers assume that government may "help" in a specific
area of social or personal life without affecting anything else. But
unintended consequences necessarily follow even narrowly aimed
social policies. Government programs disturb the natural equilibri-
um of social institutions and practices by changing or destroying

people's rational expectations. For example, according to Murray the welfare reforms of Johnson's Great Society made it both easier and more profitable for less educated people to have a child out of wedlock and go on welfare than to form a traditional family in which the father is employed full time.[16] The results were staggering increases in single-parent households and the quadrupling of black youth unemployment between 1950 and 1980 to 37 percent.[17]

Murray's conclusion, that government programs increase illegitimacy and unemployment by fostering welfare dependency, has been criticized on the grounds that the real, after-inflation value of welfare benefits has decreased since 1970.[18] But money is not the only factor relevant in determining people's actions. Leisure is one of the primary comforts of material life. More importantly, people who have become accustomed to relying on the government for support and unaccustomed to self and familial reliance will not suddenly get married and look for work because their welfare check does not go as far as it once did. Instead they will become angry that their "entitlement" has decreased in value. Political activism (along with increased crime among those who have been taught that the "system" is oppressive) is the natural outgrowth of marginal decreases in welfare benefits. Illegitimacy and unemployment will not decrease until welfare recipients once again learn the value and habits of work and family life.

If wealth and comfort are truly our goals, the family would seem to be an indefensible institution. In order to function, the family must restrict, rather than constantly satisfy, the appetites of its members. If the family is merely a convenient means for training successful workers and entrepreneurs, it is difficult to discern why parents would even make a marriage contract, let alone fulfill their parts of the bargain. Children may be cute for a time, but in material terms they can hardly compete with multiple sex partners, vacations, or a new car. Unless its traditional goal of producing adults of good character—men and women who treat others decently because it is right to do so—is valued, the family as an institution would seem counterproductive and even illegitimate.

Values and Education

In the *Nicomachean Ethics,* Aristotle argued that the family is based on the sharing by husband and wife of mutual "property" in children. According to Aristotle, parents love their offspring (and come to love one another) in large part because they share in the act of physical creation. Parents "create" children, and one naturally loves and supports that which is one's own. And it is only through the extension of familial affections to more distant relatives, friends, and neighbors that the *philia* or "friendship" of community is created and society born.

Familial property has been a central feature of Western thought and social practice. And it was not strictly a matter of *paternal* ownership of wives and children. Throughout the Middle Ages a wife had a "marital right" (now generally called the "marital debt") to her husband's conjugal activities—sex and companionship. By demanding her right, a wife could defend her husband and family against outside forces such as involuntary recruitment for service in the Crusades.

Until recent times the notion of familial property included the legal responsibility of parents for the actions of their children. It also caused most parents to feel responsible for their children's character. Parents sought to teach their children proper values and basic habits such as respect, punctuality, and the value of work. Because the purpose of the family was to produce adults of good character, failure in this task was shameful. And the task of raising children was considered both too important and too personal to be left to strangers, even to public officials or teachers in public schools. Public officials did, however, see it as their duty to enforce society's moral norms.

Social engineers, and Americans in general, have become increasingly hostile toward traditional norms or "value judgments." We no longer treat welfare dependency or even crime as "bad" but rather as dysfunctional. Character traits such as respect for law and self-reliance are judged good only to the extent that they help produce material well-being. A criminal may "not be to blame" if his crimes can be attributed to "deprivation." And the materialistic assumptions and goals of social policy mean that almost all "dysfunctional" behavior may be excused on grounds of material deprivation (or excess) and the "alienation" that supposedly goes along with it.

Blaming a criminal for his actions implies that he is *responsible* for his actions. This judgment implies that there is a model of proper behavior against which we can measure particular actions. For social engineers, such a model is "biased" because it assumes that there are particular character traits which everyone should have, regardless of race or economic conditions. Such a picture is not "value neutral."

The central assumption of value neutrality is that everyone is equal in every respect that matters. Not just race, creed, or color, but moral values and even behavior now are considered improper standards for moral judgment. Bigotry, a charge once reserved for those who judged others solely on irrelevant, inherent characteristics such as skin color, has been extended in meaning to include all who judge others on the basis of their *character.*

If everyone is equal, any measurable inequalities must be the result of some form of oppression. And the only inequalities which one is allowed to measure are wealth and comfort. So we cannot say that we have a value neutral (or tolerant and caring) educational, economic, political, or social system unless we have established an equal distribution of material goods. Value neutrality has not produced, as many feared, a moral vacuum. But it has produced an identification of justice and morality with material well-being. Freedom itself has come to mean the guarantee of material and psychological comfort.

All this means that there is no longer any role for the family to play in the socialization of children. The instrumental view of education and life's purpose has, in fact, delegitimized the family as the primary institution of child-rearing. "Good" parents let their children "choose" their own lifestyle. Good parents do not involve themselves in the decisions of their children on issues such as sexual activity (save to see to it that they learn about "safe sex"), religious belief, and career choice. Little wonder, then, that mothers and fathers see little profit in taking their children away from the television and the day-care center to raise them themselves.

Mothers and fathers also do not wish to have their own "autonomy" and material pursuits confined by the "unjust" and "merely biological" parental relationship. Mothers and fathers are too busy arguing over the distribution of household chores (or alimony) and the relative priority of their respective careers and leisure activities to concern themselves with their children's character in any event. Children's priority simply is not as high as it once was. In 1990 and 1991 polls, college freshmen rated "being well-off financially" as more important than raising a family.[19]

Many conservatives and liberals have come to accept the notion that families must be examined as essentially economic relationships. In this way they reinforce the notion that the calculator provides a more accurate means by which to judge the family's "utility" than the responsible children and hard-won marital affection that once constituted its reasons for existence.

Tocqueville argued that the familial authority of the father was natural. But the traditional patriarchy of the family left women far from powerless. Women ran the family by shaping the husband's character—by civilizing him. Women's authority was dominant in some spheres of family life and they shared authority in others. The family's "distribution of powers," while certainly reflected in sex roles, was subservient to marital affection and purpose. The traditional family existed to nurture children. It was intended to last a lifetime, in part because child-rearing takes up the attractive years of both parents, but mostly because familiarity and participation in common projects were supposed to breed affection. Fulfilling distinct roles, husband and wife were to complement one another, filling in one another's weaknesses to make each complete.

And this vision of the family is not without power even today. In part the family retains some attraction as a refuge from dangers of our age, such as AIDS. In part it remains attractive because most of us recognize that children from broken homes do less well as income earners, and also are more likely to become drug addicts, drop out of school, join gangs, go to prison, commit suicide, and commit murder.[20] In part it remains attractive because most of us find the mere pursuit of "autonomy" and money unsatisfying. Nonetheless, despite the social pressures and material lures of the single life, Americans still marry. They cohabitate and divorce, but they continue to search after something more, particularly where children are involved. According to 1990 Bureau of the Census figures, 72.5 percent of children in America under the age of eighteen live in a home headed by a married couple.

We now know that policies aimed at loosening family ties have catastrophic effects. The drive for moral autonomy has achieved just that, and resulted in massive social breakdown. Professor William Galston, now a Clinton administration domestic policy adviser, seems to recognize the problem, noting that our society requires "the right kinds of citizens possessing the virtues appropriate to a liberal democratic community." And "stable intact families make a vital contribution of such citizens."

But Galston expresses the social engineer's overriding concern for "the economic consequences of family disintegration" and is careful to rule out any return to traditional notions of personal and family responsibility. Instead, according to Galston, we must forge a new contract in America between individuals and government, whereby citizens will agree to take better care of their children in exchange for increased government support. And Galston's justification for such a new contract is clear, concrete, and pragmatic: "the best anti-poverty program for children is a stable, intact family."[21]

Social engineers overlook the fact that one cannot have a prosperous, functioning society if one is concerned solely with producing nonjudgmental pursuers of material well-being. Not even wealth can be had by those who pursue only wealth, because such pursuits are more likely to produce vice than virtue. Economic ties are fragile, and cannot bind us to one another and cause us to treat one another decently in the absence of deeper ties of family and friendship. And these deeper ties require moral judgment, based upon an understanding of traditional norms of behavior and a commitment to uphold these norms and pass them on to our children.

Notes

1. These figures are from the Department of Health and Human Services and Lynn A. Wardle, "No-Fault Divorce and the Divorce Conundrum," *Brigham Young Law Review* 79 (1991), 139–42.

2. Ibid., 97, 107.

3. Ibid., 79, 96.

4. See Thomas B. Marvell, "Divorce Rates and the Fault Requirement, *Law and Society Review* 23 (1989), 543, 546.

5. Lenore Weitzman, *The Divorce Revolution* (New York: Free Press, 1985), pp. 337–39.

6. Ibid., pp. 691–92.

7. Ibid., p. 291.

8. Ibid., pp. 592–93.

9. William James, *Pragmatism: A New Name for Some Old Ways of Thinking* (New York: Longmans, 1908), pp. 51–52.

10. Daniel Patrick Moynihan, *Family and Nation* (San Diego: Harcourt, Brace, Jovanovich, 1984), pp. 12, 25, 91–93.

11. Ibid., p. 5.

12. Ibid., p. 27.

13. Ibid., p. 9.

14. William Julius Wilson, *The Truly Disadvantaged: The Inner City, the Underclass, and Public Policy* (Chicago: University of Chicago Press, 1986), pp. 73–92.

15. Moynihan, p. 121.

16. Charles Murray, *Losing Ground: American Social Policy 1950-1980* (New York: Basic Books, 1984), pp. 159–66.

17. Ibid., pp. 26, 72–80.

18. Wilson, pp. 16–18.
19. See Amitai Etzioni, *The Spirit of Community* (New York: Crown, 1993), p. 71.
20. Ibid., pp. 70–71, 84.
21. William A. Galston, "Family Matters," in *The New Democrat* 4 (July 1992), 19–20.

Suggested Reading

Etzioni, Amitai. *The Spirit of Community*. New York: Crown, 1993.

Moynihan, Daniel Patrick. *Family and Nation*. San Diego: Harcourt, Brace, Jovanovich, 1984.

Murray, Charles. *Losing Ground: American Social Policy 1950–1980*. New York: Basic Books, 1984.

Wilson, William Julius. *The Truly Disadvantaged: The Inner City, the Underclass, and Public Policy*. Chicago: University of Chicago Press, 1986.

25

Women, Equal Rights, and the American Regime

Susan Orr

To understand the place of women in America, we must distance ourselves from the rhetorical passion that emanates from both the left and the right. We may learn something about why the question of women and equality engenders such intense emotion. But more importantly, we may come to understand something about the limits of politics, and in so doing, discover something about one of the permanent problems of politics: the difficulty that arises when human beings attempt to overcome nature.

Women, of course, have had just grievances in the past. The American regime has not always granted them their due. But much has been gained this century. Women attained full privileges as citizens of the United States in 1920 with the adoption of the Nineteenth Amendment: "The right of citizens of the United States to vote shall not be denied or abridged by the United States or by any State on account of sex." Since then, many more freedoms have been secured through the courts under the equal protection clause of the Fourteenth Amendment, as well as guaranteed through civil rights legislation. As citizens of the United States, women are now guaranteed the same rights as men. Yet feminists still refuse to declare victory.

The first thing that becomes clear in considering the equal rights movement closely is the difference between the leadership of the women's movement and their constituents. Most women consider themselves feminists of some sort. But most women think of feminism as a movement advocating equality of opportunity in the work force and in the political arena. At the same time, when confronted with many of the radical tenets that the leaders of the women's movement hold dear, many of these same women are repulsed. That the feminist agenda is radically different from ordinary women's desires will soon become clear.

There is certainly a palpable degree of frustration among American women today. Whether they consider themselves feminists or traditionalists, many women appear to be vaguely disenchanted. Evidence of this discontent is found in the endless list of new tracts published, cataloguing the injustices committed against women. Yet women today are free to pursue any career they choose; they do not need to marry to have financial security, or even to bear and raise children. In most conceivable ways, women are no longer dependent on men.

Why is this sense of frustration in American women still there? It has now been several decades since the radical phase of the feminist movement began in earnest. Almost thirty years have passed since radical feminists declared war on American society and all political institutions, because they were deemed fundamentally corrupt and oppressive to women.

Leading lights of the feminist movement like Kate Millett, Susan Brownmiller and Andrea Dworkin teach that all relations between male and female are tyrannical, none so much as the procreative act. From the feminist perspective, sex is the defining political act because it is essentially an act of power. Dworkin, for instance, defines sex as "the pure, sterile, formal expression of men's contempt for women."[1] Seen through such eyes, all sexual acts, consensual or not, become rape. And if one accepts the proposition that the defining act of marriage is a tyrannical abuse of power, the next logical step is to argue that all social order is based on a patriarchal suppression of women, perpetuated by the threat of violence. Women, as these feminists see it, have always been treated as little more than animals. As Millett writes, "The limited role allotted the female tends to arrest her at the level of biological experience."[2] According to this view, women are useful and must be controlled because they alone can produce children.

The world, according to this radical conception where the strong rule the weak, is essentially Hobbesian. But there is no necessity to this ordering of civilization. A drastic restructuring of the political world is both possible and required to ensure justice for those who are weaker and oppressed. The radical feminists have had the political will and determination to attempt to do just that.

Most women would not subscribe to such a radical understanding of the relations between the sexes. But such a view has certainly shaped much of the women's movement and the political agenda it propounds. Claiming to represent the majority of the American population, organizations like the National Organization for Women, the National Abortion Rights Action League, and Emily's List have been able to apply considerable pressure on politicians unwilling to be labeled as "anti-woman." Radical feminists have also secured tenure at universities as professors of women's studies. From these positions, they have been able to influence public policy profoundly. Both Andrea Dworkin and Catharine MacKinnon, for example, have influenced legislation and court cases concerning pornography and sexual harassment in the United States and Canada. Feminists owe such success to the fact that most Americans have not distinguished between the exercise of equal rights that most rational people agree needs to occur and the feminist movement's agenda.

As with many popular movements, the radical wing of feminism began to gain ground in the 1960s. Prominent feminist writers, like Betty Friedan in *The Feminine Mystique*, told American women, the majority of whom were housewives, that they were essentially slavish creatures, living in "comfortable concentration camps." To be fully human they must escape the confines of their homes. The traditional notion that cherished the role that women played in shaping and keeping the family together thus became an object of scorn. The home was seen as a trap in which women lived only vicariously through their husbands and children.

As a consequence of this contempt, many women did change their lives, rejecting the traditional understanding of womanhood. They left their homes and their roles as housewives and mothers to seek fulfillment in other ways. Much has changed since Friedan sounded the alarm—some for the good, some for the bad. On the one hand, improvements in technology have liberated women from much of the menial labor required to run a household in years past.[3] On the other hand, increases in what it costs to raise a family have forced many women to return to the work force when they would rather stay at home. It is certainly true that for those who wish to pursue a career, opportunities abound. Women now hold positions of importance across all professions. They are in the military, and are even in some combat positions. In fact, the 1992 elections heralded in a much proclaimed "Year of the Woman." Yet women are still angry and they are not alone in their anger.

Never have women had more freedom. Never have they been more at risk. Although more women are pursuing high-level positions in the professional and political realm, they are also becoming the objects of growing resentment. This resentment takes many forms, but one of the most ominous is that women are increasingly the victims of abuse and violence. Examples are endless—from the brutal gang rape and assault of the 28-year-old jogger in New York's Central Park in 1989 to the salacious exploits of the Spur Posse in California in 1993. Young men seem more and more willing to treat women badly.

What is even more startling is that the violence is coming not only from strangers but also from intimates. Remember that the phenomenon of "date rape" was relatively unheard of a decade ago. Now, it is no longer a rare occurrence to find adolescent males participating in the gang rape of a neighbor they have known all their lives. According to the latest statistics from the Federal Bureau of Investigation, a woman is beaten every fifteen seconds by someone she knows intimately—either a husband or a boyfriend.

The recounting of these incidents is not to suggest that violence against women is a new phenomenon, or that there isn't a greater proclivity toward violent behavior in general today. But it is certainly true that such acts are being committed at younger and younger ages, and too many are committed by adolescent males with no previous record of criminal behavior. In fact, these crimes are often committed by those who have had every material and social advantage, by those who "ought to know better." Why don't they? What has been lost? How is it that in a recent survey of junior high students, a good number of both male and female respondents thought that after a boy had spent a sufficient amount of money on a date, he deserved a sexual reward in return? Traditional protections that have been there in the past have either eroded or been taken away. In their place, something barbaric has been unleashed.

Even without considering this alarming tendency, there is a discontent among women themselves. The belief that they can have both a fulfilling career and a happy home life is no longer commonplace. Instead, women are all too often wracked with guilt over time they don't spend with their family and overwrought by stress at work, feeling as if they were shirking both roles, filling neither well. Single women who wish to marry and raise a family often despair of finding a suitable husband. Although presented with the rhetoric of an endless capacity for choice, little choice seems available to modern women.

Whatever the radical feminist movement's goals, their realization does not appear to have satisfied anyone. Women, told that they can have it all, are dissatisfied. Men are resentful, if not worse. Why is that anger there? Aristotle describes anger as *the* political passion. Is there something about this regime in particular that inspires such passion?

The animating principle of the American regime is equality. Our founding document, the Declaration of Independence, decrees it a self-evident truth "that all Men are created equal."[4] America was founded on the notion that human beings are capable of self-rule. This means that no person has the right to rule another, without that person's consent because no man or woman is so naturally superior to another that he or she may rule another as one would rule an animal. Abraham Lincoln called this principle the "sheet anchor of American republicanism." The natural equality of human beings further requires the protection of certain natural rights which are also enumerated in the Declaration, namely, the right to life, liberty, and the pursuit of happiness. The American experiment contends that these rights are best secured and maintained in a democratic republic where the citizens can rule and be ruled in turn.

Although America has never perfectly embodied the concept of equality contained within our founding document, the tendency has always been toward an ever increasing realization of the equality principle for all. The injustice of slavery was the first to be corrected, as it contradicted the principles of our regime so conspicuously. But just as it took several generations to bring the goal of equality to black Americans, it also took some time to realize that same goal for women. Yet even before the women's suffrage movement won victory with the adoption of the Nineteenth Amendment, American women were different from their European peers. Although they could not yet vote, they were certainly freer than European women. Born into a regime of liberty, their character was formed by its principles.

Alexis de Tocqueville recorded this difference as he traveled across the newly forged nation. As he noted, European women were overprotected and spoiled, causing them to be slavish and despotic in turns. In contrast, American women were granted much more freedom in all aspects of their lives and also given more respect. They were free to express their opinions, free to travel, free to marry whomever they chose. According to Tocqueville, Americans "hold that woman's mind is just as capable as man's of discovering the naked truth, and her heart as firm to face it. They have never sought to place her virtue, any more than his, under the protection of prejudice, ignorance, or fear."[5]

Tocqueville reserves his highest praise for American women by attributing the greatness of the regime to the superiority of the women who, unlike their European counterparts, were intelligent, independent, and capable of handling the rough life that was their lot. Their power resided in the hearth and home, in raising children, and hence a nation, worthy of independence. More importantly, a woman's role in maintaining the family, and thereby the regime, was understood and respected. Even before the passage of the Nineteenth Amendment, women's contribution to American politics cannot be overestimated. One only has to look to the abolitionist and temperance movements to see their influence.

Despite the natural equality of the sexes, everyone understood, until very recently, that there was also a natural difference between men and women. Tocqueville points out the fallacy of equating the two genders:

> It is easy to see that the sort of equality forced on both sexes degrades them both, and that so coarse a jumble of nature's works could produce nothing but feeble men and unseemly women . . . That is far from being the American view of the sort of democratic equality which can be brought about between man and woman. They think that nature, which created such great differences between the physical and moral constitution of men and women, clearly intended to give their diverse faculties a diverse employment; and they consider that progress consists not in making dissimilar creatures do roughly the same things but in giving both a chance to do their job as well as possible.[6]

Of course, much has changed since Tocqueville traveled across America more than one hundred and fifty years ago.

It is easy to see why the feminists have adopted the argument that women are still being denied equal rights. In fact, all our constitutional crises have centered around the question of equality. By using the rhetoric of equality in public discourse, the feminist agenda seemed familiar and hence more palatable to average Americans.

But the feminist use of the equality argument is only a facade. Their agenda goes much further.

In their writings however, they were much more candid. There, feminists declared that women were ruled through a more insidious form of slavery, insidious because most women refused to recognize their captivity. Although granted the right to vote, women had no real power. Women were still oppressed by the most egregious form of tyranny: the patriarchal institutions of marriage and the family. As Dworkin unabashedly declares, "the nuclear family and ritualized sexual behavior [i.e., heterosexuality] imprison us in roles and forms which are degrading to us."[7]

Radical feminists want the eradication of any ties to gender; in essence, to be free from nature. True freedom, for them, is freedom from any ties that bind women. To attain freedom, women have to be able to pursue their true sexual identities, free from responsibility and free from obligations to family and the raising of children. Feminism rejects a love of one's own and replaces it with a love of the self. In defining the movement in this way, we come across one of the fundamental problems in feminism itself. Most women do not want to be free from their family ties.

The root of the difficulty can be seen in two questions: Is gender natural? Are human beings completely malleable? To many, the answers would seem obvious. There are certain biological differences between men and women, mostly surrounding reproductive capacities, that cannot be gotten around. Rooted in biology, these differences manifest themselves in other ways as well. Men tend to be competitive, aggressive, warlike, and dominant. In contrast, women tend to be loving, peaceful, and nurturing. To a radical feminist, however, the gender question is not so simple. Within the movement itself, there are two competing, even contradictory, schools of thought.

The first school holds that there is no distinction between the genders. Feminists who hold to this understanding of the sexes believe that what appears different in men and women is so only by tradition or convention, not nature. Women are gentle and nurturing only because they have been taught to be subservient to male desires. To solve this inequality perpetuated by society, human beings need to put away the old robes of masculinity and femininity and strive toward a new sexual goal—androgyny. Only then will all humans be free from oppression.

Sexual relations will still exist as a means of pleasure. But all ties to reproduction will be gone. These feminists praise the advances in technology which they trust will free us from the prison of our bodies. Soon, they hope, the task of reproduction will be carried out in laboratories. Some even go so far as to insist that basic reproductive functions are not natural to either sex, but inherent in both. Through continuing evolution, they think that we will all eventually become hermaphroditic. Feminists of this stripe concede that it will be difficult to get men and women to forgo what seem to be the perfectly normal pleasures of married life (to be, in feminist terms, "breeders") in order to become new androgynously sexual beings.

The other school holds that there is indeed a difference in gender, but that the feminine gender is the superior one. All that is male is primitive, outmoded, and bad. Now that we have attained a sufficient level of civilization, we no longer need male brute strength and force. Such feminists believe that if society would only stress feminine qualities, then problems such as poverty and war would wither away. These feminists, not nearly as radical as their aforementioned sisters, seek change by incorporating women and their ways of being into the political realm.

Both these schools understand the need to revolutionize a society perceived to be inherently corrupt; they just disagree about what should be changed. They agree in their belief in the infinite malleability of human nature. As one would suspect, this contradiction within feminism leads to strange manifestations in public policy. The paradoxical nature of the feminist dilemma can be best illustrated with two recent controversies in American politics: women in combat and sexual harassment.

The first school of feminism prevailed with the issue of women in combat. The argument to put women in combat is made on the grounds that women and men can do the job equally well. Many obstacles had to be surmounted in order for women to be accepted into the military. In reality, the difficulties were not overcome, but simply ignored. At every turn, political correctness has won out over military preparedness.

To integrate women into the military successfully, much had to be changed in order for women to keep pace with their stronger male counterparts. First, the armed forces had to lower their standards in physical endurance exams so that women could pass. This is known as gender-norming. Woman are in the military serving alongside men but only because the requirements for admittance have been lowered. Women's endurance is lower than men's, as is their muscular strength, even when size is factored in. So women recruits do not have to run as far, do as many exercises, or carry packs as heavy as their male counterparts. Despite this evidence, feminists still insist that there is no natural physical difference between the sexes. No one suggests that we should sacrifice military preparedness so that blind, lame, or senior citizens can join the ranks of those in combat. But by accepting the feminist understanding of the equality of the sexes, the military has placed social engineering over combat readiness.

Without thinking, Americans have equated the notions of gender and equality. The argument is that if women are to be the equals of men, then they should be allowed to do the same things that men do. But, for the Founders, equality is not based on physical endurance but on the ability to reason. Reason is what is highest in human beings. It distinguishes human beings from animals. If equality were based on equal physical strength, then the strong would indeed be entitled to rule the weak.

Even more of a problem with women serving in the armed forces is the obvious fact that women are capable of bearing children. If we are convinced that it is a woman's patriotic duty to leave her infants and children behind for the privilege of fighting, then the importance of women to their families will have to be denigrated even further. Pregnant or nursing mothers do not make good soldiers. At any given time, however, 20 percent of women in the military are in one condition or the other. There is also the associated difficulty of placing men and women in close quarters: they tend to fraternize. The number of women serving on naval ships who returned pregnant after Desert Storm was a scandal. Certainly, we do not want pregnant women serving in combat ships. Yet the likelihood of this occurring, given the past track record, is enormous. Despite these obstacles, the Navy is aiming for warships to have 20 percent of their crews female by 1997.

The possibility of sexual assault and rape once captured also arises with women soldiers. Are not women at special risk as prisoners of war? The woman doctor who was captured by the Iraqis during Desert Storm was molested while her male comrades were forced to watch. The trauma that will be inflicted upon the women who will suffer atrocities at the hands of their captors (and the men who will be unable to protect them) has been all but ignored in the rush to quiet feminist protests of unequal treatment. It has been ignored to uphold the doctrine that there is no natural difference between the sexes.

The second understanding of gender triumphed in the debate over sexual harassment. Here, the difference between the sexes is accentuated. To be sexually harassed used to mean to be pressured to grant a sexual favor in order to receive a promotion or to keep a job. Now it can mean anything from the threat of losing one's job if one fails to have sex, to repelling an unwanted advance or mild flirtation. A man, in all innocence, can ask an associate for a date and find himself up against a charge of harassment. A man's character can be defamed by an unsubstantiated charge. Ironically, women can now exert an unjust control over men in the workplace, worse than that caused by harassment itself. No wonder there is a certain degree of resentment among men.

Keep in mind that sexual harassment is against the law. In *Meritor Savings Bank, FSB v. Vinson* (1986), the Supreme Court held that sexual harassment constitutes a violation of the Civil Rights Act. Anyone who is so harassed already has legal recourse and may lodge a complaint with the Equal Employment Opportunity Commission. However, a woman should be capable of stopping an unwanted advance that bears no threat to her job without filing a lawsuit. The law should intervene only when her job is jeopardized.

Another important concern arises when the terms of debate are redefined to be more inclusive. A crucial distinction is lost when more threatening behavior is equated with flirtation. By exaggerating and extending what constitutes harassment, we have succeeded in making it easier for truly despicable actions to go unpunished.

Feminists are actually making contradictory claims: first, that they are the equals of men in the workplace; second, that they need special protection to save them from office wolves. As critics of feminism have been only too delighted to point out, these cries of helplessness fly in the face of demands to be allowed to rule in the boardrooms of corporate America. Either women can handle themselves in the workplace, and should be treated accordingly, or they are in need of special protection.

These are just two recent controversies that illustrate the profound influence that radical feminism has had on public policy, but they depend on earlier and more telling victories. Because the feminists' desire to liberate women from male hegemony required considerable social change, they first needed to transform the existing order. And transform it they did. But the results of this change did not go as predicted. The first freedom to be procured was the freedom to be sexually liberated. In order to overthrow patriarchy, things hitherto prohibited, such as illegitimacy and both premarital and extramarital sex, needed to be made permissible. General acceptance of these behaviors strikes at the very heart of the institution of marriage, which was the intention.

The first triumph that the feminist movement can claim is making sexual promiscuity appear normal and good. One has only to look at any current woman's magazine to see this theme repeated incessantly. Of course, feminists were not alone in championing the sexual revolution, but they certainly were in the forefront. Here, the feminist strain that declared that men and women are basically the same won out as the official word on the subject. Men and women, it was argued, have the same desire for sex, the same emotional attachment to sexual involvement, and they incur the same risk. Of course, the real lives of men and women tell a different story.

The sexual revolution has been an unmitigated disaster. It has brought forth an unheard-of amount of disease and heartbreak, resulting in broken marriages, broken homes, and broken lives. Told that sex was natural and should not be confined to marriage, many Americans believed the promises of the sexual revolution and experimented accordingly. But the experiment has proved costly, and in every case, women have paid the heavier price.

Beginning with the obvious, only women can get pregnant. Once men are convinced that they are simply satisfying a women's sexual urge, the pressure to check if she is pregnant, or to take responsibility for any pregnancy, is drastically reduced. Despite every attempt to separate procreation from the reproductive act, nature seems to be able to get around our best efforts. There is no foolproof contraceptive, and it seems unlikely that there ever will be. Those with the highest effectiveness also tend to cause irreparable damage to the reproductive health of women. Another fact rarely mentioned is that effectiveness rates for contraceptives are given for only one year. If a contraceptive has an 80 percent effectiveness rate for one year, the rate lowers to 40 percent if used over ten years. So one of the most obvious results of the increase in sexual activity is that many women find themselves unexpectedly pregnant.

The number of out-of-wedlock births continues to soar at an alarming rate. The latest statistics from the National Center for Health

Statistics show illegitimate births in 1990 at an all-time high, an increase of 75 percent since 1980. In fact, illegitimate births now account for 28 percent of all births. Births, of course, fail to take into account the number of pregnancies that end in abortion. But for those illegitimate children who are born, only 20 percent of their fathers pay any regular support for their offspring. This puts a tremendous financial strain on the mother. It is little wonder that 64 percent of all never-married, single-mother households live below the poverty line.

But even if a woman doesn't get pregnant, her chances of contracting a sexually transmitted disease (STD) are rather frightening. There has been an exponential increase in the variety of these diseases over the past several decades. As with the venereal diseases of the past, the most devastating health consequences affect the female and any children she bears. Sexually active women put themselves at risk for pelvic inflammatory disease (a leading cause of sterility). Some diseases, like chlamydia and human papilloma virus, can be virtually undetectable for years (between 70 and 80 percent of all cases). And the effects of these same diseases remain with a woman for the rest of her life. Current estimates are that one in five young people is infected with an STD; in fact, 86 percent of all those infected are between the ages of 15 and 29. All of the aforementioned do not even begin to take into account the question of AIDS.

The sexual revolution also led to the instability of marriage. Once sexual activity was loosened from the bonds of marriage, the institution itself was weakened. But marriage was also made vulnerable through the help of law. Once divorce was made relatively easy, it became harder and harder for spouses to stay together through difficult times, even for the sake of their children. The divorce rate soon soared to the point where marriages now have less than a 50 percent chance of surviving until death do them part.

Today's no-fault divorce guarantees that both men and women have little control over their marital life. Each partner is at the mercy of his or her spouse. At any time, either spouse can desert the union for any reason, or for no reason at all. Even those who did not wish to participate in the sexual revolution were now affected by it. The law no longer protects the family, the foundation of stable and free society.

The rhetoric of choice when mixed with the family is a deadly combination. In fact, no one chooses his or her family. Love does not create a family: marriage, blood ties, and adoption do. But in making no-fault divorce the norm, Americans made families voluntary and amorphous associations. The consequences of this change in family structure are especially tragic for women and children. They bear the brunt of the burden.

The cry for equal rights coupled with no-fault divorce soon made it hard for women to argue effectively that they were in need of financial support when a marriage broke up. Because fault was no longer an issue, permanent support of an ex-wife was soon seen as unjust. If women and men are equal, why should a man be forced to care for a wife he no longer wanted?

In a large majority of cases (88 percent), mothers are still given custody of their children. The nominal amounts awarded for child support do not begin to cover the costs of child-rearing (in most cases less than half).[8] Now, many women must return to work, and place their children in day care, in order to make ends meet. One of the reasons that more women remain in the work force may be as insurance for the future. Their husbands may decide to divorce them later. Women are keeping themselves marketable.

One of the rallying cries of feminists today is the feminization of poverty. Statistics show that they have a point. There is an alarming increase in the number of women and their children who have become poor over the past several decades. But unfortunately, the feminization of poverty is a direct result of policies that the feminists have so eagerly championed. In the first year after a divorce, a mother's standard of living drops an average of 30 percent. A father's income, in contrast, actually increases by 13 percent. As of March 1992, there were 11 million female-headed households. In fact, the proportion of all children living in single-parent households has more than doubled from 11 percent in 1970 to nearly 25 percent in 1992. The difference in income between single-parent and two-parent families is enormous. In 1990, only about 10 percent of two-parent households were living below the poverty line. In contrast, 36 percent of all divorced, single-mother households were living below the poverty line. Over half of the children from single-parent homes live in poverty. This rate is five times higher than for other children. The median income for a two-parent family is $41,000; if the mother stays at home and does not work, $33,000. But the median income for a female-headed household is only $16,700.

There are, of course, children in two-parent homes who live in poverty. But the situation of children in poverty who live with both parents improves whenever the economy improves. Children from single-parent homes, however, remain in poverty, no matter what the economic conditions are. A practical consequence of the feminist demand for social change is widespread poverty, both economically and socially.

Poverty is not the only, or even the worst, problem that afflicts children from single-parent households. As a group, children from one-parent families exhibit above-average rates of youth suicide, mental illness, adolescent pregnancy, violence, and drug use, regardless of their income level. These are startling statistics. From everything that we know about raising children, they are always better off in a two-parent family. Single motherhood may be a choice, but it is not a blessing.

A more intangible factor, difficult to measure, is the sacrifices women will make to protect their children. Women know that the children of divorce grow up in poorer conditions, both materially and psychologically, than their peers. Once a woman realizes that stopping a divorce is next to impossible, she may become one of the slavish creatures that Friedan castigated so severely out of fear for her family's future. Because she has lost all advantage in court, she may see that she has no choice but to allow her husband to treat her badly in order to guarantee that he stays in the marriage. A similar problem arises in custody battles. Women are often forced to accept lower settlements for child support in order to ensure that their custody of the children will not be contested.

It soon becomes evident that the clear winners in the "divorce game" are men. They have every advantage, and little incentive to behave decently. The women they leave are less likely to marry again. But men remarry three times as often as the women they divorce, and they tend to marry younger women. So it is not surprising that many women are angry and feel betrayed by the very movement that promised to liberate them.

Radical feminism even diminishes sex. By declaring it to be only a biological urge which can be indulged in without consequences (with the proper equipment), feminism almost strips sex of its erotic character. It wants to free us from the limits of our bodies, but it reduces human beings to the realm of the physical. Thus, sexual partners become simple outlets for pleasure. Sex is thereby lowered to less than the animal level because animals, at least, are perpetuating their species. Despite the rise in illegitimate births, our population is not replacing itself: fewer people are having even fewer children. A further irony is that when sex is reduced to the realm of physical pleasure, men become the superior gender, for women cannot escape male superiority in strength.

Sex reminds us who we are, that is, individual men and women who are more than animals but less than gods.[9] Gender roles respond to a human need by telling us who we are. The feminists are right in their contention that men and women are different. Their error is in thinking that this difference is changeable, or that human beings would benefit from any change.

Women are sexually superior to men because women have more to do with procreation than men. So the sexual superiority of the woman is rooted in nature.[10] Men are naturally more abstracted from the consequences of the act. When men are divorced from the gender roles of husband and father, it is difficult to convince them to take responsibility for their actions or their offspring.

As we have seen, once gender is tampered with, all kinds of evils are unleashed, for there is something essentially untameable about sex. As Camille Paglia points out so coherently:

A modern assumption is that sex and procreation are medically, scientifically, intellectually "manageable." If we keep tinkering with the social mechanism long enough, every difficulty will disappear. Meanwhile, the divorce rate soars. Conventional marriage, despite its inequities, kept the chaos of libido in check. When the prestige of marriage is low, all the nasty daemonism of sexual instinct pops out. Individualism, the self unconstrained by society, leads to the coarser servitude of constraint by nature. Every road from Rousseau leads to Sade.[11]

No matter how we try, we cannot abandon gender and nature. Our efforts to escape our natural limits produce only bitter fruit.

The social experiment of the past several decades has worked to this extent: women have proved to men that they can live without them, not well, but women can survive. Woman can bear and raise children alone, although the children suffer without a father in their lives and the mother's task is made more difficult. Yet what do the men do when they have no place to channel their energies, and no compelling reason to mature? Without a proper channeling of the sex drive, men revert to brutes. Men's predatory nature is unleashed when divorced from responsibility. For Eros is a cruel master.

We began this essay by noting the increase in violence against women. This is a direct result of having men divorced from their proper role as men, or having them divorced from their gender. The increasingly brutal treatment of women is due to the radical feminist manipulation of gender which holds that men and women are the same, defines all sexual activity as rape, and demands complete autonomy from the burdens of marriage and family for women.

Radical feminism has not made men better behaved or more sensitive to women, only more disoriented, self-centered, and susceptible to violent behavior. The connection between gangs, violent crimes, and male separation from the family cannot be overlooked. They can be seen most clearly in the poorest neighborhoods where men are more thoroughly alienated from normal ties. This alienation is one that has been reinforced by public policies that discourage families from forming: programs such as Aid to Families with Dependent Children (AFDC) which penalize women financially if they marry and make men appear superfluous. Yet, as we have already discovered, marriage is one of the few proven ways out of a life of poverty. Marriage, and the family it creates, are the primary means of civilization. Built on trust, marriage requires virtues hard to come by, such as fidelity and self-sacrifice.

To be civilized, women and especially men need marriage and the family. One proof of this can be found in the fact that single men, men without families to live for, are inherently weaker than their married counterparts and they are weaker when compared to women, married or single. As George Gilder has painstakingly documented, single men are more prone to disease and ill health, and have higher rates of suicide. They die earlier from disease, accident, or crime. Their mortality rate is twice that of married men and three times that of single women. They also earn significantly less than married men, and are more likely to be unemployed. Men seem to need something beyond themselves to work for in order to prosper financially and emotionally.

We have seen some of the destruction wreaked by the radical feminist movement. But in seeing it, we can also see the reasons why it is inevitably doomed. First, radical feminism fails to understand the nature of the sexes and has not understood those it claims to speak for, women themselves. Indeed the radical feminists have always harbored an underlying contempt for things feminine. In misunderstanding women, they have failed to understand the essential nature of politics.

As those of an earlier age understood without hesitation, women are too important to any regime to be satisfied with simple citizenship. A woman's place in the political world is an essential and irreplaceable one. In order for any regime to survive, it must accomplish two essential functions: civilize the men and perpetuate the species. Both functions are carried out by women and are, in fact, inextricably linked. As Tocqueville understood, any regime needs strong women in order to endure. To guarantee the perpetuation of the polity, one needs to protect the family, a task that requires strong women, women who understand the purposes of gender. Yet the family is the very thing from which feminists want to escape. Here, as in other places, the feminists have run up against the insurmountable problem of nature.

The second failure of feminism is related to the first. When the ends of the feminist movement are examined, it becomes increasingly clear that they are different from what most women want, because most women have not divorced themselves from their natures. Most women desire enough freedom to pursue careers, and enough legal protection to ensure that they can do so without discrimination. But the family is also of great importance to them. Despite promises of liberation, the women's movement has not simply produced more freedom. Most women want the freedom to marry and stay married, which no-fault divorce denies them; the freedom to bear children, which high infertility rates make increasingly difficult; and the freedom to raise healthy and happy children with the support of a husband and father, which the modern world makes quite difficult. The feminists failure to recognize all this is the reason why they alienate so many women.

The contradiction exemplified in feminism is a problem inherent in modernity itself. Camille Paglia goes to the root of the problem, arguing that

> Modern liberalism suffers unresolved contradictions. It exalts individualism and freedom and, on its radical wing, condemns social orders as oppressive. On the other hand, it expects government to provide materially for all, a feat manageable only by an expansion of authority and a swollen bureaucracy. In other words, liberalism defines government as tyrant father but demands it behave as nurturant mother. Feminism has inherited these contradictions.[12]

In calling for complete gender equivalence, radical feminists ask for government to transcend the natural limits of human beings.

What the radical feminists asked for was the freedom to behave like men, but not real men, only really irresponsible men. And they asked for it expecting no adverse consequences.

Notes

1. Andrea Dworkin, *Intercourse* (New York: Macmillan/Free Press, 1988), p. 138.
2. Kate Millett, *Sexual Politics* (New York: Simon and Schuster, 1969), p. 26.
3. It remains true, even today, that most household chores are carried out by women.
4. It must be remembered that when Thomas Jefferson penned these words, the term "men" was understood to refer to human beings, not just the masculine gender.
5. Alexis de Tocqueville, *Democracy in America*, translated by George Lawrence (Garden City, N.Y.: Anchor Books, 1969) p. 602.
6. Tocqueville, *Democracy in America*, p. 601.
7. Andrea Dworkin, *Women Hating* (New York: Blume, 1974), p. 82.
8. Mary Ann Glendon, *The Transformation of Family Law* (Chicago: University of Chicago Press, 1989), p. 232: "In 1985, only 61% of single-parent families were awarded child support; of these, over one-quarter never received any payments, while another quarter received less than the full amount due."
9. See Maggie Gallagher, *Enemies of Eros* (Chicago: Basic Books, 1989), p. 256.
10. See George Gilder, *Men and Marriage* (Gretna, La.: Pelican, 1986), p. 9.
11. Camille Paglia, *Sexual Personae* (New York: Vintage Books, 1990), p. 14.
12. Ibid., pp. 2–3.

Suggested Reading

Dworkin, Andrea. *Intercourse*. New York: Macmillan/Free Press, 1988.
Friedan, Betty. *The Feminine Mystique*. New York: Norton, 1963.
Fox-Genovese, Elizabeth. *Feminism Without Illusions*. Chapel Hill: University of North Carolina Press, 1991.
Gallagher, Maggie. *Enemies of Eros: How the Sexual Revolution Is Killing Family, Marriage, and Sex and What We Can Do About It*. Chicago: Basic Books, 1989.

Gilder, George. *Men and Marriage*. Gretna, La.: Pelican, 1986.

Glendon, Mary Ann. *The Transformation of Family Law: State, Law and Family in the United States and Western Europe*. Chicago: University of Chicago Press, 1989.

MacKinnon, Catharine. *Only Words*. Cambridge: Harvard University Press, 1993.

————. *Toward a Feminist Theory of the State*. Cambridge: Harvard University Press, 1989.

Millett, Kate. *Sexual Politics*. New York: Simon and Schuster, 1969.

National Research Council. *Losing Generations: Adolescents in High Risk Settings*. Washington, D.C.: National Academy Press, 1993.

Paglia, Camille. *Sexual Personae: Art and Decadence from Nefertiti to Emily Dickinson*. New York: Vintage Books, 1991.

Tocqueville, Alexis de. *Democracy in America*, trans. George Lawrence. Garden City, N.Y.: Anchor books, 1969.

26

Abraham Lincoln and
Democratic Statesmanship

Joseph Alulis

The greatest service a statesman can render is to save a regime when its existence is threatened. This is the service Abraham Lincoln rendered this nation—a service he could not have performed without possessing a deep understanding of American democracy. By studying Lincoln's understanding of the challenge to the American democracy which he confronted, we can gain a better idea of the kinds of politics the American regime entails.[1] Of this challenge Lincoln observed: "I suppose almost every one knows, that in this controversy, whatever has been said, has had reference to the question of [N]egro slavery."[2] What was the challenge that Negro slavery posed to the American democracy? How was that challenge met? At the center of these questions are America's fundamental beliefs about law and rights as the groundwork of American freedom.

The Threat to Freedom: Lawlessness

For Lincoln the question of slavery, "reduced to its lowest terms," was whether slavery was to be regarded as a wrong, "a moral, a social and a political wrong," and to be treated as such. He and his party answered in the affirmative. Of himself he said, "I have always hated slavery, I think as much as any abolitionist."[3]

In his debates with Stephen Douglas,[4] Lincoln observed that the question of slavery had "shaken the government and agitated the people" for "fifty years," for the entirety of his life.[5] He grew up with the issue and was compelled to deal with it almost as soon as he entered politics.[6] We can even see the question of slavery in the background of Lincoln's earliest statement of the means by which the American regime was to be preserved, his *Address Before the Young Men's Lyceum* of Springfield, Illinois, on January 27, 1838.[7]

At the start of the *Lyceum* speech Lincoln makes clear why we wish to preserve "our political institutions." It is not simply out of "gratitude to our fathers," that is, not because they are our own, but because these institutions are good. They "conduc[e] more essentially to the ends of civil and religious liberty than any of which the history of former times tells us."[8] Our defense of these institutions is not primarily a matter of military preparedness against "some transatlantic military giant." The only serious threat to our political institutions, and thus to freedom, comes from ourselves. The only adequate response to that threat is that we make obedience to the law, our *"political religion."* Freedom is indissolubly wedded to the rule of law.

Lincoln's argument for this solution may be reduced to three propositions: (1) that the greatest threat to freedom comes from "the lawless in spirit," (2) that in order to be able to successfully resist the lawless, the people must be united, and (3) that the Constitution affords the people a solid ground upon which to make this resistance.

"Any Government" depends for its support on "the attachment of the People." That attachment depends on the government's capacity to protect the people "in their persons and property." The threat to persons and property comes from "the lawless in spirit," those who know "no restraint, but dread of punishment." Widespread disregard for the law undermines this restraint. When lawbreaking becomes popular, lawbreakers go unpunished. The lawless "make a jubilee" of this state of affairs, with the result that the people become "disgusted with a government that offers them no protection." Their attachment to popular government weakened, they will not be unwilling to see it replaced by another government that offers some prospect of security.[9]

At this point there "will not be wanting to seize the opportunity" the most lawless man of all, that man "of ambition and talent" whom Lincoln describes as a beast of prey, he of *"the family of the lion or the tribe of the eagle."* In good republican fashion Lincoln compares this man to Julius Caesar, who struck the blow that ended the republic of Rome. The "lawless in spirit," par excellence, is the tyrant. "To successfully frustrate" the designs of the lawless man of "genius," "it will require that the people be united with each other" and the best security of that union is a common attachment to "the government and laws." So Lincoln urges: "to the support of the Constitution and Laws, let every American pledge his life, his property, and his sacred honor."[10]

In this context, Lincoln indirectly addresses the question of slavery. He speaks of abolitionism, tacitly defending abolitionism. He criticizes those who lawlessly attempt to stop the abolitionists by throwing "printing presses into rivers" and shooting editors.[11] Clearly this violence falls under the ban Lincoln pronounces. But abolitionism, at least in the virulent form practiced by William Lloyd Garrison[12] and his followers, also presents a special problem. The whole point of Lincoln's speech is to inculcate "reverence" for "the Constitution and Laws." But Garrison denounced the Constitution as "a most bloody and Heaven-daring arrangement" because of its toleration of slavery.[13] In this respect, implicit in Lincoln's speech is a critique of the abolitionists as well as those who used violence against them.

Lincoln criticizes the abolitionists elsewhere for their contempt for the law. He speaks of the "just execration" meted out to those who would "tear to tatters [the Union's] now venerated constitution; . . . rather than slavery should continue a single hour." In the debates with Douglas he declares that anyone "impatient of the constitutional guarantees thrown around [slavery]" who "would act in disregard of these, . . . is misplaced standing with us."[14] He said that if elected to Congress, "I would deem it my duty" to vote for a fugitive slave law because "I have sworn to support the Constitution."[15] Less than a year before the *Lyceum* speech, Lincoln had publicly criticized abolitionism. In March 1837, in a statement entered into the legislative record of the Illinois House of Representatives, Lincoln professed the belief that though slavery was unjust, "the promulgation of abolition doctrines tends rather to increase than to abate its evils."[16] Lincoln's failure to criticize abolitionism in the *Lyceum* speech, in the context of a discussion of the relation between law and freedom, is significant for his understanding of the crisis slavery posed to the American democracy. This significance is revealed by a comparison of the *Lyceum* argument with that of James Madison in *The Federalist* as to the principal threat to liberty under a popular government.

Like Lincoln, Madison fears that under the operation of a popular government, rights may become uncertain, thereby weakening the people's support of popular government so that "some power independent of the people would soon be called for" (*Federalist* 51). Lincoln's "mobocratic spirit" and "mob law" are the counterparts of Madison's "majority faction" (*Federalist* 10). But while Lincoln fears that the citizens will not obey the laws, Madison fears that the laws themselves will be unjust. The first security for freedom for Madison is not regard for law as such, but regard for right. "Justice is the end of government . . . and ever will be pursued until it be obtained or until liberty be lost in the pursuit" (*Federalist* 51).

Lincoln is not unaware that laws may be unjust.[17] Nor does he preach respect for *any* laws regardless of content: his topic is the preservation of *our* political institutions. Those political institutions, as defended by Madison in *The Federalist,* are designed to make it less likely that the laws will be unjust, and Lincoln's praise of those institutions expresses his judgment that the Framers' design was successful. As a general rule, reverence for *these* laws is a reverence for justice and so secures freedom. What Lincoln warns against is a lawlessness that bears within itself the seed of tyranny. It is in just these terms that Lincoln describes the wrong of slavery—it "is *despotism*" and "there can be no moral right in connection with one man's making a slave of another."[18] The law which recognizes a "moral right" to enslave another person justifies despotism which is itself the antithesis of law. It, in effect, introduces lawlessness into the law.[19]

Lincoln refuses to criticize the abolitionists in the *Lyceum* speech precisely because the danger against which he warns his fellow citizens is lawlessness. Nothing is as lawless and so dangerous to the regime's freedom as slavery. In a speech during the 1858 campaign, Lincoln expresses this idea clearly in a manner that, for similarity of both thought and language, may be read as a gloss on his *Lyceum* speech:

> What constitutes the bulwark of our own liberty and independence? It is not our frowning battlements, our bristling sea coasts, . . . Our defense is in the preservation of the spirit which prizes liberty as the heritage of all men, in all lands, every where. Destroy this spirit, and you have planted the *seeds of despotism* around your own doors . . . Accustomed to trample on the rights of those around you, you have lost the genius of your own independence, and become the fit subjects of the first cunning tyrant who rises. [Italics added][20]

Lincoln could rest content with the lesson of "reverence for the laws" in 1838 because the laws were not *fundamentally* in conflict with moral right. Religious obedience to "the Constitution and Laws" is the security for liberty because the Constitution and laws are true to moral right. The challenge to the American democracy posed by Negro slavery was that under the impact of the presence of this institution among us, the Constitution and laws were being made lawless. We must consider more fully this understanding of the crisis Lincoln confronted, the cause of this transformation, and the task of the democratic statesman in the face of such a challenge.

The Place of Slavery in American Law: The *Dred Scott* Decision

One of the principal arguments of Douglas's campaign against Lincoln in 1858 is that Lincoln acted against the doctrine of his *Lyceum* speech, that he encouraged lawlessness. He did so, Douglas argued, by his "crusade against the Supreme Court of the United States because of the *Dred Scott* decision."[21] The issue here is the Court's 1857 decision, written by Chief Justice Roger Taney, that "the Constitution of the United States neither permits Congress nor a Territorial legislature to exclude slavery from any United States territory."[22] In opposition to this Lincoln stood "pledged to a belief in the *right* and *duty* of Congress to prohibit slavery in all the United States Territories."[23]

But Taney's decision, Douglas declaimed, is "the law of the land, binding on you, on me and on every good citizen, whether we like it or not." Lincoln's opposition to *Dred Scott*, Douglas charges, transforms "the government from one of laws into that of a mob." He, for his part, will "stand by the Constitution, . . . by the laws, . . . by the decisions of the court." Douglas asks: How will Lincoln "reverse that decision"? "Does he intend to appeal to violence, to Lynch law?"[24]

Lincoln contends he does not "resist" the decision as the resolution of a property dispute between Dred Scott and his master, but as a rule governing national policy. The Republicans do not intend "in any violent way [to] disturb the rights of property thus settled." But they do reject the decision as "binding on the voter, to vote for nobody who thinks it wrong" or "binding on the members of Congress or the President to favor no measure that does not actually concur with the principles of that decision."[25] Lincoln hopes to reverse the decision by the exercise of lawful political power. While the liberty of the citizen of a democracy depends on his respect for the law, democracy means that the law is of the citizen's own making.

Lincoln cites Thomas Jefferson's opinion that when the citizens surrender the authority to make ultimate decisions about constitutional matters to any other, especially to judges who are "in office for life and not responsible . . . to the elective control," they have surrendered their liberty.[26] By urging submission to *Dred Scott* not as "right upon the merits" but "simply because" it is the decision of a judge, Douglas undermines the sovereignty of the people. In fact, Douglas himself had successfully reversed court decisions by political means. "Didn't Judge Douglas find a way to reverse the decision of our [that is, the Illinois] Supreme Court, . . . ? Did he not appeal to the 'MOBS' as he calls them?" Douglas gained his title "Judge" as one of the five new members of the Illinois Supreme Court appointed to overturn the contested decision.[27]

But Lincoln carries the argument a step farther. Douglas endorsed action contrary to the decision while acknowledging that it was properly made. He insisted that, though the *Dred Scott* decision conferred on the slaveholder a right to take his "property" into the territory, the territorial legislature could "by unfriendly legislation effectively prevent the introduction of [slavery] into their midst." Lincoln calls this Douglas's "double position": to please Southern opinion, he endorsed *Dred Scott*, and to please Northern opinion, he endorsed action contrary to the decision. Douglas wished for the use of the law against others without having to obey it himself. Lincoln declared: *"There has never been as outlandish or lawless a doctrine from the mouth of any respectable man on earth."* [28]

The basis of Lincoln's resistance to the *Dred Scott* decision brings us to the critical difference between Lincoln and Douglas and to the heart of Lincoln's understanding of the crisis he faced. The decision that neither Congress nor a territorial legislature could prohibit slavery in the territories was based on the opinion that there was a "constitutional right" to hold slaves. Lincoln thought this opinion wrong and thus the decision was "improperly made." In upholding the decision, Douglas approved the opinion. The question between them was the correct understanding of the Constitution as it bears upon "the right of property in a slave."[29] Douglas contends that he seeks only to preserve the government "as our fathers made it" and that Lincoln is proposing a "revolutionary" change.[30] Lincoln agrees that the question "Why can't we leave [slavery] as our fathers place it?" expresses "the exact difficulty between us."[31]

The Constitution, for Douglas, was indifferent to slavery. The fundamental principle of our government is that each state is "to do as it pleases without meddling from its neighbors." It is "meddling" to call the institutions of other states morally wrong:

> It does not become Mr. Lincoln, or anybody else, to tell the people of Kentucky that they have no consciences, that they are living in a state of iniquity, and that they are cherishing an institution to their bosoms in violation of the law of God. Better for him to adopt the doctrine of "judge not lest ye be judged."

At Alton where the speakers addressed citizens of both free and slave states, of nearby Missouri as well as Illinois, Douglas tells his audience that peace between North and South depends on this mutual toleration of different institutions. The Union's existence was imperiled over slavery "merely that a few ambitious men may ride into power on a sectional hobby."[32]

But, for Lincoln, one "cannot logically say anyone has a right to do wrong." He added, contrary to Douglas and Taney, that the Framers of the Constitution thought slavery was wrong. The Constitution tolerates slavery because "of the difficulty—the absolute impossibility of its immediate removal" at the time the Constitution was written.[33] The southern states would not agree to a union without protection for slavery.[34] Many of the delegates opposed according slavery this protection, but they feared for the success of any republican government on this continent if the colonies were not united. Lincoln summarizes the Framers' plight: "We had slavery among us, we could not get our constitution unless we permitted them to remain in slavery, we could not secure the good we did secure if we grasped for more."[35]

The most powerful evidence Lincoln offers for this interpretation is the action of the founding generation. If they did not regard slavery as a wrong and look forward to a time when it would be eradicated, why did they provide for the end of the African slave trade and prohibit the introduction of slavery into the territories? "Why stop its spread in one direction and cut off its source in another . . . ?" By imposing restraints on the conduct of the internal and external slave trade, Congress "hedged and hemmed it in to the narrowest limits of necessity" during the first twenty years of the Union's existence.[36]

Finally, the Constitution's references to slavery employ language that shows "clear marks of disapprobation." The words "slavery" and "Negro race" do not appear in the Constitution. In those places where the Framers deal with the institution, "covert language" is used so that once slavery was abolished "there should be nothing on the face of the great charter of liberty suggesting that such a thing as [N]egro slavery had ever existed among us."[37]

So one could not say that the Constitution "distinctly and expressly affirmed the right of property in a slave." For if it is wrong to speak of ownership of human beings and if the Negro is a human being, then there can be no "slave property" in the same way there is "horse and hog property." The word property as used by the Framers of the Constitution clearly did not include "slave property." The rights of ownership of human beings the Constitution recognizes are only exceptions occasioned by necessity.[38] In short, "the plain unmistakable spirit of that age, towards slavery, was hostility to the PRINCIPLE, and toleration ONLY BY NECESSITY."[39]

Lincoln objected to the *Dred Scott* decision not only because it denied that Congress could prohibit slavery in the territories. It pointed the way to "another Supreme Court decision, declaring that the Constitution of the United States does not permit a state to exclude slavery from its limits."[40] The crisis the nation faced was that slavery was being read into the Constitution as right in principle, contrary to the true views of the Framers. The task for defenders of the nation's freedom was to "turn slavery from its claims of 'moral right,' back upon its existing legal rights and its arguments of necessity."[41]

The Framers' expectation that the institution of slavery would gradually be abolished was upset by the invention of the cotton gin in 1793.[42] This technological innovation, by making slavery more profitable, supplied it with ardent defenders. The cotton gin, in effect, tempted men to think that they might attain prosperity by doing injustice. As Lincoln put it, where slavery had previously stood, on the basis of the Declaration of Independence as morally wrong but tolerated by necessity, Douglas put it on "the cotton gin basis," as profitable and so not to be condemned.[43]

What Lincoln said he hated about Douglas's indifference to slavery as a moral wrong was that it taught men to think "that there is no right principle of action but self-interest."[44] The cotton gin, like the "evil genius" Lincoln said attended Douglas, had led "very many good men to doubt there being any advantage in virtue over vice." But real prosperity is no more compatible with vice than self-government is with slavery. When Douglas contemplated the "power and greatness" of the nation in 1858, he saw only the "smile[s]" of "Divine Providence." He forgot, as Lincoln did not, that Jefferson "trembled for his country when he remembered that God was just."[45]

For Lincoln, a "right of property in slavery" is incompatible with the Constitution because it is incompatible with security for "the blessings of liberty [for] ourselves and our posterity" (*Preamble, Constitution*). So Frederick Douglass could say of Lincoln that his opposition to slavery had its "motive and mainspring in his patriotic devotion to the interests of his own race."[46] Stephen Douglas defends his indifference to the moral status of slavery by saying that he "care[s] more" for the "rights of the white men" than "for all the [N]egroes in Christendom." But Douglass and Lincoln understood that indifference to slavery is the greatest threat to those rights. Slavery was not the business only of the states that had it. It "endangers [the liberties of the WHOLE PEOPLE] more than any, or all other causes."[47]

The "wisdom" of the Framers was their understanding that the argument of the Declaration of Independence constituted the law of freedom and to frame the nation's fundamental law in accord with it.[48] The crisis posed by Negro slavery was its erosion of the moral standard of the Declaration of Independence for the government. The *Dred Scott* decision of 1857 and "the next Dred Scott" that would follow in due course were making the law itself lawless. Lincoln did not say, as Douglas alleged, that the Constitution of 1787 was contrary to the law of God. But he did imply that Douglas and his friends were making it so. When this process was complete, the Union would no longer be capable of securing "the blessings of liberty." It would be a Union not "worthy of the saving."[49]

To Mold Public Sentiment: The Role of the Democratic Statesman

Part of Douglas's criticism of Lincoln's resistance to the *Dred*

Scott decision is that they are engaged in a race for the U.S. Senate and "under the Constitution, a Senator has no right to interfere with the decision of judicial tribunals." But Congress makes rules for the regulation of the national territories, and Lincoln had pledged to use this power, despite Taney's opinion, to prohibit slavery in the territories. He and his party would also support a candidate at the next presidential election who, if successful, would use his constitutional power to place on the Court judges committed to the Republican understanding of the policy of the Framers toward slavery.[50]

But Lincoln knew that the constitutional powers of senator, president, and judge were nothing if their exercise of these powers was not sustained by the public.

> In this age, and this country, public sentiment is every thing. *With* it, nothing can fail; *against* it, nothing can succeed. Whoever moulds public sentiment, goes deeper than he who enacts statutes, or pronounces judicial decisions. He makes possible the inforcement of these, else impossible.[51]

In this understanding of what was required to preserve popular government, Lincoln took a deeper view than *The Federalist*. Where Madison seeks to shape institutions, Lincoln seeks to shape men. In both the *Lyceum* speech and his campaign against Douglas, Lincoln's primary aim is to mold the habits, ideas, and opinions necessary to preserve liberty. The institutional devices to promote the cause of justice which Madison defends in *The Federalist* are a *necessary* but not a *sufficient* safeguard of freedom. Beneath laws and institutions and supporting them are the sentiments of the people.[52]

So Taney's decision actually required Senator Douglas's influence to be sustained. Slavery would be fastened upon the Constitution only when Douglas's attitude of moral indifference to slavery shall have "gain[ed] upon the public mind sufficiently" to assure popular support of the Court's decision. Douglas's "*general maxims about liberty*" were "preparing . . . the way for making the institution of Slavery national." These liberal maxims, "that 'whoever wants Slavery has a right to have it;' that 'upon principles of equality it should be allowed to go everywhere,'" constituted "the best instrument" to sow the seed of tyranny in the public mind.[53]

When public sentiment had been fully trained to indifference toward injustice to a class of people, the nation as a whole will have lost the strongest bulwark against injustice to itself. Douglas's maxims of liberty would have led to freedom's destruction.

> And when you have stricken down the principles of the Declaration of Independence, and thereby consigned the [N]egro to hopeless and eternal bondage, are you quite sure that the demon will not turn and rend you? Will not the people then be ready to go down beneath the tread of any tyrant who may wish to rule them?[54]

At the deepest level the crisis Lincoln confronted was a corruption of American public sentiment. The fruit of freedom itself occasions such corruption. Like Douglas, Lincoln takes pride in the fact that America is "a mighty nation." The nation at its birth had "vastly less of everything we deem desirable among men" than it did in 1858. Lincoln attributes this "rise of prosperity" to the nation's freedom. Yet there has also been a decline: "On the question of liberty, as a principle, we are not what we have been."

The rise of prosperity caused this decline: "we have grown fat." No longer fearing to be "the political slaves of King George," we have become "greedy" of the profit to be made by enslaving others.[55] This result was not unanticipated by "the Fathers of the Republic." "Wise statesmen as they were, they knew the *tendency of prosperity to breed tyrants.*" Their response was to so firmly establish in the public mind the self-evident truth of equality of right that when "in the distant future" any found it in their self-interest to deny this equality "their posterity might look up again to the Declaration of Independence and take courage to renew the battle which their fathers began."[56] On a deeper level than that of laws and institutions, the Declaration serves to sustain the nation's freedom. As long as this document is venerated by the people, its unqualified affirmation of the equality of right of all men instills in them the deepest hostility to every form of "tyranny and oppression."[57]

To protect the Union, Douglas narrowed the Declaration's scope, insisting that it applies only to whites. In defense of what he understands to be the fundamental principle of the Constitution, he belittles those who appeal to the Declaration's "abstract truth."[58] But such a defense of Union weakens freedom and this manner of protecting the Constitution subverts it. Madison in *Federalist* 51 understands that a government that runs athwart the love of justice cannot stand. To speak of the Declaration as Douglas does neglects the deepest dimension of the founding generation's statecraft, their care for the public sentiment that supports free institutions.[59]

Statesmanship, Law, and the
Universal Feeling of a Community

Opposition to slavery springs from our conviction "that all Men are created equal." But when Lincoln has asked his hearers to renew their conviction that slavery is wrong, he summons them, not to a crusade against slavery where it exists, but against slavery's extension. The equality of man as a moral right "should always be kept in view as a fundamental principle" of the law. But "conditions impose necessities upon us," in this case, the toleration of slavery as a legal right where the Constitution protects it.[60] The measure of a statesman is not the intensity of his devotion to fundamental principle, but his capacity to apply it to the conditions which he must address.

In 1858 those conditions involved the presence of a smaller population of African descent among a free people mostly European in origin and descent. The greater part of the African population was enslaved and the whole of it, in the eyes of the European population, was degraded by that fact. The institution of slavery existed in only one part of the nation. The crisis this situation posed to the nation was a corruption of public sentiment. The part of the nation that protected slavery by law was insisting that it be recognized as morally right, and the part of the nation where it had been abolished by law was becoming indifferent to its moral status. When this corruption was complete, and the nation had lost sight of the law's "fundamental principle," the equality of all human beings, the law would itself be lawless.

The task of the statesman in this crisis was to reawaken in each part of the nation a sense of the moral right of equality. Because the conditions of the two parts were different, this task of reform would also be twofold, one part addressed to those who sanctioned lawlessness, the other to those who were becoming indifferent to the lawlessness of their fellow citizens. How, in Lincoln's judgment, the democratic statesman ought to proceed in such a case may be gathered from his analysis of another reform movement, the contemporary effort to combat alcohol abuse.

This analysis occurs in a speech Lincoln delivered to the Springfield Washington Temperance Society, a group that appears to have been an 1840s counterpart of Alcoholics Anonymous. Lincoln takes as his starting point the success of the "Washingtonians," in reforming the intemperate as compared to other temperance organizations. This success, Lincoln argues, shows that "the champions engaged" and "the tactics . . . adopted" by the other groups "have not been the most proper."[61]

The traditional champions, "Preachers, Lawyers, hired agents," are lacking on two counts. There is a want of "sympathy of feeling [and] interest" between them and the intemperate. On the one hand, they have not themselves experienced the "miseries" of intemperance. On the other hand, they are assumed to have some motive other than the well-being of those whose practice they would change. The "Washingtonians," as former "victim[s] of intemperance," face neither of these barriers.[62]

Lincoln objects to the "system of tactics" that it was both injudicious in its approach and "uncharitable" in its treatment of the intemperate. It was uncharitable because it assumed that the intemperate were "incorrigible" and could have no share in the advantages of reform. Most people had too much sympathy with their fellow human beings to support such a proposal.[63]

But above all, the system of tactics was injudicious, for it relied greatly on "denunciation," an approach both "impolitic and unjust." It is impolitic because men will cling to what is harmful rather than be "driven" "even to [their] own best interest." They will "meet denunciation with denunciation." But denunciation was also unjust. Human beings are such as to regard as right the practices to which they are accustomed and "the use of intoxicating drinks" is, to us, "as old as the world itself." However harmful the use of alcohol may now be thought to be by some, until now most people thought it a good thing. This fact cannot be disregarded.

> The universal *sense* of mankind, on any subject, is an argument, or at least an *influence* not easily overcome . . . and men ought not, in justice, to be denounced for yielding to it, in any case, or for giving it up slowly, *especially*, where they are backed by interest, fixed habits, or burning appetite.[64]

The Washingtonians avoided both these errors. Their own experience taught them that the habitual drunkard was not incorrigible. Also, they knew that denunciation was unwarranted. "*They* knew that generally, [the intemperate] are kind, generous and charitable, even beyond the example of their more staid and sober neighbors." Having highlighted the role of the intemperate and now reformed, Lincoln addresses the temperate. They can help by "signing the pledge" not to drink. This action will exercise a "moral influence" on their fellows that is a "powerful engine" of good.[65]

This analysis of the best way to fight alcohol abuse reflects Lincoln's considered judgment of the best way to fight slavery. Near the end of the *Temperance* speech, Lincoln compares the "temperance revolution" with "our political revolution of '76." As the goal of the former is universal self-control, the goal of the latter is universal freedom. He caps his comparison by looking forward to the final "victory" of these revolutions "when there shall be neither *a slave* nor a drunkard on the earth."[66]

Lincoln's own approach to the problem of Negro slavery conforms exactly to the recommendations offered in the *Temperance* speech. Henry Clay is forever on his lips in the campaign of 1858, in part because Clay was a slaveholder who condemned slavery. Another example is drawn from Lincoln's speeches in Massachusetts in 1848 on behalf of the Whig presidential candidate, Zachary Taylor of Louisiana.[67]

Lincoln was not a slaveholder, but he was born in a slave state, Kentucky. He made use of that fact in the debates with Douglas. Douglas charged that Lincoln would not repeat his antislavery message in southern Illinois, in "Egypt." But at Jonesboro, the southernmost location of the debates, Lincoln reiterated his opposition to slavery extension. Having done so, he then claimed kinship with the Southern people and, in effect, charged Douglas with slandering them. Douglas thought he would be afraid to articulate his position among them, Lincoln said, because he, Douglas, having been "raised further north, . . . has some horrid idea of what this people might be induced to do."[68]

Lincoln was never so impolitic as to denounce the population of the slave states.[69] In the canvass of 1854 Lincoln was careful to include with his criticism of slavery the observation that "[the Southern people] are just what we would be in their situation."[70] In the *Temperance* speech Lincoln denies that those who "have never fallen victims" may claim "any mental or moral superiority over those who have." But he goes farther:

> I believe, if we take habitual drunkards as a class, their heads and their hearts will bear an advantageous comparison with those of any

other class . . . The demon of intemperance ever seems to have delighted in sucking the blood of genius and of generosity . . . He ever seems to have gone forth, like the Egyptian angel of death, commissioned to slay if not the first, the fairest born of every family.[71]

If one substitutes "slaveholders" or "the slave states" for "habitual drunkards," the result is provocative. In the revolution of 1776, what state might better claim to be the first or the fairest born of the American Union if not the home of Washington and Jefferson?[72] But most important, Lincoln is not so wanting in judgment as to "indulge" in wholesale denunciation of his fellow citizens as unjust.

Slavery is undoubtedly unjust as measured by moral right, but the practice of slavery in the South must be measured by the conditions that existed there. Those conditions imposed a necessity on Southern society that made the charge of injustice, in an important way, itself unjust.[73] Anyone born into Southern society before and during Lincoln's lifetime found the institution of slavery in place like "the use of intoxicating drinks" generally, "recognized by every body, used by every body, and repudiated by nobody."[74] In short, the "universal sense" of Southern society, sanctioned by custom and authorized by law, was that slavery was a moral, social, and political good. For example, Huck Finn genuinely felt he was doing something morally wrong by assisting Jim in his flight from Miss Watson.[75] Recognition of this fact requires that the statesman adopt a gradualist approach to the end of this evil.

The part the free states could play was to take the antislavery pledge wherever it had authority, within their own domain and in the national territory.[76] The 1850 legislation[77] that *did not* prohibit slavery in the Utah and New Mexico territories was understood by the advocates of slavery as a victory for their cause though they did not expect slavery to be established there. The danger in 1858 was that, under Douglas's influence, this "powerful engine" of free state opinion was being turned away from opposition to slavery, thereby giving tacit support to it.

In this turning the racial character of American slavery was of critical importance. Free state opinion would never doubt the wrongness of slavery for persons of European descent. But it might be brought to doubt the wrongness of slavery if it were a question of a "man who has a skin of a different color."[78] Racial difference combined with slavery's physical degradation of the Negro race imbued those of European descent with a near insuperable prejudice of African inferiority. If that prejudice could not be overcome, it must be separated from the idea that slavery for this people was not wrong. To do this Lincoln had to concede to racial prejudice the utmost compatible with opposition to Negro slavery.

> I have no purpose to introduce political and social equality between the white and the black races. There is a physical difference between the two, which in my judgment will probably forever forbid their living together upon the footing of perfect equality, and inasmuch as it becomes a necessity that there must be a difference, I, as well as Judge Douglas, am in favor of the race to which I belong, having the superior position . . . but I hold that notwithstanding all this, there is no reason in the world why the negro is not entitled to all the natural rights enumerated in the Declaration of Independence, the right to life, liberty and the pursuit of happiness. I hold that he is as much entitled to these as the white man.[79]

Lincoln's acceptance of racial inequality and white supremacy, however qualified, sounds harsh to our ears today. But politics is always a matter of the here and now and the crisis Lincoln faced could be resolved in no other way. In order to keep alive the sense of the wrongness of slavery, and hence the moral rightness of equality, it was necessary to sacrifice a part of equality.[80] That necessity was imposed by the feeling of the community. "Whether this feeling accords with justice and sound judgment, is not the sole question, if indeed, it is any part of it. A universal feeling, whether well or ill-founded, can not be safely disregarded."[81]

The statesman's task is to mold public sentiment. But there are limits to the extent to which he can do this. Beyond these limits the statesman who fails to accommodate public sentiment must expect the defeat of his program. In 1858 the urgent need was not to raise public sentiment to embrace the political and social equality of the races but to keep it from falling to the point where it no longer acknowledged the wrong of slavery.[82]

If public sentiment of the wrongness of slavery could be preserved in the free states and they could be brought to act upon it, then the statesman could afford to take a charitable view of the Southern people. The slaveholders themselves, as well as the Africans they enslaved, were victims of injustice, and humanity required that the statesman of the Union have a care for their well-being.

To promote a separation of slave and free states in order that, to paraphrase the *Temperance* speech, the grace of justice might abound to the just, would be "like throwing fathers and brothers overboard, to lighten the boat for our security."[83]

If the Constitution and laws were preserved from corruption, their influence could be expected, in time, to move the slave states to abolish slavery. And if this took "a hundred years," nonetheless, given the power of universal feeling in every community, no matter how unsound or ill-founded, it might be best for both races to allow the institution of slavery to be abolished in this way.[84]

A Democracy Based on Natural Law

In the struggle to preserve his fellow citizens' commitment to the "fundamental principle" of the law, equality, Lincoln relied greatly on their loyalty to their own tradition. He could base his appeal on the Declaration of Independence and ask his countrymen to renew their "ancient faith."[85] Thus the success of Lincoln's endeavor depended in part on this piece of good fortune. He had been preceded by wise statesmen who anticipated just such a crisis as this. Yet loyalty to the Fathers alone could never be adequate. Experience led some, like John C. Calhoun, to deny the Declaration's affirmation outright and others, like Douglas, to do so in a "sneaking way."[86]

Ultimately, what gives the Declaration of Independence its power is not that it is the work of the Fathers but that its message is rooted in our nature. It may be natural for us to become "greedy" in times of prosperity, but it is also natural for us to love justice at all times.[87] If the Declaration had never existed, Lincoln would have lost a rhetorical advantage, not his mainstay. That mainstay is the natural feeling of mankind. In an antislavery speech in 1854 Lincoln said, "repeal the Declaration of Independence—repeal all past history, you still can not repeal human nature." That nature fills man's heart with a hatred of slavery "and out of the abundance of his heart, his mouth will continue to speak."[88]

The "universal feeling" of a community cuts two ways. It both limits and supports the statesman's endeavor to bring legal right into conformity with "justice and sound judgment." For if that feeling is shaped by the practices to which the community is used, regardless of justice, it is also, for Lincoln, shaped by nature which inclines us to justice. So if social experience made Huck Finn believe Jim to be property, human experience made him recognize him as a man.[89] By the same token, Lincoln appeals to this universal feeling of the Southern people to keep alive the "ancient faith" in equality that belonged to them as Americans:

> you have amongst you, a sneaking individual, of the class of native tyrants, known as the "SLAVE-DEALER." . . . You despise him utterly. You do not recognize him as a friend, or even as an honest man. Your children must not play with his; they may rollick freely with the little [N]egroes, but not with the "slave-dealers" children . . . Now why is this? . . . Is there any mistaking it? . . . it is your sense of justice, and human sympathy, continually telling you, that the poor [N]egro has some natural right to himself—that those who deny it, and make mere merchandise of him, deserve kickings, contempt and death.[90]

"Universal feeling" is partly, but not entirely, a matter of social condition. A part of it is natural, though it is no less "natural" for some to be devoid of it, namely, the "lawless in spirit," the "native tyrant." Lincoln regards the power of universal feeling as the best support for "the argument in favor of the existence of an over-ruling Providence."[91] In his statesmanship Lincoln employs the idea of an over-ruling Providence as the best support for a free democratic regime. Thus, he asserts that the preservation of America's free political institutions depends first of all on a providential universal feeling, "the *love of liberty* God has planted in our bosoms."[92] By respecting universal feeling the statesman cherishes the best resource available to him to bring legal right into greater conformity with moral right.

But along with that love of liberty for ourselves goes a sense of obligation: we must not, for personal advantage, deny the good of liberty to others. The power of that natural sense of obligation or duty can be measured by Lincoln's greatest use of the idea of an "over-ruling Providence." In the spring of 1865, after four years of bloody conflict that touched the lives of every citizen with personal loss, Lincoln spoke in this way to the nation:

> If God will that [this mighty scourge of war] continue, until all the wealth piled by the bond-man's two hundred and fifty years of unrequited toil shall be sunk, and until every drop of blood drawn with the lash, shall be paid by another drawn with the sword, as was said three thousand years ago, so still it must be said, "the judgments of the Lord are true and righteous altogether."[93]

The sense of duty that accompanies our love of liberty and together with it comprises our love of justice cannot be totally abolished in us, but it can be obscured. Prosperity has a tendency to dull its ardor. The statesman's task is to devise means that nourish that love and keep it vibrant. Lincoln's complaint against Douglas is that he does just the opposite. He aids the corrupting trend of the times. "He is blowing out the moral lights around us, when he contends that whoever wants slaves has a right to hold them; . . . he is penetrating, so far as lies in his power, the human soul, and eradicating the light of reason and the love of liberty."[94]

This was the threat that constituted the crisis of the nation. Lincoln's greatest accomplishment as a statesman is that he recognized and successfully countered it. He saved the American regime by rekindling within the souls of his countrymen their natural love of liberty.

Notes

1. For an excellent discussion of this crisis and Lincoln's understanding of it, see Harry Jaffa's *Crisis of the House Divided: An Interpretation of the Lincoln–Douglas Debates* (Garden City, N.Y.: Doubleday, 1959; reprint, Chicago: University of Chicago Press, 1982).

2. *Speech at Springfield*, July 17, 1858, in *The Collected Works of Abraham Lincoln*, 8 vols., Roy Basler, ed. (New Brunswick, N.J.: Rutgers University Press, 1953), 2:507. All quotations from Lincoln are taken from the Basler edition of Lincoln's *Works*, hereafter cited as *CW*.

3. *Speeches at Quincy*, October 13, 1858, *CW* 3:254; *Speech at Chicago*, July 10, 1858, 2:492.

4. Stephen A. Douglas (1813–61), influential leader of the Democratic party in the years before the Civil War, three times elected senator from Illinois, Democratic nominee for the presidency in 1860, and a strong Unionist. Douglas's bid for reelection in 1858 was unsuccessfully contested by Lincoln. The Lincoln–Douglas debates occurred as part of that campaign, August 21–October 15.

5. *Speech at Alton*, October 15, 1858, *CW* 3:310.

6. During the years he served there, 1834–42, the Illinois state legislature dealt with the issue of slavery on a number of occasions.

7. Hereafter, *Lyceum*; citations will give only page number of *CW* 1.

8. *Lyceum*, 108. Cf. Lincoln's praise of Henry Clay whom he called his "beau ideal of a statesman": "He loved his country partly because it was his own country, but mostly because it was a free country" (*Eulogy on Henry Clay*, July 6, 1852, *CW* 2:126).

9. Ibid., 111–12.

10. Ibid., 111, 113, 114, 112.

11. Ibid., 111.

12. William Lloyd Garrison (1805–79) founded a newspaper, *The Liberator* (1831), to call for the immediate abolition of slavery. In 1832 he founded the New England Anti-Slavery Society; in 1840 he became the leader of the American Anti-Slavery Society. Garrison was deliberately aggressive in his campaign against slavery. Other opponents of slavery found Garrison's approach unduly extreme.

13. Russel Nye, *William Lloyd Garrison and the Humanitarian Reformers* (Boston: Little, Brown, 1955), 142 and 164, for Garrison's burning of a copy of the Constitution at a July Fourth celebration in Framingham, Mass., in 1854.

14. *Eulogy on Henry Clay*, July 6, 1852, *CW* 2:130; *Speech at Quincy*, October 13, 1858, *CW* 2:130, 3:255.

15. *Debates, Jonesboro*, September 15, 1858, *CW* 3:131.

16. *CW* 1:75.

17. *Lyceum*, 112–13.

18. *Speech at Peoria*, October 16, 1854, *CW* 2:266, italics added. Hereafter, *Peoria*; citations will give only page number of *CW* 2.

19. At the Constitutional Convention, in a speech that anticipates the argument of *Federalist* 10, Madison offers African slavery as an example of majority tyranny. See Madison, *Notes of Debates in the Federal Convention of 1787*, June 6.

20. *Speech at Edwardsville*, September 11, 1858, *CW* 3:95.

21. *Debates, Alton*, October 15, 1858, *CW* 3:284. Douglas's speeches in the *Debates* are included with Lincoln's in *CW*. Speeches given in the Lincoln–Douglas debates will be identified as *Debates* followed by the location. The first reference to each of the seven debates will give location and date; subsequent citations will be by location only. As all the debates are in volume three of *CW*, hereafter references to *Debates* will give page number only.

22. *House Divided Speech, Springfield*, June 16, 1858, *CW* 2:466.

23. *Debates, Freeport*, August 27, 1858, 40.

24. *Debates, Jonesboro, Galesburg, Quincy*, September 15, October 7, 13, 1858, respectively, 112, 242, 244, 267.

25. *Debates, Quincy*, 255.

26. *Speech at Springfield*, July 17, 1858, *CW* 2:517.

27. *Debates, Galesburg, Quincy*, 233, 278.

28. *Debates, Alton, Freeport*, 317, 51–52; see also, *Debates, Galesburg, Quincy*, 217–18, 268–69, 279; *Letter to B. Clarke Lundy*, November 26, 1858, *CW* 3:342.

29. *Debates, Alton, Galesburg*, 317, 231.

30. Douglas uses this language repeatedly to describe his and Lincoln's position.

31. *Debates, Jonesboro*, 117; see also, *Alton*, 308.

32. *Debates, Jonesboro, Quincy, Alton*, 114, 275, 290, 297.

33. *Debates, Galesburg, Alton*, 226, 308.
34. See especially deliberations of July 11–13 and August 8, 21–22, 1787.
35. *Speech at Chicago*, July 10, 1858, *CW* 2:501.
36. *Debates, Alton, Peoria*, 306–7, 274.
37. *Debates, Alton*, 308, 307.
38. *Debates, Galesburg, Quincy*, 230, 257.
39. *Peoria*, 275.
40. *House Divided Speech*, June 16, 1858, *CW* 2:467; see also *Debates, Ottawa, Quincy*, 27, 250.
41. *Peoria*, 276.
42. Between 1776 and 1800 the volume of raw cotton imported by England increased tenfold. In the United States, however, only a small coastal area supported the strain of cotton that could be cultivated profitably. Eli Whitney's invention of the cotton gin in 1793 permitted the profitable cultivation of other strains that could be grown throughout the South with the result that "in the four years after the gin appeared in the United States production of cotton doubled." By 1850 the United States was supplying more than 82 percent of a "vastly increased" English demand for cotton and 60 percent of the slaves in this country were engaged in its production. Avery Craven, *The Coming of the Civil War*, 2nd ed. rev. (Scribners 1957; reprint ed., Chicago: University of Chicago Press, 1966), 101–2, 110.
43. *Debates, Quincy*, 276.
44. *Peoria*, 255.
45. *Debates, Freeport, Jonesboro, Galesburg*, 44–45, 178, 220.
46. Speech at the unveiling of the Freedmen's Monument, Washington, D.C., April 14, 1876, "Appendix," *Life and Times of Frederick Douglass* (New York: Bonanza Books, 1962; reprint of rev. ed. of 1892), 484.
47. *Debates, Alton, Peoria*, 322, 270; see also, *Debates, Quincy*, 254.
48. See *Speech at Chicago*, July 10, 1858, *CW* 2:500; *Speech at Carlinsville*, August 8, 1858 *CW*, 3:79.
49. *Peoria*, 276.
50. *Debates, Quincy*, 266; *Speech at Columbus*, September 16, 1859, *CW* 3:419.
51. *Fragment: Notes for Speeches*, c. August 21, 1858, *CW* 2:552–53. For this reason, Lincoln could console himself for his loss to Douglas in 1858 with the thought that he had made an impact upon public sentiment. See his *Letter to Anson G. Henry*, November 19, 1858, *CW* 3:339.
52. Cf. Tocqueville, *Democracy in America*, J. P. Mayer, ed., George Lawrence, trans. (Garden City, N.Y.: Doubleday, 1969), 305–8, a section devoted to the thesis that "mores," a nation's ideas, opinions, sentiments, "do more than the laws" to maintain "the democratic republic in the United States."
53. *House Divided Speech*, June 16, 1858, *CW* 2:467; *Debates, Galesburg*, 233, italics added.
54. *Speech at Bloomington*, September 4, 1858, *CW* 3:90.

55. *Speech at Chicago*, July 10, 1858, *CW* 2:499; *Letter to George Robertson*, August 15, 1855, *CW* 2:318.

56. *Speech at Lewistown*, August 17, 1858, *CW* 2:546, italics added.

57. See *Letter to Henry L. Pierce and Others*, April 6, 1859, *CW* 3:376.

58. *Debates, Ottawa*, 9–10, italics added.

59. Cf. Herbert Storing, *What the Anti-Federalists Were For* (Chicago: University of Chicago Press, 1981), pp. 75–76.

60. *Debates, Alton*, 303; *Speech at Springfield*, July 17, 1858, *CW* 2:501.

61. *Temperance Address*, February 22, 1842, *CW* 1:272. Hereafter, *Temperance*; citations will give only page number of *CW* 1.

62. Ibid.

63. Ibid., 272, 275.

64. Ibid., 272–73, 274, 275.

65. Ibid., 273–74, 277.

66. Ibid., 278–79, italics added.

67. *Speeches at Lowell, Taunton, Massachusetts*, September 16, 21, 1848, *CW* 2:6, 8.

68. *Debates, Jonesboro*, 135.

69. By contrast, Garrison declared it to be his intention to "displease" people.

70. *Peoria*, 255.

71. *Temperance*, 278.

72. As a social and an economic institution slavery shaped a civilization and a character that was not without traits of "genius and generosity." See Tocqueville, *Democracy in America*, 376.

73. Cf. Thomas Aquinas, *Treatise on Law* (Chicago: Regnery, 1970), pp. 91–92: Question 96, "Of the Power of Human Law." "Now a measure should be homogeneous with that which it measures, . . . Wherefore laws imposed on men should also be in keeping with their condition, . . . [Thus] many things are permissible to men not perfect in virtue, which would be intolerable in a virtuous man." "Otherwise these imperfect ones, being unable to bear such precepts, would break out into yet greater evils."

74. *Temperance*, 274.

75. Mark Twain, *The Adventures of Huckleberry Finn*, Chapter 31.

76. See *Speech at Cincinnati*, September 17, 1859, where Lincoln professes concern that under the influence of Douglas's doctrine of indifference to the moral status of slavery, states like Ohio might repeal their prohibitions of slavery, *CW* 3:433–44.

77. Many in the North feared that the territory acquired in the Mexican War (1846–48) would expand that part of the United States in which slavery was sanctioned. This led to a proposal, the Wilmot Proviso (offered August 8, 1846 and numerous times after that), that slavery be prohibited in the new territory. The proviso passed the House repeatedly but never cleared the Senate. Southern militants threatened to secede if it was passed and a crisis ensued. The crisis grew more severe when it appeared that Zachary Taylor, the newly elected (1848) Whig president, supported the proviso. The

Compromise of 1850, a set of eight measures proposed by Henry Clay and successfully guided through the Senate by Stephen Douglas, allayed sectional strife, at least for the time, by giving each section a part, but not all, of what it wanted. By the compromise a great part of the new territory was admitted at once as the free state of California, while in the rest of the new territory, slavery was not prohibited.

78. *Speech at Cincinnati*, September 17, 1859, *CW* 3:445.

79. *Debates, Ottawa*, 16; see also *Charleston*, 145–46.

80. Gary Wills rightly notes that "Lincoln's accommodation to the prejudice of the time did not imply any agreement with the points he found it useless to dispute," *Lincoln at Gettysburg* (New York: Simon and Schuster, 1992), p. 96.

81. *Peoria*, 256.

82. *Peoria*, 265; *Speech at Columbus, Ohio*, September 16, 1859, *CW* 3:423–25.

83. *Temperance*, 275.

84. *Debates, Ottawa*, 18.

85. *Peoria*, 266.

86. *Debates, Alton*, 301–2.

87. Cf. Thomas Aquinas, *Treatise on Law*, pp. 71–72: Question 94, "Of the Natural Law," sixth article, "Whether the law of nature can be abolished from the heart of man." Thomas answers that as to "general principles," the natural law "can nowise be blotted out from men's hearts. But it is blotted out in the case of a particular action, in so far as reason is hindered from applying the general principle to a particular point of practice." This "blotting out" of secondary precepts is "either by evil persuasions, . . . ; or by vicious customs and corrupt habits." Douglas's efforts in the free states fall into the first category; the operation of the institution itself in the slave states falls into the second.

88. *Peoria*, 271.

89. See, for example, *Huckelberry Finn*, the end of Chapter 23 and Chapter 31 where Huck decides for Jim even it if is "wicked."

90. *Peoria*, 264–65.

91. *Temperance*, 275.

92. *Speech at Edwardsville*, September 11, 1858, *CW* 3:95.

93. *Second Inaugural Address*, March 4, 1865, *CW* 8:333.

94. *Debates, Galesburg*, 234.

Suggested Reading

Charnwood, Lord. *Abraham Lincoln*. New York: Henry Holt, 1917.

Jaffa, Harry V. *Crisis of the House Divided: An Interpretation of the Lincoln–Douglas Debates*. Garden City, N.Y.: Doubleday, 1959.

Lincoln, Abraham:
  Address Before the Young Men's Lyceum of Springfield, January 27, 1838.
  Address Delivered Before the Springfield Washington Temperance Society, February 22, 1842.
  Speech at Peoria, October 16, 1854.
  House Divided Speech, June 16, 1858.
  Speech at Springfield, July 17, 1858.
  Debates with Douglas, August 21–October 15, 1858.
  Speech at Edwardsville, September 11, 1858.
Potter, David M. Completed and edited by Don E. Fehrenbacher. *The Impending Crisis, 1848–1861*. New York: Harper and Row, 1976.

27

Frederick Douglass's
Constitution

Diana J. Schaub

Americans are often said to be both a legalistic and a moralistic people. Despite the litigiousness of American life, American deference to the law is, in the main, not pinched or narrow, for the reason that it does not originally stem from the conventionalist or positivist reduction of justice to legality. Instead, Americans understand justice to have an independent existence, offering a universal ground of political right. Out of the permutations of this belief in a higher law (whether divine or natural) the various strains of American moralism are produced.

In the United States, legalism and moralism can usually be brought comfortably together under one roof—the Constitution. Accordingly, it might be more accurate and more generous to say that Americans are a constitutional people. Americans revere a fundamental law of their own making ("We, the People . . ."), but that act of popular sovereignty was one endowed with a conscience. The Constitution gives formal expression to the great truth of the Declaration of Independence: the equality of all men. Constitutionalism in its fullest sense does more than limit government. By dedicating the people to a proposition, it even limits self-government. It attempts to ensure that popular government will be good government, by placing certain checks on the unbridled will of the majority.

Given the creedal character of American political life, we should not find it surprising that almost all controversial issues soon become constitutional issues. Throughout our history, no question has been more divisive than that of the rights and place of the black population in America. Just as the existence of slavery threatened to rend the Union physically, so too it threatened to rend the parchment regime by severing the relation between our two founding documents, the Declaration and the Constitution.

In the antebellum period, the breakdown of constitutionalism was clear and complete in the thought of both proslavery and antislavery factions. Southern apologists for chattel slavery were driven to reinterpret and eventually repudiate the Declaration. Chief Justice Roger Taney, for instance, in his 1857 *Dred Scott* decision, denied that the Declaration recognized the natural rights of nonwhites. Earlier, South Carolina Senator John C. Calhoun went so far as to call the Declaration's assertion of natural human equality a "self-evident lie." Stripping the fundamental principle of equality from the Constitution allowed slavery's defenders to elevate the pragmatic compromises of the Constitution into moral mandates. Thus, Taney claimed that on the basis of the Fifth Amendment's protection of the right of property, slavery was entitled to permanent protection and expansion. He perverted the intention of the Bill of Rights, transforming it from the palladium of individual liberties into a scourge in the hands of the slaveocracy. Taney neglected the fact that although there are constitutional provisions relating to slavery, nowhere in the document are slaves affirmed to be rightfully the property of another.[1]

Displaying a very strange communion of extremes, that wing of the abolitionists who followed William Lloyd Garrison accepted their enemies' reading of the Constitution. The radical Garrisonian abolitionists, like the Southern apologists for slavery, saw the Constitution as a proslavery document. In their favored language of biblical prophecy, the Constitution was "a covenant with Death and an agreement with Hell" that must be disavowed in order to uphold the revolutionary tradition of the Declaration. Like Calhoun and company, the Garrisonians saw no essential connection between the Declaration and the Constitution. While the proslavery faction denounced the Declaration, these abolitionists denounced the Constitution. The Garrisonians denied both the legitimacy and the possibility of "working within the system" for the gradual abolition of slavery. They restricted themselves to the means of moral suasion. According to the Garrisonians, the only way to work for slavery's demise was to take to the lecture platform and transform opinion. Political means such as the ballot box, elective office, and law courts were all held to be illegitimate, since they were tainted by the initial compromise with slavery. The Garrisonians sought, perhaps paradoxically, to effect massive, radical, and immediate change through the agitation of the individual conscience.

As the crisis of the Civil War approached, there were those who strove to preserve a properly articulated constitutionalism and to halt the slide into antirepublican illiberalism (whether of the antinomian or the slaveocratic sort). Abraham Lincoln was preeminent among those who spoke for the virtuous mean of constitutionalism. It must be stressed that this mean was not arrived at by splitting the difference between the two camps. The Lincolnian mean has an intransigence all its own and might be said to exist not so much between, as above, the extremes.

The one who settled for the muddy middle ground was Stephen Douglas, Lincoln's political rival in the 1850s. Douglas advocated the doctrine of "popular sovereignty." This meant leaving the subject of slavery to be dealt with by the local majority in each new state or territory. Lincoln dubbed Douglas's position the "Don't care policy," because Douglas professed not to care whether slavery was voted up or voted down. As Douglas understood the principle of majority rule, the people of America could enslave others or not as they chose. In effect, Douglas transformed the right of self-government into nothing more than "the advantage of the stronger." By counseling indifference to the question of the moral right or wrong of slavery, Douglas uncoupled the right of self-government from its mooring in the Declaration's assertion of the equality of all men. Douglas had forgotten the words of Thomas Jefferson's First Inaugural Address:

> that though the will of the majority is in all cases to prevail, that will, to be rightful, must be reasonable; . . . the minority possess their equal rights, which equal laws must protect, and to violate which would be oppression.[2]

In opposition to all those who sought to make a nullity of the parchment regime, Lincoln tried to hold together the Declaration and the Constitution. In order to prove the possibility of a nondespotic democracy, he summoned the nation to principled action on the slavery question. For Lincoln, principled action meant no compromise with respect to the wrongness of slavery. This should not be confused with the Garrisonian position: no compromise with slavery. The latter formula, which naturally metamorphosed into "no union with slaveholders," expressed a fanatical insistence upon the purity of practice. For instance, a strict Garrisonian would refuse to vote even if by that one vote slavery would be abolished, because the vote itself would have been cast under a corrupt system. Being scrupulous about the means they employed, they refused to touch the devil, even to kill him. Lincoln was not so squeamish. He was willing to accommodate himself to harsh facts and, above all, to stick with the constitutional bargain. In accordance with what was called "the federal consensus," Lincoln pledged not to interfere with slavery in states where it had long existed. However, he was resolutely opposed to any further spread of the institution into western lands. While he was prepared to make certain accommodations to the preexisting condition of slavery, he insisted that the condition be recognized and treated as an evil. The moral blame attaching to slavery must be preserved, and the institution must not be allowed to spread to unaffected areas of the nation.

Lincoln believed that his policy of physical and moral quarantine was a continuation of the approach crafted by the Founders. For Lincoln, the Constitution itself provided the model of principled action with respect to slavery. It was not a proslavery document as both Calhoun and Garrison insisted. It was not even neutral on the question, as Douglas claimed. Lincoln argued that the Founders, in order to secure the Union (i.e., gain the consent of states like Georgia and South Carolina), had accorded a measure of protection to the existing evil of slavery. But they had also, by careful draftsmanship, withheld from it moral approval. This is most clearly indicated by the fact that in the three constitutional provisions relating to slavery, the word "slave" or "slavery" is never used. Instead, those concerned are referred to as "persons." Because the Constitution did not sacrifice the principle of human equality, American practice would one day be brought into conformity with American principle. As Lincoln repeated time and again, the anomaly of slavery had originally been dealt with in such a way that "the public mind shall rest in the belief that it is in the course of ultimate extinction."[3] Lincoln's exposition of the meaning and truth of our constituting charters was an attempt to restore that nationally shared conviction of slavery's planned obsolescence.

Emancipation

While reverence for the law seemed to come naturally to Lincoln, there were others who struggled mightily before they found "political religion." Frederick Douglass (c.1817–95) was perhaps the greatest of these strugglers. The personal and intellectual odyssey that ultimately brought him to the altar of the Constitution was such that, if Lincoln is to be remembered as "the Great Emancipator," Douglass must be remembered as "the Great Self-Emancipator."

The first act of self-emancipation on the part of this famous runaway slave, abolitionist orator, and black leader was not his bodily flight north to freedom, but rather his spiritual flight, his ingenious and laborious self-education, while still a slave. As a child, Douglass had listened to his master rage that "If [a slave] learns to read the Bible it will forever unfit him to be a slave." Douglass later wrote that this speech was "the first decidedly anti-slavery lecture" he had heard, for from that moment he "understood the direct pathway from slavery to freedom."[4] With Tom Sawyer-like ingenuity, the young Douglass tricked his white playmates into revealing the secrets of the alphabet. As it happened, it was not the Bible, but a book called *The Columbian Orator* that most impressed itself on his mind. This volume was a collection of mighty speeches by the likes of Cato and George Washington extolling liberty and its blessings. Most significant for the young Douglass was the "Dialogue Between a Master and Slave" (the contribution of the editor Caleb Bingham), in which the slave's articulate and powerful condemnation of slavery wins him his freedom.

When Douglass's master hired him out for a year to Edward Covey, a man with a reputation for breaking the spirits of rebellious slaves, Douglass soon learned the limits of moral suasion and the necessity of physical resistance. He learned that in the dialogue between master and slave the slave needed more than a voice. After six months of backbreaking labor and the lash, Douglass determined not to submit to the next beating. He defended himself (never taking the offensive, but just fending off Covey's attacks) in a two-hour, hand-to-hand fight which Covey was unable to win. Covey never whipped him again. Nor did he turn Douglass over to the authorities—prevented, apparently, by his pride and financial stake in his reputation as a slave-breaker. Of this incident, Douglass said: "I had reached the point at which I was *not afraid to die.* This spirit made me a freeman in *fact,* though I still remained a slave in *form.*"[5]

In his account of these two acts of self-emancipation, Douglass suggests that the worst slavery is that of the mind and spirit, not that of the body. Indeed, the bodily slave can be freer than his master if his mind and spirit are free. Long before his body was free,

Douglass had freed his mind of ignorance and his heart of the paralyzing fear of death. In 1838, Douglass struck the blow that shattered the physical form of slavery as well, when he escaped Maryland's Eastern Shore and settled, safely and obscurely, in New Bedford, Massachusetts.

After a few years spent as a common laborer, Douglass was discovered—but not by the usual breed of slave-catcher. He was discovered instead by the Garrisonians who were eager to recruit fugitive slaves for the antislavery lecture circuit. Firsthand testimony from a "graduate from the peculiar institution, with his diploma written on his back"[6] was a most effective counter to proslavery propaganda about the mildness of slave life. Douglass accepted a position as agent of the Massachusetts Anti-Slavery Society. Despite his ardent admiration of Garrison and his newspaper *The Liberator* (by his own admission, Douglass was "[s]omething of a hero-worshiper by nature"[7]), his relations with Garrison and other presumably progressive New Englanders were far from trouble-free. Regarding him as their prize exhibit, the Garrisonians sought to keep Douglass on a short leash. They wanted him simply to recount the horrors of slavery and, they instructed, "[b]etter have a little of the plantation speech than not, . . . it is not best that you seem too learned."[8] As Douglass's oratorical powers grew, he chafed at this restriction and at the paternalism behind it. He wanted not only to retell his story, but to assess and explain it, to speak to the larger meaning of slavery, and the proper course and tactics of the fight against it.

Whatever their reservations about his rapid development (and whether those reservations were rooted strictly in concern for the cause, or in something more sinister like lingering race prejudice and envy), the Garrisonians could not hold Douglass back. In a time when Americans had a great appetite for oratory, the favorite was Frederick Douglass. His immense popularity ensured him a platform. His departures from simple narration did not, as yet, involve him in any deviation from Garrisonian dogma. He faithfully used his abilities to forward the nineteenth-century version of the seventeenth-century heresy called "come-outerism." He denounced the U.S. Constitution. He enjoined men to separate themselves from— to come out from—a corrupt church and a corrupt nation. He held it illegitimate to vote, to hold office, indeed, to engage in any political action whatsoever under the national compact.

The fears of his fellow abolitionists soon received some confirmation. The quality of his discourse and his leonine bearing were widely thought to cast doubt on his claimed slave origins. To maintain his usefulness to the cause, Douglass had to prove that he had really been a slave. In 1845, he published the first edition of his autobiography, where he disclosed the details of his former life, including his master's name and place of residence. It established him as the authentic article, but it also left the fugitive slave Douglass more than ever exposed to the danger of recapture. So he left the country and spent the next twenty months in Great Britain, rallying international sentiment against American slavery. He returned in 1847, after his freedom had been purchased for him by English friends (against the wishes of the more scrupulous Garrisonians who opposed any such complicity with the slave system). Douglass then resolved to launch his own abolitionist paper, *The North Star*, believing that

> a tolerably well-conducted press in the hands of persons of the despised race would, by calling out and making them acquainted with their own latent powers, by enkindling their hope of a future and developing their moral force, prove a most powerful means of removing prejudice and awakening an interest in them.[9]

Douglass's determination "to be a principal, and not an agent"[10] was accounted apostasy by his Boston mentors. The rift between them only worsened over time. For Douglass, now removed to Rochester, New York, independence of action inexorably produced independence of mind. He began to rethink, and then to reject, the essentials of Garrisonianism.

The starting point for his reflections can be seen in his first public address upon returning from abroad. Having been put down for a traitor in the popular press, Douglass defended the justice and the wisdom of invoking foreign aid for the overthrow of a domestic institution. His first line of defense was to assert the utter inapplicability of the term "traitor" to himself. To be a traitor, one must first belong to the collective. Douglass reminds his accusers that the laws and institutions of the United States do not even recognize him as a man, much less as a fellow citizen. He frankly admits, in fact, he insists: "I have no love for America, as such; I have no patriotism. I have no country. What country have I?"[11]

The question he poses—"What country have I?"—is the starting point of his own reflections, as well as of black American political thought generally. It is a question that does not occur to most men. For most men, in most times and places, patriotism is a natural sentiment. This was not so for America's black inhabitants. Slavery destroyed the *amor patriae* of the slaves and of some of the slaves' descendants as well.

And yet, at the same time that he draws attention to his outcast status, Douglass addresses his audience as "my fellow countrymen."[12] Moreover, he reserved a good measure of scorn for the American Colonization Society, whose many distinguished and often well-intentioned members supported the emancipation of the slaves, but only on condition of their expatriation to Africa.[13] Against both the colonizationists and those few black leaders (such as Martin R. Delany) who embraced separatism and emigration, Douglass maintained that the black man belonged in America. His birth here and his two hundred years of toil entitled him to share in America's destiny. So while he could declare himself countryless, Douglass could also declare himself (and his people) an integral part of America and its democratic experiment. In an 1849 *North Star* editorial, Douglass wrote:

> We repeat, therefore, that *we are here*; and that this is *our* country; and the question for the philosophers and statesmen of the land ought to be, What principles should dictate the policy of the action towards us? We shall neither die out, nor be driven out; but shall go with this people, either as a testimony against them, or as an evidence in their favor throughout their generations.[14]

The final sentence especially, with its biblical cadence and grandeur and its quite unbiblical opposition to any sort of exodus, shows Douglass's understanding of the black man's unique relation to America. The presence of this despised minority was a severe test of the American republic's founding creed. Of course, each new wave of immigrants was also a concrete test of American liberalism and individualism. But despite initial prejudice, the successive huddled masses (Irish, Germans, Chinese, . . .) were eventually incorporated into the body politic. By contrast, blacks seemed to be indigestible. It should be clear that Douglass's dual description of himself as both alien and familiar, both outcast and integral part, did not stem from any confusion in his own thought, but rather was necessitated by the contradictions of the existing political arrangements.

During his first years as editor of *The North Star*, Douglass kept to the official Garrisonian line. He argued that slavery drew its breath from the Constitution and that only on the Constitution's annulment could a morally acceptable and noncontradictory order be instituted. But once out of New England, Douglass had more contact with Liberty party men, Free-Soilers, and the whole crowd of political-action abolitionists. These groups subscribed to an antislavery interpretation of the Constitution and thought that slavery could be abolished through the political process. Their influence was important, for in attempting to meet their arguments, Douglass was led to reconsider "what the government of the United States is *authorized to be, and to do, by the Constitution of the United States.*"[15] In other words, he started to think about the problematic relationship between the charter of the government and the actual government.

Clearly, the interpretation of the nature of the Constitution was critical to the strategies of these two abolitionist camps. Although Douglass began his career as a Garrisonian, over time he came to repudiate the Garrisonian position and to see political action as the key to abolition. Through the writings of Frederick Douglass, we have the luxury of observing a powerful mind weighing the contending arguments and altering its convictions.

In an 1849 editorial entitled "The Constitution and Slavery," Douglass assures his readers that he still believes the Constitution to be "radically and essentially pro-slavery."[16] At the same time, he makes it clear that he is prepared to be convinced otherwise. Perhaps he is beginning to feel the irony of being leagued with the slaveholders, of having the same view of the Constitution as they had.

An anecdote will illustrate the point: Wendell Phillips, a noted Garrisonian, had published a work called *The Constitution a Pro-Slavery Compact,* which compiled the evidence (namely, the debates and material relating to slavery from the Constitutional Convention and several state ratifying conventions) that a bargain had been struck between slavery and freedom at the time of the founding. John A. Campbell of Alabama, later a member of Taney's *Dred Scott* Court, wrote to Calhoun recommending the work as "an able pamphlet . . . [which] we might circulate to great advantage excluding a few paragraphs."[17] Douglass was beginning to recognize that, by confirming and spreading the slaveholding opinion of the Constitution, the American Anti-Slavery Society was (as he later explained) "thus piling up, between the slave and his freedom, the huge work of the abolition of the Government, as an indispensable condition to emancipation."[18] Why be a revolutionary doomed to failure, when one might be a successful reformer instead? Douglass is increasingly aware that, given the American temper, the ballot box is a powerful instrument. At this point, he needs only to be persuaded that it can be a rightful one. So while he continues to denounce the Constitution as a "most foul and bloody conspiracy against the rights of three millions of enslaved and imbruted men,"[19] Douglass nonetheless invites Gerrit Smith (a prominent non-Garrisonian abolitionist) to instruct him, particularly with respect to his curious rules of constitutional interpretation.

Those rules of reading owed much to Lysander Spooner, whose *Unconstitutionality of Slavery* became one of the standard reference works of radical antislavery constitutionalism. Spooner held that the intent of the Framers was to be looked for solely in the words of the document itself (that is, not in any secondary sources, no matter how authoritative, as for example, *The Federalist Papers* or James Madison's records of the Constitutional Convention). Spooner set forth the following guidelines: (1) construe all provisions in accordance with the document's overarching purposes (in the Constitution's case, these were unmistakably spelled out in the *Preamble*); (2) take words at their plain, intelligible meaning; (3) where the language is uncertain, construe strictly in favor of natural right and freedom and never so as to give effect to a wicked purpose.[20]

The Garrisonian rule of constitutional construction was less formal. As expressed by the early Douglass:

> we shall continue to understand the Constitution not only in the light of its letter, but in view of its history, the meaning attached to it by its framers, the men who adopted it, and the circumstances in which it was adopted.[21]

In other words, it is the lawmakers' original intention, broadly gathered, and the subsequent uniform practice of the nation which should guide interpretation. For the Garrisonian Douglass, the absence of the word "slave" or "slavery" from the text of the Constitution was neither a matter of great delight nor an exegetical opportunity. In his view, the indirectness of the Framers' language only showed them to be hypocrites, ashamed of the name of their

crime, but cunning enough to devise a written charter to perpetuate it. Accordingly, Douglass at first found Spooner's reasoning quite
disingenuous. Spooner, for example, tried to construe the three-fifths
clause as applicable only to aliens and not slaves. Such semantic
feats had little connection with the "real" Constitution. As Douglass said:

> One thing is certain about this clause of the Constitution. It is this—
> that under it, the slave system has enjoyed a large and domineering
> representation in Congress, which has given laws to the whole Union
> in regard to slavery, ever since the formation of the government.[22]

Douglass here manifests the Garrisonian tendency to reason back-
wards from the practice of the government to the plan of the government, admitting of no gap between the two. The Garrisonians
were in thrall to the status quo; hence, they habitually confounded
execution and intention in this manner. Given the exceedingly conservative, precedent-bound character of the Garrisonian legal position, it is not surprising that they denounced Spooner's natural law
jurisprudence as unsound and productive of anarchy. Nonetheless,
the Garrisonians certainly present an odd spectacle. Here were men
who denounced all human government as essentially tyrannical,[23]
worrying that Spooner's attempt to solve the problem of unjust law,
by making positive law subject to the understanding of right, would
subvert all order. Echoing Wendell Phillips, Douglass warns that
granting a political role to the individual conscience will eventuate
in judge-made rather than judge-administered law, thereby destroying
the very notion of constitutional government, according to which
the written law stands supreme.

Of course, Spooner and his constitutional fundamentalists had
an answer to the Garrisonian criticisms. They held that the natural
law alone was fixed and eternal. It was the standard informing and
legitimating the artificial stability of our humanly crafted law. They
contended that the real anarchists were the Garrisonians, who saw
all government as inherently evil. Instead of trying to bring justice
and legality closer together, the Garrisonians saw the law as an
instrument of coercion devoid of justice. They endorsed a notion
of law which provided no internal bulwark against tyranny and which
converted the Constitution into nothing more than ossified majority opinion.

Douglass continued until 1851 to aver publicly that the Constitution was founded on force and fraud. But privately, he spent the two-year period following his initial confrontation with the views of Gerrit Smith studying the question. The result of his researches appeared in an editorial announcing it as his firm conviction

> that the Constitution, construed in the light of well established rules of legal interpretation, might be made consistent in its details with the noble purposes avowed in its preamble; and that hereafter we should insist upon the application of such rules to that instrument, and demand that it be wielded in behalf of emancipation.[24]

It is no understatement to say that this change of opinion transformed Douglass from an avowed enemy of the American regime into a friend—still fiercely critical, but a friend. As a sign of this, Douglass hereafter greeted his audiences as "fellow citizens."[25]

Garrison himself was greatly embittered by Douglass's defection. His outburst on hearing the news ("There is roguery somewhere!"[26]) reveals his inability to credit an honest difference of opinion. Douglass found Smith a more charitable ally. Although he always spoke well of his new friends, Douglass did not entirely adopt their reading of the Constitution. In particular, he seemed to find too strained Spooner's attempt to deny the existence within the Constitution of specific accommodations to the existing evil of slavery. Douglass preferred to minimize such evasions by combining some of Spooner's semantic strictness with a morally discriminating reinterpretation of the Founders' intent.

There were four traditionally troublesome clauses for the anti-slavery constitutionalists.

The three-fifths clause, Art. I, sec. 2(3):

Representatives and direct Taxes shall be apportioned among the several States which may be included within this Union, according to their respective Numbers, which shall be determined by adding to the whole Number of free Persons, including those bound to Service for a Term of Years, and excluding Indians not taxed, three fifths of all other Persons.

The insurrection clause, Art. I, sec. 8(15):

[The Congress shall have Power] To provide for calling forth the Militia to execute the Laws of the Union, suppress Insurrections and repel Invasions.

The importation clause, Art. I, sec. 9(1):

The Migration or Importation of such Persons as any of the States now existing shall think proper to admit, shall not be prohibited by the Congress prior to the Year one thousand eight hundred and eight, but a tax or duty may be imposed on such Importation, not exceeding ten dollars for each Person.

The "fugitive slave" clause, Art. IV, sec. 2(3):

No Person held to Service or Labour in one State, under the Laws thereof, escaping into another, shall, in Consequence of any Law or Regulation therein, be discharged from such Service or Labour, but shall be delivered up on Claim of the Party to whom such Service or Labour may be due.

As to the three-fifths clause, Douglass grants that it refers to slaves. (He does this, however, only "for the sake of the argument,"[27] reserving the possibility that "all other Persons" might fairly apply to aliens.) But he does not grant that the three-fifths clause was designed to bolster slavery or to discount the black man's humanity by two-fifths. Quite the reverse. Because under the Constitution, free blacks are counted not as three-fifths, but as wholes,[28] this provision in fact amounts to:

a downright disability laid upon the slaveholding states; one which deprives those States of two-fifths of their natural basis of representation; . . . taking it at its worst, it still leans to freedom, not to slavery.[29]

With respect to Article I, Section 8(15), granting Congress power "To provide for calling forth the Militia to execute the Laws of the Union, suppress Insurrections and repel Invasions," Douglass saw no reason to assume that this provision was designed specially to back the slaveholder with federal arms. He argued instead that the power to suppress riots and popular uprisings was an undoubtedly necessary power of government. Furthermore, he pointed out that it was a power which might one day put an end to slavery:

To our thinking, there is no part of the Constitution from which slaveholders have more to apprehend, than from this. John Quincy Adams, the most renowned statesman America has produced, gave it as his opinion twelve years ago, that this clause of the Constitution confers upon Congress the right in certain contingencies to abolish slavery in the States.[30]

As it happened, the pen-stroke that brought emancipation did indeed follow the sword-stroke, much as John Quincy Adams had prophesied it would.

To those who thought the Constitution proslavery on account of the importation clause, Douglass reminded them of the simple fact that this clause was now a dead letter. It had "expired by its own limitation"[31] decades ago. The lasting legacy of the importation clause was not to guarantee the continuance of the African slave trade, but to provide for its abolition. It was like a timebomb planted to destroy this odious feature of our national life and set to detonate twenty years after the Union had been secured. At the time of the founding, the slave trade was widely believed to be the lifeblood of slavery. The provision for action against it indicated the Framers' desire to strike at slavery itself, indirectly but decisively. Douglass concludes that the clause as a whole "looked to the abolition of slavery rather than to its perpetuity."[32]

With respect to the fugitive slave clause, Douglass refused to admit, even for purposes of argument, that the phrase "Person held to Service or Labour" was meant to refer to slaves. Like Spooner, he contended that it referred exclusively to redemptioners, a considerable class of immigrants who had obtained passage to the New World by becoming indentured servants. In defense of his reading, he cited both the provision's careful language (with its implications of contract) and the objections raised during the Constitutional Convention against admitting into the Constitution the idea of property in man—objections prompted by the brutally direct suggestion of two South Carolina delegates "to require fugitive slaves and servants to be delivered up like criminals."[33]

Douglass's approach to the fugitive slave clause reveals very clearly the limits of his moral tolerance. He could not have viewed the Constitution in a kindly light if it had obligated nonslaveholders to act as accomplices to the slave-hunting bloodhounds. Such an obligation would, to a certain degree, have nationalized slavery, for it would have broken the physical and moral quarantine in which Douglass believed the institution had been placed.

Douglass's position notwithstanding, I believe the record shows that the Framers did in fact feel compelled to accord this very significant measure of protection to slavery. But, by the circumlocutions of their draftsmanship, they managed at the same time to avoid giving moral sanction to slavery. Douglass seems to have underestimated both the pressure of circumstances and the moral finesse of the Founders. Moreover, as Herbert Storing points out, if "the fugitive slave clause was the knife by which Southern slavery cut into the North," then "the privileges and immunities clause was the knife by which Northern freedom cut into the South."[34]

Despite whatever quarrel one might have with Douglass on the particulars, his final overall view of the Constitution was right on the mark. Displaying his gift for metaphor, Douglass said:

> I hold that the Federal Government was never, in its essence, anything but an anti-slavery government. Abolish slavery tomorrow, and not a sentence or syllable of the Constitution need be altered. It was purposely so framed as to give no claim, no sanction to the claim, of property in man. If in its origin slavery had any relation to the government, it was only as the scaffolding to the magnificent structure, to be removed as soon as the building was completed.[35]

Something had gone awry, however. The scaffolding had not been torn down and it now threatened to obscure forever the building's beauty. Fortified by his antislavery interpretation of the Constitution, Douglass was at last free to turn to electoral politics as a proper and promising means to bring America to its best self. From 1851 until 1895, when death snatched him up between speaking engagements, Douglass was the premier spokesman in the struggle to secure the fundamental natural right of blacks in America (that is, liberty) and, subsequently, to secure the civil rights of black Americans.

Two Constitutions

It is necessary to say a few words about the relation of Douglass's Constitution to Lincoln's, for it would be a mistake to leave the impression that the two were identical. While Douglass did get "political religion"—that reverence for the laws to which Lincoln exhorted men in his Lyceum Address—it remained that of a particular sect. Douglass always occupied what he called "the genuine abolition ground."[36] Lincoln, despite the deliberate misrepresentations of his Southern and doughface[37] opponents, clearly did not. As Douglass pointed out, "[h]e came into the Presidential chair upon one principle alone, namely, opposition to the extension of slavery."[38] As much as he inwardly despised slavery, and as much as he did not shy from public declaration of that fact, Lincoln was nonetheless prepared to uphold the "federal consensus."

> To protect, defend, and perpetuate slavery in the states where it existed Abraham Lincoln was not less ready than any other President to draw the sword of the nation. He was ready to execute all the supposed guarantees of the United States Constitution in favor of the slave system anywhere inside the slave states.[39]

That view of Lincoln's policy led Douglass, even on such a ceremonial occasion as the unveiling of the Freedmen's Monument in Memory of Abraham Lincoln, to state that "Abraham Lincoln was not, in the fullest sense of the word, either our man or our model . . . He was preeminently the white man's President."[40] And yet it is undeniable that Douglass's people bore a special relation to Lincoln. Douglass himself said they were Lincoln's stepchildren, "children by adoption, children by forces of circumstances and necessity."[41] Lincoln's primary mission was the salvation of the Union. Abolition, which was primary for the slave and his friends, was subordinate to that project. But when the situation proved such that the one entailed the other, it too was accomplished. Thus, Lincoln came in the end to act for the whole, black as well as white. Douglass, in the largeness of his understanding, says:

> Viewed from the genuine abolition ground, Mr. Lincoln seemed tardy, cold, dull, and indifferent; but measuring him by the sentiment of his country, sentiment he was bound as a statesman to consult, he was swift, zealous, radical, and determined.[42]

Douglass's memorial address is a grateful and, above all, thoughtful acknowledgment of Lincoln's comprehensive statesmanship and a further proof of the quality of Douglass's own statesmanship.

Notes

1. For a refutation of Taney's understanding of the founding see Lincoln's "Speech on the Dred Scott Decision," 1857, and his "Address at the Cooper Union," 1860, both in *The Political Thought of Abraham Lincoln*, Richard N. Current, ed. (New York: Macmillan, 1967), pp. 84–93 and pp. 139–62.

2. Thomas Jefferson, "First Inaugural Address," in *The Portable Thomas Jefferson*, Merrill D. Peterson, ed. (New York: Viking Press, 1975), p. 291.

3. *The Lincoln–Douglas Debates of 1858*, Robert W. Johannsen, ed. (New York: Oxford University Press, 1965), p. 310.

4. Frederick Douglass, *Life and Times of Frederick Douglass* (New York: Macmillan, 1962), p. 79.

5. Ibid., p. 143.

6. Ibid., p. 216.

7. Ibid., p. 213.

8. Ibid., p. 218.

9. Ibid., p. 257.

10. Ibid., p. 264.

11. "The Right to Criticize American Institutions," speech before the American Anti-Slavery Society, May 11, 1847, in *The Life and Writings of Frederick Douglass*, Philip S. Foner, ed. (New York: International Publishers, 1975): I, 236.

12. Ibid., p. 242.

13. For an explanation of this two-pronged policy of emancipation and expatriation see Thomas Jefferson, *Notes on the State of Virginia*, Query 14.

14. "The Destiny of Colored Americans," *The North Star*, November 16, 1849, in *Writings*: I, 417.

15. "Comments on Gerrit Smith's Address," *The North Star*, March 30, 1849, in *Writings*: I, 374.

16. "The Constitution and Slavery," *The North Star*, March 16, 1849, in *Writings*: I, 366.

17. Cited in William M. Wiecek, *The Sources of Antislavery Constitutionalism, 1760–1848* (Ithaca: Cornell University Press, 1977), p. 240.

18. "The Anti-Slavery Movement," lecture delivered before the Rochester Ladies' Anti-Slavery Society, January 1855, in *Writings*: II, 352.

19. "Comments," I, 379.

20. Douglass gave the following example of strict construction in the service of personal liberty:

A law was passed there [in Connecticut] that Negroes should not be allowed to travel after nine at night unless they carried a lantern. It was resolved to cast a light upon their dark countenances. Accordingly the colored people bought lanterns and carried them but without candles in them. When hauled up for trial it was proved they were taken up with lanterns in their hands but no candles. The proof was satisfactory they had complied with the letter of the law and they were acquitted as such a law must necessarily be construed strictly. Another law was passed that Negroes should carry lanterns with candles in them. This they complied with but without lighting them and were again hauled up and acquitted.

The law was amended so as to require them to carry lanterns with lighted candles in them and anon the Negroes were found parading with lighted candles in dark lanterns and being again acquitted the Legislature gave in and let the matter drop.

It is evidently our interest to make Legislators find it difficult to enact villainy into law.

"Important Truths," speech delivered to church congregation at Harveysburg, Warren County, Ohio, May 1852, in *Writings*: V, 228.

A similar use of literalism is Portia's famous judgment against Shylock in *The Merchant of Venice*, granting him the pound of flesh, but not one drop of blood.

21. "Comments," I, 377.

22. "The Constitution and Slavery," I, 364.

23. This "no human government" doctrine was called "non-resistance" by its practitioners. It should not be confused with the technique of nonviolent direct action or passive resistance which figured so prominently in the civil rights movement of the 1950s and 1960s.

24. "Change of Opinion Announced," *The North Star*, reprinted in *The Liberator*, May 23, 1851, in *Writings*: II, 155.

25. See especially "The Meaning of July Fourth for the Negro," speech at Rochester, New York, July 5, 1852, in *Writings*: II, 181, 204. This is one of Douglass's best orations—deeply patriotic, but in an absolutely unorthodox way.

26. "Change," II, 156.

27. "The Constitution of the United States: Is It Pro-slavery or Anti-slavery?" speech delivered in Glasgow, Scotland, March 26, 1860, in *Writings*: II, 472.

28. The distinction is drawn between free and unfree, not white and black. Free blacks counted fully in the census.

29. "The Constitution of the United States: Is It Pro-slavery or Anti-slavery?" II, 472.

30. "Is the United States Constitution For or Against Slavery?" *Frederick Douglass' Paper*, July 24, 1851, in *Writings*: V, 197.

31. "The Constitution of the United States: Is It Pro-slavery or Anti-slavery?" II, 473.

32. Ibid.

33. *Notes of Debates in the Federal Convention of 1787 Reported by James Madison*, with an introduction by Adrienne Koch (Athens: Ohio University Press, 1984), p. 545.

34. Herbert Storing, "Slavery and the Moral Foundations of the American Republic," in *The Moral Foundations of the American Republic*, Robert H. Horwitz, ed. (Charlottesville: University Press of Virginia, 1977), p. 228.

The privileges and immunities clause guarantees that a citizen of an individual state is a citizen of all the states. Accordingly, a free black man who was a citizen of a northern state should have been able to travel unmolested throughout the land, including within slave states. When Missouri applied for admission to the Union, there was strenuous objection to a clause in its state constitution which barred free blacks from entering the state.

35. "Address for the Promotion of Colored Enlistments," delivered at a mass meeting in Philadelphia, July 6, 1863, in *Writings*: III, 365.
36. "Oration in Memory of Abraham Lincoln," delivered at the unveiling of the Freedmen's Monument in Memory of Abraham Lincoln, in Lincoln Park, Washington, D.C., April 14, 1876, in IV, 316.
37. "Doughface" was the name applied to Northern men with Southern principles.
38. "Oration in Memory of Abraham Lincoln," *Writings* IV, 312.
39. Ibid.
40. Ibid.
41. Ibid.
42. Ibid., IV, 316.

Suggested Reading

Douglass, Frederick. *Life and Times of Frederick Douglass*. New York: Macmillan, 1962.

Selections from Philip S. Foner, ed. *The Life and Writings of Frederick Douglass*, vols. I–IV. New York: International Publishers, 1975:

"American Slavery" 1847, I, 269–78.

"The Address of Southern Delegates in Congress to their Constituents; or, the Address of John C. Calhoun and Forty Other Thieves" 1849, I, 353–60.

"The Constitution and Slavery" 1849, I, 361–67.

"Change of Opinion Announced" 1851, II, 155–56.

"The Meaning of July Fourth for the Negro" 1852, II, 181–204.

"The Constitution of the United States: Is It Pro-slavery or Antislavery?" 1860, II, 467–80.

"Oration in Memory of Abraham Lincoln" 1876, IV, 309–19.

28

The Dilemma of Race in America

James F. Pontuso

This essay on race relations is written by a political scientist who is white. The fact that I am white and am writing this essay is somewhat embarrassing. It is often said that whites, having never experienced racism, cannot truly understand the nature of racial problems in the United States. Yet it would hardly be thought out of place if a white person who is a political scientist examined the ethnic strife in the former Yugoslavia or the religious antagonisms between Hindus and Muslims in India. Why is it awkward then for a white person to investigate the subject of race? If we attempt to understand our embarrassment over this issue, we can begin to grasp why race has posed such dilemma for this country.

Almost every generalization that has been put forward to explain America's stance on race can be seen to have exceptions. While slavery was brutal, the average life span of American slaves was far longer than that of slaves in other parts of the world. While segregation was stultifying for most, a black professional class flourished within it. While full political and civil rights have now been accorded to black citizens, these rights have not ended the race problem. During most of America's history racial prejudice dominated white opinion about blacks, yet close personal friendships between individual blacks and whites were not uncommon. In the South, legal barriers separating the races existed for many years, yet many blacks argued that white hostility toward them was actually stronger in the North. Most Americans by the 1990s claimed not to be racist, yet the vast majority still thought in terms of race.

Two examples perhaps best sum up America's curious and ironic attitude toward race. First, Thomas Jefferson, whose bold words about the rights of man written in the Declaration of Independence still inspire us today, never freed any of his slaves while he was alive and emancipated only a few upon his death. John Randolph, a slaveholder from Roanoke, Virginia, whose staunch defense of the peculiar institution led him to reject the Declaration and along with it the "principle . . . that all men are created free and equal . . . because it is not true," freed all of his slaves in his last testament and spent a sizable part of his family fortune providing property for them.

Second, Booker T. Washington, who in the latter half of the nineteenth century was the most powerful spokesman of his race, is now held in considerable disrepute because of his conservative social and economic views. His antagonist, W. E. B. Du Bois, is presently looked upon with much greater sympathy and respect. Washington's program emphasized separating the races, building a strong and independent black business class, and strengthening the family. While Du Bois did not oppose these principles entirely, he is most widely remembered for his advocacy of civil rights. The great civil rights leader Martin Luther King Jr., the foremost black leader of his day, led the most successful movement for equal rights in American history. By the 1990s King's reputation has nearly been eclipsed by that of Malcolm X, a critic of the civil rights movement and an advocate of racial separation, black economic power, and strong family values.

The problem of race between black and white is unique in the American experience. It has been with us since the earliest days of our colonial life. It is one difficulty we have seemed unable to solve.

There has been a great deal of progress, of course. Once we fought over whether masters should beat their field hands. In the 1990s we debated whether there should be more tenured black faculty at Harvard. Yet the road forward has not been an easy one. To paraphrase Frederick Douglass, while progress has been achieved, every inch has been sternly disputed. Even today, if we were graded on relations between blacks and whites, we would receive barely a respectable score.

America has earned high marks for overcoming the underlying enmities that have plagued most societies at most times in history. We have few long-standing religious, ethnic, or class conflicts. In the hotly contested battle between the sexes, America might stand as the practical model for providing women with opportunities denied them in most other places in the world. When disputes between groups have arisen, the nation has found ways to resolve them. For example, the development of American public schools, despite the disrepute into which they fell during the 1970s and 1980s, can be taken as one of our most remarkable achievements. America's schools did not merely serve to educate the children of millions of illiterate peasants from vastly divergent cultures, they also molded those students into responsible citizens, generally tolerant of each other's heritage.

America, of course, is far from ideal. Our history contains glaring examples of ethnic hostility, religious strife, and class conflict. Yet these cases seem more the exception than the rule. Surely there has been nothing in America to match the class war of the Bolshevik Revolution, the oppression of the Jews in Europe, or the ancient ethnic hatreds that reared up after the collapse of the Soviet empire. We do have instances even today of hatred aimed at certain clearly recognizable groups, such as Asians or Jews. But this antipathy does not seem to have had much of an effect on the group as a whole. Both Jews and Asians have higher average incomes than their white Christian counterparts. Blacks have not shared as fully in the American dream as have other ethnic groups. For many blacks racism and oppression have made a great difference, a legacy of poverty, crime, and hopelessness. America has hardly been the land of opportunity for them.

Race and the Principles of America

Perhaps America has difficulty living up to its ideals because its ideals are so difficult to live up to. The Declaration of Independence, from which much of our national ethos derives, proclaims that all people must be accorded inalienable rights regardless of their sex, race, religion, or ethnic group. Everyone must be given the opportunity to succeed. But the universally equal treatment that the Declaration demands each person be accorded runs counter to the way most people act.

Alexander Hamilton explained at the New York convention to ratify the Constitution:

There are certain social principles in human nature from which we may draw the most solid conclusions with respect to the conduct of individuals, and of communities. We love our families, more than we love our neighbors: We love our neighbors, more than our countrymen in general. The human affections, like solar heat, lose their intensity, as they depart the center.

This passion to cherish what is most near and like ourselves is a form of parochialism, but it is more than mere selfishness. In fact, this passion prevails against our inclination to think only of ourselves and draws us together into political communities. As such, it can be the foundation of good citizenship and of responsibility to one's friends and countrymen. By caring for one's own, however, one must exclude outsiders, since the range which human affections can be stretched does not seem to be indefinite. Other people, too, form themselves into communities, and because the interests of these various communities are sometimes at odds, there are bound to be clashes.

Some of the greatest thinkers of the past believed that universalism such as is expressed in the Declaration is impossible to put into practice. No less a writer than William Shakespeare explored this problem in two of his most celebrated works, *Othello* and *The Merchant of Venice*. Set in Venice, the most liberal and cosmopolitan republic of its day, these plays suggest that political communities must have fairly homogeneous populations. Although Othello, who is black, does a great service for the city by leading its army to victory, he is destroyed in part by the distrust and prejudice of many of Venice's leading citizens. Shylock, a Jew, is an object of almost universal hatred and contempt to the Christian Venetians. He is forced to abandoned his dearly held religion and convert to Christianity.

African slavery was introduced into the Americas because Africans were considered outsiders. When in the seventeenth century Christian Europeans began to have compunctions about enslaving fellow Christians, they turned to the non-Christian population of Africa to provide the labor force necessary to develop the natural resources of the newly conquered lands of America.

By the time of the American Revolution slavery had already become a serious moral dilemma. Jefferson wanted to include its introduction into the British colonies as one of the crimes of the British monarchy detailed in the Declaration of Independence. But this section had to be omitted from the Declaration's final draft so as not to infuriate slaveholders without whose help the Revolution might have been suppressed and liberty lost for all Americans. Hamilton and his friend John Laurens attempted to form a regiment of slaves who, by fighting for colonial independence, would become the catalyst for the emancipation of all the slaves. Yet so firmly was slavery established that neither Hamilton's scheme nor even Jefferson's reproach of the monarchy was acceptable. Slaveholders would have lost too much if they had to give up their chattels. After all, slaves were expensive. A good field hand cost more than half a year's wages for most Americans.

Slavery also supported a particular way of life, liberating plantation owners from having to perform the daily tasks necessary for survival. Many slaveholders squandered this opportunity as puffed-up aristocrats who spent a great deal of time riding horses and hunting. But slavery gave George Washington, Jefferson, and Madison the freedom to engage in political life and thereby to found a nation.

All whites, not just the owners of slaves, were fearful of retribution by slaves. As Jefferson explained in his *Notes on Virginia,* the entire sum of oppression that the colonists had suffered under the British Crown could not equal one minute of black slavery. If Jefferson's estimation were true, did not slaves have the same right to kill their exploiters as the colonists did to shoot British soldiers in order to free themselves from the king? Many whites had a dread of slave revolts, as was evident from their reaction in 1831 to the ill-fated uprising of Nat Turner and his small band of fellow slaves in Virginia. Throughout the South hundreds of blacks who took no part in the revolt and probably had no knowledge of it were shot on sight if they happened to be away from home or simply were not recognized by the whites they encountered.

Nowhere are the conflicts and uncertainties about America's attitude toward slavery more evident than in the Constitution of the United States. Later in our history, those opposed to slavery would label the Constitution of 1787 a compromise with the devil because it sanctioned human bondage. Yet the authors of the Constitution refused to mention the word slavery. They chose, instead, less onerous but more confusing ways to convey their meaning. The use of these ambiguous terms, such as "Person held to Service or Labour," is evidence of the Framers' embarrassment. They did not want to sanction slavery or racial distinctions, but they were compelled by necessity to adopt a practice entirely at odds with human liberty into a document otherwise dedicated to advancing political freedom.

The Framers of the Constitution believed that they were caught. If they had attempted to abolish slavery, the southern states probably would not have joined the Union. Those states would have formed their own political community and written a constitution which clearly justified slavery. Most of the era's leading statesmen realized that slavery was inconsistent with the spirit of liberty and should not be accorded full legal recognition. The only practical road was compromise.

When the cotton gin was invented in 1793, all hope that slavery would disappear of its own accord was lost. Cotton became the major cash crop of most southern states. Huge fortunes were made by exporting the fiber to Europe to clothe that continent's expanding population. A whole way of life, plantations, grew up around the cultivation of this plant. Cotton was a labor-intensive product and slaves provided a cheap and ready labor force. With profits to be made, slaves were imported or smuggled into the country regardless of the laws against it. With fortunes at stake, slavery was no longer merely tolerated as an unfortunate but unavoidable relic of the past. It was vigorously championed as a just and benevolent practice. As the defense of slavery grew more impassioned, so the opposition to it intensified. The clash that few really wanted became inevitable.

The Mixed Legacy of the Civil War

The debate over the peculiar institution tore the nation apart and finally caused the greatest crisis in its history, the Civil War. No nation, as Abraham Lincoln said, could exist half free and half slave. Either it would come to accept slavery and thereby abandon the principle of universal natural rights or it would abolish slavery and make its practices conform to its principles. For their part, slaveholders maintained that God had ordained slavery in the Bible and that He had singled out the black race as slaves by giving them inferior reasoning capabilities. Southerners also claimed that the burgeoning system of industrial labor in the North was actually a worse form of economic oppression than slavery. Abolitionists, such as Frederick Douglass, took it upon themselves to prove that slavery was inconsistent with the Declaration of Independence and the laws of God. Douglass's brilliantly conceived and delivered speeches put a lie to the assertion that blacks could not reason as well as whites. And as he pointed out, although industrial labor was far from perfect, the underground railroad did not move in reverse.

Bitterness and acrimony over the slave issue grew as both sides set out "moral" justifications for their views. A virtual civil war broke out in Kansas when the citizens of the then-territory attempted to decide whether to be admitted into the Union as a free state or a slave state. As tensions over the slavery question heightened, the Supreme Court handed down its decision in *Dred Scott v. Sanford* (1857). Among the many rulings that this far-reaching case made were these:

(1) Masters could legally transport their slaves into free territories and still retain ownership of them, irrespective of local laws against slavery.

(2) Congress had no power to legislate on slavery in the territories of the United States. The local inhabitants would have to decide the issue for themselves.

(3) The 1820 Missouri Compromise, a pact which controlled the spread of slavery into the western territories and which maintained sectional balance by admitting into the Union one free state for each slave state, was unconstitutional.

(4) No black person, not even free blacks living in the North, including the descendants of former slaves and some whose ancestors had never been slaves in the United States, could be a citizen of the United States.

Chief Justice Roger Taney, who delivered the opinion of the Court, reasoned that "the entire . . . African Race" was entitled to no civil or political rights whatsoever. In fact, as far as America was concerned, they had no natural rights. Taney maintained that at the time the Constitution was adopted, blacks were considered

> beings of an inferior order, and altogether unfit to associate with the white race, either in social or political relations; and so far inferior, that they had no rights which the white man was bound to respect; and that the Negro might justly and lawfully be reduced to slavery for his benefit.

Lincoln, among others, vigorously opposed the *Dred Scott* decision. He pointed out that the First Congress, many of whose members had also been delegates to the convention which authored the Constitution, had passed laws restricting slavery in the territories.

Surely these men knew what the document intended, Lincoln argued. And how could it be, he asked, that all blacks were excluded from the political community? At the time of the adoption of the Constitution, free blacks voted in a number of states, including Massachusetts, Pennsylvania, and North Carolina. These men were members of the community which constituted our political institutions and ought to share in its benefits and rights.

Lincoln insisted that slavery was wrong and that he could prove it. Would you choose to be a slave, he asked the defenders of the institution. Since no one stepped forward to volunteer, Lincoln concluded that slavery was unnatural and must be wrong. But, some insisted, there were racial differences which justified slavery. If color be the basis of slavery, Lincoln responded, be careful that someone of lighter skin than you does not put you in bondage. If intelligence be the test, you ought to be wary that someone smarter than you does not decide to make you his chattel.

People rallied to Lincoln's clear and simple message. A number of political movements joined together to form the Republican party. The Republicans opposed the extension of slavery into the territories but, because it had been authorized by the Constitution, promised to leave slavery alone in those states where it already existed. Running on this platform, Lincoln was elected president in 1860 with the smallest percentage of popular votes in American history. His election so alarmed slaveholding states that some decided to secede even before he took office. Lincoln vowed to maintain the Union at any cost. The clash, lasting nearly five years, killed and injured more Americans than any war before or since.

The Civil War decided that slavery could not be tolerated in a nation such as ours. It did not settle what to do with the former slaves. The majority of white citizens, at least those in the North, realized that blacks had won the right to be free as the result of their participation in the war. But it was unclear how fully they should share in the political community.

Jefferson's fears never materialized. There were very few instances of revenge taken by former slaves against their masters. Most blacks were willing to forget the cruelties done to them if they could be left alone to get along with their lives. Yet many found themselves in a horrible situation. The vast majority of former slaves had worked as field hands, but they owned no land on which to work their profession. Those with skilled trades had to contend with white workmen who were not happy to compete with their former underlings. All Southerners, black and white, suffered from an economy ravaged by war.

As Du Bois pointed out, Freedmen, as former slaves were called at the time, could hardly be expected to become good citizens overnight. During slavery there were laws against teaching slaves how to read and write. Every effort was made to break slaves of feelings of independence and self-reliance. The goal was to maintain them in a perpetual state of childhood. While their African heritage had long ago been ruthlessly stripped away, no attempt was made to provide a new basis for black social life. The result was a population largely uneducated, unskilled, and unschooled in ways of citizenship. But many former slaves were very eager to learn. Booker T. Washington, himself once a slave, touchingly describes in *Up From Slavery* how blacks who barely had enough to eat spent their meager earnings on schools for their children.

In response to the nearly desperate situation of many Freedmen, Congress proposed and the states adopted the Thirteenth Amendment (1865), which banned slavery from the United States; the Fourteenth Amendment (1868), which made former slaves citizens of the United States and which granted all Americans due process of law, the privileges and immunities of the law, and equal protection of the law; and the Fifteenth Amendment (1870), which guaranteed the right to vote regardless of race.

It is little wonder, given the economic devastation of the South where most blacks lived, the bitterness brought on by the war, and the federal troops permanently assigned in the South to protect the Freedmen, that hard feelings between the races would occur. What is most surprising is that during the era of reconstruction great strides were made by blacks. C. Vann Woodward writes in *The Strange Career of Jim Crow* that during Reconstruction and for some years thereafter, many public facilities and private businesses, such as restaurants, were integrated, at least for those blacks with enough money to appear "respectable." Blacks became businessmen, merchants, tradesmen, and farmers. Some were elected to hold high public office, including senator and congressman. Although for many years after Reconstruction assertions were made that these black politicians were corrupt and uneducated, in fact, the majority served with distinction and without a hint of scandal.

Whatever progress was being made came to a halt with the Supreme Court decision in *Plessy v. Ferguson* (1896). The case dealt with the issue of whether a state could require separate railroad cars for blacks and whites. The Court decided that racial segregation was not a violation of the equal protection clause of the Fourteenth Amendment so long as facilities were equal. Writing for the majority, Justice Henry Billings Brown argued that the Court could not alter long-established customs such as those associated with segregation. Laws which attempted to overcome racial hostility were futile. "Legislation is powerless to eradicate racial instincts or to abolish distinctions based on physical differences, and the attempt to do so can only result in accentuating the difficulties of the present situation." Brown also held that the forced separation of the races did not stamp "the colored race with a badge of inferiority." If blacks were made to feel subordinate by the act, it was "only because the colored race chooses to put that construction on it." Brown's decision had it both ways. Whites were justified in enacting segregation laws because they saw blacks as inferiors, but blacks should not interpret these laws as a sign of inadequacy since separation did not necessarily mean inequality.

Over the strong protests of Justice John Marshall Harlan, whose famous dissent declared that "the Constitution is colorblind," the doctrine of separate but equal became the law of the land. In clear contradiction to what Justice Brown claimed about the capacity of the law to shape mores, the decision strengthened antipathy toward blacks by giving constitutional sanction to discriminatory laws. After *Plessy* laws were quickly adopted throughout the South separating the races, but no attempt was made to make them equal.

The beginning of the twentieth century also saw the high tide of theories based on racial differences. Charles Darwin's work in biology was transferred to the social arena and used to show that blacks had not achieved as much success as whites, not because of lack of opportunity, but because the black race was at a lower stage of evolutionary development. Science was used to justify discrimination. The post-Reconstruction era also saw the rise of the Ku Klux Klan, perhaps the only successful terrorist organization in American history. The Klan thwarted the law, even going beyond the restrictive racial laws of the South, intimidating blacks through a combination of threats, open attacks, and of course, lynchings. Every effort was made to cower blacks and "keep them in their place." Not only were all public accommodations segregated, but most blacks lost the right to vote and even the right to sue in court. Although a very few blacks did retain the franchise, the one-party politics of the region ensured that their ballots counted for nothing.

It was not just the South that discriminated against blacks. While the North did not practice legal segregation, there were very few integrated areas in the United States. Social custom kept blacks from living near white neighborhoods. Opportunities were very limited. Most institutions of higher learning regularly denied admission even to the most qualified blacks. Most professions were closed to blacks either because businesses refused to hire them or because white workers refused to work with them. The vast majority of blacks could not hope for any better material rewards than those afforded by low-paying manual labor.

During this period perhaps the single most powerful black leader in American history came to prominence. Booker T. Washington (1856–1915) had quite literally lifted himself up from slavery. Born a slave, he had a burning desire to elevate himself and his people. As an adolescent during Reconstruction he left his home in West Virginia with only the shirt on his back, hoping to reach Hampton Institute in Virginia, a school founded in 1868 to educate Freedmen. He arrived at Hampton nearly starving, but availed himself of every opportunity to transform himself into an educated man and a productive citizen.

By 1893 Washington had become headmaster at Tuskegee Institute, a school he founded in 1881, and used that position as a forum to spread his gospel of individual initiative, self-reliance, manual training for blacks, and racial separation. In his famous Atlanta Exposition Speech, Washington attempted to reach out to whites by promising them a pool of hardworking, loyal, and skilled black craftsmen for their businesses. He made no demands on whites to integrate the races or even to give blacks the opportunity to vote. The speech propelled Washington into national prominence. He traveled widely presenting his views on overcoming the nation's racial problems.

Washington seemed to find cause for optimism everywhere. Whites of good will were willing to help blacks, he claimed, if blacks were ready to make the best of the help. White businesses were disposed to hire blacks if blacks showed skill and persistence in their occupations. White political leaders would eventually give blacks the right to vote if blacks showed themselves worthy of thoughtful citizenship. It is "character not circumstance that makes the man," he preached.

Washington was well aware of the difficult circumstances facing the members of his race, but he refused to dwell on anything negative. He was determined to impart a positive attitude to his followers. They would need it to overcome white hostility. If blacks were skilled, worked hard, and maintained their independence, Washington reasoned, they would have a strong sense of their own worth and not accept the view of the dominant culture that blacks were a deficient race. They would not internalize a sense of inferiority and so be held back by internal doubts and fears. Racial separation would not harm blacks if they refused to see it as a badge of subordination, but instead used it to develop their independence in the trades and in business.

The most important of Washington's critics was W. E. B. Du Bois (1868–1963), a Harvard-educated teacher and writer who, in his long and interesting life, subscribed to nearly every movement aimed at improving the condition of blacks. He was a follower of Washington, an integrationist, a Pan-Africanist, a socialist, and a Marxist. He broke with Washington in the 1890s, insisting that Washington's conciliatory rhetoric and stress on menial professions were holding blacks back. By not openly condemning white violence and bigotry against blacks, Du Bois insisted, Washington's soft words invited more attacks. Du Bois held that in a democracy, where public opinion inevitably shapes people's perceptions of themselves, segregation was bound to injure the psyche of blacks. This was especially true if blacks were relegated to menial tasks, ones which buttressed the claim of black inferiority. Du Bois argued that the franchise was critical if blacks were to protect their interests in a pluralist society such as America. He further argued for the training of best and the brightest among blacks, the "talented tenth," who would act as teachers and role models for the rest of the black community and would counter the claim that blacks were incapable of performing intellectual endeavors. The great debate between Washington and Du Bois raged on until Washington's death in 1915.

War and Race

The years immediately after Washington's death were some of the most tragic in the history of the black struggle for equality and independence. Although Woodrow Wilson is often heralded as one of the great idealists in foreign affairs, his legacy in race relations had little to do with ideals. Wilson's idealism could not prevent the United States entry into World War I.

The issue facing black Americans was whether they should enlist in the army of a nation whose laws so oppressed them. Black leaders and most black Americans saw the war as an opportunity for the advancement of blacks and so they called for black volunteers in the military. Of course, blacks had always found a place in the defense of the country. They fought in the American Revolution. The 54th Massachusetts Regiment, made famous in the film *Glory,* was but one of many black outfits that served in the Civil War. Units made up of blacks, dubbed Buffalo Soldiers, protected western settlers from Indian raids. Blacks charged up San Juan Hill with Teddy Roosevelt's Rough Riders. And it is said that General John Pershing gained his nickname "Black Jack" because he commanded a battalion of black soldiers. The practice of segregating black units, which were led by white officers, continued during World War I. Despite the obvious slight that this routine implied, blacks fought with distinction in the war.

Upon their return home black veterans expected to reap some reward for their service. Many black soldiers served in France where taboos against race-mixing were far less severe than in the United States. At the very least they hoped to be given the same opportunity for advancement that their fellow soldiers were afforded. Instead, one of the severest eras of oppression against blacks took place. The ranks of the Ku Klux Klan swelled, reaching such strength that its members could boldly march down Pennsylvania Avenue, thousands strong, regaled in white sheets. The Klan became so powerful that few Southern politicians could hope to be elected without its support. Lynching again became common. Black veterans who showed too much independence were particularly the object of the Klan's wrath. A number of race riots took place, but not of the kind we see today. Whites rioted against blacks as a way of keeping blacks in their place.

World War II had a much different effect on race relations. It was not until confronted by Nazi Germany, which proclaimed the principles of Aryan racial superiority, that many American whites came to see the nature of their own racism. Again black troops were called on to defend the nation. But this time the inconsistency between American ideals and its practices became all too clear. One example shows the problem strikingly. During the war some predominantly black units were assigned as military police to guard German prisoners of war. The Germans were moved on troop trains through the South on their way to camps in Alabama. When the trains stopped for breaks in southern states, the German prisoners were allowed to eat and drink in restaurants, but the black American soldiers guarding them were not.

The ironies of the war were not lost on a generation of black leaders. They were determined to put an end to segregation and disenfranchisement. A determined group of lawyers from the NAACP (National Association for the Advancement of Colored People, founded in 1909), including future Supreme Court Justice Thurgood Marshall, conceived a strategy of challenging legal segregation in the federal courts. Black leaders also vowed to organize blacks into an effective political instrument. They hoped that white public opinion had shifted sufficiently as the result of the war to make the success of the black struggle possible.

Race and Civil Rights

Spurred on by lawsuits filed by the NAACP's team of lawyers, the Supreme Court once again entered the tangled web of race relations. In *Brown v. Board of Education* (1954) the Court held that segregated schools violated the equal protection clause of the Fourteenth Amendment. The Court sidestepped the holding of *Plessy* by saying that in "the field of public education, separate but equal has no place." The unanimous decision ruled that segregated schools injured the "hearts and minds" of black students and generated feelings of inferiority so deep as to make separate facilities, no matter how equal in tangible ways, inherently unequal.

Both the ruling and the reasoning of *Brown* caused much confusion and controversy. Despite the strong language used to condemn segregated educational facilities, *Brown* did not require that public schools integrate immediately. The Court seemed to hesitate at making such a sweeping change in American society. Even *Brown II* (1955) did not clear up matters. Although this decision was intended to enforce compliance with the ruling in *Brown I,* it provided no clear mechanism by which the public schools would be compelled to desegregate. It ordered that desegregation be pursued with "all deliberate speed." This phrase was an invitation to recalcitrance in those states where segregation was practiced.

Not until *Green v. County School Board of New Kent* (1968) did the Court take matters clearly into its own hands and rule that compliance with *Brown* required not simply the abolition of state-

imposed segregation policies, but the effective integration of formerly segregated schools immediately. Because blacks and whites
often did not live in close proximity, the *Green* case implied that
busing would have to be employed to attain racial balance. The
Court ordered busing directly for the first time in *Swann v. Char-
lotte-Mecklenburg County Board of Education* (1971). After the order,
many white families chose to send their children to predominantly
white private schools. The pattern of separate educational facilities for the races persists in many places even today.

Many white Southerners vigorously resisted the Court's rulings.
They were especially dismayed by the Court's willingness to take
away their right of local self-government. They saw the Court as a
remote and undemocratic political entity which conceived and administered capricious policies. The ruling in *Brown* also avoided
the wider problem of Jim Crow statutes which segregated most aspects
of life in the South. But in a series of decisions handed down during the 1950s and 1960s, the Court used *Brown* as grounds for
overturning all segregation laws. White Southerners wondered out
loud how *Brown* could become a precedent for such action. Even
granting that segregated schools damaged hearts and minds of black
students, the same could not be said about not allowing blacks into
swimming pools, public parks, or cemeteries.

The *Brown* decision eventually changed the face of America. But
change did not come without struggle. Martin Luther King Jr. spear-
headed a movement that aimed as much at altering public opinion
as reversing segregation laws. In 1963 King led well-publicized
marches in Selma and Birmingham, Alabama, that confronted Jim
Crow laws with nonviolent civil disobedience. Television networks
had recently beefed-up their news staffs and had expanded their
coverage of the evening news to one-half hour. Camera crews were
on hand at the civil rights demonstrations, and viewers throughout
the nation were transfixed by scenes of peaceful marchers attacked
by police dogs and hosed down with water cannons. Race relations
were never the same thereafter.

What the Courts did not integrate, the Civil Rights Act of 1964
did. Prior to the administration of President Lyndon Johnson, himself a Southerner, civil rights legislation had been bottled up in
Congress by powerful members of the House and Senate from the
South. But Johnson was a masterful politician. He used his skills
to enact legislation that made discrimination on the basis of race
illegal in almost every aspect of American life. The Voting Rights

Act ensured that black citizens would be able to cast their ballots everywhere in the country.

While these changes were important, they did not end the race problem. Attention shifted to economic advancement. During most of America's history blacks living in both North and South had been systematically excluded from colleges, universities, law and medical schools, labor unions, boardrooms, and many of the higher paying professions. In many instances this economic discrimination was overt. Whites simply refused to work with blacks. But it was also true that an even more subtle form of discrimination hindered black advancement. Many whites believed that the majority of blacks were incapable of holding prominent occupations.

Johnson's strategy for overcoming the lack of economic opportunity was to initiate the Great Society, a huge number of programs administered by the national government aimed at giving those in poverty a chance for advancement. He hoped that by assisting poor people with nutrition programs, aid to dependent children, health benefits, housing subsidies, educational and vocational training, and loans and grants for higher education, the government could even the playing field, as he was fond of saying, and thereby eliminate poverty entirely. While blacks were not directly targeted by these programs, they would benefit disproportionately because so many fell below the poverty level.

The opportunities provided by the Great Society programs surely aided some people in climbing out of poverty. But they almost immediately created a white backlash against blacks. A perception was created that somehow most blacks were on welfare and living off the largess of the government. There were also complaints about the growth in the size of government (particularly the bureaucracy), the increase in taxes, and the intrusiveness of the national government into citizens' businesses and private lives.

Few blacks saw the programs in this way. For them these benefits were a long-overdue effort to share the nation's vast resources. They trusted the national government more than did most whites. After all, it had been the national government that had put an end to slavery, enacted constitutional amendments to protect the rights of blacks, and legislated an end to the segregation and discrimination that were so much a part of state and local law. It was the federal courts that mandated an end to racial segregation, forcing recalcitrant local governments to treat blacks as equals.

Local governments, much praised as the fountain of democracy, had traditionally been less congenial to blacks. Local officials were often more parochial and less cosmopolitan than those at the national level. They were less likely to change their ways and to see people different from themselves as equals. A number of them had been members of the Klan. The one-party system of the South also created an atmosphere in which candidates with extreme racial views were elected to local office. The difference in perspectives between black and white about the nature and extent of federal government involvement in the local and private concerns of citizens helped break the fragile national consensus that had supported the civil rights movement.

According to Charles Murray, author of *Losing Ground,* even more damning than the acrimony created by the Great Society was the effect it had on many of the recipients of assistance. Rather than helping the poor work their way out of poverty, he argues, the programs served only to make them dependent on aid. They became, as Alexis de Tocqueville predicted they would, wards of the state, no longer able to make rational and independent choices. Their initiative and self-reliance lost, far too many welfare recipients turned to thoughtless and self-destructive behavior which trapped them ever more fully in the grasp of government benevolence. Poverty was not defeated. Despite the billions of dollars that have been spent since the 1960s on programs to help the poor, exponential increases are seen in crime, violence, drug use, teenage pregnancy, and unwed motherhood. While blacks can hardly be blamed for the failure of well-intentioned but poorly drawn welfare policies, it is poor blacks who have suffered most from the stigma of welfare and the stultifying effects of an overprotective welfare state.

Some black scholars dispute Murray's claim. For instance, Coramae Richey Mann argues in her book *Unequal Justice: A Question of Color* that the true root of antisocial behavior among blacks is racism. Blacks who engage in criminal activity are "political prisoners," reacting against poverty and bigotry. Mann argues that whites and blacks are equally prone to unlawful behavior, but blacks are punished far more severely than are whites. This is evidence, she says, that the criminal justice system in America is manifestly unjust. Law-enforcement officials single out black youths for arrest and prosecution. Mann concludes that the white race uses legal codes to "maintain its hegemony" over blacks, keeping the jails full. Absent many of its young males, those who could most bring energy and vitality to their people, the black community is disorganized and demoralized.

Affirmative Action

Another controversial policy for ensuring racial equity was put in place during the 1970s. Affirmative action began innocently enough. When first introduced, it was little more than a mechanism for ensuring that minorities would be considered for employment and placement in colleges or universities. But soon affirmative action became an instrument for requiring numerical "targets" of minorities to be admitted to school or hired into a job.

The Supreme Court became involved in the issue when Allen Bakke, a white student, was refused admission to the University of California-Davis medical school despite having earned better grades and board scores than most of the minority students who had been admitted ahead of him. He sued, claiming that the policy of University of California-Davis, which denied him admission solely on the basis of race, violated his right to equal protection of the law guaranteed to him by the Fourteenth Amendment. In *Regents of University of California v. Bakke* (1978), a badly divided Court held that Bakke's rights had been infringed because the University of California system set a specific quota on the minorities to be admitted. But the Court also ruled that affirmative action procedures which did not set clear-cut quotas were constitutional. The Court reasoned that along with academic credentials and extracurricular activities, admissions committees could consider race as one aspect of a candidate's potential merit to the school. Much in the way schools seek regional heterogeneity so as to inculcate a lively exchange of views, people from different races could serve to bring diversity to the academic experience.

The *Bakke* case was used as precedent for applying affirmative action targets in employment and business contracts as well. In *United Steel Workers of America v. Weber* (1980), the Court rejected a reverse discrimination claim made by a white man against a union–employer contract that imposed a 50 percent racial quota on hiring minorities. The Court argued that under Title VII of the Civil Rights Act of 1964 voluntary quotas were permitted in order to "eliminate manifest racial imbalances in traditionally segregated job categories." The Court further expanded the use of affirmative action in *Fullilove v. Klutznick* (1980). It upheld a congressional act which set aside 10 percent of all federal grants awarded by the Department of Commerce to minority companies. Unlike *Weber,* the ruling in *Fullilove* did not rest on a finding of past discrimination, but rather on a broad congressional authority to mandate racial preferences based on the principle of proportional representation. Yet while the Court consistently upheld the constitutionality of affirmative action, it has not accepted every affirmative action remedy. In *Richmond v. J. A. Croson Company* (1989), the Court rejected a city-mandated 30 percent set-aside for minority contractors, in part because the ordinance was mandated by the city and not, as in *Fullilove,* by Congress. The Court ruled that the rights of white contractors had been violated by this law because the effects of past discrimination did not warrant so large a quota.

Studies show that most Americans of all races are opposed to affirmative action if that policy entails favoring one group over another simply on the basis of race. But there is also quite a division about what affirmative action means. Most whites are hostile toward affirmative action programs which, they argue, unfairly aid blacks who are not as qualified. Many blacks see affirmative action less as a quota system than as a mechanism for overcoming racism. Whites, so the argument goes, would never reach out to hire blacks or to accept them into colleges, universities, or businesses unless affirmative action targets compelled such behavior. Far from aiding unqualified blacks, affirmative action merely forces whites to acknowledge the merits of blacks that would, in a world dominated by whites, be overlooked. Affirmative action creates hostility because it forces whites and blacks to compete directly for scarce openings in business and higher education, not as individuals but as members of distinct races.

According to Stephen Carter, author of *Reflections of an Affirmative Action Baby,* affirmative action has created another, more subtle problem. On many college and university campuses, where one would expect the openness to new ideas and the general tolerance to prevail, racial confrontations are at their most intense. The reason, according to Carter, stems from affirmative action. If black students are accepted into school because of the "diversity" they bring to campus, then they must in fact be different and act that way. To act differently from other students means to cut oneself off from the "majority," which in most instances is white. On many campuses this segregation of the races is strictly maintained by unwritten and informal social codes. For instance, black students who join predominantly white clubs or social organizations are ostracized. On many campuses black students prefer to eat together, live together in separate black dorms, and even study together in specially created black studies programs. They wear their diversity proudly, so much so that America's most intellectually advanced institutions are almost resegregated.

Unequal and Separate?

A number of blacks argue that a certain amount of separatism is healthy and necessary. Advocates of this view reason that blacks have always had to look to white society for their ideals of beauty, virtue, and achievement. Even standards of good speech, dress, and behavior are dictated by whites. Why should blacks not celebrate their own heritage just as have many ethnic groups in America? Why should blacks have to meet the standards of a society that does not fully accept them? The yardsticks by which whites measure themselves often exclude those things at which blacks succeed, such as music, the arts, and sports. When blacks measure themselves the same way, the result can be a kind of psychological inferiority which can hinder the full development of the black individual. Although the evidence supporting separatism is mostly anecdotal, it does seem that those students trained at predominantly black colleges and even elementary and secondary students who attend schools with Afrocentric curriculum are far more apt to succeed than those who attend integrated institutions.

Some blacks also desire to achieve a kind of independence from the larger society. It is expressed in new forms of music, dance, dress, and speech. Jazz and rock and roll, for example, were originated by black musicians. Often these artistic expressions of black culture, such as jazz and rock and roll, have been adopted by the wider community. But as black art becomes more broadly accepted, it loses its character as a representation of the black community. Blacks then seek to escape the dominance of white society by conceiving a wholly new form, as rap musicians have transformed rock and roll.

Yet independence and separation have costs. When blacks attempt to establish their own culture and distinct society, they must exclude outsiders, i.e., whites. Naturally this separation and group identity causes similar feelings of distinctiveness and separation among whites. Those whites who seek to ameliorate racial tension actually feel hurt when blacks exclude them and associate them with white racists. Separatism also gives white racists an excuse for their attitudes against blacks. They can claim that blacks are seeking to advance the interests of their race against whites, so whites are entitled to do the same.

The issue of the best means to achieve black advancement points to an important struggle within the black community. Poor blacks and people who claim to speak for poor blacks argue that middle-class blacks have sold out to the white power structure and culture. They have "made it" because they "act white." They are accused of forgetting their African roots, abandoning their black identity, and leaving poverty behind without giving any help to the poor.

Many middle-class blacks, although often less vocal, maintain that an identification with poverty and with the ethos of the urban poor is misguided. This group often claims that dominant forms of the media create and reinforce racial stereotypes by presenting blacks as if all were poor, uneducated, or social misfits. So poor is the general image of blacks that Japanese businessmen are often surprised to find blacks working in responsible positions.

Much of what blacks have achieved has been ignored. White historians are just beginning to acknowledge the many contributions that blacks have made to the advancement of the nation. We rarely ever hear that one of the fastest-growing groups among black Americans are those families earning over $50,000 a year. Some middle-class blacks find the identification with poverty and with the spokesmen of the poor stifling. As Justice Clarence Thomas has argued, it simply is not true that all blacks must hold the same opinions.

What Do We Think About Race?

Most whites do not think much about race unless the issue arises directly. Because they do not think a great deal about race, they do not consider themselves racist. Yet when they do think about blacks, they often associate them with crime, violence, poverty, and personal and social irresponsibility. They believe that they are judging blacks fairly and treating them no differently than they would treat whites who behaved badly. Many whites think themselves sympathetic to blacks who are hardworking, upright, and honest. Whites see black celebrities, such as Michael Jackson, Bill Cosby, and Bo

Jackson, as a sign that the system works and that anyone with talent and drive can get ahead.

Many whites are embarrassed by the issue of race because it is the one area where the principles of the Declaration, the principles in which most Americans believe, have not worked very well. They find it difficult to talk to blacks about the issue. They know that blacks, if they wish to do so, can bring up any number of examples to show that America has not lived up to its own ideals. Whites do not want to be confronted by the past injustices of their race and the failure of their ideals. They do not want to have to defend the fairness of America.

Many blacks, too, are embarrassed by the race issue because they must constantly prove themselves, not simply as individuals, but as blacks. They are asked to do much more than prove their personal worth. They must overcome the pervasive attitude that somehow the majority of their countrymen do not fully trust them. They are still unwelcome in their own land. They too hold the principles of the Declaration—the view that each person should be judged by his or her own abilities—as their guiding conviction. Yet they wonder whether there will ever be a time when the color of their skin does not enter into the calculation of their merit.

The relationship between black and white in America is similar to that of partners in a difficult marriage. Both sides recognize that the other partner is important to them. They see many good things about the relationship. Yet there are so many hurts, so many slights, and so many wrongs that "reconciliation" will not come easily. Unlike companions in a real marriage, however, there is no way for blacks and whites to divorce. Our mutual fates are forever intertwined. There are many cordial relationships between black and white. When we know each other, work together, play sports together, the issue of race is mostly forgotten. Even though we seem unable to live up to our principles, most Americans, both black and white, have the same fundamental belief that the content of one's character counts more than the color of one's skin.

Acknowledgment

This essay was prepared with a grant from Hampden-Sydney College.

Suggested Reading

Carter, Stephen L. *Reflections of an Affirmative Action Baby.* New York: Basic Books, 1991.

Du Bois, W. E. B. *Souls of Black Folk.* Millwood, N.Y.: Kraus-Thomson, 1980.

Malcolm X. *The Autobiography of Malcolm X,* with Alex Haley. New York: Grove Press, 1965.

King, Martin Luther, Jr. "Letter from Birmingham Jail."

Washington, Booker T. *Up From Slavery.* Garden City, N.Y.: Doubleday, 1963.

Woodward, C. Vann. *The Strange Career of Jim Crow.* 3rd rev. ed. New York: Oxford University Press, 1965.

29

The Dissident Criticism
of America

Peter Augustine Lawler

My purpose is to consider the best available radical criticism of
the American regime. To be radical means to get to the root of the
matter. Genuinely radical thinkers are only quite rarely revolutionaries. They have a balanced appreciation of the strengths and weaknesses of existing order, and they know that human life will never
be perfected. If the existing regime is decent but flawed, the appropriate political strategy is to reform it, not destroy it. Revolutions always do great harm, and only under extraordinarily oppressive circumstances can they reasonably be expected to do more good
than harm.

But the critics I will consider were revolutionaries. They were
dissidents, or those who illegally and fundamentally resisted communist totalitarianism. They worked for revolutionary change because they really did live under extraordinarily oppressive rule. They
were fundamental critics of communism, but they are also friendly
critics of America. They admire America's devotion to liberty and
democracy. But they also see within our regime self-destructive
tendencies that may make it increasingly difficult for us to defend
our liberty.

We find it especially difficult to listen to such criticism today.
Americans, like all peoples, have more than a touch of national
chauvinism. We are too quickly irritated when anyone from the outside
questions our view of our fundamental principles or our way of
life. Today especially, such criticism strikes us as implausible.

Our belief was that the radical alternative to liberal democracy
was some comprehensive form of socialism or communism. But that

alternative is gone, and radical criticism now seems to be impossible. It goes without saying that the remaining debates, such as whether we should have national health insurance, are not radical.

President George Bush, in the wake of the fall of communism, spoke confidently of a "new world order," a global alliance of liberal democracies led by the moral example and military might of the United States. Francis Fukuyama wrote an unusually theoretical best-seller, *The End of History and the Last Man*, which claimed to prove that there were no legitimate alternatives to liberal democracy left in the world. Fukuyama actually claimed even more. Perhaps existing liberal democracies, such as the United States, are the final goal of all human striving.

But, for the dissidents, even the victory in the Cold War does not show that American democracy is perfect or, in some respects, even humanly worthy. Their criticisms are partial, but radical.

The two most eloquent and profound of the dissidents are the Russian Alexander Solzhenitsyn and the Czech Václav Havel. Each gave a noteworthy address articulating carefully and powerfully his criticism of America. Solzhenitsyn spoke at the Harvard commencement in 1978. Havel spoke to a joint session of Congress in 1990.

Solzhenitsyn, born in 1918, is a very prolific novelist and historian. He won the Nobel Prize for Literature in 1970. His writing is almost always animated by the desire to expose the lie of communist ideology and to rebuild Russia into a home fit for human beings. His *Gulag Archipelago*, published in three volumes in the 1970s, awakened the West to the magnitude of the lie. He spent a number of years in a Soviet labor camp and was finally expelled from the Soviet Union in 1974. He has lived in the United States since 1976, but plans to return to Russia soon.

Havel, born in 1936, is an internationally known playwright and essayist. His writing shows a deep appreciation of the problems encountered by the greatest contemporary philosophers. He was frequently jailed by Czech authorities for his dissident activities. His most recent arrest was on October 27, 1989, just two months before he assumed the presidency of the newly noncommunist Czech and Slovak Republic. The Czechs and the Slovaks separated into two nations in January 1993, and Havel is now the president of the Czech Republic.

I am going to consider Solzhenitsyn's Harvard address, "A World Split Apart," rather briefly, and give more attention to Havel's address to Congress. I have several reasons for proceeding this way. First,

Solzhenitsyn's main concern was the West's, and particularly America's, capacity to defend human liberty by resisting communism. This concern is no longer ours. Havel's address concerns the post-Cold War world. Second, Solzhenitsyn, although he said he spoke as a friend to America, may have used a rhetoric too extreme for his purpose. Americans, for the most part, did not consider the substance of his criticisms with open minds. Havel's criticisms are made gently, ironically, and indirectly, and certainly America has been more open to them.

Finally, Solzhenitsyn is far more hostile to American culture than Havel. Havel is a much more Western and cosmopolitan figure, who admires and enjoys rock music, contemporary literature and films, and so forth. These cultural differences are relatively superficial, but they do make Havel's moral and political criticisms seem more friendly or sympathetic. The differences are superficial enough that an overview of Solzhenitsyn's key criticisms actually serves as a good introduction to Havel. On the fundamental questions, Havel is very much indebted to Solzhenitsyn.

Solzhenitsyn on Courage, Well-Being, and Responsibility

The heart of Solzhenitsyn's address is his observation that "the most striking feature" about the West to an "outside observer" is a "decline in courage." He means primarily "civic courage," which he defines as the willingness "to risk one's precious life for the common good." He believes that the West, including America, is losing its capacity to defend its liberty.

But Solzhenitsyn goes on to show that the decline of courage is merely a symptom. The real disorder is an excessive, habitual concern for material well-being at the expense of everything higher. The history of the modern West is characterized by progressively less cultivation of the soul or "voluntary self-restraint." The "most precious possession" of human beings, "our spiritual life," is disappearing.

Solzhenitsyn already sees some evidence of this excessively materialistic orientation in the founding principles of modern states. He mentions the American Declaration of Independence, in which he sees the American Founders beginning a project in "the pursuit of happiness." The Americans, over time, have developed a more and more simply materialistic understanding of what happiness is. The founding project, Solzhenitsyn says, is completed with the "welfare state." In the welfare state, human beings enjoy unprecedented abundance and liberty. They should be happy, if the theory of the Founders were true.

But Solzhenitsyn observes that experience has shown that this modern psychology is flawed. It ignored a fundamental scientific fact. Too much comfort and prosperity—"a high degree of habitual well-being"—is bad for any "living organism." Too much attention to bodily well-being is bad even for the body.

The West today is characterized by a "weakening of the human personality." Because of this individual weakness, it is failing to achieve even the modest goal of comfortable self-preservation. Individuals are unable to secure their bodies' safety against violence and criminality.

"To defend oneself," Solzhenitsyn asserts, "one must be ready to die." He adds that the people suffering under and resisting communism have "firmer and stronger" personalities than people in the West, because they are better able to face death. America, as a result, is "not a model" for possible postcommunist development by the Russian people.

The excessive pursuit of material well-being or happiness has also actually made the American people extremely unhappy. Living without much courage or genuinely spiritual life, they are full not of enjoyment but of anxiety and fear. They are anxious about their status in a world dominated by material competition. They are much more afraid of death than ever before, because they seem to have so much more to lose. They have deprived themselves of the gifts of God and nature—spiritual life and courage—that are the preconditions for what happiness is possible for human beings. "Only by the voluntary nurturing in ourselves of freely accepted and serene self-restraint," Solzhenitsyn contends, "can man rise above the stream of materialism."

Another sign, for Solzhenitsyn, of the absence of courage and spiritual life that make possible voluntary self-restraint is the West's excessive legalism, especially in America. Self-restraint or self-rule has been too largely replaced by the fearful rule of law. America is a litigious society because it is not a particularly courageous or spiritual one.

Almost gone is the perception of a duty to go beyond what the law requires. Evil is blamed on "misguided social systems" and not on personal irresponsibility. The ability of the human being to rise voluntarily above determination by his environment, and so really to choose between good and evil, is too generally denied. Because we deny the very possibility of personal responsibility, it is becoming more rare and unreliable. No one expects it or counts on it. Everyone, Solzhenitsyn says, is excessively aware of his rights, but no one speaks seriously of duties.

Solzhenitsyn, most radically, traces the error informing modern psychology and politics to "the very foundation of modern thought," which is "the prevailing Western view of the world which arose with the Renaissance and found political expression since the age of Enlightenment." He calls this turn in thought "humanistic autonomy" or "anthropocentricity," the view that man is free "from any force above him."

The modern definition of man is without "the concept of the Supreme Complete Entity" to "restrain our passions and our irresponsibility." Man is defined without God and self-restraint. But experience has shown that if he is without "a sense of responsibility to God and society," to what is above him, he cannot help but enslave himself to what is below him, matter or environment.

The premise of this anthropocentric way of thinking is that man has no higher "task" than "the achievement of happiness on earth." But it turns out that this apparently low and simple goal cannot be achieved by human beings. Solzhenitsyn reminds us that "If man were born only to be happy, he would not be born to die."

The only way human beings can achieve this goal of earthly happiness is to forget about their mortality, and so to have no need for courageous and spiritual responses to that knowledge. So Solzhenitsyn says that the goal of "carefree consumption" can be achieved only through "a total engrossment in everyday life." Human beings must be led not to think about their futures, but only to enjoy the present. They must be reduced to a less than human condition.

Solzhenitsyn says this "total engrossment" was the goal of the Communist party in the East and commercialism in the West. He found an "unexpected kinship" between Western humanism and communism. His deepest fear is that the West will be unable to defend human liberty because it has almost forgotten what that liberty is.

But Solzhenitsyn's hopeful conclusion to his Harvard Address is that human liberty has a future. He says that the modern world is coming to be seen for what it is, an excessively materialistic over-reaction to the too excessively spiritual society of the Middle Ages. He calls for a new "spiritual effort" based on human reflection on these two forms of excess. It might produce a "new height of vision" that will do justice to both "our physical nature" and "our spiritual being."

So Solzhenitsyn does not criticize American materialism in order to destroy it. He wants its great successes to be preserved by being incorporated in a more comprehensive or higher vision of what it means to be a human being. He does not oppose human liberty, but he wants to have it better understood. Solzhenitsyn's sometimes excessive criticisms of American excesses actually aim at a moderate result.

This moderation is clear in Solzhenitsyn's program for postcommunist Russia, in his book, *Rebuilding Russia*. There he sees the importance of private property and enterprise for the development of the human personality. He asks only that the Russian movement away from socialism and toward privatization proceed cautiously so that profit-taking and banks do not become "the hidden masters of all life."[1] Finally, economic development must be put in its place, which is far from the highest one: "The strength or weakness of a society depends more on the level of its spiritual life than on its level of industrialization. Neither a market economy nor even general abundance constitutes the crowning achievement of human life."[2] That the economic goods are not the highest goods, of course, does not mean that they are not good at all.

Solzhenitsyn also chooses democracy as the best form of government for the Russians today. He does so in full view of its weaknesses, and he cites Alexis de Tocqueville, among others, to show that he is alive to the dangers it poses to liberty. Democracy, properly understood, must be compatible with liberty. Solzhenitsyn approves of former President Ronald Reagan's view that "[d]emocracy is less a system of government than a means of *limiting* government, preventing it from interfering in the true sources of human values that are found only in family and faith."[3]

But Solzhenitsyn is also critical of the impersonality and irresponsibility of Western democracies, where many or most citizens do not vote at all and many others vote whimsically or in ignorance. He favors for Russia "the democracy of small areas."[4] This democracy is of properly human dimensions, where voters and elected officials can be expected to act responsibly and be held accountable.

President Havel's Gift to America

Havel addressed Congress as president of the Czech and Slovak Republic, seeking economic and political assistance. He acknowledges the economic and political superiority of the Americans, as well as their generosity. He says his people have much to learn from the Americans on "how to educate our offspring, how to elect our representatives, and the ways how to organize economic life so that it will lead to prosperity and not to poverty."

Havel adds that the Americans may have one lesson to learn from the Czechs and Slovaks, a philosophical one. It seems, at first, that this lesson is not very important. For the most part, Havel really does regard the American people as a model for the development of his own. He seems very far from Solzhenitsyn's strong criticisms.

But then Havel introduces his genuine point, the dependence of political life on philosophy. He says his speech has two parts. The first "is from a political point of view." The second "is from a point of view we might call philosophical." The difference turns out to be between the particular policies that usually make up political life and the human foundations of that life. Only from the second point of view can human beings see why they might accept "political responsibility."

Havel offers this point of view as a gift from his people, one required by simple justice or perhaps his people's pride. They must find "something to offer" in return to those who are "well-educated, powerful, and wealthy." The Czechs and Slovaks have learned something from their "bitter experience" of "human suffering" and "above all enormous humiliation." What they know, which the Americans do not, seems to come from an aspect of their experience that is strikingly inferior and unfortunate.

But Havel finds "something positive" in his people's experience. They have "a special capacity to look, from time to time, somewhat further" than those who "live a somewhat normal life." Someone "pinned under a boulder," as the Czechs and Slovaks were by the oppression of communism, "has more time to think about his hopes than someone who is not trapped that way."

According to Havel, the extraordinary suffering, oppression, and degradation of the Czechs and Slovaks have actually been good for thought. The American example shows that, when life is ordinary, comfortable, and relatively unconstrained, more than superficial thought is rare. The Americans seem to have plenty of time to think, but their normal lives prevent them from doing so.

In Havel's other writing, he shows that the specifically modern view is that political institutions that guarantee peace, freedom, and prosperity will produce human progress in all areas, including thought. Perhaps the most important product of the leisure provided by technology is time for reflection. But Havel's view is that modern liberal democracy has not usually been good for thought, because profound or genuinely truthful thought requires far more than leisure.

Havel opposes this modern view (which he, like Solzhenitsyn, says originated in the Renaissance) with the wonderful example of the Czech philosopher Jan Patocka, who died as the result of his brutal treatment by the police while being interrogated for his dissident activities. Havel asks whether it is "not symptomatic that the best-known victim of 'the struggle for human rights' was also our most important philosopher" in Czechoslovakia.[5] He says there must be some relation between Patocka's great political courage and his profound thought.

Havel remembers that Patocka once wrote, "a life not willing to sacrifice itself to make life meaningful is not worth living." Havel used that memory to define a humanly worthy life. It is one which is "capable of sacrificing something, in extreme cases, everything, of the banal, prosperous life—that rule of 'everydayness,' as Jan Patocka used to say—for the sake of that which gives life meaning."[6] Patocka and Havel agree with Solzhenitsyn that it is courage that raises human beings above being determined by material need alone. It is what makes possible a meaningful or spiritual life. It is what makes self-defense in every respect possible.

Courage, or the willingness to sacrifice everything, is especially required for genuinely human thought. It is what allows human beings to think about and come to terms with what they really know about their existence. Ordinarily, they tend toward self-forgetfulness. They want to lose themselves, especially their knowledge of their mortality, in what Patocka calls "everydayness" or what Solzhenitsyn calls "total engrossment" in the moment.

Havel's conclusion is that only "intellectual and moral courage" makes it possible to live a human life in light of the truth. Without that courage, "nothing is worth anything." Whenever a human being identifies morality with expediency, or what is required to preserve himself comfortably, he always "in the depth of his spirit . . . feels that nothing matters."[7]

So what the Czech and Slovak dissidents have to offer the "free world," which is what the world not dominated by communism used to call itself, is "the idea that a price must be paid for truth, the idea of truth as a moral value." They have acquired a "sense of responsibility" that "grows out of . . . certain moral experiences that compel one to transcend the horizon of one's personal interests" in the direction of courage. The result is "a relatively higher degree of inner emancipation" than human beings ordinarily experience.[8] Havel says his people are more free, morally speaking, than the Americans. For that reason, they are better situated to think about and act in response to their responsibility as human beings.

Havel concludes his address to Congress by giving an American example of this extraordinary freedom for responsibility. He calls attention to our Founders, the authors of the Declaration of Independence, the Constitution, and the Bill of Rights. They, our "best minds," did not hesitate to assume "practical responsibility" for their ideas. So their "great documents" still "inspire us all . . . to be citizens."

Thomas Jefferson's words in the Declaration concerning the foundation of government in consent, Havel says, "were a simple and important act of the human spirit." They were an *act*, because they were the foundation for the Americans' dissident resistance in 1776. Havel says: "What gave meaning to the act . . . was the fact that the author backed it up with his life. It was not just his words, it was his deeds as well."

Havel implicitly suggests that we Americans ought to wonder whether our Founders articulated the proper relationship between words and deeds. Did they make clear the human meaning or spirit of their doctrine of consent? This foundation must be found in courage or the willingness to sacrifice everything, and not as the modern Jefferson sometimes said, in the material desires for security and comfort.

Jefferson, whatever he may have said, clearly knew to be true what Havel elsewhere says Czech and Slovak dissidents knew: "one idea is rooted in our common awareness; that the inability to risk, *in extremis*, even life itself to save what gives it meaning and a human dimension leads not only to the loss of meaning but finally and inevitably to the loss of life as well."[9] As Solzhenitsyn explains, beings who are too attached to well-being cannot even defend their bodies, much less their souls.

Havel's Great Certainty

Havel's view is that the "free world" does not understand properly the relationship between human thought and deed. He tells Congress of "the one great certainty" that his dissident experience has given him: "Consciousness proceeds being, and not the other way around, as the Marxists claim."

This must certainly have been news to Congress, as it is to us, if only because neither we nor the members of Congress are accustomed to such philosophical language. But one thing is clear immediately. The Americans, Havel says, are much less certain than Havel and the other dissidents that Marxism is untrue.

The Marxist view is that human consciousness, or our understanding of ourselves and the world, is determined by impersonal forces beyond human control and responsibility. So consciousness is determined by "being," which the Marxists identify with the power of these impersonal forces. This view dominates, in a number of forms, the sophisticated social scientific thinking of educated Americans. We are all influenced by the powerful, impersonal explanations of psychologists, sociologists, and economists. The implication of their view is that human beings are neither free nor responsible for what they think or do.

Marxism, for Havel as for Solzhenitsyn, is nothing but the very extreme version of this characteristically modern thought. The excesses of this thought still have great influence over us, even with the disintegration of communism. "We are still," Havel says to Congress, "under the sway of the destructive and vain belief that man is the pinnacle of Creation, and not just part of it, and therefore everything is permitted." What distinguishes our civilization, Havel agrees with Solzhenitsyn, is this anthropocentric arrogance. We believe there are no limits to what human beings may do.

But Havel elsewhere explains that this radical or unlimited claim for freedom actually causes human freedom to disappear. Human beings tend to believe that they can "play" with or use without moral responsibility the power of science. They can do so because God, who was thought to put moral limits on what human beings can do, seems now to be nothing but a "subjective illusion." Man might actually replace God.

Man arrogantly came to believe he could use the power of science to recreate the world. He could "therefore plan for a life of happiness for all." He could conquer human misery, including even the unhappiness that comes with consciousness of death.[10]

It seems that those who play God can do whatever they please. But they are not really God. They are limited, for example, by the power of science. That power depends on matter's obedience to the predictable laws of nature. It is impersonal. It cannot account for human freedom.

The scientist's power depends on human beings not having particular personalities or identities. So the scientist ends up even denying his own personality or identity. Human freedom disappears into a "system," ruled by no one in particular. Marxism claims to be in the service of human freedom. But it really understands human beings to be completely enslaved to the economic system.

The Marxists claim to have a view of human freedom in the future. It is a utopia, a world of complete freedom which has existed nowhere so far. This utopian vision, Havel says, is of "a heaven on earth." It will be a world without evil and human suffering.[11] It will be a world without criminals, because there will be no crime. It will also be, Havel contends, a world without human beings.

"In an ideally homogeneous society," Havel observed when he was in prison for his dissident activities, "there will be no criminality because there will be no human life." The aim of communist totalitarianism, in his experience, was simply to stamp out "individuality" as criminality. Life becomes a "standardized nothing." In such a society, "prison" becomes "a 'correctional institute': a wastebasket for peculiar humans and their bizarre stories."[12] Being free, having one's own will or identity, is an error that must be corrected. In such a society, there is more freedom in prison than anywhere else.

For Havel, the modern, systematic denial of human freedom and responsibility reached its extreme form under communist totalitarianism. But it also exists as a tendency in the West, including America. Solzhenitsyn, Havel says, describes better than anyone else "the illusory nature of freedom in the West," because it is not "based on personal responsibility." The result is a "chronic inability . . . to oppose violence or totalitarianism." There is also very little genuinely political life. Human beings seem "incapable of . . . transcending concerns about their own personal survival to be proud and responsible members of a polis, making a genuine contribution to the creation of its destiny."[13] We tend to view the political com-

munity as existing for our comfortable self-preservation, or to protect our rights, and we have little of the pride that comes from the
proud and responsible performance of our duties as citizens.

Havel appreciates the fundamental difference between communist regimes, which aimed at being wholly systematic, and Western
democracies, which exhibit only systematic tendencies. Because the
West, including America, is still animated to some considerable extent
by personal freedom, Havel assumes that it is open to and can respond to his criticism. He hopes to inspire resistance to the general
weakness of the modern world, which is "the general unwilling-
ness of consumption-oriented people to sacrifice some material
certainties for the sake of their own spiritual and moral integrity."[14]

Havel's dissident experience makes him certain that modern human
beings are not determined by some scientific or technological system. He says to Congress that "[f]rom time to time we say that the
anonymous megamachinery which we have created for ourselves
no longer serves us, yet we still fail to do something about it." The
fact is that human beings need not ever submit to "anonymous"
rule. They can always exercise responsibility wherever they are.

Higher Responsibility

Our view of the world tends to keep us from seeing everything
that is true about human existence. It is an obstacle to our understanding of what it means to be a human being. So Havel tells
Congress, "we still don't know how to put morality ahead of politics, science, and economics." That is because we still do not understand "that the backbone to all our actions—if they are to be
moral—is responsibility." Responsibility, finally, is to "the order
of Being, where all our actions are indelibly recorded and where,
and only where, they will be judged."

This must also have been news to Congress. It is quite difficult
to understand everything that Havel means by "the order of Being." We know, he says in another place, that "we touch eternity in
a strange way," that "the world is more than a cluster of improbable accidents." He also says that "responsibility is always 'higher
responsibility.'"[15] We know we are part of an ordered whole, and
not the highest part. This knowledge, whether or not it includes
belief in a personal God, is enough to give moral order and direc-

tion. One cannot properly define man, as Solzhenitsyn says, without some "concept of the Supreme Complete Entity."

"The interpreter or mediator between us and this higher authority," Havel tells Congress, "is what is traditionally referred to as human conscience." This experience human beings have of conscience is reliable enough to be the foundation of accepting "the burden of responsibility." Havel acknowledges that this experience seems vague to us because it is personal. But he asks that we trust him and it. He asks that we not trust the assertion of modern science that conscience and personal experience are not trustworthy.

The greatest gift of the dissident experience to America is that it shows that the personal experience of conscience can still be trusted. Havel says elsewhere that the courageous and truthful example of Solzhenitsyn shows that "it is still possible to oppose personal experiences . . . to 'innocent' power and unmask its guilt." Solzhenitsyn showed that it is never true to say no one is responsible for brutal use of power. Someone always is. So it is becoming clear "that wholly personal categories like good and evil still have their unambiguous content."[16]

The dissident experience can be the foundation of a reconstitution of the modern world on a humanly worthy or spiritual foundation. The acknowledgment of conscience and personal responsibility does not mean a rejection of the genuine modern achievements of prosperity, democracy, and the idea of rights. This nuanced thought leads Havel to political recommendations for the Czechs very similar to those Solzhenitsyn made to the Russians.

Democracy should be oriented around "small communities" of human proportions where the rule is personal responsibility and not seemingly impersonal and unaccountable institutions.[17] The modern view of the free market, properly understood, shows that private property is indispensable for personal responsibility and pride in one's work. As Havel wrote recently, because "everything belongs to someone . . . someone is responsible for everything." The replacement of socialism with private property means the abandonment "of control and discipline . . . in favor of self-control and self-discipline."[18]

But Havel, with Solzhenitsyn, cautions that the "free market" does not "contain the meaning of human life." It is only a part, and by no means the highest part, of the plurality or diversity which is that life. Most important, for Havel, is "the general cultural level of everyday life," its ability to rise above the thoughtless uniformity of "everydayness."[19] He says political leaders should elevate the cultural level through their rhetoric, their example, and sound public policy.

Havel, like Solzhenitsyn, takes heart in the deterioration of the modern way of viewing the world, and he views the collapse of communism as just one part of that world's general exhaustion. But he, again like Solzhenitsyn, is no reactionary, hoping for the restoration of some past world. The opportunity is here to go forward. Havel concludes his remarks to Congress by saying "history has accelerated. I believe once again it will be the human mind that will notice this acceleration, give it a name, and transform those words into deeds." He suggests that Jefferson's great act needs to be repeated. The relationship between words and deeds needs to be reformulated, and deeds based on those words can transform the world.

There is one very obvious criticism of this hopeful conclusion. Havel suggests to Congress that only extraordinary or "founding" circumstances of some sort or another bring human beings of great moral and intellectual excellence, such as Jefferson and Havel, to power. But it seems likely that the effect of the dissident experience will quickly fade as the Czech Republic and even Russia become part of the West. The remarkable president-playwright-poet-philosopher Havel will likely have quite ordinary successors. It is not at all clear that anything has happened recently that can transform through resistance the tendencies toward irresponsibility in the West, including America. But Havel, extraordinary even among founders for the close connection he sees between philosophical reflection and practical responsibility, remains to inspire us beyond everydayness.

Conclusion

I leave it to you to decide how complete and convincing the dissident criticism of America is. Criticism from outside is always open to the countercriticism that the outsiders do not really know us. In this case, that countercriticism is readily inflamed by the perception of ingratitude. The newly won freedom of the Czechs and the Russians is a product of the Americans' resolute use of their power during the Cold War as much as or more than dissident resistance. Do Havel and Solzhenitsyn properly understand or appreciate the spirit that produced the American resistance to communism? Our resistance may not have required many extraordinary sacrifices, but it was rather constant and determined.[20] The dissident critics may not have grasped the extent or depth of our spiritual resources.

But I do think that we can turn to Havel and Solzhenitsyn for the most radical and revealing description of our weaknesses, even if their presentation of them is exaggerated. There is much truth in the charge that our thought and action are too much enslaved to a world dominated by the "everydayness" of the life of consumers in a world dominated by high technology. Our language is weak in making moral distinctions, and it is becoming weaker. We are suspicious of calls to courage and sacrifice for the good of our souls. Because we are not particularly courageous, we are personally irresponsible and find it difficult to cultivate voluntary self-restraint. Our social institutions, such as the family, church, and local communities, deteriorate as a result.

Despite the fact that we are sometimes quite ready to defend our personal liberty, we often prefer impersonal theories such as Marxism and other forms of social and economic determinism to the truth about human responsibility. We do not experience ourselves very strongly as bound to something or someone higher. So we often do find it difficult to resist determination by material forces in thought and deed.

We do not have the strong sense of practical responsibility that would lead us to participate readily in a vigorous and proud political life. We are also very weak spiritually, and so we are unhappy and anxious in the midst of our prosperity. We long, whether we acknowledge it or not, for a world constituted clearly by the distinctions between good and evil and man and God. But these unsatisfied longings do not reduce us to victims of an atheistic, meaningless time. Our personal experiences, if we tell ourselves the truth about them, can still be the foundation of personal responsibility. The struggle to acknowledge and act upon that responsibility still exists. It is the foundation of a humanly worthy understanding of liberty.

Notes

1. Alexander Solzhenitsyn, *Rebuilding Russia: Reflections and Tentative Proposals*, trans. A. Klimoff (New York: Farrar, Straus, and Giroux, 1992), p. 37.

2. Ibid., p. 49
3. Ibid., pp. 64–65.
4. Ibid., p. 82.
5. Václav Havel, *Open Letters: Selected Writings 1965–90*, trans. P. Wilson and others (New York: Knopf, 1991), pp. 275–76.
6. Ibid., p. 263.
7. Václav Havel, *Letters to Olga*, trans. P. Wilson (New York: Knopf, 1988), p. 261.
8. Havel, *Open Letters*, p. 177.
9. Ibid., p. 311.
10. Ibid., pp. 252–55.
11. Ibid., pp. 254–56.
12. Ibid., p. 340; Havel, *Letters to Olga*, p. 312.
13. Havel, *Open Letters*, p. 208.
14. Ibid., p. 145.
15. Václav Havel, *Disturbing the Peace: A Conversation with Karel Hvizdala*, trans. P. Wilson (New York: Knopf, 1990), p. 182; Havel, *Summer Meditations*, trans. P. Wilson (New York: Knopf, 1992), pp. 5–6.
16. Havel, *Open Letters*, p. 270.
17. See Havel, *Disturbing the Peace*, pp. 16–17; *Summer Meditations*, p. 103; *Open Letters*, pp. 173, 211–12.
18. Havel, *Summer Meditations*, p. 62; *Open Letters*, p. 211.
19. Havel, *Summer Meditations*, p. 14.
20. Solzhenitsyn acknowleged that "the preponderance of responsible people in government preserved the West" by winning the Cold War (Address to the International Academy of Philosophy in Liechtenstein, September 14, 1993).

Suggested Reading

Ericson, Edward R., Jr., *Solzhenitsyn and the Modern World*, Washington, D.C.: Regnery Gateway, 1993.

Havel, Václav. "Address to U.S. Congress," *Congressional Record-House* (February 21, 1990), pp. H392–95.

Lawler, Peter Augustine. "Havel on Political Responsibility," *The Political Science Reviewer* (Fall 1993).

Pontuso, James F. *Solzhenitsyn's Political Thought*. Charlottesville: University Press of Virginia, 1990.

Solzhenitsyn, Alexander. "A World Split Apart," *East and West*, trans. I. Alberti. New York: Harper and Row, 1978.

Index